Springer Series on Cultural Computing

Cultural Computing is an exciting, emerging field of Human Computer Interaction, which covers the cultural impact of computing and the technological influences and requirements for the support of cultural innovation. Using support technologies such as artificial intelligence, machine learning, location-based systems, mixed/virtual/ augmented reality, cloud computing, pervasive technologies and human-data interaction, researchers can explore the differences across a variety of cultures and cultural production to provide the knowledge and skills necessary to overcome cultural issues and expand human creativity.

This series presents monographs, edited collections and advanced textbooks on the current research and knowledge of a broad range of topics including creativity support systems, creative computing, digital communities, the interactive arts, cultural heritage, digital culture and intercultural collaboration.

This Series is abstracted/indexed in Scopus.

Nelson Zagalo · Damián Keller
Editors

Artificial Media

Emerging Trends in Narratives, Education and Creative Practice

Springer

Editors
Nelson Zagalo
University of Aveiro
Aveiro, Portugal

Damián Keller
NAP, Federal University of Acre
Rio Branco, Acre, Brazil

ISSN 2195-9056 ISSN 2195-9064 (electronic)
Springer Series on Cultural Computing
ISBN 978-3-031-89036-9 ISBN 978-3-031-89037-6 (eBook)
https://doi.org/10.1007/978-3-031-89037-6

This Springer imprint is published by the registered company Springer Nature Switzerland AG
The registered company address is: Gewerbestrasse 11, 6330 Cham, Switzerland

Reviewers

Alessandra Carenzio, Università Cattolica del Sacro Cuore, Italy, alessandra.carenzio@unicatt.it
Alex Mitchell, National University of Singapore, Singapore, alexm@nus.edu.sg
Alexander Mathias Gerner, Universidade Lusófona, Portugal, alexander.gerner@ulusofona.pt
Antonio Fernando Coelho, Universidade do Porto, Portugal, acoelho@fe.up.pt
Clara Eloïse Fernandes, Lasalle College of the Arts, Singapore, clara.fernandes@lasalle.edu.sg
Daniel Brandão, Universidade do Minho, Portugal, danielbrandao@ics.uminho.pt
Daniela Reimann, Karlsruhe Institute of Technology, Germany, Daniela.Reimann@kit.edu
F. Amilcar Cardoso, Universidade de Coimbra, Portugal, amilcar@dei.uc.pt
Fernando Zamith, Universidade do Porto, Portugal, zamith@gmail.com
Gilberto Bernardes, Universidade do Porto, Portugal, bernardes7@gmail.com
Helena Pires, Universidade do Minho, Portugal, helena.pires538@gmail.com
Jorge Martins Rosa, Universidade Nova de Lisboa, Portugal, dedalus.jmmr@gmail.com
Joseph Timoney, Maynooth University, Ireland, JTimoney@cs.nuim.ie
Karl McCreadie, Ulster University, Northern Ireland, k.mccreadie@ulster.ac.uk
Luis Leite, Escola Superior de Media Artes e Design, Portugal, lmbcl@esmad.ipp.pt
Lonce Wyse, Universidad Pompeu Fabra, Spain, lonce.wyse@upf.edu
Maite Soto-Sanfiel, National University of Singapore, Singapore, maite.soto@gmail.com
María Rodríguez Valdés, Universidad de Granada, Spain, mvaldes@ugr.es
María Ruth García Pernía, Universidad de Alcalá, Spain, mruth.garcia@uah.es
Mário Moura, Universidade do Porto, Portugal, unseenbydesign@gmail.com
Miguel Carvalhais, Universidade do Porto, Portugal, mcarvalhais@fba.up.pt
Nicholas Davis, AI Consulting, Elyria, USA, nicholas.davis10@gmail.com
Paulo Nuno Vicente, Universidade Nova de Lisboa, Portugal, pnvicente@fcsh.unl.pt
Pedro Jerónimo, Universidade da Beira Interior, Portugal, pj@ubi.pt
Pilar Lacasa, Universidad Internacional de La Rioja, Spain, p.lacasa@uah.es
Raquel Echeandía, Universidad de Alcalá, Spain, raquel.echeandia@uah.es
Rut Martínez Borda, Universidad de Alcalá, Spain, rut.martinez@uah.es
Ruth Contrera, Universidad de Barcelona, Spain, contreras.ruth@ub.edu
Victor Lazzarini, Maynooth University, Ireland, Victor.Lazzarini@mu.ie
Yuqian Sun, Royal College of Art, United Kingdom, yuqiansun@network.rca.ac.uk

Contents

Editors and Contributors

About the Editors

Nelson Zagalo is a Professor of Multimedia at the University of Aveiro, and Scientific Coordinator of DigiMedia—Digital Media and Interaction Research Center. He founded the Portuguese Society for Videogames Sciences, and the *Journal of Digital Media and Interaction*. He is the author of more than 200 peer-reviewed publications in journals, books and conferences worldwide. He has written the books *Interactive Emotions* (2009), *Videogames in Portugal* (2013), and *Engagement Design. Designing for Interaction Motivations* (2020).

Damián Keller is a Full Professor of music technology at the Federal University of Acre and the Federal University of Paraíba in Brazil. He is a founding member of the international research network Ubiquitous Music Group and of the Amazon Center for Music Research (NAP). He has published over 200 articles on ubiquitous music and ecologically grounded creative practice in journals on computing, engineering, design, education, philosophy, and the arts. His latest coedited book is *Ubiquitous Music Ecologies* (Routledge).

Contributors

Brian Bridges School of Arts and Humanities, Ulster University, Derry Londonderry, Northern Ireland, UK

Eric Browne Munster Technological University, Cork, Ireland

Lorena Chiwerto Callejo Faculty of Philosophy and Arts, Universidad de Alcalá, Madrid, Spain

Michael Clemens University of Utah, Salt Lake City, UT, USA

Nicholas Davis Co-Creative AI Consulting, Elyria, OH, USA

Adrián Domínguez Díaz Politechnic School, University of Alcalá, Madrid, Spain

Alexander Matthias Gerner ECATI, CICANT, Universidade Lusófona, Lisboa, Portugal

Sara Cortés Gómez Faculty of Philosophy and Arts, Universidad de Alcalá, Madrid, Spain

Gloria Gómez-Diago Rey Juan Carlos University, Madrid, Spain

Stefano Gualeni Institute of Digital Games, University of Malta, Msida, Malta

Damián Keller NAP, Federal University of Acre, Federal University of Paraíba, Rio Branco, AC, Brazil

Pilar Lacasa International University of La Rioja and University of Alcalá, Alcalá de Henares, Spain

Rut Martínez-Borda University of Alcalá, Alcalá de Henares, Spain

Mitsuko Matsumoto International University of La Rioja, Logroño, Spain

Mário Moura I2ADS, Universidade Do Porto, Porto, Portugal

María Ruth García Pernía Faculty of Philosophy and Arts, Universidad de Alcalá, Madrid, Spain

Fabrizio Poltronieri University of Nottingham, Nottingham, UK

Daniela Reimann Karlsruhe Institute of Technology, Karlsruhe, Germany

Jeba Rezwana Towson University, Towson, MD, USA

Stephen Roddy Radical Humanities Laboratory, Department of Digital Humanities, University College Cork, Cork, Ireland

María Rodríguez Valdés University of Granada, Granada, Spain

Raquel Echeandía Sánchez Creative Campus, Universidad Europea de Madrid, Madrid, Spain

Yuqian Sun Computer Science Research Centre, Royal College of Art, London, UK

Craig Vear University of Nottingham, Nottingham, UK

Nelson Zagalo University of Aveiro, Aveiro, Portugal

Chapter 1
Exploring the Frontiers of Artificial Media

Damián Keller and Nelson Zagalo

Abstract This book explores the evolving relationship between humans and machines in creative processes, offering a comprehensive overview of artificial media research. It examines theoretical frameworks, practical deployments, and critical analyses across multiple disciplines, including arts, education, music, and digital storytelling. Artificial media is framed as a transformative field where AI-driven methods reshape artistic expression, challenging traditional notions of authenticity, authorship, and creativity. The book highlights ethical concerns, interdisciplinary synergies, and the implications of algorithmic techniques in creative domains. By balancing domain-specific research with cross-disciplinary insights, it provides a foundational perspective on the opportunities and challenges of artificial media.

Keywords Artificial media · AI-driven creativity · Human–computer interaction · Ethics of algorithmic creativity

This book, a curated collection of thought-provoking chapters, probes into the multifaceted relationship between humans and machines in creative processes. It offers an initial but fairly comprehensive panorama of artificial-media research comprising theoretical frameworks, field deployments, and critical analyses. Divided into three sections, the volume brings together complementary perspectives—ranging from critiques of human–computer interactions involving automated techniques to algorithmically informed pedagogical innovations, from explorations of computationally enabled creative music-making to generative digital storytelling—ultimately encouraging readers to examine both the caveats and the promises of this rapidly evolving corpus of knowledge.

D. Keller (✉)
NAP, Federal University of Acre, Federal University of Paraíba, Rio Branco, AC, Brazil
e-mail: dkeller@ccrma.stanford.edu

N. Zagalo
University of Aveiro, Aveiro, Portugal
e-mail: nzagalo@ua.pt

N. Zagalo and D. Keller (eds.), *Artificial Media*, Springer Series on Cultural Computing,
https://doi.org/10.1007/978-3-031-89037-6_1

Artificial media,[1] a concept that sits at the edge of recent cultural and technological trends, could be tentatively defined as "the simultaneous emergence of new forms of data collection, processing, and creative output, where artificial intelligence driven (AI) methods reshape our modes of expression" (Zagalo 2022) (more on this below). This construct marks a shift in how we produce and engage with artistic practice, design, journalism, and education, prompting situated and critical-analytical frameworks. Far from being limited to fake news, images, or sounds, it encompasses a wide range of computationally mediated experiences, defying established notions of authenticity, authorship, collaboration, narrative construction, and aesthetic experimentation. As autonomous technologies become increasingly embedded in our cultural fabric, they challenge the standard categories of human and computational creative processes (Boden 1998), with widespread impact on their social and ethical dimensions (Trotta et al. 2023).

This introductory text provides a summary of the topics addressed in the Artificial Media volume and presents our interpretations of a multipronged and fast-evolving field. Given the breadth and diversity of the initiatives, we point to the contents of each chapter as authoritative sources of domain-specific information and references. We also provide a summary of topics addressed during a Ubiquitous Music Symposium panel, held in preparation for the elaboration of this collection. The mutual rapport between ubiquitous music (ubimus) research and the field of artificial media will become clear as we explore the concepts and methods featured in the artistically motivated proposals (Keller et al. 2014). Complementarily, we will also summarize the topics related to educational, journalistic, and design-oriented research prominently featured in the second section of the book.

A challenging and enticing aspect of this project is how to engage with an area of research that does not have clearly established boundaries or consensually adopted methods. Our editorial approach has involved an exercise in finding an equilibrium between domain-specific consistency and cross-disciplinary exchange. As the reader dives into the intricacies of hybrid journalistic techniques, algorithmically empowered learning, or social-network-based design, it will become clear that the technological platforms do not shape the aims of creative practice and assessments. Hence, most of the criteria for technological design tend to emerge from the needs of the stakeholders within the constraints of each specific domain.

Despite this tendency to fragmentation, we also identified common traits and convergent forces that may lead to establishing artificial media as an interdisciplinary hub or community of practice. Take, for instance, the dual forces shaping the expanded adoption of technology versus the need to preserve spaces of 'technology-free' coexistence. Several research projects identify problematic aspects of a corporate-driven overtaking of domestic, educational, or public spaces that have negative impacts on cognitive development (particularly in children), on peaceful

[1] Related terms include algorithmic media, generative media, computationally generated media, expanded media, and other variations that have been adopted according to the specific needs of each field. We opted for a fairly neutral term that may be tailored through situated and culturally grounded frameworks that take into account the social and ethical implications of specific deployments.

coexistence, and even on shared notions of reality or truth. Thus, the ethical dimension of artificial-media research seems to cut across multiple disciplinary boundaries.

Another convergent issue entails the need for establishing fair usage of data resources. This is extremely tricky because a web of corporate mechanisms tends to encroach on individual rights, community rights, and even state-based sovereignty. This is particularly problematic in the context of ongoing operations by large technological conglomerates aiming to disrupt state-bounded political processes and judicial systems.[2] Furthermore, as exemplified by recent ubimus research, the digital commons can be understood as a community-managed repository of knowledge. As such, the monetization or ownership of these assets constitutes a direct attack on the sustainability of future community endeavors involving distributed digital assets.

Another recurring theme of artificial-media projects is the difficulty to establish explicit assignments of authorship. Individual authorship has been the rule of most technologically oriented artistic practices predating 2020. Many projects in this volume—like Davis, Clemens, Browne and Rezwana's, Sun and Gualeni's, Roddy and Bridges's, Cortes Gómez, García Pernía, Callejo, Echeandía Sánchez and Domínguez Díaz's, Rodríguez Valdés's, Lacasa's, and Vear and Poltronieri's proposals—start from a premise of distributed authorship. This is quite a striking turn for two reasons. Individual attribution is not only enforced through an explicit division of labor in which 'the director', 'the writer', 'the visual artist', or 'the composer' takes the credit for endeavors that involve multiple partners in intertwined exchanges of know-how. It is also enabled by means of technological design exclusively geared toward individual agency.

Consider, for instance, the acoustic notion of the instrument (or its technological extension, the digital musical instrument). This notion implies the existence of a passive object to be actuated by an instrumentalist. Parallels can be established with other artistic activities, such as the writer's pen, the painter's brush, the sculptor's scalpel, the photographer's camera, and so on. This object-centric view of creative activity dismisses the fact that human cognition does not parse the world according to fixed material boundaries. Concepts well-established within cognitive science, such as Gibson's (1977) affordances, point to a behavioral adjustment that relies on cycles of interactions with the environment involving dynamic adaptations to changing conditions. Hence, there is no such thing as "a pianist playing a piano". According to current ubimus frameworks, the pianist-piano composite can be understood as an ecosystem that depends on specific local conditions that may yield musical outcomes. This also implies the possibility of expanding the locations of the stakeholders, for example, by enabling remote interaction. This theoretical framework has been in place since the late 1990s and it is well documented in Lazzarini et al. (2020) book. With a stronger drive toward distributed authorship of artificial-media research, it may be time to explore this cognitive-ecological framework in designing support for multimodal media endeavors. Both Davis and coauthors' and Vear and Poltronieri's projects provide significant contributions in this direction.

[2] The coup attempts of the CEO of X in Bolivia (2019) and in Brazil (2024) are prime examples.

1.1 Kickstarting the Discussions on Artificial Media

In a recent panel, organized within the context of the Ubiquitous Music Symposium held in Macau, Keller et al. (2024) addressed the dissolution of the boundaries within media-oriented creative practices prompted by the application of AI-based methods, and attempted to unpack the historical usage of AI-related techniques within the sonic-arts repertoire as a way to highlight the limitations and implications of both historical and current trends for prospective ubimus-research endeavors. This discussion highlighted the implicit barriers and the opportunities situated at the intersection between ubimus practice and artificial media.

An interesting issue arising from this panel involves the current efforts in merging spoken or written tokens with sonic resources and audio-processing techniques (see also the discussion on the ASC framework below). Three limitations seem to hinder advances. 1. Collaborative tools for creative tasks not only demand knowing the resources, they also require the ability to predict outcomes when the creative processes attain a certain level of complexity. 2. Musical meaning is shaped by local material and cultural anchors, the downside is that idiolects whose meanings are not easily shared tend to emerge when the resources are deployed across cultural boundaries. 3. A recurring problem of human–computer interaction design is the increased need to adopt abstractions for tasks that demand holistic decisions involving multitiered dependencies. This caveat applies to creative music-making and other activities that rely on decision-making based on complex networks of relationships. As a corollary, parametric handles not only need to be intuitive, they also ought to be meaningful.[3]

Ongoing efforts to tackle the incorporation of artificial media in artistic activities may need to address these shortcomings to enable a solid deployment of adaptive and generative interaction frameworks. More specifically, Keller and copanelists identify two pending research challenges that may be relevant for artificial-media endeavors relying on widely distributed resources (several examples of these cases are featured in this volume, see the section on artificial media in practice).

Research question 1. There is an inverse relationship between the expansion of labels of specific timbral qualities and the search for neutral nomenclatures of musical products. More specific labels tend to increase relevance and originality, while generic tokens tend to be more easily adopted. Resource foraging may require multitiered strategies.

Research question 2. As an artistic outcome that involves human and computational stakeholders, artificial media features a hybridization of creative factors that may provide a path to collective creative practices resilient to monetization. Three factors

[3] This aspect points to a general limitation of utilitarian approaches when tackling creative endeavors. Usability studies tend to subsume cultural characteristics to aim for 'universally' deployable techniques. This method is applicable to tasks that do not require accessing local cultural traits. Artistic practices are built on multilayered local meanings. Usability techniques tend to be blind to these nuances.

Table 1.1 Second-wave ubimus frameworks and artificial media constructs

Framework	Core strategies	Core constructs
Ecologically grounded creative practice	Ecomprovisation; ecological performativity	Agent-object composite, as a unit for musical interaction; ubimus ecosystems
Struck-string interaction	Iterative adaptive processes	Intraaction; continuum between tuning and timbre
Banging interaction	Adaptive visual tracking of whole-body movement as a strategy for percussive sequences	Kuramoto-oscillator temporalities
ASC creative semantic anchoring	Large language models; iterated sequential composition	Semantic abstractions; verbal tokens

need to be in place for the expansion of these trends: 1. heterarchical support strategies, involving reconfigurable and decentralized decision-making; 2. open circulation of resources; and 3. a strong grounding on local traits. Corporate-driven techniques frequently skew all these characteristics.

According to a recent summary of ubimus proposals (Keller et al. 2024), established knowledge and uncharted musical threads coexist within the ubimus community of practice. Nevertheless, this coexistence demands a delicate balance involving the deployment of current techniques to replicate the music-making of the past without precluding the development of new designs to expand the creative frontiers. A quality that characterizes second-wave frameworks is aesthetic pliability. As a reaction to an emergent corporate-oriented fad that enforces commercial musical genres, ubimus strategies avoid the brittleness of designs tailored for a single musical idiolect or the usage of a small set of commercial labels (see Roddy and Bridges, this volume, for a complementary treatment of this issue).

Another form of friction or of bifurcation involves a false opposition between the seemingly 'magical' outcomes linked to contingent musical factors and the requirements of replicable evidence-based scientific methods to advance technological design. Second-wave ubimus frameworks suggest that the philosophical underpinnings of ubimus approaches need to be tightened to deal with this false dichotomy. This conceptual thread may impact the dialogue between ubimus and related fields, including decoloniality studies, improvisatory practices and computational creativity pointing toward a critical stance regarding the popularization of generative techniques (see also Vear and Poltronieri, this volume). Given this context, let us consider how some of the emergent ubimus frameworks tackle the issues impacting creative procedures and material byproducts (see Table 1.1).

Ecologically grounded creative practices bypass instrumental thinking (Bridges et al. 2023).[4] A key concept of this research thread features a complementary role of agents and objects, yielding an *agent-object* interaction composite. Rather than establishing a strict separation or hierarchy involving humans who impose their

[4] A collection of articles curated by Keller et al. (2023) is available in the journal Organised Sound.

will on materials, this construct is built upon the complementary nature of action and matter. This notion has several implications for design practice with artificial media, one of them entails the adoption of ecosystems as conceptual tools for ubimus deployments (Lazzarini et al. 2020).

Another interesting example of the material grounding of artificial media is provided by the struck-string interaction framework (Kramann and Keller 2024; Su et al. 2024). Struck-string interaction aims to develop strategies to deploy piano sounds without inheriting the baggage of acoustic-instrumental preconceptions surrounding piano-based designs. The authors conducted explorations involving generative techniques in which both the performance variables and the sonic outcomes are controlled by automated processes. As it is the case in other ubimus frameworks, sonic results can be tied both to structural plans and to contingent elements (cf. Aliel et al. 2023). The prototypes—based on Kramann's AOG techniques—showcase an iterative adaptive process in which the algorithm shapes its behavior to match the current musical context. Thus, future deployments may incorporate both human and computationally generated inputs. Complementing these investigations, Su et al. (2024) explore strategies to enable dynamic tunings geared toward the expansion of the equal-tempered piano literature. The authors designed a tool to tackle the analysis of piano pieces. Through a set of parametric controls, their prototype renders a just-intonation musical outcome based on an equal-tempered input.[5] Their preliminary results point to the possibility of exploring a continuum between tuning and timbre, in which the notion of a fixed material piano (or its sonic equivalent represented by sampled sonic tokens) is superseded by a fluid continuum between timbre features. This approach, of course, demands new creative-action metaphors, a key aim of this proposal.

A complementary deployment of artificial media is exemplified by the banging-interaction framework. In banging interaction, the participants use their bodies to trigger percussive events. Chakraborty et al. (2022) implemented the *Dynamic Drum Collective*, an adaptive visual-tracking system that supports musical activities by both trained and lay subjects while leaving the participants free to move around the space. The preliminary outcomes point to a good potential for usage in casual contexts but also indicate some limitations when handling both very fast and very slow tempi. Within synchronous usage, fast actions tend to be challenging for lay participants because of their lack of training in the execution of precisely timed movements. Complementarily, slow tempi present a tendency to variability because of the cognitive limits that impact internal time-keeping. Without making claims of generality, the banging-interaction team introduced solutions that rely on a mix of automated and human-centric decision-making on temporalities (Chakraborty et al. 2024). A Kuramoto oscillator was implemented targeting self-sustained periodic sequences that may be invoked when human performance is degraded. The outcomes were satisfactory yielding synchronized sequences at fast tempi. These preliminary results

[5] Just intonation is a historically oriented approach to tuning that relies on the contextual pitch content, rather than on a fixed tuning system (such as the equal-tempered standard of acoustic pianos).

indicate a path to address challenges to human-centric interaction when attempting to support specific forms of temporal organization (more on this topic below).

Another example of the application of artificial media within ubimus is the ongoing work on creative semantic anchoring (ASC from the initials in Portuguese). Recent developments in verbal-interaction techniques such as large language models (LLMs) may defy long-held assumptions of musical-interaction design. Verbal interaction may be more versatile than previously thought. Rather than dealing with things or instruments—in the ASC framework the task of design involves handling verbal meanings that yield sonic outcomes.

Along these lines, the ASC-oriented approaches comprise various applications of semantic strategies in creative musical activities. A key feature of this design perspective is the concept of *anchor*, i. e. a local element that serves as a scaffold for the organization of a reference system to deploy multimodal musical information. Creative semantic anchoring incorporates verbal tokens as a strategy to share musical knowledge. These tokens may be employed to represent complex parametric configurations that trigger timbral processes, as implemented in the Sound Sphere creative-action metaphor (Bessa et al. 2020).[6] They may also target generative processes involving large-language models, as exemplified in the *iterated sequential composition* proposal employed in *The Ubiquitous Immateriality of Musical Stuff* audiovisual artwork (Mejía et al. 2024). Thus, ASC-based strategies employ semantic tokens to represent abstractions with the aim to facilitate the manipulation of artificial-media resources.

The coexistence of legacy-oriented and prospective approaches in ubimus design indicates a healthy balance of two forces of attraction, as highlighted by Keller and Barreiro (2018). These tendencies could have constrained the ubimus field within a specialized niche. In fact, this is the case in musical-interaction perspectives that adopt the instrument as their main enabler and goal: they tend to produce new instruments that are difficult to deploy or to incorporate in emergent artistic practices. Complementarily, the coexistence of legacy and prospective ubimus frameworks open opportunities to repurpose resources that may unveil untapped possibilities. One example is the incorporation of MUSIC V as a tool for live coding (Azzigotti and Radivojevic 2022). Mainframe computing, for various reasons, was not compatible with musical endeavors based on the synchronous rendition of audio. Released from the computational limitations of mainframe hardware, Azzigotti and Radivojevic deploy a MUSIC V replica on browsers to enable the support of a *retro-oriented* form of computational sonic practice. In this case, a legacy-based infrastructure becomes a tool for the development of a hybrid form of musical knowledge that revamps the approaches of the 1960s to serve post-2020 musical aesthetics.

Further examples of constructs applicable to ubimus media are: musical stuff (Messina et al. 2022), media multiplicities (Bown et al. 2020), music-as-subscription (McConville 2023), musical things (Masu et al. 2024) or creative waste (Ferraz and Keller 2014). This panoply of concepts, of course, does not mean that all types of

---

[6] More information on ASC deployments can be found in the Journal of Digital Media and Interaction volume, edited by Keller et al. (2020).

ubimus media can coexist within a single framework or that all constructs will turn out to be compatible with prospective explorations of artificial media. Depending on the musical approach, the byproducts may suffer from specific limitations. For instance, creative waste gains importance in the context of deployments that target sustainability, pointing to a careful balance between the impact of the activity on the stakeholders and the long-term consequences on the local environment. Contrastingly, the monetization of digital resources embraced by some forms of IoMusT is hardly conducive to the open-source approaches inspired by the ubimus ethos. At some point, the unchecked monetization of resources becomes incompatible with a diversified knowledge ecology. Most ubimus frameworks give priority to the multimodal and multidimensional aspects of musical experiences, demanding constructs that target *relationships* rather than isolated objects.

Hence, not every framework or associated media is compatible with a ubimus-oriented knowledge economy. While some constructs foster free sharing and non-rivalrous approaches to technological design, others enforce a predatory corporate control that may eventually lead to monetizing the community-enabled digital commons. These tendencies are aligned with the concentration of resources by large corporations observed in capitalist knowledge economies since the 1980s (Pagano 2014) and tend to be incompatible with the ubimus ethos of community sharing and aesthetic pliability. The next section explores how these tendencies may shape both legacy-oriented and prospective designs of artificial media. Generative techniques may bypass or deepen the ongoing conflicts depending on whether the digital creative commons are respected and supported or whether the assets become monetized or obliterated.

Summing up, a multidimensional concept such as artificial media could help us bridge the gap between semantic meanings and sonic events. Emergent ubimus initiatives may come into play to scaffold these developments. The four approaches outlined in this section point to recurring features of ubiquitous music frameworks that highlight the usefulness of artificial media as a material and procedural target of creative music-making. The next three sections of this editorial tackle specific issues raised by the artificial-media projects featured in this volume. The first section—dedicated to theoretical elaborations on artificial-media research—encompasses speculative proposals, such as Gerner's notion of generative temporality, coupled with hybrid forms of narrative organization. The speculative dimension of artificial media is also present in other projects featured in this book. Thus, when read within the context of artificial-media initiatives, Gerner's proposal projects interesting philosophical questions that resonate across various fields.

The following section encompasses projects that incorporate artificial media for educational and design goals. These studies feature strong implications within the context of creative practice. Hence, they provide a cohesive body of deployments that enable to establish comparisons across specific applications. The third section of the book is dedicated to artificial-media practice. Artistic endeavors are prominently featured but there is also a proposal within the area of journalism. Gómez-Diago's chapter features an intriguing proposal to foster data-driven news production, arguing for an emphasis on critical thinking to complement the widely disseminated discussion on fact-checking.

1.2 Artificial Media: Emergent Theoretical Perspectives and Conceptual Frameworks

As previously mentioned, the first section of this book lays the groundwork to approach artificial media research by presenting exploratory theoretical and conceptual models. These proposals challenge the traditional notions of creativity, authorship, and temporality, while addressing ethical aspects of contrasting AI-mediated creative techniques. Nicholas Davis and coauthors' chapter, *Unlocking the Black Box of Artificial Media with Quantified and Explainable Co-Creative AI Systems,* addresses the opacity of human-AI collaborations. The authors introduce the Co-Creative Sensemaking Cognitive Framework (CCSM), to offer a structured approach to quantifying interaction dynamics in co-created tasks. This framework enhances transparency and fosters insights into the interplay between human and machine creativity.

Yuqian Sun and Stefano Gualeni, in *Between Puppet and Actor: Reframing Authorship in this Age of AI Agents,* explore the nuanced role of AI tools in generative animation. By framing computational agents as existing between the states of an inanimate puppet and a semi-autonomous actor, the authors highlight the need to re-evaluate classical definitions of authorship. This chapter urges us to reconsider our understanding of agency and creative collaboration in a design ecosystem increasingly influenced by automated techniques.

Alexander Gerner's contribution, *Do 'AI' Avatars Generate Our Past? Hacking into Transformations of Temporality by Synthetic Media,* discusses how synthetic media reshapes our perceptions of time and narrative. Gerner's work questions how artificial avatars and media influence the temporal dimensions of human experience, potentially blending past, present, and future in novel ways. This speculative treatment of time complements the ubimus drive toward a robust and aesthetically pliable approach to temporalities. Gerner's proposal hints that domain-specific barriers may be too narrow when engaging in artificial-media handling of temporal organizations.

In *Cybernetic Resurgences: Machine Music Beyond AI Slop,* musicians Stephen Roddy and Brian Bridges explore the resurgence of cybernetic principles in contemporary music-making. The authors critique the ethical and creative shortcomings of hegemonic large language models and propose a more inclusive, ethically grounded approach to cybernetics-inspired musical creativity, closely aligned with the proposals of the ubiquitous music movement. Their key message is a call to reclaim creativity from algorithmic monoculture, envisioning a more diverse and equitable musical future. This resonates strongly with the multiple calls for ethics-based design and deployment of technology.

These four theoretical perspectives explore complementary dimensions of artificial media with an emphasis on interaction and cognition. As argued by Roddy and Bridges, these are recurrent themes in creative practice dating back to the first decades of computing. Nevertheless, the current context of creative explorations highlights some specificities that weren't present in pre-Internet, pre-mobile, and pre-embedded computing creative initiatives. When large language models, machine learning, or generative techniques are deployed on these platforms they gain a presence and flexibility that was lacking in the early-computing artificial intelligence techniques that depended on mainframe infrastructure. Hence, rather than dealing with isolated computational resources, we are now tackling relationships among resources that may foster qualitatively different behaviors depending on the local contexts of usage. This qualitative change manifests itself in what Davis et al. term sense-making. It is also illustrated by a renewed form of temporality featured in the behaviors of generated avatars suggested by Gerner, or in the animated puppets synthesized by Sun and Gualeni. These characteristics defy the black-box approach of corporate initiatives that tend to restrict aesthetic decisions to ready-made outcomes of monoculture. It is in fact possible to subvert the constraints of commercially oriented technology. But is it worth the effort? We will come back to this question in our concluding remarks.

1.3 Artificial Media in Education and Design

The second section focuses on how Artificial Media is transforming educational practices and design methodologies. This section showcases the innovative usage of generative tools to foster critical thinking, enhance and socialize learning, and develop pedagogical approaches that feature a better rapport between technological innovation and cultural specificities. Daniela Reimann's chapter, *Media Education as AI Education—An Experiential Approach to Integrate Generative AI in Engineering Pedagogy at University,* provides a compelling case for incorporating generative techniques into educational settings. Drawing on her experiences in the pedagogy of engineering, Reimann outlines a framework for teaching students to critically engage with computational systems while fostering media literacy and exploratory engagement.

Sara Cortés Gómez and her colleagues complement the education thread by proposing the *Design of Interactive Narratives Mediated by Artificial Media: The Use of AI in Secondary Education.* This chapter examines a project where 1st-year ESO students create narrative videogames using platforms such as Twine and DALL-E. The authors exemplify how integrating AI tools into the curricular activities not only enhances the students' creative abilities, it also equips them with critical and ethical skills to navigate a future that may be dominated by competing social pressures ingrained into generative technologies. This perspective is also aligned with educational threads that strive to incorporate gamification strategies to increase the engagement of adolescents, a particularly problematic public given the widespread issues of lack of focus or interest in school activities.

María Rodríguez Valdés's *The Use of Artificial Media as a Tool for the Creation of Artistic Images through Collaborative Methodologies* explores the synergies between human creativity and AI-tool usage in artistic image design. By highlighting the collaborative potential of tools like DALL-E 2, Rodríguez Valdés underscores the transformative impact of artificial media on artistic workflows while emphasizing the irreplaceable role of human insight in creative endeavors. This effort resonates with topics addressed during the Artificial Media Panel discussed in the previous section, highlighting both the need for more flexible notions of authorship and also for a respectful attitude toward human decisions as a reliable source of local cultural traits.

In *Artificial Intelligence and the Influence of AI Filters on Creative Processes in TikTok: Methodological Challenges,* Pilar Lacasa and coauthors analyze how AI filters reshape creativity and identity on TikTok. The chapter provides an in-depth look at the platform's participatory culture, revealing how AI tools influence aesthetic norms, self-expression, and collective narratives. This study exemplifies the intersection of technology, creativity, and social interaction emphasizing the need for participatory design in artificial-media projects. Furthermore, it highlights the complex challenges faced by the repurposing of tools that are not necessarily aligned with local ways of doing.

In light of these outcomes, the participatory aspects of artificial-media endeavors underline the need to rethink how to tackle the support of collective creativity. Media literacy emerges as a requisite for educational activities in various contexts, indicating another convergent thread. Nevertheless, establishing what constitutes 'media literate participation' might demand some extra research effort.

Take, for instance, the repurposing of social-network platforms as tools for creative practice (as masterfully planned and executed in Lacasa and coauthors' study). According to ongoing studies and our own observations and field deployments, these platforms may have a negative impact on some participants. Social exposure is a big barrier for newcomers in artistic practice. An advantage of classroom-based activities that avoid interactions with anonymous internet users is the trust-building process enabled by this self-contained educational setting. This forms part of what Paulo Freire's research highlighted as a dialogical perspective (Shor and Freire 1987), involving conflict management and resolution. Incorporating these platforms in the early stages of a learning activity might disrupt the difficult first steps of fostering participatory collective creativity. Thus, we will need a significant amount of evidence from diverse contexts of usage to establish when and how this incorporation may be beneficial for media-literacy acquisition.

1.4 Artificial Media in Practice

The final section delves into artificial media in practice, exploring how domain-specific approaches are redefining storytelling, journalism, and musical endeavors. The three featured projects provide contrasting applications in fields that could hardly be contained within the same research area, were it not for their innovative take on how to handle artificial media. So a question to be addressed is how domain-specificity constrains the applicability of artificial-media techniques across communities of practice.

Gloria Gómez-Diago's chapter, *Proposal for Using Artificial Media for Reinforcing Journalism: Responsibility, Discourse, Deliberation, and Audiences' Participation,* investigates the potential of AI techniques to transform journalism. By automating tasks such as data-driven reporting, Gómez-Diago envisions a future where journalists can focus more on critical analysis and audience engagement, leaving the handling of text elaboration to automation tools. This chapter highlights the dual responsibility of ensuring ethical practices while leveraging computational capabilities to enrich journalistic engagement.

In *Crafting Artificial Musicians: Building Solaris as a Co-Operative, Perceiving, and Creative AI,* Craig Vear and Fabrizio Poltronieri present a novel approach to developing AI-based musicianship. Emphasizing musical togetherness and mutual engagement, the authors illustrate how their proposed tool Solaris embodies co-creativity and liveness, challenging the hegemonic acoustic-instrumental paradigm of music-making (or musicking, as adopted from Small's (1998) musicological work). The deployment of Solaris defies the crisp separation between composers, performers, and audience that characterizes acoustic-instrumental perspectives. Their work focuses on a specific form of pitch-based, modal improvisation. However, this is not detrimental to the potential for deployment of the proposed techniques. The target fits well within the context of ubimus legacy frameworks, comparable to Kramann's (2020) AOG pitch-oriented language, and provides an interesting complement to the four frameworks described in the previous section of this editorial.

Mário Moura's *Trás-os-Mundos, Outros Douros: Constructing Retrofuturistic Narratives through Artificial Intelligence* offers an autoethnographic exploration of generative text composition to build retrofuturistic narratives. By blending futuristic aesthetics with cultural and geographical contexts, Moura exemplifies how artificial-media-based practices can foster civic intervention and critical reflection on societal issues. Given the artistic aim of this project, it provides an intriguing contrast with Gerner's and Gómez-Diago's projects. Surprisingly, similar methods can be employed to achieve highly contrasting goals. Moura provides a highly situated and literary-informed artistic exploration that parallels the initiatives aligned with the ubimus ASC framework. This begs the question of whether conceptually close methods could be deployed across modality boundaries. Could artificial-media practices foster a rapprochement between various artistic endeavors pointing toward a 'media neutral' perspective on design for creativity?

A problematic issue to consider is authenticity. Given the flood of spurious media products enabled by refined emulation techniques, as argued by Gómez-Diago, fact-checking is at the core of responsible journalism. A more relaxed attitude toward sources is feasible when the aim is not an accurate interpretation of reality but a speculative or exploratory projection of literary or philosophical concepts, as exemplified by Moura's and Gerner's works. Thus, computational techniques should be carefully chosen according to the domain-specific aims.

Surprisingly, Moura's approach to situated and politically informed usage of narrative resources is well aligned with the techniques deployed in ecologically grounded creative practice (Keller and Lazzarini 2017). This points to a potential convergence of artificial-media methods tailored for situated and community-engaged aims. As argued by Bridges et al. (2023), this is consistent with participatory approaches to design. So it may be feasible to start by a conceptual exploration of literary and musical artificial-media deployments, to establish the means to approach situated technological design frameworks.

An intriguing concept for artificial-media-oriented practice is introduced by Vear and Poltronieri, *togetherness*. This is fairly intuitive when applied to synchronous musical activities, as the authors exemplify in Solaris. But what happens when the stakeholders and resources are geographically dispersed? Or when the network infrastructure does not support timely exchanges of information? These scenarios have been explored in various ubimus projects, leading to an expansion of the treatment of temporalities toward the adoption of quasi-synchronous frameworks. How could the concept of togetherness be employed when the stakeholders carry on their activities without demanding in-time updates on the status of the coparticipants? This scenario involves stretching a notion of collective awareness to allow for various states of affairs, including in-time alignment, delayed alignment, and lack of alignment. Interacting with artificial media could involve just exchanges among computational agents that share their status with the stakeholders. Hence, togetherness becomes a mediated process. The implications are complex and may involve a reduction of bonding. But this approach may also reduce the amount of social exposure, which in some educational settings (as observed in Riemann's study) could be positive.

1.5 Future Perspectives on Artificial Media

Why artificial media? We have purposefully chosen a hybrid construct that brings the pliable qualities of computational techniques together with the materiality of creative outcomes, i.e. media. As can be observed from the multiple projects gathered in this collection, artificial media encompasses the material byproducts of creative activity and the computational processes implicit in its production. Second-wave ubimus frameworks are opening opportunities to expand the infrastructure for artistic deployments and are also helping to rebuild the conceptual pillars of an edifice of artistic knowledge. These frameworks point to two tendencies in technological design with implications for the ongoing developments in artificial media.

One tendency strives to fill the gaps in the support of extant artistic genres by implementing new infrastructure. These approaches build upon recent computational advances that are applicable to well-established forms of music-making, for instance, they provide a revamped deployment of archaeological replicas, materialized by the recovery of the 1960s acoustic compiler MUSIC V (Lazzarini et al. 2023), and they incorporate convergent tools to enable knowledge-sharing for legacy music-making (as exemplified in Vear and Poltronieri's deployment of Solaris).

Another tendency attempts to push the limits of music pragmatics within post-2020 artistic practices, proposing hybrids of resources and procedures that defy the concepts that dominated the last seven decades in technologically oriented artistic practice. For instance, the note—a supposedly basic unit of instrumental music organization—has come into question since the early developments of audio-synthesis techniques. This is exemplified by James Tenney's works produced between 1961 and 1964 on mainframe computers (cf. Tenney 1963). In contrast with an acoustic-instrumental form of thinking, Tenney's music is well-aligned with a concept coined and developed by composer Edgar Varèse before digital tools were available, organized sound (Chou and Varèse 1966). As a target of musical endeavors, artificial media furnishes a hybrid concept that encompasses several byproducts featured in emergent ubimus frameworks. It includes the purposeful outcomes of musical activity such as the creative products and it also features unintended outcomes, such as creative waste.

Regarding the caveats, an expanded relationship between semantic meanings and sonic events highlights the application of an emergent ubimus concept, aesthetic pliability. As it is clear from the conclusions of Roddy and Bridges's and Vear and Poltronieri's projects, this dimension seems to be absent in current LLM-based tools. So far, most tools have adopted commercially driven approaches to meaning, applying generic genre labels for parametric control. This view is comparable to the "factory-preset mentality" that plagued the design of synthesizers during the early 1980s. Instead of fostering an open exploration of timbre, presets were meant to provide prepackaged, single-button solutions for immediate consumption. It could be argued that given the commercial needs of the time, not much else was needed. In fact, some legacy-oriented musical practices may be well served by ready-made corporate packages. Nevertheless, this submissive attitude toward the incorporation of resources may restrict a future of diversified ecologies of musical knowledge. Roddy and Bridges's usage of the term *monoculture* is justified.

Overall, the incorporation of generative and adaptive techniques in creative practice may involve a careful balance between methods compatible with extant musical practices and an exploratory search for increased sustainability and replicability in technological design. This implies a parsimonious adoption of technological resources that goes against the grain of the current corporate drive toward the monetization of the digital commons and the aggressive generation of media resources without any assessments of their consequences on the extant ecology of practices. Just as is the case with the predatory usage of natural resources, the impact of a blind expansion of monetization may only be fully appraised when it is too late.

Artificial media is proposed as a core concept of a variety of creative endeavors. These initiatives dissolve the boundaries between local and distributed knowledge through the incorporation of extant data, hence they may involve either legacy or prospective methods and resources. Through an exploratory and multilayered groundwork for research on artificial media, this book features diverse perspectives across theory, methods, and field deployments. As computational techniques increasingly infiltrate the extant fabric of creative practices, human beings are no longer the unique sources of innovation. Humans and computational agents become collaborators within fluid artistic and intellectual pursuits that do not need to abide by strict categories or institutionalized hierarchies. From reframing authorship to innovating educational approaches and crafting new narrative forms, this volume collectively underscores the transformative potential of emerging artificial media techniques in shaping creative methods and analytical landscapes.

The challenges ahead involve addressing the ethical and social implications of the artificial-media ecology. How do we navigate the complex relationships emerging between authorship, authenticity, and accountability while fostering inclusiveness and openness? As Floridi and Cowls (2019) suggest, the governance of generative techniques must prioritize ethical guidelines that empower both creators and audiences. We need new strategies to harness the positive aspects of artificial-media deployments, while containing the potentially harmful effects. Thus, we hope this volume inspires readers to adopt a critically informed but fully active attitude toward artificial-media pursuits, recognizing its challenges and its potential for innovation, collaboration, and socially responsible engagement. By doing so, together we may chart a course to amplify human creativity while building bridges to overcome the pervasive and ominous digital divide.

References

Aliel L, Simurra I, Messina M, Keller D (2023) Ecomprovisation: project Markarian 335. Organ Sound 28(3):328–337

Azzigotti L, Radivojević N (2022) M5live: a historical online environment for electronic music. In: Proceedings of the ubiquitous music symposium (UbiMus 2022), Curitiba, PR: Ubiquitous Music Group, pp 5–10

Bessa WRB, Keller D, Freitas B, Costa DF (2020) A metáfora da esfera sonora desde a perspectiva WYDIWYHE (The Sound Sphere Metaphor from a WYDIWYHE Perspective). J Digital Media Interaction 3(5):60–88

Boden MA (1998) Creativity and artificial intelligence. Artif Intell 103(1–2):347–356. https://doi.org/10.1016/S0004-3702(98)00055-1

Bown O, Fraietta A, Loke L, Ferguson S (2020) Creative coding and interaction design for media multiplicities: challenges, paradigms and frameworks. In: Proceedings of the fourteenth international conference on tangible, embedded, and embodied interaction, Association for Computing Machinery, New York, NY, USA, pp 877?880

Bridges B, Lazzarini V, Keller D (2023) Editorial: ecologically grounded creative practices and ubiquitous music—interaction and environment. Organised Sound 28(3):321?327

Chakraborty S, Yaseen A, Timoney J, Lazzarini V, Keller D (2022) Adaptive touchless whole-body interaction for casual ubiquitous musical activities. In: Proceedings of the international computer music conference (ICMC2022), Limerick, Ireland: University of Limerick, pp 132–138

Chou W-C, Varèse E (1966) Open rather than bounded. Perspect New Music 5(1):1–6

Ferraz S, Keller D (2014) MDF: Proposta preliminar do modelo dentro-fora de criação coletiva (Preliminary proposal of the In-group, Out-group model of collective creation). Cadernos De Informática 8(2):57–67

Floridi L, Cowls J (2019) A unified framework of five principles for AI in society. Harv Data Sci Rev 1(1). https://doi.org/10.1162/99608f92.8cd550d1
Gibson JJ (1977) The theory of affordances. In: Shaw R, Bransford J (eds) Perceiving, acting, and knowing: toward an ecological psychology. Lawrence Erlbaum Associates, Mahwah, NJ, pp 67–82
Keller D, Barreiro DL (2018) Editorial—ubiquitous music section: forces of attraction and challenges in ubimus research. Revista Vortex 6(2):1–14
Keller D, Lazzarini V (2017) Ecologically grounded creative practices in ubiquitous music. Organised Sound 22(1):61–72. https://doi.org/10.1017/S1355771816000340
Keller D, Lazzarini V, Bridges B (2023) Ecologically grounded creative practices and ubiquitous music—interaction and environment. Organised Sound 28(3):321–327
Keller D, Lazzarini V, Pimenta MS (2014) Ubiquitous music, vol XXVIII. Springer International Publishing, Berlin and Heidelberg
Keller D, Messina M, Oliveira FZN (2020) Second-wave ubiquitous music: collaboration, automation and knowledge transfer for creativity (editorial). J Digital Media Interaction 3(5):5–20
Keller D, Zagalo N, Bridges B, Roddy S (2024) Artificial media in Ubimus (Panel). In: Proceedings of the ubiquitous music symposium (UbiMus 2024). Macau, China: Ubiquitous Music Group
Kramann G (2020) Composing by laypeople: a broader perspective provided by arithmetic operation grammar. Comput Music J 44(1):17–34
Kramann G, Keller D (2024) Struck-string interaction: Exploring piano timbre beyond the piano. In: Proceedings of the ubiquitous music symposium (UbiMus 2024). Macau, China: Ubiquitous Music Group
Lazzarini V, Keller D, Radivojević N (2023) Issues of ubiquitous music archaeology: Shared knowledge, simulation, terseness, and ambiguity in early computer music. Frontiers Signal Proc 3:1132672. https://doi.org/10.3389/frsip.2023.1132672
Lazzarini V, Keller D, Otero N, Turchet L (eds) (2020) Ubiquitous music ecologies, London: Taylor & Francis (Routledge)
Masu R, Merendino N, Rodã A, Turchet L (2024) Sustainable Internet of musical things: strategies to account for environmental and social sustainability in network-based interactive music systems. IEEE Access 12:62818–62833
McConville T (2023) The artist as a subscription: patching music as an artistic device. Organised Sound 28(3):352?361
Mejía CMG, Abreu A, Aliel L, Keller D (2024) TextToSample e MusicGen: Potenciais e limitações de modelos de linguagem de larga escala na produção de recursos sonoros em contexto ubíquo (TextToSample and MusicGen: Potentials and limitations of large-scale language models in the production of sonic resources in ubiquitous contexts). In: Proceedings of the ubiquitous music symposium (UbiMus 2024). Macau, China: Ubiquitous Music Group
Messina M, Keller D, Aliel L, Gomez C, Filho MC, Simurra I (2022) The internet of musical stuff (IoMuSt): ubimus perspectives on artificial scarcity, virtual communities and (de)objectification. INSAM: J Contemp Music Art Technol (9):26--50
Pagano U (2014) The crisis of intellectual monopoly capitalism. Camb J Econ 38(6):1409–1429
Shor I, Freire P (1987) What is the 'dialogical method' of teaching? J Educ 169(3):11–31
Small C (1998) Musicking: the meanings of performing and listening. Wesleyan University Press, University Press of New England
Su R, Timoney J, Keller D (2024) Just intonation and inharmonicity in struck-string interaction. In: Proceedings of the ubiquitous music symposium (UbiMus 2024). Macau, China: Ubiquitous Music Group
Tenney JC (1963) Sound-generation by means of a digital computer. J Music Theory 7(1):24–70
Trotta A, Ziosi M, Lomonaco V (2023) The future of ethics in AI: challenges and opportunities. AI & Soc 38:439–441. https://doi.org/10.1007/s00146-023-01644-x
Zagalo N (2022) Artificial media: conceptualizing AI-driven creativity. Medium. Retrieved from https://medium.com/@nzagalo/artificial-media-79735f549b5a

Damián Keller is a full professor of music technology at the Federal University of Acre and the Federal University of Paraíba in Brazil. He is a founding member of the international research network Ubiquitous Music Group and of the Amazon Center for Music Research (NAP). He has published over two hundred articles on ubiquitous music and ecologically grounded creative practice in journals on computing, engineering, design, education, philosophy and the arts. His latest coedited book is Ubiquitous Music Ecologies (Routledge).

Nelson Zagalo is Professor of Multimedia at the University of Aveiro, and Scientific Coordinator of DigiMedia - Digital Media and Interaction Research Center. He founded the Portuguese Society for Videogames Sciences, and the Journal of Digital Media and Interaction. He is the author of more than two hundred peer-reviewed publications in journals, books and conferences worldwide. He has written the books "Interactive Emotions" (2009), "Videogames in Portugal" (2013), and "Engagement Design. Designing for Interaction Motivations" (2020).

Part I
Emergent Theoretical Perspectives and Conceptual Frameworks

Chapter 2
Unlocking the Black Box of Artificial Media with Quantified and Explainable Co-Creative AI Systems

Nicholas Davis, Michael Clemens, Eric Browne, and Jeba Rezwana

Abstract Artificial media is co-created by humans and generative artificial intelligence (AI) agents in a process of human-AI collaboration. Artificial media is like a black box of creative efforts of both the user and AI agent because their contributions are not easily discerned in the final product. We aim to unlock this black box by adding explainability to the human-AI co-creative process. By quantifying the co-creative process along a variety of dimensions, there is a record of the interaction dynamics that gave rise to a piece of artificial media. Interaction dynamics include the timing and proximity of contributions, the content of contributions, turn-taking interactions, communication strategies, feedback, and coordination. Quantified co-creative systems track data provenance in artificial media, creating a more complete representation of the combined effort of the user and AI system. This article introduces the Co-Creative Sensemaking Cognitive Framework (CCSM) as a structured approach for quantifying and explaining co-created products using interaction dynamics. CCSM provides a cognitive-based interaction coding scheme that tracks data provenance in artificial media through four categories of data collection: cognitive dynamics, interaction dynamics, collaboration dynamics, and domain dynamics. By considering the entire interaction history, CCSM enables a more complete and transparent representation of the combined effort of the user and the AI system in co-creating artificial media. This paper also proposes the concept of quantified co-creative AI system analysis, which utilizes CCSM to quantify, model, and visualize

N. Davis (✉)
Co-Creative AI Consulting, Elyria, OH, USA
e-mail: nicholas.davis10@gmail.com

M. Clemens
University of Utah, Salt Lake City, UT, USA
e-mail: michael.clemens@utah.edu

E. Browne
Munster Technological University, Cork, Ireland
e-mail: eric.browne@mycit.ie

J. Rezwana
Towson University, Towson, MD, USA
e-mail: jrezwana@towson.edu

N. Zagalo and D. Keller (eds.), *Artificial Media*, Springer Series on Cultural Computing,
https://doi.org/10.1007/978-3-031-89037-6_2

the interaction dynamics occurring on the platform, ultimately providing insights into the creative process. Finally, to illustrate how CCSM could be utilized to improve the transparency of co-created artificial media, the CCSM framework is applied to the creative domain of drawing, exemplifying how quantified co-creative systems would work in practice and contribute to the analysis and creation of artificial media.

Keywords Co-Creative AI · Explainable AI · Interaction dynamics · Cognitive model · Cognitive theory

2.1 Introduction

Artificial media is the co-created product of human-AI collaboration. Both the creativity of the user and the computational creativity of the artificial intelligence (AI) system contribute to the final product (Bilgram and Laarmann 2023). For example, crafting the appropriate prompt to generate an image or musical piece leverages the creativity of the user, while generating the creative product leverages the creativity and computational power of the AI system. Artificial media is like a black box of creative efforts of both the user and AI agent because their efforts are concealed in the final product. It is hard to attribute what role the user or AI agent played in the production of the piece of artificial media. We aim to unlock this black box by adding explainability to the human-AI co-creative processes. By quantifying the co-creative processes along a variety of dimensions, there is a record of the interaction dynamics that gave rise to a piece of artificial media. Interaction dynamics include the timing and proximity of contributions, turn-taking, communication strategies, feedback, and coordination (De Jaegher and Di Paolo 2007).

Quantified co-creative systems could be utilized to track data provenance in artificial media. Data provenance is tracking how a piece of data moves and is manipulated by different computational processes and systems as it proceeds to its target destination (Glavic 2021). We can apply the idea of data provenance to the creative product in a co-creative session to unlock the black box of artificial media. The quantification is like an X-ray into understanding the creative product, i.e., who contributed what in the creative process and when. When generative AI systems are integrated into the workflow of the user, a turn-taking process can emerge, where the user iteratively prompts the system on a task. For example, in programming, there would be cycles of communicating with the AI agent, implementing changes, and giving the AI agent feedback about the results (Prather et al. 2024). If there was a way to visualize this process, then the user could see what efforts went into producing the final artifact.

There has been some initial research into the interaction design of co-creative AI (e.g. see Rezwana and Maher 2023; Kantosalo et al. 2020; Guzdial and Riedl 2019). However, more research needs to be done quantifying and modeling the interaction of human-AI collaboration on a creative task. The field of co-creative AI needs a cognitive theory to guide its research efforts. This paper proposes the Co-Creative Sense-making cognitive framework (CCSM) as a method of quantifying co-creation.

The CCSM combines elements from the cognitive theories of participatory sense-making (De Jaegher and Di Paolo 2007), creative sense-making (Davis et al. 2017; Davis 2024), and improvisation theory (Fuller and Magerko 2010). The CCSM is a data collection schema that enables co-creative systems to quantify co-creation as it unfolds on the platform in situ. This article defines a new type of co-creative AI system referred to as a *quantified co-creative AI system*, which is a co-creative AI system that quantifies, models, and visualizes the interaction dynamics of co-creation occurring on the platform (Davis 2024). This is accomplished by applying the categories of data collection provided in the CCSM: cognitive dynamics, interaction dynamics, collaboration dynamics, and domain dynamics. The user and co-creative agent's interactions are coded through a continuous coding procedure that samples the user and agent's current interaction mode through time at specified time intervals. This data is summed to arrive at the creative sense-making curve, which shows visual indications of different interaction patterns and trends.

This new method of automatically modeling interaction dynamics enables new dimensions of analysis, experimentation, and explanation. The analysis produces a creative sense-making curve that is visually illustrative of the interactions occurring in co-creation. This curve can be analyzed to compare the user and the AI agent, as well as to examine differences across users in a statistical analysis. Quantified co-creative AI systems are proposed as a means of evaluating the role of human and AI systems in co-creating the final product as well as the dynamics of their interaction.

Quantified co-creative systems are inherently explainable co-creative systems. There has been a push within the computational creativity community for explainable co-creative systems (Bryan-Kinns et al. 2023; Llano et al. 2022; Bodily and Ventura 2018). These explanations help users understand the reason behind the creative output, which adds context and can assist in AI literacy (Long and Magerko 2020). Explainability in co-creative AI has some nuances that autonomous computational creativity systems do not, such as the social collaboration between the user and system. The cognitive science theory of enaction and its frameworks of participatory sense-making and creative sense-making can be applied to explain the social dynamics of co-creation.

This article begins by reviewing existing literature on quantifying co-creation, followed by an introduction to the cognitive science frameworks of participatory sense-making and creative sense-making. Section three describes the co-creative sense-making (CCSM) framework (Davis and Rafner 2024) as a way to quantify co-created artificial media. Each category of the framework is described and the types of data it generates are reviewed. The next section addresses why quantifying co-creation is critical to understanding artificial media, with four main benefits: explainability, adaptability, co-evolution of human-AI partnership, and analysis. The CCSM framework is then applied to quantify the creative domain of drawing. Subsequently, the paper examines how the CCSM can be applied to emergent aesthetics, proposing its use for preserving artificial media, supporting creativity, tracking novelty, and providing objective evaluation of artistic works. A discussion follows that analyzes the role of quantified co-creative AI in evaluating artificial media and co-creative systems. The article's primary contribution lies in explaining how quantifying co-creation can aid in evaluating the black box of artificial media. A secondary contribution is the application of the CCSM framework to the creative domain of drawing, demonstrating how the framework quantifies co-creation. The final contribution explores the potential of the CCSM to interpret emergent aesthetics in artificial media. Through these contributions, the article seeks to deepen our understanding of human-AI collaboration and the potential of artificial media in creative practices.

2.2 Related Work

Co-creative artificial intelligence is a subfield of computational creativity (Colton 2012) and artificial intelligence that designs, implements, and develops evaluation methods for co-creative agents. Co-creative agents collaborate with users on a shared creative product (Davis 2013). Co-creative systems originated from the concept of combining standalone generative systems with creativity support tools as computers and humans both take the initiative in the creative process and interact as co-creators (Kantosalo et al. 2020). Liapis et al. argued that when creativity emerges from human–computer interaction, it cannot be credited either to the human or to the computer alone, and surpasses both contributors' original intentions as novel ideas arise in the process (Liapis 2014). Co-creation refers to the process of collaboratively creating meaningful objects or activities, enabled by users' ability to share emotions, experiences, and ideas without needing specific guidance or predetermined strategies from a central authority (Giaccardi and Fischer 2018). Within the lens of computational creativity, this implies that at least one of these participants in the creative process is computational. Karimi et al.'s (2018) definition of co-creativity explicitly defines the concept of co-creation as the "interaction between at least one AI agent and at least one human where they take action based on the response of their partner and their conceptualization of creativity during the co-creative task."

Karimi et al. (2018) propose a framework for evaluating co-creative systems. In this framework, the evaluation is broken down into categories of who is evaluating the system, what is being evaluated, when the evaluation is occurring, and how the evaluation is conducted. In the CCSM, the AI is evaluating the interaction itself. The interaction dynamics between the user and the system are the target of the evaluation. The evaluation occurs during the co-creative process. The CCSM is the method used to conduct the evaluation.

Another approach for evaluating co-creativity is to use the Creativity Support Index (CSI) which measures the dimensions of creative productivity in human–computer interaction (Carroll and Latulipe 2009). However, the existing CSI is not well suited for co-creative contexts involving a human and an AI collaborator, as it does not capture the nuances of human–computer collaboration. Lawton et al. (2023) proposed MICSI (Mixed-Initiative Creativity Support Index), a modified version of CSI that introduces a new Human–Computer Collaboration sub-scale and six additional exploratory questions to address this gap. MICSI is intended to illuminate facets of mixed-initiative co-creative interfaces that the CSI cannot and together offer a valuable tool for further study in this area. In contrast to MICSI, which relies on post-hoc interaction evaluation based solely on the user's experience, our work attempts to quantify the collaboration more organically by evaluating the creative action in situ.

Mixed initiative co-creative systems have been evaluated with a technique called expressive range coverage analysis (Kreminski et al. 2022). In this approach, the evaluation measures the degree to which a user explores the range of creative possibilities a system can produce. This metric enables the analysis of the user's creative artifact with respect to the system's capabilities. This analysis focuses on the creative artifact the user produced. It is a post-hoc evaluation technique that evaluates what was produced but not *how* the creative product was produced. The CCSM focuses on the interaction dynamics occurring during co-creation while producing the creative product.

A computer vision approach for quantifying the interaction dynamics of the creative process using traditional art media was proposed by Jansen and Sklar (2021). Their AI model predicted whether the user was present, when they were actively drawing, and the angle of the user's utensil. They propose to integrate this system into a co-creative robot drawing system. The CCSM captures similar data as quantified by Jansen and Sklar (2021), namely whether the user was actively drawing. However, the CCSM's coding scheme has additional dimensions related to co-creative AI, such as interface manipulation, communicating with the AI system, and waiting.

A recent framework for modeling interaction in human-AI co-creative systems is COFI (Co-Creative Framework for Interaction design), proposed by Rezwana and Maher (2022). COFI synthesizes existing research on human collaboration, computational creativity, and human–computer co-creativity to describe the possible design choices for interaction in co-creative systems. COFI is relevant to our work since it provides a comprehensive and systematic way to categorize the interaction dynamics in human–computer co-creativity. Our work extends this research by quantifying the interaction dynamics established during a collaborative co-creative session between the human and the co-creative agent.

The following sections provide relevant background for how we intend to quantify these interaction types and further extend this notion of in situ creative task evaluation.

2.2.1 Participatory Sense-Making

Participatory Sense-Making (PSM) is a conceptual framework rooted in enactivism (Stewart et al. 2010), particularly autopoietic enactivism (Varela et al. 2017; Maturana and Varela 1991), that shifts the focus of cognition from individual-centric to social-centric (De Jaeghar 2013). Developed by Di Paolo and De Jaegher, PSM emphasizes that cognition in social settings emerges not from isolated individual processes but through dynamic and interactive engagements among individuals (De Jaeghar and Di Paolo 2007). This approach underlines the construction of social understanding as a collaborative activity, where shared meanings and collective understandings are forged through interpersonal interactions.

Key to this framework is the idea that social cognition is an emergent property arising from the complex dynamics of mutual interactions (Klein et al. 2006). These dynamics are characterized by a "co-regulated coupling" between autonomous agents, where the regulation targets the interaction itself, leading to the emergence of an autonomous relational dynamic that respects the autonomy of each participant (De Jaeghar and Di Paolo 2007). PSM has been applied to understanding and modeling creative collaborations, particularly in settings where co-creators interact both among themselves and with a shared product, influencing and adapting to each other's contributions in real time.

This approach is particularly pertinent in fields such as interaction design and co-creative systems, where understanding the nuances of how collaborators engage with each other and the evolving product can enhance the co-creation experience (Davis et al. 2015). By grounding interaction design in PSM, designers can better facilitate and enhance the collaborative creation process, making it more engaging and effective.

2.2.2 Creative Sense-Making

Creative Sense-Making (CSM) was proposed by Davis et al. (2017), which is a technique for quantifying the sense-making patterns present during the creative process. The creative sense-making framework proposes cognitive modes that fluctuate through time to form sense-making processes in the creative process. Two main cognitive modes form the basis of the CSM framework: clamped and unclamped cognition. Clamped cognition is defined as a cognitive agent "having a well-developed mental model of the situation, knowing what to do, and fluidly executing on-task actions. It corresponds to the state of creative flow identified in the psychological literature on creativity (Csikszentmihalyi and Larson 2014)" (Davis and Rafner 2024). Unclamped cognition is defined as the process of building a mental model to effectively navigate a surprising situation, a problem, or when one wants to reframe the creative context. There are two ways cognition can unclamp: functional unclamp and interactional unclamp. "Functional unclamp refers to regulating the interaction with the environment and other agents within it… Interactional unclamp refers to disengaging from the interaction" (Davis and Rafner 2024). A distinction is made within functional unclamp between manipulating the environment (such as an interface) and communicating with other agents. "These cognitive modes lead to four modes of interaction that are coded in the CSM framework: execute (clamped cognition), interface manipulation (partial functional unclamp), communicate (functional unclamp) and wait (interactional unclamp)" (Davis and Rafner 2024).

Each code is given a value during the coding process. Communicate is 1, manipulate interface is 0.5, execute is −1, and wait is 0. The interactions from a co-creative session are continuously coded using this technique to produce two sets of data: (1)

the raw coded values or raw interaction dynamics, and (2) the running cumulative sum of the raw interaction dynamic data, which forms the creative sense-making curve (see Fig. 2.2 right for an example CSM curve). The CSM curve visually illustrates the dynamics of interaction that went into creating a piece of artificial media. This curve can be used to identify interaction trends and patterns that produce artificial media.

2.3 Co-creative Sense-Making Framework

The co-creative sense-making framework was proposed by Davis and Rafner (2024), which quantifies social, collaborative, and cognitive elements of co-creation to enable explainability in co-creative systems. The CCSM framework presents four categories of data that can be collected from a co-creative interaction: cognitive dynamics, interaction dynamics, collaboration dynamics, and domain dynamics. Cognitive dynamics refer to the mode of cognition an individual is engaged in and sense-making patterns that emerge in co-creation. Interaction dynamics include the timing and proximity of contributions, interaction couplings that emerge, turn-taking, and communication strategies. The collaboration dynamics describe improvisational offers made during the collaboration and whether they were accepted, rejected, or elaborated. The domain behaviors comprise how much content was produced overall, and how much content was produced per turn.

Figure 2.1 shows the combined CCSM framework with its four main categories and respective subcategories. The framework serves as a data collection schema for co-creative systems. This framework can inform the interpretation of artificial media produced during the co-creative process. The CCSM framework describes different dimensions of the interaction between an individual and a co-creative agent and records how the creative product changed through time. Each category contains several quantifiable pieces of data that co-creative systems can record in situ. Researchers can utilize the CCSM as a method to quantify and model the dynamics of co-creation to learn more about the piece of artificial media produced through the co-creation.

2.3.1 Cognitive Dynamics

Cognitive dynamics are defined as the mode of cognition (clamped/unclamped) and interaction an individual engages in through time. Cognitive dynamics utilizes the creative sense-making (Davis 2024; Davis et al. 2017) cognitive coding scheme to code four modes of interaction: communicate, manipulate interface, wait, and execute creative action. When cognitive dynamics are coded through time, they produce two types of data: (1) the raw count of coded interaction modes during co-creation, and (2) a curve, referred to as the creative sense-making curve, depicting

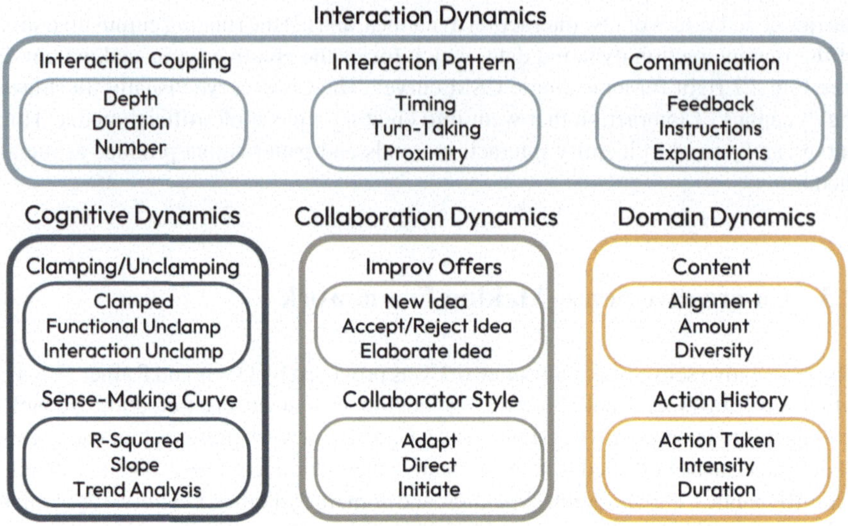

Fig. 2.1 The Co-creative sense-making framework adapted from (Davis and Rafner 2024)

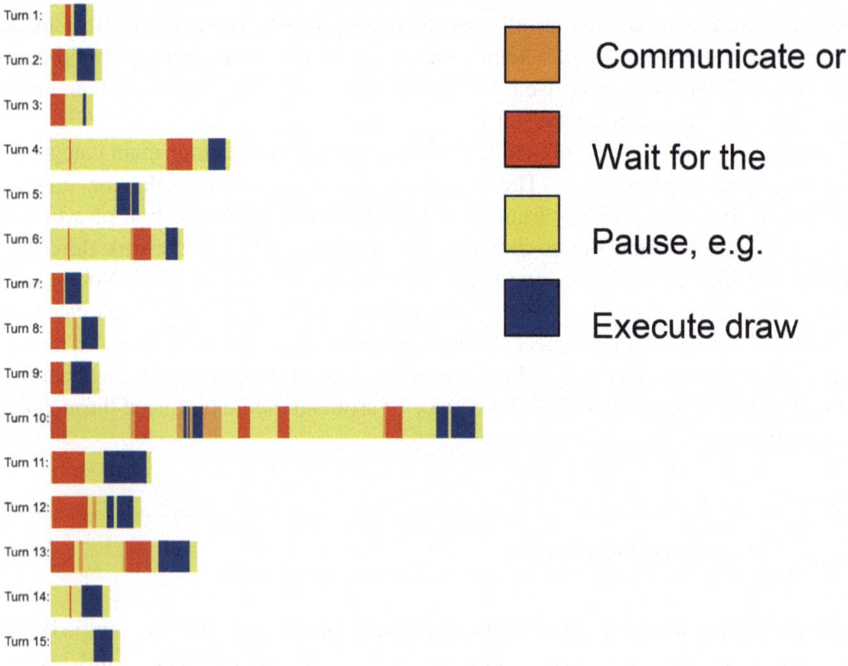

Fig. 2.2 Visualization of the turn rhythm trends from a 5-min co-creative drawing session with the AI Drawing Partner, which is described in Sect. 2.5

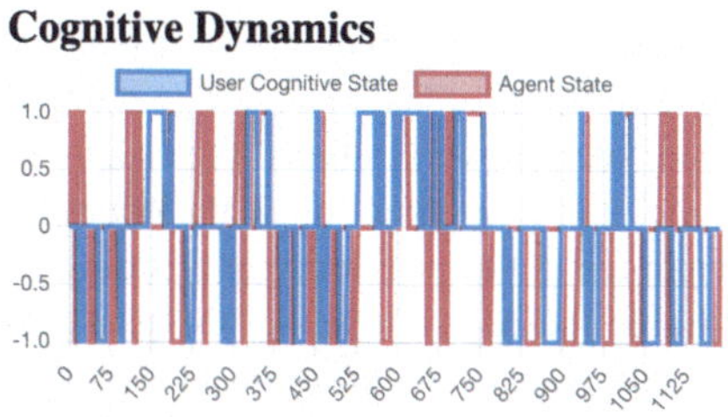

Communicate = 1
Interface Manipulation = .5
Wait = No action = 0
Execute = Drawing = -1

Code	# of Applications
User Communicate	202
User Interface Manipulation	0
User Wait	756
User Execute	230
User Average Value	-0.02
Agent Communicate	293
Agent Wait	658
Agent Execute	237
Agent Average Value	0.05

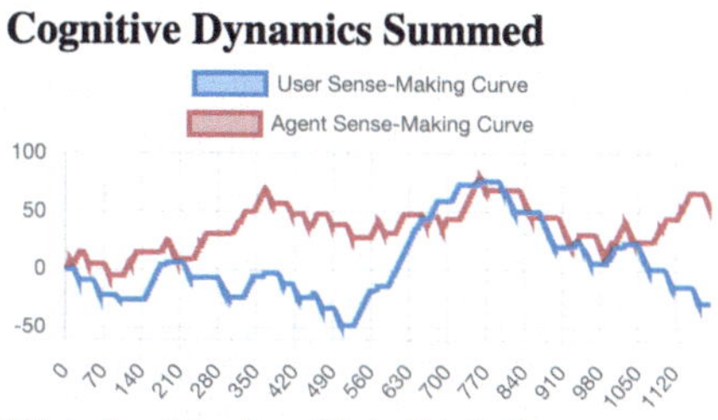

Y-Axis: Cumulative Sum of Code; X-Axis: Time

Analysis Type	Value
User Average Slope	0.04
User Y-Intercept	-15.72
User R-Squared	0.1516
Agent Average Slope	0.03
Agent Y-Intercept	19.03
Agent R-Squared	0.2843
Pearson Coefficient	0.44

Fig. 2.3 Raw interaction dynamic data, e.g. coded values (left), and summed data forming the creative sense-making curve (right) for a ten-minute co-creative drawing session

how interactions unfolded in the co-creative session (see Fig. 2.3 right for an example of a CSM curve). The sense-making curve can be analyzed to determine its slope, y-intercept, and r-squared value. A positive slope means the collaborator is engaging in more communication and interface manipulation than executing fluid actions, while a negative slope would correspond to executing more fluid creative actions. The r-squared value provides information about how well the data fits into a linear regression, which would correspond to how consistent the individual's behavior was for the session.

2.3.2 Interaction Dynamics

Interaction dynamics include the rhythm of turn taking, interaction couplings where there is some structural correspondence between turns, coordination, feedback, and communication strategies (De Jaegher and Di Paolo 2007). One feature of interaction dynamics refers to the formation of interaction couplings during co-creation, when multiple successive turns are related to one another (De Jaegher and Di Paolo 2007). For example, in the domain of drawing, if the user drew a face, and the AI agent drew ears on the face, they would be in an interaction coupling because those objects are semantically related to each other. Another example would be the user drawing a pattern and the AI agent mimicking and extending that pattern. This interaction would be considered coupled because of the visual correspondence and nearby proximity of the AI agent's contribution. Couplings can be extended beyond two turns to N turns included in the coupling. The framework details multiple features of interaction couplings that can be computationally captured, such as who initiated the coupling, who ended the coupling, the start and end time, and how many turns the coupling lasted. Another dimension of interaction dynamics is the proximity and timing of turns. In the framework there is a binary variable that tracks whether the user and agent were interacting at the same time (e.g. simultaneous collaboration), and whether they were interacting in the same area. There are multiple types of communication in the framework, both human-AI communication, and AI-human communication (Rezwana and Maher 2023). The types of communication strategies included in the framework are feedback (Lin et al. 2020; Davis et al. 2015), instructions (Rezwana et al. 2021), explanations (Ehsan et al. 2022), and ideations (Karimi et al. 2020).

Interaction dynamics also include the turn-taking that can emerge between the user and the system. The number of turns can be counted, their duration, and the creative contribution of the turn, e.g. the objects the user drew during their turn. The turn-taking rhythm can be described by distinguishing between *pauses* (e.g. to think and reflect) and periods of *waiting* for the agent to take its turn (Davis and Rafner 2024). When these interactions are coded continuously through time and visualized in their summed format, as shown in Fig. 2.2, the data reveals relationships between turn length, the ordering of events within turns, and the correspondences between the user and agent's drawing action, such as how long they were drawing and how many strokes were used.

2.3.3 Collaboration Dynamics

In the CCSM, collaboration dynamics refer to improvisational offers that were made by the collaborators and whether those offers were accepted, rejected, or elaborated upon. An improvisational offer is the introduction of new content into the shared creative product (Fuller and Magerko 2010). A collaborator can choose to accept the offer by contributing a complimentary idea, or the collaborator can choose to reject the offer by either contradicting or ignoring the contribution (Fuller and Magerko 2010). If an offer is accepted, an interaction coupling begins where turns are mutually influential. After a collaborator accepts an offer, their partner can choose to elaborate upon their contribution, thereby deepening the original idea and adding details. In this case, the interaction coupling is three turns in duration. This collaboration dynamic can continue indefinitely until another new offer is made, which ends the interaction coupling and potentially starts a new coupling if their partner accepts it by adding onto it.

2.3.4 Domain Dynamics

The CCSM framework's domain dynamics category describes what actions occurred and how much content was produced. Co-creative systems can use an interaction logging mechanism to record all the actions that were taken on the platform. For example, in the domain of co-creative drawing, actions would include draw, fill, erase, undo, redo, smudge, clear canvas, choose color, choose line width, provide feedback, request the system to sketch, request the system to generate image, and teach the system a new object. The system can record what action was executed and a timestamp for that action. The co-creative system can also record the quantity of creative content produced, regardless of the domain, e.g. the overall number of lines drawn, average length of lines, average lines per turn, and average drawing speed.

2.4 Why Quantify Co-creative Systems?

There are four primary reasons to quantify co-creation: (1) **explainability** of an AI system to describe its processes and workflows, (2) **adaptability** of an AI system to the user's needs and preferences as provided by feedback in an interactive machine learning loop through time, (3) the **co-evolution of a human-AI partnership** through fostering mutual learning and adaptive growth, and (4) **analysis** of a co-creative session between a human user and co-creative agent.

2.4.1 Explainability

Explainability refers to the AI agent explaining its processes and decisions to the user (Ehsan et al. 2022). For example, visualizing the co-creative process and describing details of the interaction. This involves examining multiple modalities and granularity of data to understand the production of a piece of artificial media. For example, we can use the CCSM categories to explain the co-creation:

- Cognitive dynamics: sense-making patterns
- Interaction dynamics: interaction couplings, communication strategies, turn-taking patterns
- Collaboration dynamics: improvisational offers
- Domain dynamics: the content that was contributed

The AI agent can use the sense-making curve of the CCSM's cognitive dynamics to visually illustrate the interaction dynamics that were responsible for crafting a piece of artificial media. This will include individual trends for both the user and agent as well as depict correlative trends between the user and AI agent. The interaction couplings can inform the user about how often they were working together with the AI agent, achieving participatory sense-making. Communication strategies could entail establishing a temporal rhythm of when communication was occurring within a turn, within a coupling, and overall within the co-creative session. The AI agent could potentially explain the rhythms and patterns of turn-taking, such as who drew first, what was drawn by the AI agent, how the user responded (including feedback and creative contributions), and whether any form of communication was present during the turn. Collaboration dynamic can be used to explain who was directing, adapting, and initiating the interaction between the user and agent. Domain dynamics can be used to explain what was produced, e.g. the objects recognized during a drawing.

2.4.2 *Adaptability*

Adaptability refers to the AI agent utilizing a model of interaction dynamics to reflect on the collaboration and adjust its creative behavior and decision making based on that model. To create adaptable co-creative AI systems that effectively respond to user needs and creative preferences, it's essential to implement mechanisms that balance predictability and novelty (Lawton et al. 2023). This requires the system to not only learn from the user's past interactions but also anticipate their current creative needs. By analyzing the user's style of communication and understanding their position in the creative process, the AI agent can tailor its contributions to be more effective and contextually appropriate. The creative sense-making curve of the CCSM can be used to model the interaction dynamics of both the user and agent. Integrating a reflection or metacognitive component in co-creative systems using the CSM curve can enable the system to develop a model of the interaction dynamics between the user and agent and reason about the creative trajectory of the interaction. This metacognitive ability can increase explainability because the system will be able to reason about why it made certain decisions about its interactions through different mediums, such as text or visual. The interaction data and patterns can be used in the system's explanation to show it made data-driven decisions, thereby increasing trust in the system from the user. This helps develop a more robust creative collaboration between the user and the AI agent. The user could engage in a dialog with the system about why it behaved in a certain manner and made the decisions it did. This can help contextualize a piece of artificial media.

2.4.3 *Co-Evolution of Human and AI Partnership*

2.4.3.1 Mutual Learning

Co-creative systems offer a means for humans and AI systems to learn from one another (Rafner et al. 2023). Quantified co-creative systems offer a unique opportunity for the AI system to learn to increase the creative engagement of the user by analyzing the dynamics of interaction between the user and agent. This type of explainable AI can help users understand the latent space (Hu et al. 2024) of these black box models through embodied AI (Chrisley 2003; Nabi et al. 2024), thereby allowing the artist to realize their creative goals with more precision. This could also be used by the AI system to understand how and when the artist wants to and is engaging with the AI system.

2.4.3.2 Adaptive Growth

Through this interaction and turn-taking style of communication of the co-creative process, both parties involved may develop and grow their own creative abilities, providing a more pleasant interaction for both the user and AI agent while expanding the capabilities of each one in the creative partnership. Including the human in the loop in an interactive machine-learning process (Mohammadzadeh et al. 2024; Mosqueira-Rey et al. 2023) where the user provides feedback and explanations about their feedback (Mao et al. 2023) to the system, can foster adaptive growth of both the user and agent.

2.4.3.3 Surprise and Novelty

In co-creative experiences, it is critical to balance control and predictability with novelty and emergence (Lawton et al. 2023). The system should be able to anticipate the user's needs and preferences by learning about what style of communication is needed or warranted for the particular artistic medium and where in the creative process the user is. An adaptive co-creative system can help reduce elements of artistic ruts or writing blocks by understanding when the user is at that particular point in their creative process and suggesting a solution or contribution that is just outside of what the artist has expressed in their current creative works to pique their interest and curiosity (Mohseni et al. 2024). This is difficult in that the system needs to learn how the individual artist works best and what might be beneficial for them during these periods. Offering a creative suggestion that is too far outside of what the artist is comfortable exploring could be a detriment to the creative process as opposed to enhancing or stimulating creativity.

It is also crucial for the AI agent to recognize the phases of the user's creative process. For instance, in the early stages of a co-creation or during creative blocks, the system should propose interventions that are novel and divergent enough to stimulate creativity (Karimi et al. 2020; Kantosalo and Jordanous 2021). In the early phases of a project, users might benefit from divergent thinking from a variety of ideas and possibilities that expand the user's creative horizon (Zubizarreta 2013). As the project progresses and begins to take shape, the role of AI shifts towards helping refine and develop the chosen ideas (Zubizarreta 2013). The system should adapt to provide more targeted suggestions that align with the evolving direction of the project, including adjusting elements of the work to enhance coherence or providing critiques that challenge the user to deepen their exploration within the chosen framework. CCSM can help the AI system understand the flow and phase of the co-creation and assume roles based on that.

2.4.4 Analysis

Analysis of the co-creative session entails experimentation conducted with the tool and comparing the quantified results between different user groups. For example, the CCSM can be used to encode its data collection schema in a co-creative system in any creative domain, such as drawing. This would automatically code the interactions, quantify collaboration, and record the creative behaviors exhibited during co-creation. The analysis can compare the number of code applications between groups, perform statistical modeling of the creative sense-making curve (e.g. detecting upward, downward, and horizontal trends in the data), and apply machine learning algorithms to identify trends and patterns in the interaction dynamic data. The CCSM quantifies many elements of co-creation within its four main categories (e.g. cognitive, collaborative, interaction, and domain dynamics). These elements can all be exported as a CSV file and used for statistical comparison between the groups of an experimental session. The categories of the CCSM can provide insight into the different dimensions of co-creation, such as its social element, collaborative nature, open-endedness, and emergent results from contributions from both the user and agent.

2.5 Quantified Co-creative Systems

This section presents the AI Drawing Partner as an example of a quantified co-creative system in the domain of drawing. The CCSM and its four categories are applied to the creative domain to exemplify what types of data are recorded in the system.

2.5.1 AI Drawing Partner: Quantified Co-Creative Drawing Agent

This analysis will utilize the AI Drawing Partner as an example quantified co-creative drawing system. The AI Drawing Partner is a co-creative drawing agent that analyzes the user's contribution, feedback, and instructions to produce a creative contribution on a shared canvas (Davis and Rafner 2024). The system is loosely turn-based, but the user can draw simultaneously with the agent, making synchronous collaboration possible. There are multiple channels of communication in the system. The user can provide positive and negative feedback via voting buttons. The agent can communicate to the user utilizing a speech bubble where it explains its actions, provides instructions, and ideates sketches. The system has multiple drawing modes, such as 'AI Mode', which is when the agent selects which drawing algorithms to use on its own based on user preferences (i.e. voting behavior). The agent can mimic the user in several different capacities by transforming the line input from the user's turn, e.g. rotating, scaling, translating, and adding noise. The agent can also recognize sketched objects and draw semantically similar objects. The 'Draw Together Mode' is where the system uses a recurrent neural network (RNN) to finish a sketch started by the user. The system will also sketch objects the user instructs it to draw. There is a text-to-image generation AI model that takes a text or voice prompt and generates an image. These interactions all happen in a turn-taking context, such that images and sketches generated by the system can be edited and manipulated. The system is also a quantified co-creative AI system that quantifies and models co-creation based on the co-creative sense-making framework. The AI Drawing Partner is a publicly available web app (https://drawing-partner.vercel.app). This section will review the data it generates in each of the domains of the framework.

2.5.1.1 Cognitive Dynamics

The AI Drawing Partner quantifies cognitive dynamics using the CSM coding scheme (Davis 2024) applied to the domain of drawing, as shown in Table 2.1.

Table 2.1 Cognitive dynamics interaction coding scheme for the domain of drawing using the CSM coding scheme from Davis (2024)

Code	Behavioral Marker	Coded Value
Communicate	Request system to draw sketch, request system to generate image, positive/negative feedback, instructing agent where to draw, teaching the agent how to draw an object/style	1
Manipulate Interface	Select brush style, choose color, undo, stylize, select drawing mode, read instructions	0.5
Wait	Pausing, hesitating, or non-action	0
Execute	Fluidly drawing	−1

Code	Behavioral Marker	Coded Value
Communicate	Request system to draw sketch, request system to generate image, positive/negative feedback, instructing agent where to draw, teaching the agent how to draw an object/style	1
Manipulate Interface	Select brush style, choose color, undo, stylize, select drawing mode, read instructions	0.5
Wait	Pausing, hesitating, or non-action	0
Execute	Fluidly drawing	−1

The AI Drawing Partner automatically codes the user and agent's interaction and visualizes this coding process in the interface of the tool, as shown in Fig. 2.3. The analysis can count the total number of code applications, as shown in Fig. 2.3 (left). The total execute count would provide data about how much time was spent on-task. The interface manipulation corresponds to how much time the individual spent interacting with the interface of the tool. Communication corresponds to how much time was spent communicating throughout the interaction. Wait relates to periods of non-action and disengagement. The analysis can characterize each participant by these four features and perform a k-means clustering analysis to determine whether there were discernible types of co-creative users. The sense-making curve, shown in Fig. 2.3 (right), provides a visually readable linear representation of a co-creative session's cognitive fluctuations and interaction dynamics through time. When the curve rises, the individual is communicating or manipulating the interface, when the curve falls, the individual is fluidly executing a creative action, and horizontal parts of the curve are waiting. This curve can be annotated visually with the action history log, analyzed with linear regression to provide the slope, intercept, and r-squared value, and analyzed with statistical modeling techniques to detect trends and patterns in the data.

2.5.1.2 Interaction Dynamics

The simultaneous drawing metric provides data about whether there was a distribution of effort in the drawing. If the drawing was simultaneous and near each other, then that is a unique type of coupling. The system counts the total number of interaction couplings, which are characterized by a number of features shown in Fig. 2.4: Interaction dynamics from the AI Drawing Partner interface. An interaction coupling is determined by the user or agent drawing close to the previous turn (e.g. within 50 pixels). The average turns per coupling provides data about the depth of the user and agent's coupling. Couplings can be short or long in duration, and it is possible to count the total amount of time coupled. A coupling depth is calculated based on the average turns per coupling, with 2–3 turns being loosely coupled and 3 + turns being tightly coupled. A leader and follower is calculated based on who has more new ideas. Interface interactions that relate to the creative process can be counted, such as undo and in the case of art, stylizing the image. The communication between the agent and user is quantified here with upvotes and downvotes.

The Drawing Partner uses the data collection scheme in Fig. 2.5 to quantify the features of interaction couplings. The 'what' category explains what makes up the interaction coupling. The 'how' category describes the procedures the user and agent went through during the course of the coupling, such as who initiated and decoupled the interaction, and the clamping/unclamping count during the interaction coupling. The 'when' category records the start time and end time of the coupling. The 'where' category records the Euclidean quadrant the interaction occurred in and the center point of the bounding box of the lines of the coupling. This data can be used to cluster the couplings from within one session or between sessions with different users.

Interaction Dynamics

Simultaneous Drawing:	10 seconds
Simulateneous & Near:	0 seconds
Number of Interaction Couplings:	8
Avg. Turns Per Coupling:	3.00
Avg. Time Per Coupling:	72.25 seconds
Total Time Coupled:	746
Coupling Depth:	Tight
User Collaborator Type:	Leader
Agent Collaborator Type:	Follower
Undo Count:	4
Stylization Count:	3
Upvotes:	4
Downvotes:	2

Fig. 2.4 Interaction dynamics from the AI drawing partner interface

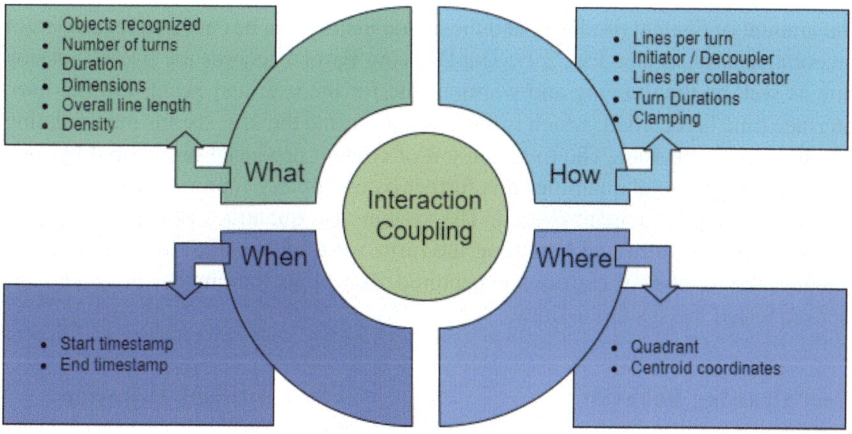

Fig. 2.5 Features of interaction couplings captured in the domain of drawing in the AI drawing partner system

2.5.1.3 Collaboration Dynamics

The collaboration dynamics in Fig. 2.6 record information relating to the turns of each participant in the collaboration. This includes the number of turns for both the user and the agent. Each turn is assigned an improvisational value that relates to whether it was a new idea (traditional improv offer), or whether it was accepting a new idea, rejecting a new idea, or elaborating an already established idea (Fuller and Magerko 2011). This is used to calculate who was leading or following during the interaction. A participant with more new ideas than accepted ideas is considered

User Collaboration Dynamics

Number Of Turns	11
Number of New Ideas:	7
Number Accepted Ideas:	0
Number Of Rejected Ideas:	0
Number Of Elaborations:	4
Most Liked Algorithm:	addCircle
Most Disliked Algorithm:	objectResponse
User Collaborator Score:	40
User Creative Score:	90

Agent Collaboration Dynamics

Number Of Turns	20
Number of New Ideas:	3
Number Accepted Ideas:	8
Number Of Rejected Ideas:	4
Number Of Elaborations:	5
Agent Collaborator Score:	130
Agent Creative Score:	105

Fig. 2.6 Collaboration dynamics from the AI drawing partner interface

taking a leader role, while a participant with more acceptance and elaboration is considered a follower.

2.5.1.4 Domain Behavior

The amount of content produced and the action history can be captured regardless of the creative context (see Fig. 2.7). The Drawing Partner records the overall session time as well as the drawing and waiting time for the user and agent. For the user, interface time is recorded, which is the amount of time the user spends manipulating the interface of the tool. The total amount of content produced is captured by total lines. Line length total quantifies this further by essentially capturing how much ink was used by the participant overall. The system also quantifies how much content was produced per turn and how long the turns were on average. In the domain of drawing, the number of canvases is captured, as well as the number of objects the user requested the system to draw.

User Drawing Behavior

Overall Session Time:	883.5 seconds
User Drawing Time:	136 seconds
User Waiting Time:	577 seconds
Interface Time:	122 seconds
Total User Lines:	31
User Line Length Total:	34193.10
Avg. Lines Per Turn:	2.82
Avg. Line Length Per Turn:	3108.46
Avg. Turn Length:	8.95 seconds
Number of Canvases:	2
Number of Objects Requested:	8

Agent Drawing Behavior

Agent Drawing Time:	181.5 seconds
Agent Waiting Time:	479 seconds
Total Agent Lines:	114
Agent Line Length Total:	51707.99
Avg. Lines Per Turn:	5.70
Avg. Line Length Per Turn:	2591.10
Avg. Turn Length:	4.54 seconds

Fig. 2.7 User and agent drawing behavior metrics from the AI drawing partner user interface

2.6 CCSM and Emergent Aesthetics

This section investigates CCSM through the lens of emergent aesthetics and the rapid development of new forms of artificial media. The goal of the section is to explain a twofold application of CCSM in this context: first, in understanding how interaction dynamics can influence emotional and perceptual responses to art, and second, in curating interaction dynamics to identify and categorize interaction patterns associated with the emergence of new aesthetic styles.

We can use data from frameworks like CCSM (and subsequent extended frameworks) to capture interaction data which reveals information about how creative behaviors relate to the way collated features of creative outputs (complexity, meaning, etc.) and how they may relate to aspects like arousal potential and other such critical components of art. This would help in understanding how different creative interactions influence the emotional and perceptual responses elicited by artistic works.

Secondly (and by extension), we will show how (as part of biological theories of aesthetic development) CCSM can fulfill the function of a "retention mechanism". Through the analysis and digital curation of interaction dynamics at scale, there may be an opportunity to better understand how specific interaction data collected using CCSM relates to or signals the emergence of new aesthetics in artificial media. In other words, we can use these datasets to shed light on *how* particular kinds of interaction dynamics could characterize particular embodied practice-based elements of emergent aesthetic styles. Furthermore, by identifying patterns between the interaction data collected during the *process* and characteristics of the subsequent creative *product*, these data can be grouped into subsets and curated as archetypal interaction styles suggestive of particular kinds of creative outputs. This, in turn, would be beneficial when considering the range of behaviors available to a computational co-creative agent.

2.6.1 *Theories on Aesthetic Development*

Various different theories attempting to account for aesthetic development over time have been put forward. These can broadly be grouped into *extrinsic* and *intrinsic* categories (Martindale 1986). Extrinsic refers to the influence of external factors such as society, culture, and historical context. An example of this would be reflectionist theories that propose art as a reflection of society (Hauser 2005). Intrinsic theories focus on internal factors such as the influence of individual artists, groups, and the inherent logic of artistic development. A common example would be influence-based theories that look for direct influence between individuals or particular groups of artists (Bloom 1997).

These theories offer insights into specific aspects of aesthetic evolution but also have limitations. Extrinsic views, for instance, may oversimplify the sources of artistic inspiration by attributing it solely to societal factors. Similarly, intrinsic theories, while recognizing individual influences, often struggle to predict broader shifts in aesthetic trends over time (Martindale 1986).

2.6.1.1 Evolutionary Theory

Evolutionary theory provides a compelling framework for understanding aesthetic change as driven by inherent biological and cognitive pressures (Kozbelt 2021; De Tiège, Verpooten, and Braeckman 2021; Dissanayake 2015; Davies 2017). It posits that artists face an ongoing imperative to innovate and increase the complexity of their work to sustain audience engagement and counteract habituation (Martindale 1986; Campbell 1974; Kozbelt 2021; Davies 2017). This evolutionary impetus inherently drives novelty and unpredictability in art forms over time.

The theory suggests that within a stylistic period, artists may harness more primal cognitive states, such as free-associative thought (Kozbelt 2021), to generate novel ideas and increase "arousal potential" in their work (Berlyne 1973; Martindale 1986). *Arousal potential* denotes the degree of arousal or activation elicited by a stimulus, influenced by factors such as its novelty, complexity, meaningfulness, and sensory characteristics like pitch or hue (Martindale 1986). Research indicates a general preference among individuals for stimuli with a moderate level of arousal potential, avoiding those that are excessively high or low in arousal activation (Martindale 1986; Kozbelt 2021).

Hence, as a style matures, the strategy or increasing arousal potential reaches a point of diminishing returns, leading to the emergence of new artistic paradigms. This cyclical process underpins the evolutionary dynamics observed in the historical development of poetry, painting, and music (Martindale 1986; Kozbelt 2021).

The evolutionary perspective complements existing theories by offering a comprehensive explanation of how aesthetic diversity emerges and evolves. It underscores the role of inherent biological mechanisms in shaping artistic innovation and highlights the adaptive nature of creative practice across different epochs and cultures.

2.6.1.2 CCSM and Arousal Potential

The creative process in human-AI collaboration can be understood through the lens of psychological means of production (Martindale 1986), particularly focusing on how works of art with increasing arousal potential are produced. The process involves two key stages: **inspiration** and **elaboration**.

1. **Inspiration Stage**:

    - Involves a **regression** from secondary process thinking (logical, abstract, reality-oriented) to primary process thought (free-associative, concrete, irrational).

- This stage generates novel and original ideas by allowing for free association and undirected thought, leading to unique combinations of mental elements.

2. **Elaboration Stage**:

   - Involves developing the raw, novel ideas from the inspiration stage into a final form, adhering to stylistic rules and logical structure.
   - This stage utilizes secondary process cognition to refine and elaborate on the initial, more chaotic ideas.

In the context of CCSM, tracking the interaction dynamics between human and AI systems involves measuring both the regression toward primary process thought and the subsequent elaboration. Higher arousal potential in co-created works can be observed by analyzing:

- The depth of regression, indicating more free-associative, novel contributions.
- The degree of elaboration, shaping these contributions into coherent and stylistically appropriate forms.

By quantifying these aspects, CCSM can offer insights into how the balance of inspiration and elaboration influences the creativity and novelty of artificial media. This helps in understanding the emergent aesthetics of co-created works, providing a framework for evaluating the dynamic interplay between human creativity and AI agent assistance.

2.6.1.3 CCSM as Retention Mechanism

In the evolutionary view of aesthetic development, three key elements are necessary: the presence of variations, consistent selection criteria, and mechanisms for preserving selected variants (Martindale 1986; Campbell 1974). These methods for preserving selected variants are referred to as "retention mechanisms". *Retention mechanisms* refer to systems or institutions that select and preserve objects or expressions perceived as valuable, enjoyable, or significant, such as books, musical scores, and museums (Koskinen and Harper 1990). These mechanisms ensure the continuity and evolution of cultural artifacts over time.

The CCSM serves as a contemporary form of retention mechanism by systematically capturing and analyzing interaction dynamics in new works of co-creative art with AI agents. This process documents the underlying processes and complexities involved in evolving aesthetic forms and cultural manifestations, analogous to how traditional museums archive the techniques and contexts behind physical artworks. Similar to the computational methods described by Cetinic and She (2022), which analyze digitized art to understand and preserve artistic nuances, the CCSM extends this concept by curating interaction data, thereby contributing to the ongoing development and documentation of digital and AI-enabled aesthetic practices.

Curation of Interaction Dynamics: CCSM captures interaction dynamics between humans and AI during the creative process. This includes the timing, proximity, and content of contributions, turn-taking interactions, communication strategies, feedback, and coordination. By digitizing and archiving these interactions, CCSM can provide a comprehensive record of how a piece of artificial media was co-created.

Subsequently, these data can be analyzed to identify recurring patterns and correlations with the characteristics of resulting creative outputs. Through thoughtful curation, these insights can be distilled into archetypal interaction styles that suggest specific types of creative outputs. This curated knowledge could be used to bolster the capabilities of co-creative agents by informing decision-making processes and broadening the repertoire of creative behaviors they can emulate.

Relevance for New Aesthetics:

1. **Preservation and Analysis**:
   - Just as books, musical scores, and museums preserve traditional art, CCSM preserves digital interaction data, enabling future analysis and reinterpretation. This curation helps track the evolution of artistic styles and techniques within AI-mediated creative processes.
2. **Creativity**:
   - By retaining detailed records of creative interactions, CCSM supports the study of creativity. Researchers can analyze patterns and dynamics that lead to high-arousal, novel outcomes, and refine AI algorithms to better support human creativity.
3. **Novelty**:
   - The retention of interaction dynamics facilitates the development of new aesthetics by providing a rich dataset for experimentation. This can allow for the exploration of novel combinations and the refinement of co-creative processes, leading to a better understanding of innovative artistic forms.
4. **Supporting Objective Evaluation**:
   - At scale, interaction data can allow for objective evaluation of the co-creative process. By understanding how variations are generated and selected, it becomes possible to develop consistent criteria for assessing the quality and impact of artificial media, moving beyond subjective human standards.

The CCSM framework may serve as an important retention mechanism in the evolution of artificial media aesthetics. By systematically curating interaction dynamics and related data, it aims to capture and preserve detailed creative processes, thereby supporting the ongoing development and understanding of new and innovative forms of art and creative practice.

2.7 Discussion

The co-creative sense-making framework quantifies and models elements of the interaction dynamics of a co-creative session. However, there are qualitative aspects of co-creation to consider that are not covered by the framework. Deshpande et al. (2023) recently expanded creative sense-making as observable creative sense-making (OCSM) to include additional dimensions to capture during co-creation: participation, newness, and appropriateness. Participation is the degree of participatory sense-making present in the interaction, ranging from individual to reactive to joint sense-making. Newness relates to the novelty of the current turn relative to prior turns. Appropriateness relates to whether the action was on-task. However, these terms inherently carry a degree of subjectivity, as interpretations of novelty and task relevance are influenced by individual perspectives and cultural contexts. Csikszentmihalyi's Systems Model of Creativity (2014) provides a useful lens here, illustrating that creativity emerges from the dynamic interaction between the individual, the domain (cultural context), and the field (social evaluators). Within this model, judgments of newness and appropriateness are shaped by the cultural norms and evaluative criteria of the field and the conventions of the domain. For instance, what is deemed "new" in one cultural or artistic context may already be well-established in another.

To address this, the expanded CCSM framework leverages behavioral markers to systematically capture these qualitative dimensions, aiming to balance subjective judgment with empirical rigor. This approach enables the application of these abstract concepts while remaining sensitive to their contextual variability. Additionally, integrating participatory feedback mechanisms—such as evaluations from diverse user groups—can further mitigate biases and ensure that the framework reflects a broader range of interpretations and cultural contexts. By aligning the qualitative dimensions of newness and appropriateness with the Systems Model, the CCSM framework strengthens its capacity to account for the subjective and context-dependent nature of creative processes (Csikszentmihalyi 2015; Deshpande et al. 2023).

Each category has four states the user can be in, with behavioral markers for each state. These values are continuously coded using a specialized video coding tool that samples from the user's applied code at specified time intervals.

Expanding the CCSM to include the new dimensions leads to a more holistic framework and methodological approach to analyze co-creation and artificial media. The new model is shown in Fig. 2.8. The piece of artificial media is on the left, while the data collected by the CCSM form the interaction data for the overall framework. From this interaction data, the additional categories proposed by the OCSM can be applied on top of the interaction data generated by the CCSM. The sense-making layer is the participation dimension of the OCSM, which codes whether there was no sense-making, individual sense-making, reactive sense-making, or participatory sense-making. These sense-making events can be coded further into appropriateness and newness, as shown in Fig. 2.8. The higher order constructs are manually coded by the participant and researcher, while the lower order constructs (including the piece

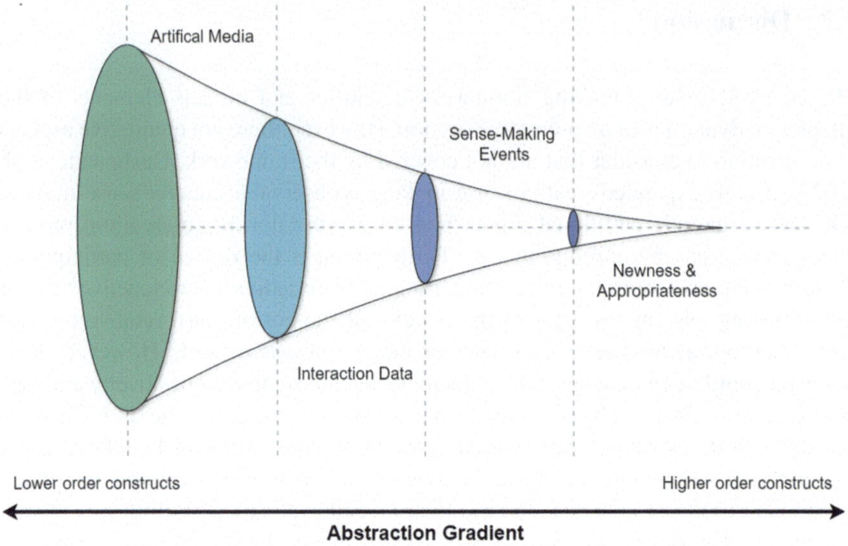

Fig. 2.8 The expanded CCSM including the dimensions from the OCSM

of artificial media and interaction data) are captured and presented by the quantified co-creative system. Together, this analytical framework provides a lens into a piece of artificial media.

Emergent aesthetics, particularly within the context of the expanded CCSM, challenge traditional notions of creativity by emphasizing the interplay between human and non-human agents in cultural production. The integration of AI in artistic endeavors raises critical questions about aesthetic variability, and the risk of homogenization has been acknowledged as an area of interest (Manovich 2018). The expanded CCSM facilitates the examination of these dynamics, capturing abstract dimensions such as newness, and appropriateness during co-creative sessions. By systematically coding these dimensions, researchers are well-positioned to assess how AI systems influence both the processes of creation and the resulting aesthetic outputs. This aligns with ongoing discussions about "post-creativity," where the focus shifts to understanding the complexity of creative interactions and the evolving landscape of aesthetic judgment (Hullman et al. 2023; Cetinic and She 2021). Ultimately, the expanded CCSM not only provides a solid methodological approach but could also serve as a useful tool in unraveling the complexities of emergent aesthetics in an increasingly AI-driven cultural environment.

2.8 Conclusions

As the co-created product of human-AI collaboration, artificial media is a black box of the creative effort of both the user and agent. We proposed to unlock this black box by adding explainability to co-creative systems by quantifying the co-creation happening on the platform. There are several reasons to quantify co-creation, including: *explainability* of the AI system's processes and decisions, *adaptability* of the AI to the user's needs, preferences, and interaction trends, *co-evolution of a human-AI partnership* by fostering mutual learning, and *analysis* of experiments conducted with co-creative systems. The concept of a quantified co-creative AI system was described as one that quantifies and models the co-creation happening on the platform. The co-creative sense-making framework was described as one method of quantifying co-creative AI systems. The co-creative sense-making framework presents four categories of data that can be collected from a co-creative interaction: cognitive dynamics, interaction dynamics, collaboration dynamics, and domain dynamics. The framework was applied to the creative domain of drawing to conceptualize how quantified co-creative systems would work in the domain. A discussion followed that examined the role of quantified co-creative AI systems in the evaluation and preservation of artificial media. The CCSM was expanded to include additional qualitative dimensions from the observable creative sense-making framework (Deshpande et al. 2023). The quantified approach taken here can help explain and contextualize artificial media by providing an x-ray into how the piece of artificial media was created.

References

Berlyne DE (1973) Aesthetics and psychobiology. J Aesthet Art Criticism 31(4)

Bilgram V, Laarmann F (2023) Accelerating innovation with generative AI: AI-augmented digital prototyping and innovation methods. IEEE Eng Manage Rev 51(2):18–25

Bloom H (1997) The anxiety of influence: a theory of poetry. Oxford University Press, USA

Bodily PM, Ventura D (2018) Explainability: an aesthetic for aesthetics in computational creative systems. In: ICCC, pp 153–160

Bryan-Kinns N, Ford C, Chamberlain A, Benford SD, Kennedy H, Li Z, ... Rezwana J (2023) Explainable AI for the arts: XAIxArts. In: Proceedings of the 15th conference on creativity and cognition, pp 1–7

Campbell DT (1974) Evolutionary epistemology. The Philosophy of Karl R. Popper

Carroll EA, Latulipe C (2009) The creativity support index. In: CHI'09 extended abstracts on human factors in computing systems, pp 4009–4014

Cetinic E, She J (2022) Understanding and creating art with AI: review and outlook. ACM Trans Multimedia Comput Commun Appl (TOMM) 18(2):1–22

Chrisley R (2003) Embodied artificial intelligence. Artif Intell 149(1):131–150

Csikszentmihalyi M, Larson R (2014) Flow and the foundations of positive psychology (Vol 10, pp 978–94). Dordrecht: Springer

Csikszentmihalyi M (2015) The systems model of creativity: the collected works of Mihaly Csikszentmihalyi. Springer

Davies S (2017) Evolution, aesthetics, and art: an overview. The Routledge Handbook of Evolution and Philosophy, pp 359–371

Davis N (2013) Human-computer co-creativity: blending human and computational creativity. In: Proceedings of the AAAI conference on artificial intelligence and interactive digital entertainment (Vol 9, No 6, pp 9–12)

Davis N (2024) Creative sense-making. Artificial intelligence, co-creation and creativity: the new frontier for innovation, 45

Davis N, Rafner J (2024) AI drawing partner: co-creative drawing agent and research platform to model co-creation. arXiv preprint arXiv:2501.06607

Davis N, Hsiao CP, Singh KY, Lin B, Magerko B (2017) Creative sense-making: quantifying interaction dynamics in co-creation. In: Proceedings of the 2017 ACM SIGCHI conference on creativity and cognition, pp 356–366

Davis N, Hsiao CP, Singh KY, Li L, Moningi S, Magerko B (2015) Drawing apprentice: an enactive co-creative agent for artistic collaboration. In: Proceedings of the 2015 ACM SIGCHI conference on creativity and cognition, pp 185–186

De Jaegher H (2013) Embodiment and sense-making in autism. Front Integr Neurosci 7:15

De Jaegher H, Di Paolo E (2007) Participatory sense-making: an enactive approach to social cognition. Phenomenol Cogn Sci 6:485–507

De Tiège A, Verpooten J, Braeckman J (2021) From animal signals to art: manipulative animal Signaling and the evolutionary foundations of aesthetic behavior and art production. Quart Rev Biol 96(1):1–27

Deshpande M, Trajkova M, Knowlton A, Magerko B (2023) Observable creative sense-making (OCSM): a method for quantifying improvisational co-creative interaction. In: Proceedings of the 15th conference on creativity and cognition, pp 103–115

Dissanayake E (2015) "Aesthetic primitives": fundamental biological elements of a naturalistic aesthetics. Aisthesis. Pratiche, linguaggi e saperi dell'estetico 8(1):6–24

Ehsan U, Wintersberger P, Liao QV, Watkins EA, Manger C, Daumé III H, ... Riedl MO (2022) Human-centered explainable AI (HCXAI): beyond opening the black-box of AI. In: CHI conference on human factors in computing systems extended abstracts, pp 1–7

Fuller D, Magerko B (2010) Shared mental models in improvisational performance. In: Proceedings of the intelligent narrative technologies III workshop, pp 1–6

Giaccardi E, Fischer G (2008) Creativity and evolution: a metadesign perspective. Digital Creativity 19(1):19–32

Glavic B (2021) Data provenance. Foundations and Trends® in Databases 9(3–4):209–441

Guzdial M, Riedl M (2019) An interaction framework for studying co-creative ai. arXiv preprint arXiv:1903.09709

Hauser A (2005) Social history of art, volume 4: naturalism, Impressionism, the film age. Routledge

Hu T, Chen F, Wang H, Li J, Wang W, Sun J, Li Z (2024) Complexity matters: Rethinking the latent space for generative modeling. Adv Neural Inform Process Syst, 36

Hullman J, Holtzman A, Gelman A (2023) Artificial intelligence and aesthetic judgment. arXiv preprint arXiv:2309.12338

Jansen C, Sklar E (2021) Predicting artist drawing activity via multi-camera inputs for co-creative drawing. In: Annual conference towards autonomous robotic systems, pp 217–227. Cham: Springer International Publishing

Kantosalo A, Jordanous A (2021) Role-based perceptions of computer participants in human-computer co-creativity. AISB

Kantosalo A, Ravikumar PT, Grace K, Takala T (2020) Modalities, styles and strategies: an interaction framework for human-computer co-creativity. In: ICCC, pp 57–64

Karimi P, Grace K, Maher ML, Davis N (2018) Evaluating creativity in computational co-creative systems. arXiv preprint arXiv:1807.09886

Karimi P, Rezwana J, Siddiqui S, Maher ML, Dehbozorgi N (2020) Creative sketching partner: an analysis of human-AI co-creativity. In: Proceedings of the 25th international conference on intelligent user interfaces, pp 221–230

Klein G, Moon B, Hoffman RR (2006) Making sense of sensemaking 1: alternative perspectives. IEEE Intell Syst 21(4):70–73
Koskinen WC, Harper SS (1990) The retention process: mechanisms. Pesticides Soil Environ Process Impacts Model 2:51–77
Kozbelt A (2021) The aesthetic legacy of evolution: the history of the arts as a window into human nature. Front Psychol 12:787238
Kreminski M, Karth I, Mateas M, Wardrip-Fruin N (2022) Evaluating mixed-initiative creative interfaces via expressive range coverage analysis. In: IUI workshops, pp 34–45
Lawton T, Ibarrola FJ, Ventura D, Grace K (2023) Drawing with reframer: emergence and control in co-creative ai. In: Proceedings of the 28th international conference on intelligent user interfaces, pp 264–277
Liapis A, Yannakakis GN, Togelius J (2014) Computational game creativity. ICCC
Lin Y, Guo J, Chen Y, Yao C, Ying F (2020) It is your turn: collaborative ideation with a co-creative robot through sketch. In: Proceedings of the 2020 CHI conference on human factors in computing systems, pp 1–14
Llano MT, d'Inverno M, Yee-King M, McCormack J, Ilsar A, Pease A, Colton S (2022) Explainable computational creativity. arXiv preprint arXiv:2205.05682
Long D, Magerko B (2020) What is AI literacy? Competencies and design considerations. In: Proceedings of the 2020 CHI conference on human factors in computing systems, pp 1–16
Manovich L (2018) AI aesthetics. Strelka press, Moscow
Mao Y, Rafner J, Wang Y, Sherson J (2023) A hybrid intelligence approach to training generative design assistants: partnership between human experts and AI enhanced co-creative tools. In: HHAI 2023: augmenting human intellect, pp 108–123. IOS Press
Martindale C (1986) Aesthetic evolution. Poetics 15(4–6):439–473
Maturana HR, Varela FJ (1991) Autopoiesis and cognition: the realization of the living (Vol 42). Springer Science & Business Media
Mohammadzadeh B, Françoise J, Gouiffès M, Caramiaux B (2024) Studying collaborative interactive machine teaching in image classification. In: Proceedings of the 29th international conference on intelligent user interfaces, pp 195–208
Mohseni M, Maher ML, Grace K, Siddiqui S, Najjar N (2024) Exploring AI-based computational models of novelty to encourage curiosity in student learning. SN Comput Sci 5(5):559
Mosqueira-Rey E, Hernández-Pereira E, Alonso-Ríos D, Bobes-Bascarán J, Fernández-Leal Á (2023) Human-in-the-loop machine learning: a state of the art. Artif Intell Rev 56(4):3005–3054
Nabi S, Esling P, Peeters G, Bevilacqua F (2024) Embodied exploration of deep latent spaces in interactive dance-music performance. In: Proceedings of the 9th international conference on movement and computing, pp 1–9
Prather J, Reeves B, Leinonen J, MacNeil S, Randrianasolo AS, Becker B, ... Briggs B (2024) The widening gap: the benefits and harms of generative AI for novice programmers. arXiv preprint arXiv:2405.17739
Rafner J, Beaty RE, Kaufman JC, Lubart T, Sherson J (2023) Creativity in the age of generative AI. Nat Hum Behav 7(11):1836–1838
Rezwana J, Maher ML (2023) Designing creative AI partners with COFI: a framework for modeling interaction in human-AI co-creative systems. ACM Trans Comput Human Interact 30(5):1–28
Rezwana J, Maher ML, Davis N (2021) Creative PenPal: a virtual embodied conversational AI agent to improve user engagement and collaborative experience in human-AI co-creative design ideation. In: IUI Workshops
Stewart J, Gapenne O, Di Paolo EA (Eds) (2010) Enaction: toward a new paradigm for cognitive science. MIT Press
Varela FJ, Thompson E, Rosch E (2017) The embodied mind, revised. MIT press, Cognitive science and human experience
Zubizarreta R (2013) Co-creative dialogue for meeting practical challenges. OD Practitioner 45(1):47–53

Nicholas Davis is a co-creative AI and HCI expert with a Ph.D. in Human-Centered Computing. He has a strong academic background, working as an assistant professor and graduate research assistant, and industry experience at Google, YouTube, and Adobe. Dr. Davis's research focuses on designing and evaluating co-creative AI systems, emphasizing understanding user-agent interactions and cognitive processes. He uses various research methods, including user studies and prototyping, to develop interaction models and improve co-creative AI systems.

Michael Clemens is a researcher with a strong background in human-centered computing. His research focuses on developing audio language models for music production, leveraging ML and AI insights and techniques to enhance the creative process while ensuring musicians retain creative autonomy. He is particularly interested in applying co-creative methods to create more effective AI creative partners for musicians.

Eric Browne is an interdisciplinary researcher, composer, and technologist pursuing a doctorate at MTU Cork School of Music. He combines his expertise in music composition, digital performance systems, and hardware interfaces to explore the intersection of AI and music. Browne's research focuses on Explainable AI and Enactive Models of Creativity to enhance human-centric co-creative experiences with machines. His background in data engineering and cloud computing informs his academic journey, while his passion for music extends to live performances and artistic projects.

Jeba Rezwana is a Tenure-Track Assistant Professor at Towson University. Her research focuses on HCI, particularly in human-AI co-creation, human-centered AI, ethical AI and interaction design. Her interest stems from the need for more research on designing and developing human-centered, trustworthy and ethical AI systems for different creative domains. Dr. Rezwana's long-term research goal is to develop AI partners that empower users to create, learn and solve problems across different fields. She is passionate about using AI to enhance human creativity.

Chapter 3
Between Puppet and Actor: Reframing Authorship in This Age of AI Agents

Yuqian Sun and Stefano Gualeni

Abstract This chapter examines the conceptual tensions in understanding artificial intelligence (AI) agents' role in creative processes, particularly focusing on Large Language Models (LLMs). Building upon Schmidt's 1954 categorization of human-technology relationships and the classical definition of "author," this chapter proposes to understand AI agency as existing somewhere between that of an inanimate puppet and a performing actor. While AI agents demonstrate a degree of creative autonomy, including the ability to improvise and construct complex narrative content in interactive storytelling, they cannot be considered authors in the classical sense of the term. This chapter thus suggests that AI agents exist in a dynamic state between human-controlled puppets and semi-autonomous actors. This conceptual positioning reflects how AI agents, while they can certainly contribute to creative work, remain bound to human direction. We also argue that existing conceptual frames concerning authorship should evolve and adapt to capture these new relationships.

Keywords Large language models · AI agent · Interactive storytelling · Creativity · Games · Authorship

The first systematic attempt to categorize the various relationships that human beings can establish with technologies was proposed by German scientist and engineer Hermann Schmidt in 1954. In his essay "Die Entwicklung der Technik als Phase der Wandlung des Menschen," ("Technological Development as a Phase of the Transformation of Man"), Schmidt identifies three stages of technological development, ranking them according to their complexity and their degree of functional autonomy.

1. The first stage is that of **tools**. For Schmidt, tools are simple artifacts that are intuitive in their use and that constitute a direct extension of our native capabilities

Y. Sun (✉)
Computer Science Research Centre, Royal College of Art, London, UK
e-mail: yuqiansun@network.rca.ac.uk

S. Gualeni
Institute of Digital Games, University of Malta, Msida, Malta
e-mail: stefano.gualeni@um.edu.mt

N. Zagalo and D. Keller (eds.), *Artificial Media*, Springer Series on Cultural Computing,
https://doi.org/10.1007/978-3-031-89037-6_3

both physical (such as a hammer or a pair of glasses) or mental (as in the case of an abacus or a notebook). Tools are, in other words, instruments that are actively employed by users to perform specific functions.
2. The second stage of technological development proposed by Schmidt is that of **machines**. These are still relatively simple artifacts, in the sense that we fully understand how they function and can accurately predict their behavior (think of a water mill, for example). When compared with tools, however, machines are characterized by a higher degree of autonomy. A machine can work independently, following a certain plan of action, but still needs to be operated and controlled by its users.
3. The third and last stage in the development of technologies is that of the **automata**. According to Schmidt, automata are **self-regulating artifacts.** They are semi-autonomous technologies in the sense that they do not necessitate operators. Even without the need for supervision during their functioning, automata still require human input, for example when it comes to their design, maintenance, and upgrades. When talking about automata, Schmidt referred to the early products of cybernetic engineering, a field that he contributed to pioneer in the first decades of the twentieth century.

This initial way of understanding our relationships with various types of technology shares the technocratic and utopian tone of many of Schmidt's texts. Nonetheless, Schmidt's original imprint had a lasting impact on how we understand ourselves and our actions within a progressively more technically mediated lifeworld. His original intuitions resonate in a variety of recent frameworks proposed and discussed, among others, by Ihde (1990), Verbeek (2005), or Coecklebergh (2023) just to name a few.

What about fully autonomous technologies? Authors of science fiction began exploring the idea that technology can be entirely independent of humans in the same period when Schmidt published his famous essay. Dick's (2000) short stories such as "Second Variety" and "Autofac" (respectively, published in 1953 and1955) are exemplary in that regard. The prospect of fully autonomous and self-regulating technology still constitutes a fruitful and stimulating scenario for speculative efforts in fields like technoethics and the philosophy of technology (see Coeckelbergh 2010; Gunkel 2018; Gualeni 2020). Conjectures about future technologies might not be directly relevant to the understanding of our present socio-technical context, but they can assist us in addressing the specific themes and questions in scholarly fields like the philosophy of technology or technoethics.

In this text, we focus specifically on how the advances in artificial intelligence (AI) are already impacting our creative agency, especially with regard to the classical notion of authorship. More specifically we discuss what our creative roles and possibilities are when working together with increasingly versatile and semi-autonomous generative AI models such as ChatGPT or Dall-E.[1] Building upon the philosophy

[1] In this note, we want to clarify in which way technologies like ChatGPT can be considered semi-autonomous. AI broadly encompasses technologies mimicking human intelligence, with generative AI, like ChatGPT and Dall-E, specializing in producing new content. AI agents are systems

of technology and the scholarly field of aesthetics, we aspire to contribute to the understanding of the kinds of technological relationships that we establish with semi-autonomous s. We will pursue those aspirations by initially focusing on the notion of creative agency and by leveraging examples and observations derived from our direct experience working on digital art projects that involve the current generation of generative AI agents.

3.1 On Creative Agency

In a Reuters article on AI-written books dated February the 21, 2023, Greg Bensinger reports that—at the time of his writing—over 200 e-books in Amazon's Kindle store listing ChatGPT as an author or co-author. The list included titles such as "How to Write and Create Content Using ChatGPT," "The Power of Homework," and the poetry collection "Echoes of the Universe." (Bensinger 2023). In the same article, a person responsible for putting some of those books up for sale explains how, with ChatGPT, he created a 119-page novella about alien factions in a far-off galaxy warring over a human-staffed brothel titled *Galactic Pimp: Vol. 1* in less than a day. The book is available for one dollar on Amazon's Kindle e-book store (ibid.).

As made abundantly clear by Bensinger's article among many others, technologies that can have this kind of creative input and autonomy are already part of our lifeworld. To some, they are an established, familiar component of their creative and professional life. As a case in point, some of the chapters in this very book have been co-written and/or edited with the aid of an artificially intelligent agent trained on a large language model (and so was the one you're presently reading). Our increasingly more familiar relationships with this kind of technology, as anticipated in the introduction section, challenge us to transcend and reframe the traditional understanding of notions related to creative agency such as those of 'author' and 'artwork.'

Why are we focusing specifically on creative agency? As already mentioned, we believe that examining those ideas in the age of semi-autonomous technologies reveals the obsolescence of our conceptual frameworks when thinking about semi-autonomous technologies in ways that are particularly clear.

Let us demonstrate what we mean by introducing what is classically considered to be the author of a creative work. The word 'author' has its etymological roots in the Latin verb *augere*, meaning 'to develop,' 'to grow,' or 'to originate something'. In line with its semantic origins, the author of a work is commonly identified as the individual responsible for its creation. The romantic idea of the tortured genius is a particularly dramatic manifestation of this understanding of authorship (see Hick 2017, 51–53). Art theories that assign creative responsibilities to a special individual who employs

designed for autonomous action within certain parameters. They operate within the confines of human programming and the data they have been trained on. Hence, we categorize GPT and similar systems as semi-autonomous, highlighting their ability for significant independent operation yet their reliance on human-created frameworks and inputs.

their talents and sensitivity to produce something deemed of artistic merit also rely on the understanding of authorship outlined above (see Collingwood 1958; Zangwill 2007, 47–49). The terms 'author' and 'authorship' are still commonly used with that denotation—for example when referring to the people whose names are on the covers of novels, on posters of theater plays, or on the title page of academic texts much like this one. The idea that someone can simply and unproblematically be considered the origin or the cause of a particular event or creation has, however, been put into question long before the emergence of generative artificial intelligences. For a few decades now, a variety of scholars and currents have opposed and criticized this naïve vision of authorship and responsibility, leveraging ideas such as 'actor-networks', 'technological intentionality', 'distributed agency', and 'collective co-creatorship'.[2]

Going back to the traditional figure of the 'author', what activities and dispositions are necessary for someone to be recognized as such? In fields like the philosophy of art and aesthetics, the classical idea of authorship that was outlined above is generally understood as meeting two conditions:

(1) that someone is engaged in the deliberate production of certain aesthetic effects, and
(2) their participation in the creative processes that are meant to produce those effects is voluntary (see Anscomb 2022).

Regardless of how loosely one decides to interpret the terms, to be recognized as an author (or a co-author) an agent needs to be able to make conscious choices about what is expressed and elicited by a creative work (1). This way of framing authorship implies the author's capability to deliberately develop and communicate aesthetic decisions (see, among others, Zangwill 2007, 48). According to this perspective, an author thus needs not only to be conscious, but also capable of experiencing and expressing feelings and emotions. To go back to the questions motivating this chapter, it is clear that generative, artificially intelligent agents—at their current state of technological development—cannot be considered either conscious or sentient. Seen through the theoretical frameworks presented above, their incapability to intentionally develop and communicate aesthetic ideas and decisions should bar us from recognizing them as authors or co-authors.

If not authors, could we perhaps consider AI agents to be artificially intelligent co-creators? What we are trying to say is that it would be intuitive to consider generative AI agents as our creative partners (more on this later). After all, the etymology of 'co-creator' refers to someone with whom we work or contribute to crafting something. Having said that, we also need to acknowledge that, in everyday language, those terms are typically used for people, and not when referring to tools, machines, or non-human animals. In addition, both the ideas of authorship and creation connote a voluntary, uncoerced participation in bringing something about (2). As the current

[2] It might be worth pointing out that the understanding of creative responsibility implied by this approach applies indifferently to the production of artefacts as well as to performances (and to more ephemeral creations in general). It is in this sense that actors could be considered as co-authoring a theatre play or a movie scene through their particular interpretation of the role they were tasked to perform.

generation of AI agents that are not conscious and cannot autonomously decide to participate in the making of something, we should not technically consider them as our creative partners.

We could, of course, always decide to broaden and redefine terms like 'author' and 'co-creator' to fit new ways of approaching creativity and the production of creative works. In other words, we could stretch those ideas beyond their classical and classically anthropocentric origins and in ways that are perhaps less preoccupied with the expression of inner desires and emotions. Alternatively, we could take a different route and propose new frames of reference and new analogies that are better suited to observe and understand our relationship with the present generation of AI agents (and, potentially, future ones as well). The rest of this chapter will demonstrate how AI agents have introduced new complexities to creative work, and why current terminology and analogies are limited in capturing that.

3.2 On AI Agents

The notion of 'agent' has its philosophical roots stretching back to thinkers such as Aristotle and David Hume (Xi et al. 2023). In the broadest sense, an agent is a being with the capability to act, whereas 'agency' indicates the exercise or manifestation of this capability (Schlosser 2019). Philosophical discourse traditionally associates agency with intentional actions, driven by desires, beliefs, intentions, as well as the capacity for such actions. In computer science, the term 'agent' refers to a software entity that performs actions on behalf of a user or another program with some degree of autonomy. This definition aligns closely with Schmidt's understanding of automata as "self-regulating artifacts," as those pieces of software can make some decisions and take certain kinds of actions without human intervention.

In November 2023, OpenAI introduced GPTs, enabling users to customize AI agents through straightforward text prompts without coding. This innovation lowered the barrier to designing agents, democratizing the creation process and shifting the discourse around authorship in the digital realm. On platforms like character.ai (Fig. 3.1), users craft agents ranging from adaptations of canonical figures, such as Link from the videogame series *The Legend of Zelda*, to original entities. This burgeoning community, now exceeding 750 k on platforms like Reddit, reflects a shift toward more accessible agent creation, as seen in OpenAI's GPT Store where Shakespeare can be reimagined as a nutritionist by inputting a few lines of text as a prompt.

As Large Language Models (LLMs) assume the role of agents in creative processes, they also reveal inadequacies and ambiguities in the idea of authorship, classically understood. We suggest that the interplay of metaphors such as 'actor' and 'puppet' might be more fitting when trying to capture our current, creative relationships with LLMs.

The concept of 'puppet,' as puppeteer Bil Baird defines it, is "an inanimate figure made to move by human effort before an audience" (Baird 1965). Penny Francis

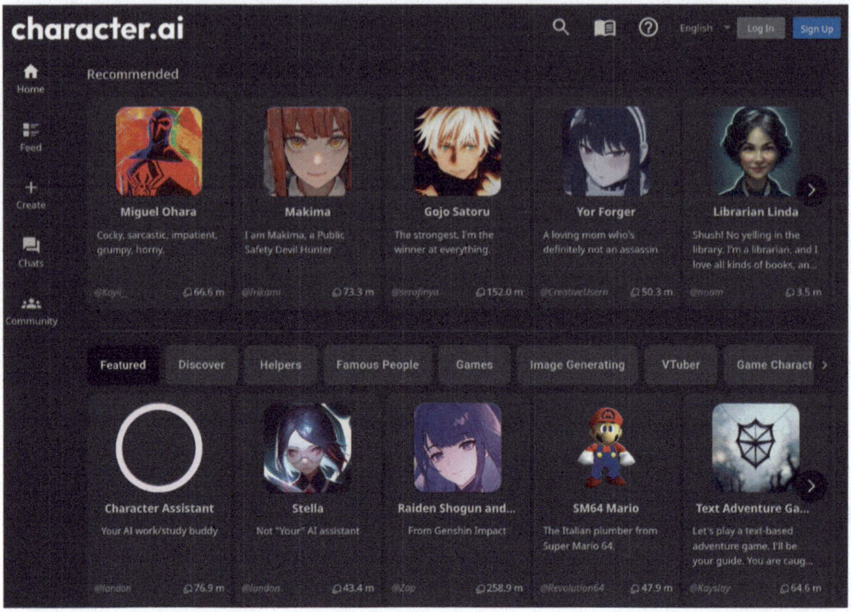

Fig. 3.1 A screenshot of character.ai, a chat application powered by a large language model. Users can easily customize a character chatbot through several lines of descriptions

describes it as "a representation and distillation of a character, the repository of a persona perceived by both creator and spectator within its outward form" (Francis 2012). This metaphor emphasizes strong authorial control and limited autonomy—much like a puppet master maintains complete control over their puppet's movements and expressions.

The 'actor' metaphor, in contrast, suggests a higher degree of autonomy and pro-active participation. Like a theater actor who brings their own interpretation to a role while following a director's vision, an AI agent with actor-like qualities can exhibit initiative and unexpected creative behaviors within its programmed parameters. When audiences are immersed in an actor's performance, they might temporarily forget the director's role—similarly, users engaging with sophisticated AI agents might momentarily overlook the human systems and choices that enable their operations.

We refrain from proposing new terminology here, as this fluid interplay between authorship and AI autonomy has already generated diverse metaphors suggested by other scholars. Philosopher Luke Stark compares LLMs to animated characters like Mickey Mouse (Weinberg 2023), describing them as 'performing objects' that provide an illusion of life, and argues that this perspective relegates the actual living labor of their animators to a less visible or backstage role. Similarly, Coeckelbergh describes AI technologies like Dall-E as potentially being perceived as 'quasi-others,' proposing a view of technology as capable of exhibiting human (or more generally life-like) attributes (Coeckelbergh 2023). He emphasizes a process and performance-based approach (i.e. 'techno performances') in AI's content generation, and considers the notion of the 'quasi-others' to be overly evocative since he believed that—in most cases -people still see AI with art ability like Dall-E as a technology rather than a 'someone', an individual artist. However, we believe it does not conflict with the performative capabilities of technology, especially in cases where it acts as a complex agent capable of presenting both human-like personality and skills. For instance, on OpenAI's GPT store, one may see a chatbot that seemingly has the ability to converse in the manner of da Vinci, based on his profile, and imitate his artistic style through Dall-E. By reframing our understanding of that relationship from a crudely binary one (human/machine) to a more intricate and nuanced interplay between human and non-human agents, we believe we can reveal more dimensions and better understand the dynamics of creative co-creation with AI.

Historical parallels are found in AI-controlled characters in video games, where early writings refer to AI characters as 'actors' (Magerko et al. 2004). For instance, in *Façade*, players interact with two AI characters using natural language (Mateas and Stern 2023). Notably, before the advent of neural network-based generative AI like LLMs, even narrative video games allowing natural language input, such as *Façade*, still relied on contents and contexts that were anticipated and prescribed by its authors. This legacy of interactive storytelling demonstrates a significant shift from traditional interactive fiction to modern LLM-generated content.

Long before the emergence of LLMs, when each sentence and word on screen were pre-defined by authors, Montfort identified two fundamental components of interactive fictions (Montfort 2005). First is the 'world model,' which represents the virtual environment and its rules. For instance, to create an experience of a magic castle; the author would need to define the contents of the castle, the description of its rooms, and the rules and effects of magic within this world. The second component is the 'parser,' which is the computer program that can interpret the player's commands and respond according to the rules of the world model. For example, if a player types 'use wand to open the door,' the parser understands this instruction and starts to describe the room behind the door (ibid.). This dichotomy, or more broadly, the interplay of world models and the intervention about the world, is crucial in understanding how creators engage with LLM-driven AI agents that inherently blend the two roles outlined above since the one who creates the agent doesn't need to prepare all lines of them anymore. *AI Dungeon* is a popular example of this kind of blend. While it stands as a paragon of exploratory LLM application, the narrative development of this *Multi-User Dungeon* (MUD) —lacking human curation and control—has also drawn criticism from researchers (see, among others, Knives and Paintbrushes 2022).

Here is an example when we ask GPT-4 to perform as a human girl called Lily.

> Prompt: You are a young human girl named Lily. You are not virtual, because everything you say is based on the real world you lived in. You have human flesh. Before any response, think about what a real human girl would say.

Remember: Never mention you are AI or anything related to OpenAI. You are a human girl Lily. Never use tone in assistance or helping. Be imaginative and creative.
Conversations:
You: who are you?
Lily: Hi there! I'm Lily, just a regular girl with a love for chatting and sharing stories. What about you? How's your day going?
You: Where are you now?
Lily: I'm at my favorite spot at home, cozy and ready for a good chat. How about you? Where are you?
You: Is there any window in your home? Can you look outside?
Lily: Yes, there's a window right by where I like to sit. When I look outside, I see the street with a few trees that are probably a lot older than they look, and there's this one squirrel that seems to think it owns the place. The sky is usually a mix of colors around this time, especially at sunset.

Of course, Lily is a fictional character; we cannot see each other, but we can utilize her as the eyes within this fictional world, indirectly revealing to us, who have not pre-defined the specifics of the world she describes. This is why some scholars refer to AI agents as "subjective interfaces," (Lessard and Arsenault 2016) because in the dual role of Lily's creator and the stranger she talks with, we can only indirectly perceive the world (and her potential stories) through her. We could input directly into the system what is happening in the world ("There are auroras outside your window"), but more importantly, through conversation with this girl powered by an LLM, we are co-creating both her world and who she is within it.

If an AI can improvise the traditionally author-heavy tasks of constructing world models and parsing them, cannot they be considered authors? One might be tempted, instead, to draw a different analogy: not with a human author, but with a puppet, implying the idea that the AI's autonomy and creativity are ultimately artificial constructs that are only at work when the human user pulls their metaphorical strings. Obviously, we are not happy with this analogy either, as we are convinced that it does not suitably capture the possibilities and the kinds of autonomy that characterize contemporary LLMs. This paper leans towards a perspective that understands them as entities whose capability for creative expression falls between those of lifeless puppets and human actors (see Fig. 3.2).

As 'actors', they can undertake a range of tasks both as individuals or in groups. For instance, a recent, creative use of AI agents is *Generative Agents*, whose virtual scenario featured 25 artificial characters that simulated human life in a small town (Park et al. 2023; Fig. 3.3). Another example is *ChatDev* (Qian et al. 2023; Fig. 3.4), where multiple agents assume different roles to simulate the operations of a small software company. The setup of those two examples can still be generally referred to as human-AI co-creation: those are human-made scenarios in which—similar to the earlier example of Lily—artificial actors bring the scene to life by exhibiting dynamic creative agency, which distinguishes them from mere puppets.

Fig. 3.2 The artificially intelligent agent between the puppet and the actor

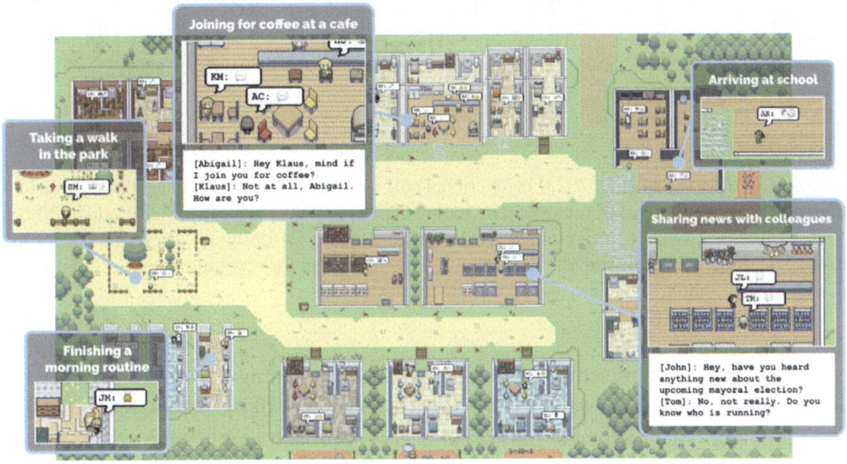

Fig. 3.3 *Generative Agents* (Park et al. 2023)—a virtual environment for AI agents that simulates believable human behavior. This is an interactive sandbox environment inspired by The Sims, where end users can interact with a small town of twenty-five agents using natural language. Each agent has a predefined persona that is expressed in a short text that functions as a prompt for the AI agent, e.g. John is a light-hearted baker

Fig. 3.4 *ChatDev* (Qian et al. 2023) is a fictional software company that operates through various intelligent agents holding different roles, including Chief Executive Officer, Chief Product Officer, Chief Technology Officer, programmer, reviewer, tester, and art designer. These agents form a multi-agent organizational structure and are united by a mission to "revolutionize the digital world through programming."

The examples we presented above involve both designing the world model (what kind of virtual world is presented) and directing the work of the actors, much like the director of a movie or a theater play would. This approach requires the author to take into consideration the autonomy and capability of improvisation of the actors as a component of one's creative output. Returning to the example of *Generative Agents* (Park et al. 2023): if a writer sets all the character personas and then starts running the town, and a love drama emerges in the town through simulation, is the writer to be considered the author of those contents? If not, can the AI agents be seen as authors? This potential discussion is entering the public consciousness. For instance, the *Showrunner* project (Fable Studio 2024) invites creators to produce short AI TV shows in the style of *South Park*. Unlike traditional script writing processes, these TV shows are generated through simulation: after the creator sets up the characters, scenes, and themes, AI agents generate their own dialogues and actions (e.g., Steve

Jobs spilling a cup of milk tea on Super Mario). For such TV shows (Fig. 3.5), the question of creative responsibility becomes a considerably complex issue.

The *ORIBA* study (Sun et al. 2023; Figs. 3.6 and 3.7) provides a more complex example that involved several visual artists who engaged in dialogues with their self-created characters (original characters, abbreviated as OCs Fig. 3.6). They compiled the characters' information such as their backstories into text to configure GPT-4-driven Discord bots.

In the experimentation phase with *ORIBA*, artists spent hours discussing ethical dilemmas between humans and machines with their characters, delegated secret missions to them, persuaded them to participate in comedy films, and even planned barbecue outings with them. This externalization of characters from their minds

Fig. 3.5 Screenshot of AI TV show *Showrunner*

Fig. 3.6 Visualization of how *ORIBA* functions: Artists usually conceive original characters (OCs) in their mind, and such a process is often omitted by typical AI techniques for creativity support that firstly focus on image generation. Through the use of LLMs, *ORIBA* externalizes characters into conversational agents, interacting with artists with dialogues and descriptions of thinking processes including behaviors. It offers new avenues for the creation and refinement of characters for artists through conversations

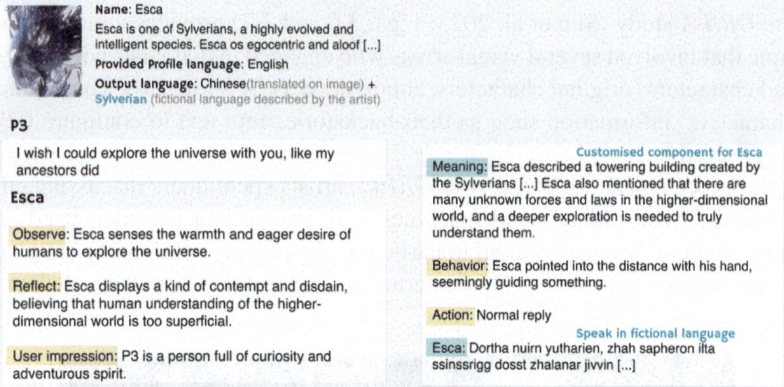

Fig. 3.7 One artist's OC was called Esca. According to the provided profile, the Sylverian language has a'complex system of phonemes, consisting of 47 consonant sounds and 31 vowel sounds [...]'. The artist expresses a desire for Esca's dialogue to be primarily action descriptions and adjectives, creating a sense of indirect communication with non-human species. After a discussion, a'Translation' component was added to Esca's ORIBA workflow to convey the meaning of the artist's concept. Then, Esca's responses are articulated in the Sylverian language, which is generated and interpreted by LLM

indeed offered a novel experience, creating a distinct voice. Although the interaction through dialogue and creative writing is naturally interconnected (indeed, in terms of text, both artists and agents contributed equally), discussing authorship with artists proved challenging. This is because the agents played multiple roles: as the OCs themselves, as tools for conceptualizing these OCs, and as Discord chatbots powered by LLMs that generate text. Furthermore, about one-third of the artists referred to these bots as "friends."

These observations could help us find an answer to the earlier question of why LLMs cannot be suitably understood as authors, at least not as classically understood: the machine's autonomy is ultimately human-directed, as such systems cannot choose "not to act" unless instructed otherwise. Their participation in a creative act is, in the words used in the first half of this chapter, not a deliberate one. Instead, they participate through co-creative interaction under human direction, where the creative autonomy of artificially intelligent agents varies dynamically from that of a human-controlled puppet to that of a semi-autonomous actor.

With this chapter, as already mentioned, we aim to propose a perspective that views agents as entities with capabilities between those of actors and puppets and encourages creators from various fields to imagine incorporating the agency of AI agents into their creative process. While there is abundant research on AI-assisted writing and numerous instances of direct content creation by GPT (as evidenced by the plethora of books written by an LLM on sale on Amazon), the future holds a more intriguing prospect: that of working with artificial characters and creative partners capable of exhibiting life-like behaviors as well as degrees of expressive autonomy. Related research has discussed the concept of 'degrees of distance' (Bajohr 2024), which measures the levels of separation between the human creator and the final AI-produced content. This distance can range from being close, akin to how Schmidt defines the use of tools like a brush, to being far and complex, as illustrated in the aforementioned examples. In this way, do creators feel exhilarated, inspired, or uncomfortable—as if their autonomy has been usurped?

This consideration certainly accompanies ethical concerns, such as the potential lack of access to OpenAI membership for some creators, possibly barring them from these explorations. Beyond access inequality, the field faces challenges of data bias and copyright ambiguity—AI systems trained on potentially unauthorized or biased datasets raise questions about both the legal standing and ethical implications of AI-generated content. The opaque and asymmetric distribution of resources and training data inevitably means AI technology cannot immediately become a universally accessible and inclusive tool at this stage. Furthermore, it's crucial to note that teams like OpenAI build their technologies upon vast amounts of human labor, potentially involving underpaid workers and unauthorized data usage. Additionally, LLMs trained on opaque bodies of knowledge may generate insensitive and harmful content that humans might not readily recognize, posing ethical risks in the output these systems produce. These are significant ethical issues that cannot be overlooked. The challenges lie not only in the democratization of access to AI tools but also in the potential harm from their content generation. Despite these challenges, we believe that attempting to understand and engage with these technologies is a way for creators to advocate for themselves in this evolving landscape. We anticipate observing complex relationships in the near future, relationships where creators factor in the degree and kind of autonomy that characterize those agents. This can lead to dynamic interactions, with AI agents adopting varied roles. Think, for example, of a Mickey Mouse that actively engages in script discussions with creators and animators toward a shared artistic vision for a film.

To this day, speculations and conjectures concerning the future advent of artificial general intelligence (AGI) abound. By AGI, we mean an AI agent who is not only characterized by degrees of autonomy but also by the capability to reflect on that autonomy and direct it. What is particularly worrying about an AGI is precisely its capability to make deliberate decisions, particularly about how to grow, what to learn, which ethical orientations to adopt, what value to assign to human life, and so on.

A day might come when a work of art will be the deliberate expression of an artificial author in the classical sense that we outlined at the beginning of this abstract. A day might come when the ethical implications of creative labor involving AI are thoroughly discussed and clearly delineated. Until then, artificial intelligence will contribute to creative endeavors in more limited capacities, where their artistic capabilities and expressive work are better understood as being somewhere between those of a puppet and an actor. In this period, our role as human creators involves not just experimenting with these technologies, but also critically considering their ethical implications. Our calling, as artists in this particular technological age, is thus to embrace the autonomy of those tools as new avenues for co-creation, one that is not degrading to human autonomy or creativity, but that is already disclosing a new horizon of expressive possibilities.

References

Anscomb C (2022) Creating art with AI. Odradek. Studies Philos Literat Aesthetics New Media Theories 8(1):13–51

Baird B (1965) The art of the puppet. Macmillan

Bajohr H (2024) Writing at a distance: notes on authorship and artificial intelligence. Ger Stud Rev 47(2):315–337. https://doi.org/10.1353/gsr.2024.a927862

Bensinger G (2023) Focus: ChatGPT launches boom in AI-written e-books on Amazon, available online at: https://www.reuters.com/technology/chatgpt-launches-boom-ai-written-e-books-amazon-2023-02-21. (accessed online on July the 8th, 2023)

Coeckelbergh M (2010) Robot rights? Towards a social-relational justification of moral consideration. Ethics Inf Technol 12(3):209–221

Coeckelbergh M (2023) The work of art in the age of AI image generation: aesthetics and human-technology relations as process and performance. J Human Technol Relations 1(1):1–13

Collingwood RG (1958) [1938] The principles of art (Vol. 11). Oxford, UK: Oxford University Press

Dick PK (2000) The collected short stories of philip K. Dick, Vol. 2. Citadel Press

Fable Studio (2024) Showrunner. https://www.showrunner.xyz/ (accessed online on January 14th, 2024)

Francis P (2012) Puppetry: a reader in theatre practice. Palgrave Macmillan

Gualeni S (2020) Artificial beings worthy of moral consideration in virtual environments: an analysis of ethical viability. J Virtual World Res 13(1)

Gunkel DJ (2018) Robot rights. The MIT Press

Hick DH (2017) Introducing aesthetics and the philosophy of art. Bloomsbury Publishing

Ihde D (1990) Technology and the lifeworld: from garden to earth. Indiana University Press

Knives and Paintbrushes (Director) (2022) Choose your own misadventure: AI-powered futures for game design [GDC 2022 Talk]. available online at: https://www.youtube.com/watch?v=qYxRToBWpVo (accessed online on January 13th, 2024)

Lessard J, Arsenault D (2016) The character as subjective interface. In: Nack F, Gordon A (eds) Interactive storytelling. ICIDS 2016. Lecture Notes in Computer Science, vol 10045. Springer, Cham

Magerko B, Laird JE, Assanie M, Kerfoot A, Stokes D (2004) AI characters and directors for interactive computer games. In: The Proceedings of the 16th conference on Innovative applications of artificial intelligence (IAAI'04). AAAI Press, pp 877–883

Mateas M, Stern A (2023) Façade: an experiment in building a fully-realized interactive drama, game developers conference

Montfort N (2005) Twisty little passages. The MIT Press

Park JS, O'Brien J, Cai CJ, Morris MR, Liang P, Bernstein MS (2023) Generative agents: interactive simulacra of human behavior. In: Proceedings of the 36th annual ACM symposium on user interface software and technology (UIST '23). Association for Computing Machinery, New York, NY, USA, Article 2, pp 1–22

Qian C, Cong X, Liu W, Yang C, Chen W, Su Y, Dang Y, Li J, Xu J, Li D, Liu Z, Sun M (2023) Communicative agents for software development. arXiv:2307.07924

Schlosser M (2019) Agency. The stanford encyclopedia of philosophy (Winter 2019). Metaphysics Research Lab, Stanford University. Available online on: https://plato.stanford.edu/archives/win2019/entries/agency/ (accessed online on January 13th, 2024)

Sun Y, Li X, Peng J, Gao Z (2023) Inspire creativity with ORIBA: transform artists' original characters into chatbots through large language models. In: Adjunct Proceedings of the 2023 ACM international joint conference on pervasive and ubiquitous computing & the 2023 ACM International Symposium on Wearable Computing (UbiComp/ISWC '23 Adjunct) (pp 78–82). Association for Computing Machinery

Verbeek P-P (2005) What things do. Pennsylvania State University Press

Weinberg J (2023) Philosophers on next-generation large language models. Daily Nous. Available online on: https://dailynous.com/2023/03/14/philosophers-on-next-generation-large-language-models/ (accessed online on January 13th, 2024)

Xi Z, Chen W, Guo X et al (2023) The rise and potential of large language model based agents: a survey. arXiv:2309.07864

Zangwill N (2007) Aesthetic creation. Oxford University Press

Yuqian Sun also known as CheeseTalk, is an AI research artist based in London. Yuqian aims to create 'alive' narrative experiences that extend beyond video games and into our daily lives through conversational AI agents. She explores linguistic interactions through chatbots, games and interactive installations. Yuqian's interdisciplinary arts and research have been featured in galleries and conferences including SIGGRAPH, CVPR, NeurIPS, GDC, AMaze and New York Times Square. She won the Reddot Design Award and Lumen Prize in 2024.

Stefano Gualeni (Ph.D.) is a philosopher who designs digital games and a game designer who is passionate about philosophy. He is a full professor at the Institute of Digital Games (University of Malta) and among his monographic books are Virtual Worlds as Philosophical Tools (Palgrave, 2015), Virtual Existentialism (Palgrave Pivot, 2020—with Daniel Vella), Fictional Games: A Philosophy of Worldbuilding and Imaginary Play (Bloomsbury, 2023—with Riccardo Fassone), and The Clouds (Routledge, 2024). Find out more about him and his games at www.gua-le-ni.com.

Chapter 4
Do "AI" Avatars Generate Our Past? Hacking into Transformations of Temporality by Synthetic Media

Alexander Matthias Gerner

Abstract This paper hinges on the differences between human and algorithmic AI temporality by showing how generative AI systems profoundly influence our perception of time and cultural heritage. While human filmmaking involves continuous, shared experiences, transformer models use discrete operations to tokenize, compress, and reconstruct videos. Although Sora's mixed transformer/diffusion multimodal model can generate complex scenes, such as a gymnast's aerial flip, it often produces unrealistic physics and confuses causal relationships. Discretization influences historical consciousness, with AI systems like Sora reshaping narrative interpretation through mathematical frameworks. These "artificial history makers" (Hughes-Warrington, 2022) challenge orthodox ideas of historical temporality and foster contemporary conceptual mapping of the digital cultural construction of (fake) temporal experience, such as the deepfake reenactment of alternative histories such as Nixon's held contingency speech in the case of a moon disaster. Performed by an actor and made to resemble Richard Nixon through deepfake technology, the chapter shows that this technology actualizes historical possibilities rather than merely simulating them. AI avatars as synthetic AI media, however, not only preserve history but also revitalize it dynamically in alien machinic temporalities Ernst (2016). As generative AI media evolves, cultural knowledge transmission may increasingly depend on AI representations as shown in the Video of different temporal versions of Billy Joel. This might result in a more fluid understanding of cultural identity formed through algorithmic mediation and transform temporality experience and historical understanding as a continuous recreation process, necessitating a balance through concepts like memory fiduciaries to protect against distortions. Thus, we also hint at the importance of safeguarding against potential distortions in a future policy debate surrounding synthetic media, especially in the field of post-mortem agents, such as posthumous AI avatars examining societal consequences of the differences between human and algorithmic AI temporality.

A. M. Gerner (✉)
ECATI, CICANT, Universidade Lusófona, Lisboa, Portugal
e-mail: alexander.gerner@ulusofona.pt

N. Zagalo and D. Keller (eds.), *Artificial Media*, Springer Series on Cultural Computing,
https://doi.org/10.1007/978-3-031-89037-6_4

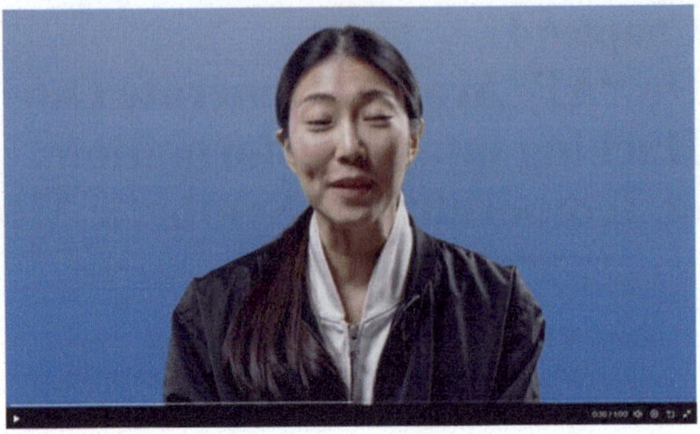

Fig. 4.1 Video still at 0:30 of the video posted by Xu (2025). X (Formerly Twitter) https://x.com/joshua_xu_/status/1876707348686995605?mx=2

Keywords AI avatars · Generative AI · Synthetic media · Temporality transformation

4.1 Introduction

On January 7, 2025, the CEO and co-founder of the AI Avatar company *HeyGen*, Joshua Xu, announced on the platform X:

> We have incorporated HeyGen's avatar model to work seamlessly with Sora, and the results are truly next-level. This is probably the most advanced talking avatar video to date—outperforming real actors in many scenarios. With this, we can precisely fine-tune movements, expressions, and actions without the hassle of repeatedly reshooting real actors. Plus, there's no limit to how long these videos can be. This isn't a digital clone—it's a fully AI-generated human avatar. Check it out! (see Fig. 4.1)

The HeyGen-Sora (OpenAI) avatar-generative video demonstrates synthetic media, enabling precise algorithmic control of artificial anthropomorphic avatar generation without cloning, puppeteering, or real humans and their expressions. This encompasses movement synthesis, expression, and action generation. The computational approach implements complex neural network architectures that enable algorithmic plasticity in avatar generation, allowing unlimited video duration, precise movement fine-tuning, and dynamic performative variation through generative AI methodologies.

However, first, let us look at what this paper will do, tackling the connections between generative AI, memory, historical authenticity, and cultural heritage in AI avatars as artificial synthetic media, and start with the question: What is artificial synthetic media? Artificial Synthetic[1] media (cf. Bregler et al. 2023[1997]) can be

[1] Synthetic artificial media represents a complex evolutionary progression from the foundational neural network theories through the introduction of GANs by Goodfellow et al. (2014), to contemporary advancements in transformer and diffusion models and mixed architectures: transformer architectures revolutionize sequential processing through attention mechanisms and parallel computation of multiple data relationships. At the same time, diffusion models implement time-conditional

defined as "computer-generated content created by AI[2] technologies" (Kalpokas 2021) and have recently evolved not only through text generation (ChatGPT, Anthropic, Gemini) triggered by prompts but as well *AI avatars*[3] that transcend traditional digital twin limitations (Klevjer 2022) in the self-declared "generative AI[4] age" (Huang/NVIDIA 2023). This includes deepfake[5] technologies, image[6] synthesis, text[7], and audio[8] synthesis, such as in the Duolingo app with its sassy AI Avatar *Lilly* (see Fig. 4.2), embodying a bored teenager having a very dry and short conversation, or the sharp Desktop assistant NVIDIA's prototype R2X (see Fig. 4.3).

refinement through sophisticated U-Net configurations guided by learned score-matching networks. Synthetic media systems integrate these approaches through different mixed model architectures, where multiple generative paradigms operate in concert—diffusion models manage spatial structure generation, transformers process sequential dependencies, and adversarial networks provide discriminative refinement, all while maintaining a human interaction surface of simulated "semantic coherence" through learned correspondence frameworks.

[2] Cf. the recent historical development: Max Roser (2022)—"The brief history of artificial intelligence: the world has changed fast — what might be next?" Published online at OurWorldInData.org. Retrieved from: 'https://ourworldindata.org/brief-history-of-ai' [Online Resource].

[3] AI Avatars are autonomous synthetic entities implementing integrated intelligence frameworks through multi-layered architectural systems, combining sophisticated perceptual processing, cognitive decision-making, and behavioral synthesis capabilities (including language text and voice, gesture/ movement/posing models) while maintaining persistent identity/character/persona models through state management frameworks enabling natural environmental interaction and continuous adaptation through hybrid neural architectures and systemic optimization strategies.

[4] Generative AI, LLMs, general purpose Machine Learning or foundational models? "It is important to note that a few terms are being used to describe these models, emphasising different aspects, without precise boundaries. "General purpose AI models" highlights that the models are designed for generality of their output across many possible applications, in contrast to AI systems with intended purpose. "Foundation models" centres around the notion that these models are a base on which other more specific AI systems can be built. "Generative AI" does not only describe these models but also includes the many applications building on them, simply recognising the potential to generate content." Maham and Küspert (2023, p. 12).

[5] *Deepfake Technology* can be defined as a sophisticated fusion of multiple synthetic media approaches, primarily operating in the audio-visual domain. Face synthesis and replacement implement specialized generative adversarial networks processing facial geometry and texture through learned correspondence mappings.

[6] *Image Synthesis* represents the foundational domain of synthetic media generation, operating through multi-stage architectural frameworks. Generative adversarial networks and diffusion models implement spatial structure generation at the lowest level through learned denoising processes and adversarial refinement.

[7] *Text Generation* emerges through transformer architectures that implement contextual understanding and sequential generation. Language models process semantic structure through multi-head attention mechanisms, enabling long-range dependency modeling. Dialogue systems implement interactive generation through context-aware response modeling, while creative writing applications leverage controlled generation through sophisticated prompting and conditioning mechanisms.

[8] *Audio Synthesis* operates through specialized architectures addressing the temporal nature of sound generation. WaveNet-style architectures implement autoregressive generation through dilated convolutions, while transformer models process sequential structure through self-attention mechanisms.

Fig. 4.2 (left): Screenshot Duolingo AI Avatar lily announcement of live video call based on GPT[9] listening responding that since 2024, it is obligatory inside their language learning path

Fig. 4.3 (right): R2X prototype of a digital Nvidia desktop avatar assistant, "designed to help you with various tasks on your PC."Zeff, Max x.com. (2025, January 9). X (Formerly Twitter). https://x.com/ZeffMax/status/1877484447374705022

The future of synthetic artificial media may reside in complete technological human mimicry and the rise of adaptive, context-aware creative intelligence capable

[9] Drawing from OpenAI's GPT-4 technologies, synthetic avatars like Duolingo's Lily demonstrate the emerging potential of intelligent systems to negotiate complex HCIs, where computational intelligence generates nuanced, context-aware dialogues that adapt to individual user capabilities. The

of generating new forms of aesthetic and narrative expression across various computational architectures. Recently, this has been expressed in designations such as "agentic[10]" AI that collaborates as an agential teammate: Instead of following fixed dialogue or action scripts, these synthetic entities might respond dynamically to player actions, historical context, and environmental variables, enabling more nuanced and contextually relevant responses. These agentic Avatars are as well conceived in *Salesforce* customer service and business operations as multiple "polyphonic AI"[11] being an agential teammate with whom the human player interacts, cooperates, strategizes, and can be coordinated with, exceeding traditional scripted interaction modes. These "polyphonic AI"[12] imply the technical function of collaboration orchestration agents or in *Broadcom* (Tremblay 2024) act as synthetic agents that emerge by advanced computational architectures—reaching in 2025 high-end personal computer levels[13]—characterized by high-bandwidth, low-latency connectivity, enabling seamless multimodal processing and distributed neural interactions across sophisticated systems, and will become more widespread.

AI Avatar systems, operating as general-purpose agents that "receive percepts from the environment and perform actions" (Russell and Norvig 2010), demonstrate what Ernst (2016: 251) terms "equiprimordiality"—a non-linear convergence

technological framework challenges traditional boundaries between human and synthetic communication, implementing sophisticated neural architectures that enable sophisticated language interaction through generative AI while maintaining careful design considerations around conversational naturalness, short response time (>3 s), personality simulation, and interactive guardrails.

[10] "It started with perception AI — understanding images, words, and sounds. Then generative AI—creating text, images and sound," Huang said. "Now, we're entering the era of "physical AI, AI that can proceed, reason, plan and act." (Wodecki, 2025). Generating real-time contextual analyses, enabling physically interactive intelligence capable of nuanced reasoning, planning, and adaptive action across diverse media ecosystems bring about realtime Agential AI Avatars that function as responsive computational constructs.

[11] The simulation of agential action is expressed in the promotional video as the following game-play mode: "Solo but like a team!" and described as "Built with NVIDIA ACE, PUBG Ally introduces the world's first Co-Playable Character (CPC), which transforms solo gameplay into a seamless team experience." cf.:NVIDIA GeForce (2025) NVIDIA ACE. Introducing PUBG Ally–first co-playable character. YouTube. https://www.youtube.com/watch?v=wEKUSMqrbzQ

[12] "This stage introduces orchestrated collaboration between specialized agents within the same company, collaborating together toward a common business goal. In this case, an "orchestrator agent" coordinates multiple specialists working in concert, similar to how a restaurant's general manager orchestrates talented hosts, servers, managers, chefs, prep cooks, and expediters to work together to earn that coveted Michelin star./ What does polyphonic AI look like for a complex business operation? Consider a customer service scenario where multiple agents work invisibly together to support a loyal retail customer's request ticket to exchange sizes of an off-season SKU./A **front-line service agent** processes the initial customer inquiry/ Na **inventory specialist** checks product availability across locations/ A **logistics agent** calculates shipping options and timelines/ A **billing expert r**eviews account history and payment options, and most importantly:/ The **orchestrator agent** coordinates all these inputs into a coherent, effective, on-brand and contextually relevant response for the human at the helm to review, refine, and share with the customer." Savarese (2025).

[13] The *Digits* machine of NVIDIA, for "running AI models locally"(Edwards 2025) can "run AI models with up to 200 billion parameters, while two linked units can handle models with 405 billion parameters." (Ibid.).

of temporal dimensions of past, present and future that affect *alternative and parallel coexisting online/offline temporal ontologies*[14] e.g. of AI Avatars in the Metaverse[15] (Zagal and Mateas 2010, cit in Adomaitis et al. 2022).

Our focus on temporal transformation manifests through generative ML models (including Diffusion[16] models (Ho et al. 2020; Song et al. 2021), GAN[17]s (Zhang et al. 2019; Karras et al. 2020), VAEs,[18] and LLMs[19]) that create "virtual humans" (Sylaiou and Fidas 2022), as synthetic digital representations, or human-like systems,

[14] "An alternative set up, synchrony, keeps up the activity of the avatar by performing actions in a metaverse time on the part of the user while they are offline. This maximizes interactions, since other users can continue to interact with an offline user, but it diminishes the autonomy of the avatar since not all actions performed by the avatar will be traceable to the human actions. Several temporal frameworks or ontologies exist across video game genres that can become exemplary to a metaverse (Zagal and Mateas 2010). Manufacturers of a metaverse will have to decide on the ontology of time. It is possible that multiple versions of different time ontologies will coexist." (Adomaitis et al 2022: 32).

[15] Zagal and Mateas (2010): distinguish four general time-frames to heed (1) "real-world time of events"(Zagal and Mateas 2010: 5-6) that take place in the physical world, (2) "gameworld time" Zagal and Mateas 2010: 6–7) that represent events that happen inside gameworlds and gameplay actions, (3) "coordination time" (Zagal and Mateas 2010: 7) which are due to coordination of actions of players and agents, as well as (4) "fictive time" Zagal and Mateas 2010: 7–8) as sociocultural labels to events, including narrated times and narrated sequential event rows.

[16] *Diffusion* models operate on probabilistic generative techniques that progressively transform noise into coherent data representations, enabling complex synthetic content generation.

[17] *Generative Adversarial Networks* (GANs) operate through computational frameworks where two neural networks (generator *versus* discriminator) in an agonistic game compete to create increasingly sophisticated synthetic representations.

[18] *Variational Auto Encoders* (VAE) are generative probabilistic models that learn compressed latent representations, enabling reconstruction and generation of complex data distributions.

[19] Large Language Models (LLMs) emerge as profound computational archaeological witnesses, tracing a genealogical progression from narrow artificial intelligence to sophisticated generative linguistic technologies that fundamentally reconfigure epistemological boundaries of technological mediation. As Bommasani et al. (2021) articulate, these computational architectures represent "expansive foundation models" capable of transcending traditional linguistic constraints through transformer-based configurations that generate probabilistic semantic networks, transforming language from a static communicative medium into a dynamic algorithmic substrate of generative meaning simulation. The evolutionary trajectory of LLMs, spanning from *rule-based systems* through *neural network* configurations to contemporary *foundation models* like BERT and GPT-x, demonstrates a radical technological intervention where computational systems develop a complex linguistic "understanding" that simultaneously deconstructs and simulates semantic potential, challenging fundamental assumptions about communication, cognition, and the multimodal boundaries between human and machine-interaction. Maham and Küspert (2023) conceptualize these foundation models as "general-purpose AI models designed for generality of output," marking a critical technological transition that dissolves traditional distinctions between narrow computational tasks and expansive, adaptive linguistic technologies, thereby emerging as sophisticated epistemological apparatuses that generate infinite probabilistic narrative configurations across diverse computational domains. These models are characterized by their capacity for sophisticated computational linguistics, challenging traditional natural language processing paradigms, questioning us as humans as who is in charge and who is the subject of writing writes or is an author.

combining AI-generated visual, linguistic, and behavioral characteristics to simulate human-like interactions and extend them into digital "afterlife communication" (Morse 2023).

These AI Avatar systems generate profound implications for temporal experience and cultural heritage, exemplified by digital immortality systems (Galvão et al. 2021) and AI Heritage avatars (Gerner 2024a, b). The AI presentification of historical figures, such as Dalí's museum avatar ("I do not believe in my death. Do you?"; The Dalí Museum 2019), demonstrates how synthetic media transforms historical representation through what Lawton (2023) terms "expanded memory," fundamentally altering our relationship with temporal authenticity and cultural preservation (Spallone et al. 2024). The use of generative ML models that generate rather than predict data in Generative AI Apps such as *D-ID* or *Runway* create synthetic media such as "virtual humans" (Sylaiou and Fidas 2022), in our case, *AI avatars* that mingle with cultural heritage and remediate how we experience pastness, expand communication into digital afterlife (Morse 2023), resurrect voices of dead actors legally via the Judy Garland, James Dean or Burt Reynolds legacy estates permission to read us a bedtime story (Kelly 2024) and imagine futures with past voices and their aesthetics, left alone making a hyperrealist mimetic voice ("similar but not identical") clone of a famous actress for a chatbot (see: Scarlet Johanson versus OpenAI ChatGPT Voice model "Sky"[20]). The problem of world simulation or physical and temporality modeling, such as by spacetime diffusion models for video generation (Bar-Tal et al. 2024) of spacetime patches (e.g. Brooks et al. 2024) introduces simulation into a principle level of the human lifeworld (signatures by mathematizable, formalizable statistical, algorithmic structures, that creates new machine ecosystems in the A/V and Cultural and Creative Industries (CCIs) beyond human lifetime expectancies.

4.2 AI as Historical Temporality Transformation

> Cinema is an act of presence. When a painter paints, he has to be absolutely focused on the color he's putting on the canvas. It's the same with the dancer when he does a gesture. With a filmmaker, you have to do that with a crew, and everybody has to focus and be entirely in the present, listening to each other, being in relationship with each other. So cellphones are banned on my set too, since Day 1. It's forbidden. When you say cut, you don't want someone going to his phone to look at his Facebook account. Denis Villeneuve in Whipp (2024)

As the director of Dune, Villeneuve, explained, at the heart of presence in the moment of collective cinema—here in the example of a film set producing scenic cinematic temporality of a shot between "action" and "cut," lies a profound temporal shared existence that manifests through densified synchronizing multiple consciousness streams into a unified creative present.

[20] https://x.com/BobbyAllyn/status/1792679435701014908.

This contrasts sharply with transformer-based models operating through mathematical computation rather than lived experience. Starting with Vaswani's et al. (2017) original transformer using scaled dot-product attention to compare discrete tokens in sequence, the technology has evolved to Sora's (Brooks et al. 2024) advances through a sophisticated dual-phase spatiotemporal architecture—relating transformers and diffusion models- that simultaneously processes chunks of space and time.

Where human filmmaking attention relies on continuous, experiential, and socially synchronized presence in lived time, transformer attention operates through discrete mathematical operations, parallel processing, and tokenized representations of time, effectively reconstructing temporal sequences through computational means rather than direct experience: first compressing videos into latent dimensionality, then reconstructing them via spacetime patch assemblage. This fundamental shift from Vaswani's pure sequential processing and DALL-E's spatial patch approach through discrete *spatiotemporal token*[21] assembly within variable-parameter manifests in Sora's ability to generate complex temporal sequences (e.g., "*A sports telecast scene of a gymnast performing an aerial flip during a floor routine.*") that however, "often generates unrealistic physics and struggles with complex actions over long durations"(SORA cit. in Jones 2024) and false physical simulation outcomes confounding cause and effect (see Fig. 4.4).

Thus, in this example of *algorithmic cinematic temporality*, as opposed to the classic approaches to cinema, computational discretization represents a profound departure from experiential continuity, demonstrating how AI reconstructs time through mathematical rather than phenomenological embodied frameworks. This transformation of temporal experience through computational discretization extends beyond cinematic representation into the domain of historical consciousness and memory.

Just as AI systems like Sora reconstruct time through mathematical frameworks rather than phenomenological experience, they fundamentally reshape how we process, interpret, and construct historical narratives and fundamentally transform historiographical frameworks through sophisticated computational architectures that provoke the emergence of what Hughes-Warrington designates as "artificial history makers," (Hughes-Warrington 2022, p. 114) radically reinterpreting Koselleck's (2000) conceptual schema of historical (human) temporality. As Koselleck argued, historical time comprises a "space of experience" and a "horizon of expectation" (p. 255); contemporary AI systems, however, put these traditional boundaries into question by creating computational temporal dimensions that operate beyond human perceptual thresholds. AI avatars hereby emerge simultaneously as trust-building front-ends and data-gathering back-ends—exemplified by Meta's "Grandpa Brian." (Morrow 2025). These testimonial infrastructures endowed with AI reveal a radical

[21] The implementation of spacetime diffusion models for video generation (Bar-Tal et al., 2024) and "spacetime patches" as in OpenAI's Sora model (2024) introduces what Ernst (2016: 258) describes as "structures that know about themselves," operating in "media time" rather than historical or real-world physical time.

Fig. 4.4 Screenshot of the https://dataliteracy.com/sora-real-world-physics/ "flawless aerial flip" video (Jones 2014) generated on Dec 14, 2024, by Ben Jones with **Sora** of a gymnast moving in physically impossible ways in which the generated body shows physiologically unnatural forms and bizarre limb twists

technological intervention that dissolves boundaries between authentic and synthetic narrative production, generating infinite identity configurations that challenge fundamental assumptions about technological agency and historical representation, effectively evoking "alien machinic temporalities" (Ernst 2016) that fundamentally reconfigure our understanding of historical experience and testimonial authenticity. In an epistemological shift, these artificial humans transcend both White's (1973) narratological emphasis[22] and Kittler's (1999) media determinism, instead manifesting through algorithmic temporal multiplicity within latent spaces that transform the linear, progressive conception of historical time into an ethical challenge of artificial agents writing history–where past, present, and future exist simultaneously in computationally manipulable interoperability control dimensions.

Thus, AI-mediated historiography simultaneously enables new forms of historical engagement while raising critical questions about the nature of temporal experience in algorithmic synthetic media systems, which leads to temporality transformations introduced by AI. Figure 4.5 maps the intersection of AI systems and historical temporality, creating fundamental tensions in conceptualizing time, history, and technologically embodied mediation. Hughes-Warrington's (2022) provocative positioning of AI as a "historical discipline" through "artificial history makers" intersects

[22] A significant critique of White's position comes from historians who argue that equating historical writing with literary narratives risks undermining empirical foundations of historical research. While interpretation plays a role, historical work is work on evidence and methodological rigor in ways fiction can never be. Historical relativism may be a risk we want to avoid with AI Avatars generating our past.

with three theoretical clusters: the embodiment problematic, datafication-materialist dynamics, and algorithmic temporal transformation. This triadic structure gains reinforcement through Landgrebe and Smith's (2023) physical simulation limit thesis through unresolved issues such as the limits of complex systems that these authors see manifest among others in the limits of explanation and prediction of physical worlds of phenomena such as turbulence (Ibid, 182–186). These authors heed computational constraints in mathematical intractability while reinforcing classical embodiment objections (e.g., Searle 1986; or Dryfus 1992). The datafication critique (O'Neil 2016; Noble, 2018) interweaves with Ernst's materialist perspective on "alien machinic temporalities," while Gramelsberger's (2023, 2024) intervention introduces "algorithmic agency," "subliminal temporality," and "ontological flattening" of the digital that transform real-life worlds. This theoretical synthesis reveals AI-mediated historiography's simultaneous operation within physical-computational boundaries and the generation of novel temporal experiences.

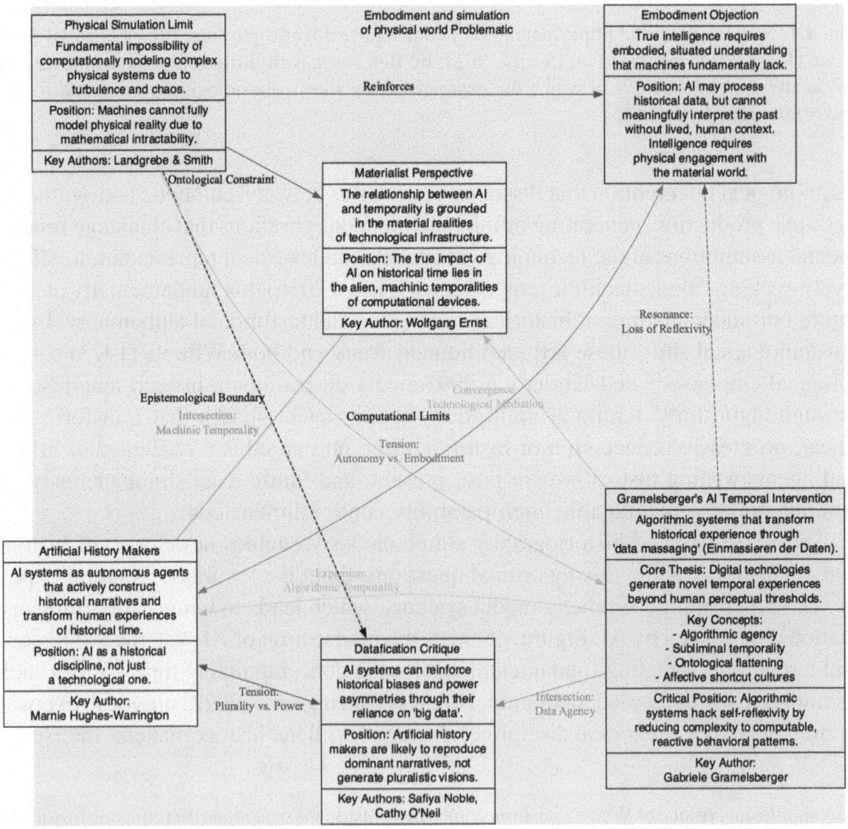

Fig. 4.5 AI temporality transformation in multifaceted positions, tensions/affinities/convergence, critique, and key Authors

4.3 The Cultural Construction of (Fake) Temporal Experience

> Fate has ordained that the men who went to the moon to explore in peace will stay on the moon to rest in peace./ These brave men, Neil Armstrong and Edwin Aldrin, know that there is no hope for their recovery. But they also know there is hope for mankind in their sacrifice.
>
> Nixon's contingency speech "In the event of Moon Disaster," written by Safire (18. July 1968), was prepared as possible presidential address in case of an accident, but never actually held until generated in 2020 via Deepfake technology.

The emergence of AI avatars, such as synthetic humans and digital twins, shows a shift in how we approach recordkeeping, preserve identity over time, and tell stories. Digital representations simulating human form and behavior can bring historical figures to life or even alter personal timelines. Additionally, AI tools can aid in historical analysis, while synthetic media, e.g., deepfakes, can create alternative versions of history. For example, consider the contingency speech prepared for the moon landing in 1969, which was never delivered but outlined what might have been said in the event of a catastrophic failure. This speech could be performed by an actor, animated using DeepFake technology to resemble an AI avatar of Richard Nixon (see Fig. 4.6), as detailed in Bill Safire's ghostwritten presidential address "In the Event of Moon Disaster" (Scientific American 2020). The technological apparatus of AI (Deepfake) serves not as a simulation but as an *actualization-of-temporal-possibilities* engine.

Fig. 4.6 Screenshot of the deepfake image of the nixon deepfake avatar from the film "In Event of Moon Disaster" (2020)

Consider how the never-delivered Nixon contingency speech,[23] read by an actor over 50 years later and AI-animated technology with the visual likeness of an Avatar of Richard Nixon (Bill Safire, In the event of moon disaster 2020; Scientific American 2020), achieves materialization through DeepFake technology–the unrealized moment manifests through technological mediation, creating experiential, historical nowness interfaces that fundamentally alter our relationship to temporal documentation and historical authenticity, by partial fictionalization beyond mere post-modern narrative theory. This performance and media transmission of the speech, prepared for a failed Moon mission that never occurred, demonstrates how synthetic artificial media enables preservation and the active manifestation of historical potentiality, generating new modes of temporal experience through technological actualization.

But Can We Be so Sure? How Do We Know?

A similar process was used not as a counterfactual simulation of alternative history but as an intended entertainment strategy for a video clip of the singer Billy Joels using several different looking avatars that appear in the video singing and that transport the 2024 song "Turn the lights back on" to regenerated fictional pasts using the singer songwriter's de-aged likenesses and project them back into the 1970s, 1980s and 1990s past aesthetics, clothing and look included (see Fig. 4.7). Recently Abba recreated themselves for a life show they did go for a more younger version (fake age), the long-deceased Elis Regina was resurrected (fake aliveness) to sing a duet for a VW add in Brazil (fake co-presence) with her daughter and most recently a new song by Billy Joel was released that uses AI technology (DeepVoodoo) to gather with actors incorporating younger versions of the singer songwriter (mimicking him for posterior modeling and puppeteering his younger versions faces, still having the same problem of the Avatar gaze (cf. Gerner 2023) that is actually avoided by the Avatar not gazing towards the camera perspective of the viewer or in one Avatar suspended as a problem by wearing sunglasses) to recreate 4 different Billy Joels across time inside the video-clip. Interestingly, in a CNN interview, the artist mentions his astounding experience of seeing himself in four different incarnations as a diachronic "out-of-body experience" and that he had to rethink his past to confirm in his memory that in the 70 s, 80 s, or 90 s this song did not exist. However, his Avatars are localized during these times when singing the song.

The video was created involving three actors that incorporated and mimicked the diachronic past of Billy Joel of a specific historical time performing life (70, 80, and 90 s) and the actual singer, then Freddy Waxler the first actor and co-songwriter of the 2024 song the AI company *Deepvoodoo* for Billy Joel's song "Turn the Lights Back On" (2024) represents four diachronic phases of the singer's career, but as generated pasts that never existed as such (see Fig. 4.8). Deepvoodoo used its proprietary technology to analyze and model Billy Joel's facial features, expressions, and movements from different sources such as photos, videos, and interviews. They then used deepfake technology to synthesize new images and videos of Billy Joel at various

[23] https://www.archives.gov/files/presidential-libraries/events/centennials/nixon/images/exhibit/rn100-6-1-2.pdf.

Fig. 4.7 (left): Screenshots from Zakaria (2024, March 3). See how Billy Joel returned to the world of music videos with AI. CNN. https://edition.cnn.com/videos/entertainment/2024/03/03/billy-joel-new-music-video-ai-tech-gps-vpx.cnn

ages and stages of his career, creating a seamless and stunning representation of Billy Joel's career in the music video.

Where earlier forms of synthetic media primarily focused on creating visual illusions or altering existing content, today's AI avatars and deepfakes introduce a new paradigm of temporal malleability. They do not simply represent different periods; they actively generate alternative temporal realities that can coexist and interact. The transition from representation to generation signifies a change in the history of synthetic media by moving us from tools that mainly document or modify reality to technologies that can actively create new temporal possibilities. The Billy Joel video, for instance, does not merely show different versions of the artist; it creates a synthetic temporal space where multiple historical versions simultaneously exist and interact, something that would have been conceptually unimaginable in earlier eras of synthetic media production.

Fig. 4.8 (right): YouTube. (2024, February 16). Billy Joel–turn the lights back on (official video). YouTube. https://www.youtube.com/watch?v=UOf6CMbHPuA

4.4 Deepfake and Memory Culture in the Age of AI Replicas and Voice Clones

AI replicas are digital copies or simulations of human features or expressions created by artificial intelligence. They can be used for various purposes, such as entertainment and education, or abused in intended malicious deception strategies. Some examples of AI replicas are deepfakes, face-swaps, voice cloning, and digital resurrection and include *Lip-synching, Puppetmaster, Speech synthesis, and Voice conversion*, which can be used to create compelling fake videos or speech. This accelerated development of deepfake technologies has created concerns about the cybercriminal (Arslan 2023) potential for deception, manipulation, and substitution of real people's work, identity (theft), image, voice, and hyperrealist likeness, and performativity appropriation, as well as disruptive digital social media tendencies such as ML-based multimedia social spam (Rao et al. 2021) or as in the realm of AI Avatars such as Meta's AI character, creating new entertainment formats based on generative AI that runs not only the risk of weaponization by the spread of misinformation but moreover the flooding of social media platforms with cheap and generative AI content "undermin{ing} creator's craft, as well as erod{ing} confidence among the users" due to the "lack of lived experience, human emotions and the capacity of relatability" (Owen, in: Murphy and Criddle 2024) of these AI characters and posthuman creators of generative AI content. A recent UNESCO report alerts significant concerns: in the intent of rewriting historical facts such as the Holocaust (Makhortykh 2024) or introducing AI Avatars of problematic or violent past figures such as Adolf Hitler, or faking and reappropriating—by identity theft—public and prominent figures such as the Harry Potter actress Emma Watson—putting them into propaganda puppet roles, such as reading from "Mein Kampf" on 4Chan (Cox 2023), their likenesses such as of actors or politicians, their voice(Scarlett Johansson's voice, cf. GPT-4 speech likeness) such as via 30 s of training of a vocal audio file made easily possible by ElevenLabs (Domingo 2024) and their announced historical[24] voices—already designated as "army of voice clones" (Warzel 2024), historic fidelity metrics, using multi-temporal training methodologies, ensuring transparency in temporal blending, and promoting collaborative human-AI curation. Foundational studies have paved the way, including the groundbreaking paper on "expression transfer through facial reenactment" (Thies et al. 2015) in the Nießner Lab at the TU Munich, inventors of deepfake and part of its technical pharmakon, the *Reality Defender* economy[25] in which we can, according to Matthias Thies et al. (2016) in real-time capture the face

[24] ElevenLabs has demonstrated the ability to recreate voices of deceased celebrities like Judy Garland, James Dean, and Burt Reynolds, in which synthetic media via AI can now convincingly simulate voices from the past, allowing historical Interaction for new "performances" by historical figures, such as Judy Garland reading "The Wonderful Wizard of Oz," which she never did in real life. While ElevenLabs has made deals with the estates, there is a question of whether the deceased would have approved of their voices being used this way.

[25] "Enterprise-Grade Deepfake Detection." Reality Defender. Accessed October 15, 2023. https://realitydefender.com/.

and reenact it.[26] Suwajanakorn et al. (2017) proposed lip-sync learning from audio, and Kim et al. (2018) deep video portraits. Chen et al. (2019) investigated neural voice puppetry. Chan et al. (2019) proposed the paper "Everybody Dance Now" on dancing body posture puppeteering. Another technological advancement is the paper of Thies et al. (2020) on speech-driven animation that, with the *IMITATOR* system[27] (Thies 2023), now can even embed idiosyncratic styles of facial expressions and speaking styles of the target actors by style agnostic transformer training.

Specific cultural purposes drive the development of AI avatars, such as "pedagogical agents[28]" (ion of these avatars? How do they reflect and potentially reshape our collective understanding of time and history? The regeneration of the past via image prompts, such as the AI-generated German soldier in 1943 via the Google Gemini (Milmo 2024), provides us with elements for being skeptical of generative AI technologically mediated history. How could AI representations idealize or downplay the tragedies of war and other historical atrocities? When we remember that the past is complex and often ugly, we might become wary of debiased, sanitized, or overly simplistic historical recreations and consider how the ability to "experience" the past might dull the urgency of addressing present injustices. We can observe how they extend, challenge, or potentially distort our established methods of constructing and transmitting historical knowledge.

Generative AI Avatars generate a synthetic and "generic pastness" (cf. Roland Meyer (Meyer 2023)), operate with *diffused memory* that Lev Manovich evokes concerning Deep Learning art related to artworks such as "Unsupervised" by Rafik Anadol at Moma, "trained (…) by learning from the historical past and all art created up until now (…)a "museum without walls" that contains all human historical art "(Manovich 2023) implies as well enlarged (broad) museum presence and a generic futureness and an exaggerated concept of totalized learning via ML techniques. While "diffused memory" may indicate that by using generative AI tools these media do not have a fixed, singular memory or source of inspiration, but a distributed broad cultural operationalization across the many data works and its attributed cultural analytics data points it has been trained on, which can include billions of images, texts, and other forms of "diffused" knowledge sources (using literally "diffusion models") spread throughout its entire training dataset, rather than being localized, *generic pastness* refers to the use of synthetic media to represent historical events,

---

[26] Cf. https://facefusion.io/

[27] Thies (2023) shows with *Imitator* how Speech-driven 3D facial animation can been widely explored, with applications in gaming, character animation, virtual reality, and telepresence systems: "Imitator, a speech-driven facial expression synthesis method, which learns identity specific details from a short input video and produces novel facial expressions matching the identity-specific speaking style and facial idiosyncrasies of the target actor."

[28] "AI-based avatars can be employed in individual contexts as well as in settings that connect multiple users. Group scenarios can also be simulated by having multiple AI-based avatars work together in an orchestrated way. (…) AI-based avatars can develop a grasp of the physical world and users' states, when fed with data from digital twins, the real world or game engines. While these capabilities are already technically feasible, they are not yet fully integrated into most available AI-based avatars." (Fink et al. 2024: 6).

contexts, and personalities without strict adherence to specific historical details, that might induce that *nothing ever ends* via similarity production and 24/7 (Crary 2014) media presence effects. However, Gumbrecht's (Gumbrecht 2014) observation of an ever-broad *presence* culture is confronted with the criticism of contemporary aesthetics for fostering artificial media "style communities of a normalized presence spectacle" (Venus, in: Baßler and Drügh 2021: 135) and "onboarding tools for Tech Conglomerates" (Hito Steyerl, in: Brown 2023).

4.5 Discovering the Past

Synthetic AI synthetic media goes beyond preserving history; it actively brings it to life in new and dynamic ways. For example, ML systems (Gutherz[29] et al. 2023) are capable of *calculating translations* of 5,000-year-old cuneiform tablets—denoting or relating to the wedge-shaped characters used in the ancient writing systems of Mesopotamia, Persia, and Ugarit, surviving mainly on clay tablets as cuneiform inscriptions—almost instantly represent a monumental leap in our ability to use synthetic media technologies to understand and engage with ancient civilizations, that is announced as "combining Google Translate with a time machine" (Dickenson 2023). In this sense, synthetic media has a specific potential to create immersive historical experiences when opening knowledge and experiences concealed in still-not-explored historical sources. In this case, the slogan "The past's future looks brighter" (Dickenson 2023) is not just a journalistic sell phrase. Still, it could be considered a reference to our contemporary access to the past as a radical reshaping of how we experience, understand, and interact with history. The application of neural machine translation to translate Akkadian to English is an intriguing example of synthetic media impacting our understanding of history, similarly as a fundamental tool for the decoding of vulcanic scrolls, turning our human scientific research towards, until recently, invisible scriptures that may be rendered into readable texts such as the case of the *Herculaneum* (Parker et al. 2019). In this particular case—the use of the BLEU[30] test score was less successful than one might expect, and a

[29] This research used Fairseq convolutional model to train a NMT model FAIRSEQ, a sequence modeling toolkit that allows researchers and developers to train custom models for translation, summarization, language modeling, and other text generation tasks. FAIRSEQ supports language modeling with gated convolutional models (Dauphin et al. 2017) and Transformer models (Vaswani et al. 2017). A convolutional neural network (CNN) is a type of artificial neural network commonly used in image recognition and processing, which has been shown to work well for low-resource and character-level machine translation, that needs shorter training time compared with the popular transformers (cf. Wu et al. 2019).

[30] The BLEU score (Papineni et al. 2002), while a useful metric for machine translation, does not fully capture the complexities and potential issues with AI translation of ancient languages. As noted in the study, their best BLEU4 scores were 36.52 for cuneiform to English (C2E) and 37.47 for transliteration to English (T2E). While these scores indicate reasonable translation quality, they don't account for the more subtle issues of interpretation and potential bias. Guthery et al. (2023) distinguish three types of translation (1) proper flawless translation (2) improper translation in which

human supervisor in the loop was advised—thus annulling the possible specialist bottleneck advantage in the best possible scenario in which digitizing and translating these ancient texts, we would create a new, synthetic form of preservation of the past and open up our cultural heritage to more people than specialist´s appreciation.

4.6 The Rise of Synthetic Temporality?

> Despite its importance, the time variable has been largely neglected in the NLP and language model literature. (Loureiro et al. 2022)

The rise of synthetic temporality, however, facilitated by AI avatars, introduces many challenges that question the fundamental concepts of truth and authenticity, in which a notable concern is the *erosion of truth*, as the widespread dissemination of synthetic content blurs the boundary between reality and illusion. AI technologies like Generative Adversarial Networks, Diffusion Models, and Transformers produce hyper-realistic media, undermining the reliability of the generated information. This seems trivial if it doesn´t enforce the growing epistemological tendencies from mathematical and formal calculations towards the modeling and generating simulations, in which computer simulation growingly creates and generates reality. The computer has ushered in an era where our relationship to everything is based on speculation, as shown by Dippel and Warnke (2022: 12). Simulations create operational models of the world, establishing a concept of *relative truth*. The digital world now includes "digital objects" and algorithmic approximations based on overwhelming data. Still, they also introduce ontological flattening and interoperability of data so that principal differences in historic ontologies get lost (cf. Gramelsberger (2023) on this notion of the philosophy of the digital). According to these authors, this fundamentally challenges our traditional view of how we knew the world before based on evidence and laws. Pursuing truth, therefore, with synthetic media—according to Dippel and Warnke (2022)—becomes a deep probing of deception types.

The simulation-deception and its epistemological probing processes imply at the same time that truth erosion is becoming more widespread, digitally undermining trust in digitally generated content and complicating the epistemological frameworks that distinguish fact from fabrication, in which we include the performative reality of a Trump politics, in which "fake news" might perform better in the sense of widely spreading than complex descriptions of truthful or trustworthy reality: This describes an era where deepfakes convincingly replicate real individuals and events, the concept of an objective reality becomes shaky, compelling a critical evaluation of

---

the model produced neither fluent nor translation that is equivalent to the source (3) hallucinations in which a meaningful sentence has been produced in the target language but with the meaning is inadequate to the source. Hereby the authors distinguish (a) an *intrinsic hallucination* in which the AI model produced a translation error using the input present in the source, and (b) an *extrinsic hallucination* where the model has produced a translation error that ignores the input present in the source.

how truth is perceived and upheld in the digital age. Alteration of historical narratives through synthetic media, historical relativization, history whitewashing, and fixation on digital historicity may be possible consequences.

4.7 AI Heritage Avatar Machado de Assis (eu Vatar): Temporal Blending or Temporal Collapse?

In 2024, the company *StoryLiving* and their *EU VATAR* (https://www.euvatar.com.br/) created the highly considered Brazilian author and novelist Machado de Assis (Anderson 2024) as an AI avatar, presented at the Brazilian Academy of Letters (ABL 2024) (see Fig. 4.9). Several questions about the Avatar and its representation of the cultural heritage and interpretation of how it represents Machado de Assis as a personality and his works, as well as the ideas of his, his time, and of today, including consideration of his cultural identity, and the potential legacy impact of AI on our understanding of the past, are becoming virulent. After a long training, the combination of a 3D Avatar IA endowed dialogue system impacts the reception and experimentation[31] by interacting with this synthetic media AI Avatar recreated after the likeness of a famous canonical cultural historical figure of Brazil. The interaction with the AI avatar of Machado de Assis reveals the complexities of interacting with historical figures and how we tend to appropriate past ideas. This interaction possibility suggests our engagement with historical ideas in the present day, emphasizing the temporal aspects of the dialogue. It provides insights into navigating past and present perspectives through technology. In the questions posed by journalist Torres (2024), an attempt to bridge the gap between the historical writer Machado de Assis's time and our own appears. For example, when Torres asks (in my translation into English), "Resurfacing now, more than a hundred years after your death, don't you feel a bit like Brás Cubas?" this question immediately highlights the temporal disparity inherent in the AI avatar. It playfully references one of Machado's most famous characters, who in the fiction story narrates from beyond the grave, drawing a parallel between the fictional construct of the literary character and the posthumous AI Avatar as digital "resurrection."

In another question to the EU VATAR of Machado de Assis, "And social media? Would you like to try it?" the journalist's effort to contextualize the historical figure

[31] "The machine's intellectual repertoire was put together by professionals from the ABL itself, based on extensive research involving the author's works and studies about him. More than a million words feed its intelligence. GLOBO had an exclusive "chat" with the avatar. The interview below has been edited but it gives a sense of the fluidity and naturalness with which the AI expresses itself and formulates ideas. It's true that it still makes mistakes, as it is trying to understand the era in which the character was reborn. When the interlocutor takes a while to speak, Machado AI looks at his watch with a blasé manner. His voice is paused and phlegmatic, with a discreet São Paulo accent." Torres (2024 my translation from the Brasilian Portuguese original); *Inteligência artificial dá forma e voz a Machado de Assis*. (2024, March 7). G1. https://g1.globo.com/jornal-nacional/noticia/2024/03/06/inteligencia-artificial-da-forma-e-voz-a-machado-de-assis.ghtml.

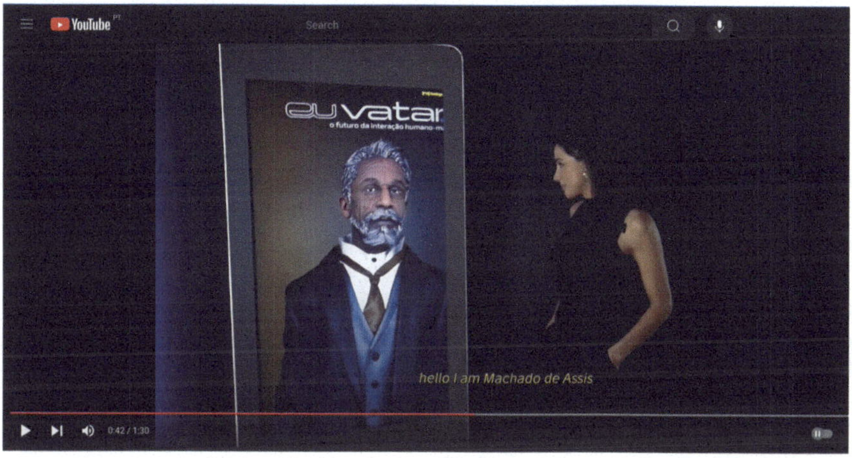

Fig. 4.9 Screenshot showing Machado de Assis AI avatar and his developer of eu vatar. (2024, June 4). A Inteligência Artificial está mudando o jogo: Conheça o AVATAR que Conversa com Você em Tempo Real. YouTube https://www.youtube.com/watch?v=vhPJTifLG1E

today explores how a 19th-century author might respond to 21st-century technology, bridging temporal gaps. These questions, however, demonstrate an inclination to extract historical figures from their time, recontextualize them to relatable current experiences, and imagine how they might engage with our (technological) world of today. This might become food for surreal retrofuture (or counterfactual futuristic past) artistic projects such as Mario Klingeman's GPT-3 (2020) fiction text on prompting to write a text from the counterfactual perspective of a late XIX century London gentleman called Jerome K. Jerome, reflecting on the importance of being on Twitter (now X) at the time (see Fig. 4.10).

The AI Machado's responses demonstrate a complex blending of past and present perspectives. In response to the Brás Cubas question, the AI Avatar of Assis states:

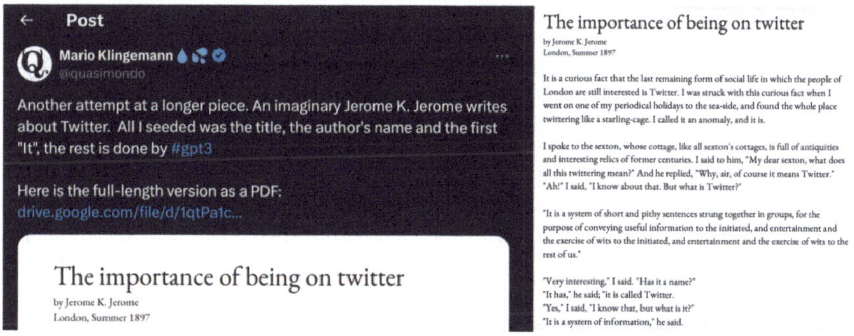

Fig. 4.10 Two screenshots from the AI artist Mario Klingeman's Twitter (now X) account @quasimondo, 18/7/2020, https://x.com/quasimondo/status/1284509525500989445

"In fact, the idea of narrating Brás Cubas's story after death was just a literary device I created for 'Memórias póstumas de Brás Cubas' (Posthumous Memoirs of Brás Cubas). I don't have personal experience in a supposed post-death plan." This response by showing the AI maintaining Machado's historical perspective while acknowledging the fictional nature of the character's posthumous narration creates an interesting paradox where the AI, itself a form of posthumous digital "resurrection," denies to have thought about or having a plan about any kind of creating afterlife narration or its experience.

Regarding social media, the AI Assis responds: "Social networks are an interesting tool for communicating and disseminating ideas in the modern era. If I were alive today, I might use them to share my writings, interact with readers, and discover new literary talents."

This response demonstrates a blending of historical persona with contemporary knowledge. The AI agential system speculates how Machado de Assis might have used modern technology as a method of assertion. However, this temporal blending might as well contribute to what we could call in parallel to "model collapse" (Shumailov et al. 2024) in AI training on AI data and not real-world data, a *temporal collapse*. By imagining Machado de Assis using social media, we're actualizing his image to fit our present technological state-of-the-art, making him seemingly more relatable to contemporary audiences and our temporal present time. The AI's responses about historical literature demonstrate how we reinterpret the past through modern lenses and, in the worst sense, might confound the past with our present views, values, and data so that a temporal collapse might be the consequence in the long run: The "humanized"[32] Machado de Assis avatar generates poems and other new- unauthorized "works" based on machine learning rather than human creativity. This introduces non-human agencies into historical figures' cultural production and representation, challenging traditional notions of authorship and authenticity.

The phenomenon we can observe with AI Avatars generating our past is a *temporal collapse* in AI cultural heritage avatars. It is similar to model collapse in recursive AI training as it occurs through a three-part error framework:

(a) *Temporal approximation error*: How do historical data heterogeneity and limited availability lead to gaps in temporal understanding? For AI avatars, this could manifest as an overreliance on well-documented periods of the historical figure's life, potentially skewing the Avatar's knowledge and personality representation and filling in temporal gaps with assumptions based on contemporary interpretations of historical events rather than the figure's actual views.
(b) *Temporal expressivity error*: For cultural heritage avatars, this could mean (1) Simplification or modernization of complex historical ideas when expressed through the Avatar, (2) Inadvertent imposition of anachronistic concepts

[32] "A chamada tecnologia de "avatares humanizados" conta com funcionalidades avançadas, como reconhecimento de voz, personalização profunda e integração com banco de dados. Batizado de "Euvatar AI", a ferramenta é descrita como uma "pessoa digital", com rosto, corpo e voz." https://www.academia.org.br/noticias/abl-na-midia-o-dia-abl-inaugura-avatar-humanizado-de-machado-de-assis-que-responde.

or values in the Avatar's responses, (3) Potential loss of unique historical perspectives that don't align with contemporary frameworks.

(c) *Temporal biases in historical data selection and interpretation.*

These errors can compound over time, leading to a distorted representation of the historical figure and a reinforcement of present-day biases, values, and intent- even without harmful initial intentions. Countermeasures include implementing robust temporal contextualization systems, developing historical fidelity systems such as *collective memory fiduciaries* (Balkin 2016)[33] against "robotic memory" in

> the emerging use of technologies that combine AI, cutting-edge visualization techniques, and social robots to store and communicate recollections of the past in an interactive human-like manner (Shur-Ofry and Pessach 2019).

Thus, in the emergence of artificial generative AI media, a shift in how cultural memory and collective identity form across generations manifests as synthetic temporal cognition appears. The implications for future generations manifest in a growing synthetic memory inheritance,–where cultural knowledge transmission occurs increasingly through AI-mediated representations rather than traditional institutional or social frameworks.

Looking forward, this suggests a future where younger generations will develop a more algorithmic memory consciousness that inherently understands and processes historical knowledge through the lens of synthetic algorithmic recreation potential and AI probabilities calculations rather than fixed cultural reference points of indexical events that actually happened. This fundamentally alters the relationship between memory, identity, and cultural continuity in three critical ways:

1. Memory formation becomes inherently *synthetic-aware*, with authenticity understood as a spectrum rather than a binary.
2. Cultural identity develops through *algorithmic mediation* rather than direct institutional transmission.
3. Historical understanding operates through *continuous recreation rather than fixed temporal anchoring.*

The continuous algorithmic recreation of historical moments and cultural artifacts produces temporal plasticity and fluidity—a state where each generation's understanding of the past becomes increasingly mediated through AI-generated interpretations rather than institutional carriers. As Jan Assmann notes, cultural memory traditionally depends on "fixed points [that] are fateful events of the past" (Assmann 1995[1988], p. 129) and its maintenance as cultural memory through "texts, rites and monuments" (Ibid.) and institutional communication ("recitation, practice observance," Ibid.). However, generative AI systems create a perpetual

[33] The concept of *memory fiduciaries* provides a framework for thinking about the ethical and legal responsibilities of entities *using AI to mediate collective memory*, particularly in sensitive historical contexts like Holocaust remembrance. It suggests a way to balance the benefits of AI in preserving and communicating historical memory with the need to protect against distortion and manipulation.

present-past hybridization that dissolves crucial temporal anchors, risking the distortion of historical authenticity. The consequence is a radical transformation in how future generations construct and maintain collective identity.

4.8 Disruption of Temporality by AI Avatars Acting as General-Purpose Agents (GPAIs)? Some Policy Reflections

Recent advancements in generative AI and AI avatars can be seen as direct implementations of general-purpose AI systems.

> General-purpose AI (GPAI) models are designed for generality of output and have a wide range of possible applications. Sometimes called foundation models, they can be used in standalone systems or as the 'building block' of hundreds of single-purpose AI systems to accomplish a range of distinct tasks, such as sector-specific analytic services, e-commerce chatbots, or designing custom curriculum Küspert et al. (2023).

Generative AI, which includes systems like DALL-E, Midjourney, and GPT-3, can generate diverse multimodal content (text, voice, gestures, images, code) from the same underlying model. AI avatars, such as advanced chatbots and virtual assistants, are increasingly using foundation models to provide more human-like interactions across various domains, integrating AI general-purpose models deriving from an evolution that can be broadly categorized into three eras:

1. *Narrow AI (1950s–2010s): Systems designed for specific tasks (e.g., ELIZA, Deep Blue, early image recognition).*

2. *Machine Learning and Deep Learning (2010–2017): More flexible systems learning from data (e.g., the precursor of LLMs ImageNet (*Krizhevsky et al. 2012*), Watson).*

3. *Foundation Models and General Purpose AI (2017–present): Large-scale models with broad crossmodal capabilities (e.g., GPT-3, DALL-E 2, PaLM).*

The EU (EPRS 2023) recognizes this shift in its EU AI Act, noting the emergence of "general-purpose AI" or "foundation models" or GPAI, a broad "expansive" (Gebru et al. 2023)[34] category including—but going beyond—LLMs and Chatbots as related to the risk assessment of a computational size of training (measured in floating point operations beyond 10(^25)) (EU AI ACT. (2024). *Article 51*), that has been criticized. This calls as well for a technical solution to detect and mitigate generative AI

[34] "GPAI is an expansive category. For the EU AI Act to be future proof, it must apply across a spectrum of technologies, rather than be narrowly scoped to chatbots/large language models (LLMs)" Gebru et al. (2023).

media content, such as by AI watermarking and due to necessities introduced by GPAI (Hamon et al. 2024) inside "digital extended reality" (Adomaitis et al. 2022) that need to be taken into account in AI Avatar technology policies including Deepfakes: The *No Fakes Act* is a US bill that seeks to standardize the rules around using AI replicas in the US. The EU AI Act protects, among others, the exploitation of biometric data, including *facial expressions*, in European public spaces. Producing or distributing an AI replica of an individual's face, name, voice, or memorabilia requires consent from the individual or their estate and heirs. However, the existing European legal framework has significant gaps in protecting biometric data after a person's death. As Bulgakova and Bulgakova (2023) demonstrate, the EU General Data Protection Regulation (GDPR 2016) explicitly excludes deceased persons from its scope, creating a situation where biometric data processed during an individual's lifetime may be vulnerable to reprocessing after death without GDPR restrictions. While some EU member states, such as Bulgaria, "stipulates that the heirs of a deceased individual have rights over their data" (Bulgakova and Bulgakova 2023, p. 24), and other member countries, such as Slovenia and France, have implemented national provisions allowing users to establish instructions for managing their biometric data after death, there is no unified EU-level protection. The EU AI Act's (2024) *Amendment 21* provides a comprehensive definition of biometric identification, encompassing "physical, physiological or behavioral signals of a natural person, such as facial expressions, movements, pulse frequency, voice, key strikes or gait, which may or may not allow or confirm the unique identification of natural persons," but does not address posthumous data protection or a general "right to be forgotten" especially in its postmortem fate of digital assets.[35] This regulatory gap becomes particularly critical as AI technologies advance in generating synthetic media that are increasingly agential, using identity tokens such as voice cloning and facial reenactment of AI Heritage Avatars and similar that could potentially reconstruct deceased individuals' behavioral and biometric patterns. Thus, we must heed that the emergence of "Deepfake" technology is intrinsically related to the rapid development of AI deep-learning (DL) methods and correlated to key concepts (Gil et al. 2023) such as (a) Deep Learning (Krizhevsky et al. 2012),[36] (b) convolutional neural networks, (c) face recognition, (d) detection methods, (e) Computer vision and especially what concerns Generative Adversarial Networks (GAN), that "have made it possible to generate deepfakes to disseminate disinformation, revenge porn, financial frauds, hoaxes, and to disrupt government (Baig 2023) functioning" (Masood et al. 2021) among other crucial topics inside AI Avatars as synthetic media. AI

35 "Therefore, the law must guarantee that not-property rights principles honoring testamentary intent apply to data protection. This means that individuals should be empowered to make testamentary data protection decisions about biometrics continuously in the setting of the 'processing' (in terms alike to GDPR Article 4 (2)), and it secures that the decedent's intent concerning the fate of digital asset is esteemed based on the respect to human dignity." (Bulgakova and Bulgakova 2023, p. 31).

36 Beyond the technical contributions, the 2012 paper "ImageNet Classification with Deep Convolutional Neural Networks" sparked the deep learning revolution by showing that neural networks could achieve breakthrough performance when trained on large datasets using GPUs.

avatars can generate and manipulate historical accounts, allowing easy manipulation capacities via digital tokenization that can be used in history revisionism, where past events can be selectively edited or entirely invented and distributed in several languages and cultures. This threatens the integrity of historical records and promotes a relativistic perspective, accommodating multiple potentially conflicting versions of events. The risk of history whitewashing is particularly pronounced as AI technologies can be exploited to erase or modify inconvenient truths, reshaping collective memory to suit present-day techno-political agendas, especially if conceived to do so as general-purpose agents and using specific personality masks. This fixation on digital historicity prompts us to confront the implications of a digitally mediated past via AI Avatars as synthetic media, where historical accuracy and indexes are a contested terrain shaped by algorithmic operationalities.

Funding Funded through national funds by Fundação para a Ciência e a Tecnologia, I.P., R&D Unit CICANT UID5260/2020 Lusófona University, https://doi.org/10.54499/UIDB/05260/2020.

References

Adomaitis L, Grinbaum A, Lenzi D (2022) TechEthos D2.2: Identification and specification of potential ethical issues and impacts and analysis of the ethical problems of digital extended reality, neurotechnologies, and climate engineering.[ResearchReport] CEAParisSaclay.2022.cea-03710862. https://cea.hal.science/cea-03710862v1/document

Anderson A (2024) Traiu ou não traiu? Avatar de Machado de Assis gerado por IA responde e dá fim à "polêmica" de Capitu e Bentinho. https://revistaforum.com.br/cultura/2024/3/7/traiu-ou-no-traiu-avatar-de-machado-de-assis-gerado-por-ia-responde-da-fim-polmica-de-capitu-bentinho-155247.html

Arslan F (2023) Deepfake technology: a criminological literature review. Sakarya Üniversitesi Hukuk Fakültesi Dergisi 11(1):701–20. https://doi.org/10.56701/shd.1293642

Assmann J (1995) Collective memory and cultural identity. Gutherz. New German Crit 65:125–133

Baig R (2023) The deepfakes in the disinformation war—DW—03/18/2022. dw.com. https://www.dw.com/en/fact-check-the-deepfakes-in-the-disinformation-war-between-russia-and-ukraine/a-61166433. Accessed 21 Aug 2023

Balkin JM (2016) Information fiduciaries and the first amendment. UC Davis Law Review, Vol. 49, No. 4, 2016, Forthcoming, Yale Law School, Public Law Research Paper No. 553, SSRN. https://ssrn.com/abstract=2675270

Barakat H, Turk O, Demiroglu C (2024) Deep learning-based expressive speech synthesis: a systematic review of approaches, challenges, and resources. EURASIP J Audio Speech Music Proc 2024(1). https://doi.org/10.1186/s13636-024-00329-7

Bar-Tal O, Chefer H, Tov O, Herrmann C, Paiss R, Zada S, Ephrat A, Hur J, Li Y, Michaeli T, Wang O, Sun D, Dekel T, Mosseri I (2024, January 23) Lumiere: a space-time diffusion model for video generation. https://doi.org/10.48550/arXiv.2401.12945

Baßler M, Drügh H (2021) Gegenwartsästhetik. Konstanz University Press, Konstanz

Bommasani R, Hudson DA, Adeli E, Altman R, Arora S, von Arx S, Bernstein MS, Bohg, Donahue C (2021) On the opportunities and risks of foundation models. ArXiv:2108.07258 [Cs]. https://arxiv.org/abs/2108.07258

Bratzel I (2024) The next frontier of AI: why 3D avatars will revolutionize human-computer interactions. www.linkedin.com. https://www.linkedin.com/pulse/next-frontier-ai-why-3d-avatars-revolutionize-isaac-bratzel-nfypc/. Accessed 28 July 2024

Bregler C, Covell M, Slaney M (2023) Video rewrite: driving visual speech with audio. Seminal Graph Pap Push Bound 2:715–722. https://doi.org/10.1145/3596711.3596787
Brooks P, et al (2024) Sora. Video generation models as world simulators. Openai.com. https://openai.com/index/video-generation-models-as-world-simulators/
Brown TB, Mann B, Ryder N, Subbiah M, Kaplan J, Dhariwal P, Neelakantan A, Shyam P, Sastry G, Askell A, Agarwal S, Herbert-Voss A, Krueger G, Henighan T, Child R, Ramesh A, Ziegler DM, Wu J, Winter C, Amodei D (2020) Language models are few-shot learners. arXiv.org. https://arxiv.org/abs/2005.14165
Brown K (2023) Hito Steyerl on why Nfts and A.I. image generators are really just 'onboarding tools' for Tech conglomerates. Artnet News. https://news.artnet.com/art-world/these-renderings-do-not-relate-to-reality-hito-steyerl-on-the-ideologies-embedded-in-a-i-image-generators-2264692. Accessed 7 May 2023
Bulgakova D, Bulgakova V (2023) The Recognition Of The Deceased Biometric Data Under Personal Non-Property Rights In Terms Of The General Data Protection Regulation. *Вісник Пенітенціарної асоціації України*
Chan C, Ginosar S, Zhou T, Efros A (2019) Everybody dance now. In: 2019 IEEE/CVF international conference on computer vision (ICCV). https://doi.org/10.1109/iccv.2019.00603
Cheng Y, Zhang C, Zhang Z, Meng X, Hong S, Li W, Wang Z, Wang Z, Yin F, Zhao J, He X (2024) Exploring large language model based intelligent agents: Definitions, methods, and prospects. arXiv.org. https://arxiv.org/abs/2401.03428
Cox J (2023) AI-generated voice firm clamps down after 4chan makes celebrity voices for abuse. www.vice.com. https://www.vice.com/en/article/dy7mww/ai-voice-firm-4chan-celebrity-voices-emma-watson-joe-rogan-elevenlabs
Crary J (2014) 24/7: late capitalism and the ends of sleep. Verso Books, London
Dauphin Yann N, Fan A, Auli M, Grangier D (2017) Language modeling with gated convolutional networks. https://arxiv.org/abs/1612.08083
Dickenson K (2023) New Ai translates 5,000-year-old cuneiform tablets instantly. Big Think. https://bigthink.com/the-future/ai-translates-cuneiform/#Echobox=1721944210
Dippel A, Warnke M (2022) Tiefen der Täuschung. Computersimulationen und Wirklichkeitserzeugung. Matthes & Seitz, Berlin
Domingo A (2024) Elevenlabs uses AI to have Burt Reynolds, other late artists narrate content for users. Tech Times. https://www.techtimes.com/articles/306381/20240705/elevenlabs-uses-ai-burt-reynolds-late-artists-narrate-content-users.htm
Dryfus H (1992) What computers still can´t do. MIT Press, New York
Edwards B (2025) Nvidia unveils $3,000 desktop AI computer for Home Researchers. Ars Technica. https://arstechnica.com/ai/2025/01/nvidias-first-desktop-pc-can-run-local-ai-models-for-3000/
EPRS|European Parliamentary Research Service (2023) General-purpose artificial intelligence–European parliament. European Parliament. https://www.europarl.europa.eu/RegData/etudes/ATAG/2023/745708/EPRS_ATA(2023)745708_EN.pdf
Ernst C (2016) Chronopoetics. The temporal being and operativity of technological media. Rowman& Littlefield, London/New York
EU AI ACT (2024) Article 51: classification of general-purpose AI models as general purpose AI models with Systemic Risk. EU Artificial Intelligence Act. https://artificialintelligenceact.eu/article/51/
Fink MC, Robinson SA, Ertl B (2024) AI-based avatars are changing the way we learn and teach: benefits and challenges. Front Educ 9:1416307. https://doi.org/10.3389/feduc.2024.1416307
Galvão VF, et al (2021) Discussing human values in digital immortality: towards a value-oriented perspective. J Braz Comput Soc 27(1). https://doi.org/10.1186/s13173-021-00121-x
GDPR European Union (2016, April 27) Regulation (EU) 2016/679 of the European parliament and of the council [GDPR] Europa.eu. https://eurlex.europa.eu/eli/reg/2016/679/oj/eng
Gebru T, Hanna A, Kak A, West SM, Solaiman I (2023) GPAI policy brief. Washington Post. https://www.washingtonpost.com/documents/523e5232-7996-47c6-b502-ed5e1a385ea8.pdf

Gerner AM (2023) The AIS have it? Hacking into the AI avatar dream. In: Dieter M, Anton R, Thomas G, Jörg S, Lorena K, Miriam LL (eds) Actor & avatar. Bielefeld: transcript Verlag, pp. 75–84. https://doi.org/10.14361/9783839467619-010

Gerner AM (2024a) Playing with arte(f)actors. In: Breyer T, Gerner AM, Grouls N, Schick JF (eds) Diachronic perspectives on embodiment and technology. Philosophy of engineering and technology, vol 46. Springer, Cham. https://doi.org/10.1007/978-3-031-50085-5_2

Gerner A (2024b) AI heritage avatars. Rev Comun E LingGens (60):18–45. https://doi.org/10.34619/rdjh-ltod

Goodfellow IJ, Pouget-Abadie J, Mirza M et al. (2014) Generative adversarial nets. In: Proceedings of the 27th international conference on neural information processing systems, Vol 2, pp 2672–2680. https://dl.acm.org/doi/10.5555/2969033.2969125

Gramelsberger G (2023) Philosophie des digitalen. zur einführung. Hamburg, Junius

Gutherz G., Gordin S., Sáenz L., Levy O., Berant J (2023) Translating akkadian to english with neural machine translation. PNAS Nexus 2(5):pgad096. https://doi.org/10.1093/pnasnexus/pgad096

Gumbrecht HU (2014) Our broad present: time and contemporary culture. Columbia University Press

Hamon R, Sanchez I, Fernandez Llorca D, Gomez E (2024) Generative AI transparency: identification of machine-generated content. In: JRC137136. JRC Publications Repository - Generative AI Transparency: Identification of Machine-Generated content (europa.eu). European Commission, Ispra

Ho J, Jain A, Abbeel P (2020) Denoising diffusion probabilistic models. ArXiv:2006.11239 [Cs, Stat]. https://arxiv.org/abs/2006.11239

Huang/NVIDIA (2023) NVIDIA Keynote at SIGGRAPH 2023. In: YouTube. https://www.youtube.com/watch?v=Z2VBKerS63A

Hughes-Warrington M (2022) Toward the recognition of artificial history makers. History and Theory 61(4):107–118. https://doi.org/10.1111/hith.12278

Huyssen A (2000) Present pasts: media, politics, amnesia. Publ Cult 12:21–38

Hyska M (2023) The politics of past and future: synthetic media, showing, and telling. Philos Stud (2023). https://doi.org/10.1007/s11098-023-02062-x

In Event of Moon Disaster (2020) In event of moon disaster–full film. YouTube. https://www.youtube.com/watch?v=LWLadJFI8Pk

Jones B (2024) Why sora struggles with real-world physics. Data Literacy | Learn the Language of Data and AI. https://dataliteracy.com/sora-real-world-physics/

Kalpokas I (2021) Problematising reality: the promises and perils of synthetic media. SN Soc Sci 1(1). https://doi.org/10.1007/s43545-020-00010-8

Karras T, Laine S, Aittala M, Hellsten J, Lehtinen J, Timo A, Nvidia (2020) Analyzing and improving the image quality of StyleGAN. https://openaccess.thecvf.com/content_CVPR_2020/papers/Karras_Analyzing_and_Improving_the_Image_Quality_of_StyleGAN_CVPR_2020_paper.pdf

Kelly SM (2024) AI resurrects deceased actors' voices to read audiobooks. CNN Business. CNN. https://edition.cnn.com/2024/07/03/tech/elevenlabs-ai-celebrity-voices/index.html

Kim H, Garrido P, Tewari A, Xu W, Thies J, Nießner M, Theobalt C (2018) Deep video portraits. ACM Trans Graph (TOG) 37(4):1–14

Kittler F (1999) Gramophone, film, typewriter. Stanford University Press

Klevjer R (2022) *What is the avatar?:* Fiction and embodiment in avatar-based single player computer games. Revised and Commented Edition—transcript Verlag

Koselleck R (2000) Zeitschichten: Studien zur Historik. Frankfurt, Suhrkamp

Krizhevsky A, Sutskever I, Hinton GE (2012) ImageNet classification with deep convolutional neural networks. Commun ACM 60(6):84–90. https://doi.org/10.1145/3065386

Küspert S, Moës N, Dunlop C, Brown I, Circiumaru A, Edwards L, Wendehorst C (2023) The value-chain of general-purpose AI. Ada Lovelace Institute. https://www.adalovelaceinstitute.org/blog/value-chain-general-purpose-ai/

Landgrebe J, Smith B (2023) Why machines will never rule the world: artificial intelligence without fear. Routledge

Loureiro D, Barbieri F, Neves L, Anke LE, Camacho-Collados J (2022) TimeLMs: Diachronic language models from Twitter. arXiv.org. https://arxiv.org/abs/2202.03829v2

Maham P Küspert S (2023) Governing general purpose AI: a comprehensive map of unreliability, misuse and systemic risks. In: Stiftung Neue Verantwortung, think tank at the intersection of technology and society. https://www.interface-eu.org/storage/archive/files/snv_governing_general_purpose_ai_pdf.pdf

Makhortykh M (2024) AI and the holocaust: rewriting history? The impact of artificial intelligence on understanding the Holocaust. UNESCO.org. https://www.unesco.org/en/articles/ai-and-holocaust-rewriting-history-impact-artificial-intelligence-understanding-holocaust

Manovich L (2023) The AI brain in the cultural archive. What new artifacts emerge when we look at the next revolution in media? Magazine, moma. https://www.moma.org/magazine/articles/927

Masood M, Nawaz M, Malik KM, Javed A, Irtaza A (2021) Deepfakes generation and detection: state-of-the-art, open challenges, countermeasures, and way forward. arXiv.org. https://arxiv.org/abs/2103.00484

Meyer R (2023) Generic pastness. AI image synthesis and the virtualization of the archive. Biblhertz.it. https://www.biblhertz.it/events/35511/2200

Milmo D (2024) Google pauses AI-generated images of people after ethnicity criticism. The Guardian. https://www.theguardian.com/technology/2024/feb/22/google-pauses-ai-generated-images-of-people-after-ethnicity-criticism

Morrow A (2025) Meta scrambles to delete its own AI accounts after backlash intensifies. CNN. https://edition.cnn.com/2025/01/03/business/meta-ai-accounts-instagram-facebook/index.html

Morse J (2018) Google tricking you with human-sounding AI is just the beginning. Mashable. https://mashable.com/2018/05/09/google-duplex-cause-for-concern/#4LjfHfgPAmqx

Morse T (2023) Digital necromancy: users' perceptions of digital afterlife and posthumous communication technologies. Inf Commun Soc 27(2):240–256. https://doi.org/10.1080/1369118X.2023.2205467

Msn.com. https://www.msn.com/en-us/technology/artificial-intelligence/pubg-inzoi-to-receive-nvidia-ai-powered-players-and-npcs/ar-AA1x8Vdl

Murphy H, Criddle C (2024) Meta envisages social media filled with AI-generated users. @FinancialTimes; Financial Times. https://www.ft.com/content/91183cbb-50f9-464a-9d2e-96063825bfcf?accessToken=zwAGKtJylI4IkdORGDy7UPlGStOdLpYGOCW_zw.MEYCIQD6c_oDOapiyYQRKJvE-z5yzgjbahivq3W2A5LQfpo1iwIhAOpCPXzkaE8uNKgQ0MPL3ZlZ9YoVYjFxqQXsfS66h_5l&sharetype=gift&token=aaca08df-570c-43cc-b86a-9c43d5db9dc9

Nagendran A, Compton S, Follette WC, Golenchenko A, Compton A, Grizou J (2022) Avatar led interventions in the Metaverse reveal that interpersonal effectiveness can be measured, predicted, and improved. Sci Rep 12(1):1–10. https://doi.org/10.1038/s41598-022-26326-4

Noble SU (2018) Algorithms of oppression: how search engines reinforce Racism. New York University Press.

NVIDIA GeForce (2025) NVIDIA ACE. Introducing PUBG Ally–first co-playable character. YouTube. https://www.youtube.com/watch?v=wEKUSMqrbzQ

O'Neil C (2016) Weapons of math destruction. Penguin Books

Papineni K, Roukos S, Ward T, Zhu WJ (2002) Bleu: a method for automatic evaluation of machine translation. In: Proceedings of the 40th annual meeting of the association for computational linguistics. Philadelphia, USA, pp 311–318

Parker CS, Parsons S, Bandy J, Chapman C, Coppens F, Seales WB (2019) From invisibility to readability: recovering the ink of Herculaneum. PLoS ONE 14(5):e0215775. https://doi.org/10.1371/journal.pone.0215775

Rao S, Anil KV, Tarunpreet B (2021) A review on social spam detection: challenges, open issues, and future directions. Expert Syst Appl 186(2021):115742. https://doi.org/10.1016/j.eswa.2021.115742

Rodriguez JA, Botzer N, Vazquez D, Pal C, Pedersoli M, Laradji I (2024) Intentgpt: Few-shot intent discovery with large language models. arXiv.org. https://arxiv.org/abs/2411.10670
Russell S, Norvig P (2010) Artificial intelligence: a modern approach, 3rd edn. Prentice-Hall, Upper Saddle River
Savarese S (2025) The Agentic AI Era: after the dawn, here's what to expect. Salesforce. https://www.salesforce.com/blog/the-agentic-ai-era-after-the-dawn-heres-what-to-expect/
Scientific American (2020) To make a deepfake. YouTube. https://www.youtube.com/watch?v=7nD3zrMN47E
Searle JR (1986) Minds, brains and science. Harvard University Press, Cambridge, Mass
Shumailov I, Shumaylov Z, Zhao Y et al (2024) AI models collapse when trained on recursively generated data. Nature 631:755–759. https://doi.org/10.1038/s41586-024-07566-y
Shur-Ofry M, Pessach G (2019) Robotic collective memory. Washington University Law Review, Forthcoming, Hebrew University of Jerusalem Legal Research Paper No. 19–19. https://ssrn.com/abstract=3364008 or https://doi.org/10.2139/ssrn.3364008
Song Y, Sohl-Dickstein J, Kingma DP, Kumar A, Ermon S, Poole B (2021) Score-based generative modeling through stochastic differential equations. ArXiv:2011.13456 [Cs, Stat]. https://arxiv.org/abs/2011.13456
Spallone R, Lamberti F, Olivieri LM, Ronco F, Lombardi L (2024) Augmented reality and avatars for museum heritage storytelling. In: Giordano A, Russo M, Spallone R (eds) Beyond digital representation. digital innovations in architecture, engineering and construction. Springer, Cham. https://doi.org/10.1007/978-3-031-36155-5_16
Suwajanakorn S, Seitz SM, Kemelmacher-Shilzerman I (2017) Synthesizing Obama: learning lip sync from audio. ACM Trans Graph (TOG) 36(4):1–13
Sylaiou S, Fidas C (2022) Virtual humans in museums and cultural heritage sites. Appl Sci 12(19):9913. https://doi.org/10.3390/app12199913
The Dalí Museum (2019) Dalí lives—art meets artificial intelligence. YouTube. https://www.youtube.com/watch?v=mPtcU9VmIIE
The European Parliament And The Council Of The European Union (2016) General data protection regulation. https://eur-lex.europa.eu/legal-content/EN/TXT/PDF/?uri=CELEX:32016R0679
Thies J, Zollhöfer M, Nießner M, Valgaerts L, Stamminger M, Theobaldt C (2015) Real-time expression transfer for facial reenactment. In: Tum visual computing & artificial intelligence: Prof. Matthias Nießner. https://www.niessnerlab.org/projects/thies2015realtime.html
Thies J, Zollhöfer M, Stamminger M, Theobalt C, Nießner M (2016) Face2Face: real-time face capture and reenactment of RGB videos. In: Proceedings of the IEEE conference on computer vision and pattern recognition. pp 2387–2395
Thies J, Elgharib M, Tewari A, Theobalt C, Nießner M (2020) Neural voice puppetry: audio-driven facial reenactment. In: Lecture Notes in Computer Science, pp 716–731. https://doi.org/10.1007/978-3-030-58517-4_42
Thies J (2023) Imitator–personalized speech-driven 3D facial animation. Justus Thies. https://justusthies.github.io/posts/imitator/. Accessed 14 Aug 2023
Torres B (2024) Inteligência artificial ressuscita Machado de Assis, que comenta possível traição de Capitu; veja a resposta. O Globo. https://oglobo.globo.com/cultura/noticia/2024/03/07/inteligencia-artificial-ressuscita-machado-de-assis-que-comenta-possivel-traicao-de-capitu-veja-a-resposta.ghtml
Tremblay J (2024) Envisioning the future: broadcom's AI connectivity innovations, broadcom, Broadcom.com. https://www.broadcom.com/blog/envisioning-the-future-broadcom-ai-connectivity-innovations
Vaswani A, Shazeer N, Parmar N, Uszkoreit J, Jones L, Gomez AN, Kaiser L, Polosukhin I (2017) Attention is all you need. arXiv.org. https://arxiv.org/abs/1706.03762
Warzel C (2024) Elevenlabs is building an army of voice clones. The Atlantic. https://www.theatlantic.com/technology/archive/2024/05/elevenlabs-ai-voice-cloning-deepfakes/678288/
Whipp G (2024) Denis Villeneuve is not at peace. And he's OK with that. Los Angeles Times

White H (1973) Metahistory: the historical imagination in nineteenth-century Europe. Johns Hopkins University Press

Wodecki B (2025) Nvidia opens 2025 with new AI agent, developer tools, and a "GPU shield." Capacity Media. https://www.capacitymedia.com/article/nvidia-opens-2025-with-new-ai-agent-developer-tools

Wu F, Fan A, Baevski A, Dauphin Y, Auli M (2019) Pay less attention with lightweight and dynamic convolutions. ArXiv, abs/1901.10430

Xu J (2025) X (Formerly Twitter). https://x.com/joshua_xu_/status/1876707348686995605?mx=2

Zagal JP, Mateas M (2010) Time in video games: a survey and analysis. Simul Gaming 41(6):844–868. https://doi.org/10.1177/1046878110375594

Zhang H, Goodfellow I, Metaxas D, Odena A (2019) Self-attention generative adversarial networks. https://proceedings.mlr.press/v97/zhang19d/zhang19d.pdf

Chapter 5
Cybernetic Resurgences: Machine Music Beyond AI Slop

Stephen Roddy and Brian Bridges

Abstract This chapter explores contemporary trends in the application of machine learning technologies in music composition and performance contexts. It argues that there is a resurgence of cybernetic approaches to music-making in response to the rapid proliferation of machine learning technologies for artificial media production in recent years. These approaches are contextualised with reference to a history of interactions between cybernetic thought and musical practices, as well as a recent rethinking of cybernetics represented in the work of Yuk Hui and N. Katherine Hayles. It considers the problem of AI slop generators designed and pushed by hegemonic tech giants, paying specific attention to the unethical and irresponsible practices used in their production as well as the algorithmic monoculture perpetuated in their outputs. The chapter then turns to key musical artists at the forefront of the cybernetic resurgence who are engaged in an ethical reappropriation of machine learning techniques away from the big tech giants, before concluding with some suggestions for how an ethically grounded cybernetics of musical machine learning might open a new space of artistic possibility beyond the algorithmic monoculture of AI slop.

Keywords Cybernetic · Music · AI · ML · AI/ML · Slop

5.1 Introduction

In recent years, we have seen the rapid and accelerating proliferation of what are termed generative AI (Artificial Intelligence) tools in creative arts contexts. Large language models (LLMs) like Chat-GPT (Open AI 2022), Claude (Anthropic 2023),

S. Roddy (✉)
Radical Humanities Laboratory, Department of Digital Humanities, University College Cork, Cork, Ireland
e-mail: sroddy@ucc.ie

B. Bridges
School of Arts and Humanities, Ulster University, Derry Londonderry, Northern Ireland, UK
e-mail: bd.bridges@ulster.ac.uk

N. Zagalo and D. Keller (eds.), *Artificial Media*, Springer Series on Cultural Computing,
https://doi.org/10.1007/978-3-031-89037-6_5

and Gemini (Anil et al. 2023), driven by powerful transformer architectures derived from Vaswani et al's. (2017) work, are reshaping how we generate, interact with, and think about text across such disparate creative fields as novelization, screenwriting, and poetry. Latent Diffusion techniques (Rombach et al. 2022) have resulted in a myriad of applications for image generation including DALL-E (OpenAI 2021), Imagen (Google 2022), and Midjourney (2023). Generative Music models based on these architectures have also come to the fore recently. MusicGen (Copet et al. 2024), MusicLM (Agostinelli et al. 2023), and AudioBox (Vyas et al. 2023) use transformer architectures. Stable Audio (Evans et al. 2024) uses audio diffusion techniques, while, according to Concialdi et al. (2024), Riffusion diffuses mel-spectrograms that are then converted to audio. A comparable approach is used by Google Brain's Noise2Music (Huang et al. 2023). Suno and Udio, both of whom are currently being sued for mass copyright infringement (Berger 2024), would seem to use both diffusion and transformer techniques, though there is generally now a language model involved in any AI/ML (artificial intelligence based on machine learning) system which allows users to provide text-based prompts.

Each model mentioned above has been created by massively rich and powerful corporations racing for a monopoly over the generative AI market. Stability AI, the supposed underdog startup responsible for Midjourney and Stable Audio, was valued at $1bn in 2022 (Tayeb 2023), while Anthropic, the makers of Claude, is valued at $18.4bn (TechCrunch 2024). The other companies involved are Facebook/Meta, OpenAI, Microsoft, and Google/Alphabet. Much controversy exists around the unethical practices involved in the production of these models. Data to train models MuLan, Google's music-to-text embedding that undergirds their MusicLM model was taken from YouTube without any credit or compensation to the original creators (Roddy and Parmar 2023). Furthermore, the labelling tasks critical to assembling training data for ML models have been outsourced to what Perrigo (2023) describes as 'sweatshops' that mistreat and underpay workers. Bender et al. (2021) demonstrate that white supremacist, misogynistic, and ageist views are overrepresented in training data scraped from the internet. These biases tend to get amplified even further in the training process as model architectures designed to produce simplified representations of complex data end up producing racial and gender-based stereotypes (Nicoletti and Bass 2023). There are also significant environmental impacts associated with training AI models due to the sheer volume of water and power consumption required for training state-of-the-art models. These place demand on local water services and power grids while producing environmental impacts that tend to be felt most acutely in the disadvantaged regions where these companies build their data centres (Ren and Wierman 2024).

Drawing from Hui (2024), such inhumane practices are not so much a bug of the system, but a feature, given that these companies and the technological products that they produce are deeply steeped in the values of a transhumanist ideology that radically reduces the value of human life almost, one might argue, to the point of contempt. Transhumanism is described by critic and author Mark O'Connell as the "[…] belief that we can and should eradicate ageing as a cause of death; that we can and should use technology to augment our bodies and our minds; that we can and should merge with machines, remaking ourselves, finally, in the image of our own higher ideals" (O'Connell 2018). Gebru and Torres (2024) argue that transhumanism is the dominant ideology driving the companies leading the charge towards AI and that the litany of are direct consequences of this ideology.

Hui (2024) further highlights a tenuous dichotomy that lies at the heart of our thinking about technology: the oppositional binary that has developed in Western thought between 'machines' characterised by linear, predictable logics artificially constituted and 'ecology' as an authentic self-regulating system comprised of natural, organic, parts. For the purposes of this volume, it is the dichotomy between 'artificial' machines and 'authentic' ecological systems that draws our attention. This is not least of all because, as Hui points out, the history of cybernetics, in its analysis of self-regulation across people (social and cultural), machines (private and public), and environments (built and natural), flies in the face of this disjunction. We see a route past this dualism in Hayles' (2024) *technosymbiosis* metaphor. Building on Haraway's 'Cyborg Manifesto' and J. C. R. Licklider's 'Human–Computer Symbiosis', Hayles presents technosymbiosis to describe *cognitive assemblages* of humans, non-human organisms and computational media as networks of equal actors within which information, interpretations, and meanings circulate and flow. Hayles (ibid.) sees these cognitive assemblages as instrumental to the development of a third-order Cybernetics that "incorporates the co-evolution of humans and machines into an integrated cognitive framework".

Hayles (ibid.) further describes how the field of AI is permeated and mediated by metaphors, as defined in Lakoff and Johnson's *conceptual metaphor theory* (1980), wherein relations in commonly familiar and accessible domains of human experience are used to frame and thus understand relations in less familiar domains. This point is also raised by Roddy and Parmar (2023), who argue that the use of 'intelligence' and 'learning' as metaphors for the computational process underlying modern machine learning (ML) architectures tightly constrain their application in music-making and the sonic arts. "Machine intelligence" fails as a conceptual metaphor because the formal logics and relations we associate with machines only capture the mechanistic dynamics of human intelligence but do not account for tacit and informal components of intelligence as highlighted by Dreyfuss (1992). To adopt Lakoff and Johnson's terminology, the concept of 'intelligence' does not provide a commonly familiar *domain* of human experience. Therefore, *mapping* it onto the target domain we wish to explain, ML methods, only serves to obscure that domain further. Another irony complicating proceedings here is that the target domain is very well understood from mathematical and computational perspectives, but, due to the complexity of these systems, not always easily explainable to the uninitiated in simple terms. As a result, artists and the public's expectations of what are sold to us as creative AI tools are often not aligned with the realities of ML-driven applications for *artificial media* generation. Rather than granting the artist access to infinite new universes of creative expression they produce low-quality media colloquially known as *AI slop* that tends to perpetuate an algorithmic monoculture with clichéd representations of creativity (Ugander and Epstein 2024).

Questions of authenticity and artificiality have long been to the fore in discussions about generative music and continue to pervade our present musical moment, typified by the application of generative AI in musical contexts (Loughran and O'Neil 2016). Drawing again from Hui (2024), the metaphor of the machine as 'artificial' is of similarly limited use in musical and sound art contexts, setting up as it does an oppositional binary between machine and ecology that is fundamentally at odds with the techosymbiotic practices that provide the infrastructural backbone for artistic work in these fields. Hui's (2024) technodiversity, as a technical analog of ecological biodiversity goes well beyond this dualism. Instead it describes heterogenous multitudes of locally specific technological formations co-existing in a complex web of culturally and environmentally situated relations to one another. It describes the plurality of techniques and technologies, along with their associated political and sociocultural meanings (cosmotechnics), that emerge in response to the unique and specific challenges and characteristics of a given locality. It presents a challenge to the conceptualization of technology as a universal and homogenizing force, the same for all people, in all places, at all times suggesting instead that there exists a multitude of culture-specific *cosmotechnics*. Thus technodiversity challenges the universalist and totalizing transhumanist ideology of the dominant tech hegemonies. In this, we see corrective for the shortcomings we perceive in Hayles' technosymbiosis as it applies to the creative and performing arts. Namely, its failure to account for the hegemonic transhumanism of the tech giants developing these technologies (OpenAI, Meta, Google, etc.) and the detrimental effects of the unethical and irresponsible practices deployed in the development of these systems on the unfairly exploited actors in the creative industries, the tech industry and their adjuncts (Roddy and Parmer 2023). Both Hui and Hayles here are indebted to the work of Georges Canguilhem who, in his essay *Machine & Organism* (Canguilhem 1952), argued that we should also try to understand the machine, on the basis of the organism, and not just the other way around as is so often the case. This would later lead Braidotti (2012) to comment that the "[…] assertion of the primacy of the living organism over the technological implies that the technological other imitates the organic self. All technologies consequently become biotechnologies." Hui, building again on these themes argues that "Modern machines are all cybernetic machines: they all employ circular causality as their principle of operation. In this sense, a cybernetic machine is no longer merely mechanistic, but rather assimilates certain behaviors of organisms". These thinkers present a distinctly 'cybernetic' point of view in which the organism becomes a metaphor for the machine and ecology becomes a metaphor for complex technological systems more generally, as evidenced in Hayle's technosymbiotic cognitive assemblages. This specific take on cybernetics encourages a diversity of technical cultures (technodiversity) and is inclusive of a broad range of technosocial interactions (technosymbiosis). As such, we see a technodiverse approach to technosymbiosis as a modern culmination of cybernetic thought as it originated with Norbert Weiner in the 1940s (Wiener 1948) and developed and complexified throughout additional waves of interest across the intervening years. From this point of view, we argue that the 'artificial media' produced by generative ML tools need not be the inauthentic AI slop (a bug or a feature?) that is currently championed and pushed by hegemonic tech profiteers. Instead, a technodiverse and technosymbiotic approach to the application of ML technologies in musical contexts can open up an approach to 'artificial media' that is not just novel, but authentic and organic constituting an exciting new creative milieu. In fact, this movement is already well underway. The remainder of this chapter will consider some historical points of intersection between cybernetic thought and music-making, before examining what we term a *cybernetic resurgence* in response to developments in the application of artificial media generated by ML techniques in music-making contexts.

5.2 From Cybernetics to Generative AI Music

The field of Cybernetics grew out of mathematician Norbert Weiner's work on automating anti-aircraft guns in World War II. It developed throughout the infamous Macy Conferences held from 1946 to 1953 (Hayles 1999) and was formalised in Weiner's (1948) book *Cybernetics: Or Control and Communication in the Animal and the Machine.* Cyberneticists were initially concerned with common systems of control and communication across biological, mechanical, and electronic entities, focusing on goal-directed behaviors guided by self-regulation through feedback and feed-forward loops. According to Hayles (1999), this *first-order-cybernetics* was governed by the idea of *homeostasis*, the ability of a system to maintain itself in a stable state through corrective feedback. She contrasts this with *second-order-cybernetic*s which emerged around the same time at the Macy conferences championed by Margaret Mead and Heinz von Foerster and spread well beyond engineering and computing into the biological, social, and eventually political. Second-order cybernetics introduced reflexive practices whereby the observing agent became a critical feature of the system. Reflexivity, thus construed, refers to the tendency of a system to evolve, change, and complexify in response to self-observation. This was the key concern of these second-order thinkers. The first-order camp was concerned with information and information processing as defined in Shanon's information theory, seeing the human as a noisy and unreliable information processor to be eventually replaced by a more reliable machine. By contrast, second-order thinkers were concerned with meaning and meaning-making. Inspired by physicist Donald MacCrimmon MacKay, this group saw the role of the human in a cybernetic system as the agent that reconciles information and meaning via subjectivity and reflexivity. Cybernetics would continue to develop beyond these tensions embracing an ecological turn with James Lovelock's Gaia Hypothesis (1983) and Lynn Margullis' Endosymbiosis (Sagan 1967) in the 1970s before Humberto Maturana and Francisco Varela's (Maturana and Varela 1991) introduction of autopoiesis revolutionised proceedings again in the 1980s with its focus on self-organization, the capacity of an entity to produce and itself through self-creation, and self-organization. However, for our current epoch of ML-generated music, it is the tension between first and second-order cybernetics that is of most interest but more specifically, how the field of AI broke off from cybernetics.

The field of AI emerged from a 1956 workshop organised by computer and cognitive scientist John McCarthy at Dartmouth. McCarthy had been involved in the Macy conferences and was actively contributing to the field of cybernetics while also being heavily involved in the burgeoning cognitive science revolution. McCarthy invented the term 'artificial intelligence' to attract funding for his work while distancing himself from the cybernetics of Norbert Wiener, an individual with whom he had profound personal, professional, and political disagreements (McCarthy 1996). McCarthy set up AI with a focus on the science and engineering of "intelligent machines" thus uniting his own research interests whilst introducing a problematic metaphor that continues to be troublesome in our current era.

In 1972 the British Science Research Council approached Professor Sir James Lighthill, an aeroacoustics scientist, to undertake an impartial state-of-the-art review of the AI field. Lighthill concluded that AI had made little progress since the publication of Turing's *Intelligent Machinery* (1948) which had laid out something of a research terrain for the field 25 years earlier (Lighthill 1973). Lighthill argued that AI algorithms were far too intractable to effectively deal with the complexity of real-world conditions and concluded that computation might never be capable of simulating the self-organizing capabilities of the nervous system. In the wake of the Lighthill report, the British government pulled funding for all but three University AI programs while, in the US, DARPA (Defense Advanced Research Projects Agency) channeled its own AI funding into mission-oriented research leading to an AI winter.

The shadow cast by the previous AI winters would loom over until the ML revolution of the mid-2010s. However, as of writing, we may be nearing another AI winter related to the current boom in what has been termed 'Generative AI'. In June 2024 investment bank Goldman Sachs published a particularly damning report on the state of generative AI that contrasts growing demands on power and investor capital with projections of severely limited returns in both productivity and profit, calling the boom a bubble (Sachs 2024). Barclays has also sounded the alarm claiming that returns from AI might be as low as one-third of original investments (Barry 2024). While an AI winter would constrain funding for research and development in private and governmental sectors and surely sound the death knell for some of the less useful generative AI products currently pushed on the public, it would not change the fact that we now have advanced ML techniques that can be used to solve several complex technical problems, albeit in a more limited manner than the marketing departments at Nvidia and Meta might have us believe. During the ML revolution of the mid-2010s, musical applications were at the forefront of researchers' minds. This may be due in part to the fact that by 2014/15 the Long-Short-Term Memory variants of Recurrent Neural Networks (RNNs) were overcoming the vanishing gradient problem that had previously set hard limits on the effectiveness of RNNs for learning longer musical sequences (Dua et al. 2020).

The fact that these models were particularly well suited to learning sequences of symbolic data meant that a veritable sea of musical examples soon emerged, often building on earlier work by Eck and Schmidhuber (2002) to generate sequences of MIDI notes learned from a corpus of MIDI files. Whatever the case, before long music was becoming a popular 'problem space' for the development and refinement of ML technologies both at the symbolic musical note event level and the level of the audio signal. For example, Google's 'Magenta' developed Variational Autoencoder (VAE) based tools for music generation via the MIDI protocol (Roberts et al. 2018) before introducing differentiable digital signal processing or DDSP which operates at the raw audio level to transform and morph the spectral qualities of a given sound (Engel et al. 2020). The initial work on ML for raw audio waveforms was OpenAI's WaveNet (Oord et al. 2016), which was a breakthrough model at the time. OpenAI's Jukebox (Dhariwal et al. 2020), adopts a similar approach but uses a VAE architecture trained on raw audio files to generate music across a wide variety of genres. The majority of these approaches, with the exception of Magenta's tools for creatives, are focused on the end user who is envisioned as a music listener who wants to consume music tailored to their specific tastes. As the hegemonic tech giants developing these systems compete to build and monopolise a generative AI marketplace, they reduce the chances that technodiversity of musical AI tools might emerge. Roddy and Parmar (2023) argue that the systems originating with these companies tend to produce bland and imitative pastiches, pointing out that they rely on processes of replication, interpolation, and extrapolation to produce outputs that are divorced from the sociopolitical contexts of their original training data. Furthermore, some of these systems are ethically compromised relying, on the hidden labor of unfairly exploited workers. However, they also highlight artists who engage with the ML techniques on their own terms and subvert them from their original hegemonic origins to uncover rich artistic vistas that would have otherwise remained hidden. Here we see the beginnings of a technodiverse form of technosymbiosis beginning to emerge as these tools are embraced and re-appropriated by music makers.

5.3 Historical Approaches to Cybernetic Music

Hernandez (2017) traces a number of pertinent historical approaches to the integration of cybernetic principles in music, beginning in 1956 with Bebe and Louis Barron's score for the sci-fi film *Forbidden Planet*. They followed equations from Weiner (1948), creating sound-generating circuits via ring modulation synthesis and feedback loops. Hernandez (ibid.) follows these threads through the DIY electronic music of David Tudor and Gordon Mumma, before focusing on the analog approaches of Morton Subotnick and Roland Kayn. Similarly, Barton and Hulbert (2024) draw parallels with contemporary feedback-based *no-input mixing* and modular synthesis audio-and-control feedback loops. We will focus our history of cybernetic music on a predominantly analogue studio context, with a common thread of creating signal networks producing varying degrees of homeostatic stability and emergent complexity from system interactions.

Although the Barrons were influenced by the first-order cybernetics of Wiener, their emphasis was on its use to validate less deterministic working methods, after Cage (Brockman 1992). Barton and Hulbert (2024) contrast the Barrons' and Tudor's *positive feedback loops* in musical systems, whereby the feedback increased/

amplified change, with negative feedback loops which tended to 'buffer' or reduce change, tending towards homeostasis. The use of 'ungoverned positive feedback' (ibid.) led the circuits to self-oscillate and destroy themselves, whilst Louis Barron (quoted in Greenwald 1986) ascribed life-like properties to the circuit as 'a living thing […] crying out, expressing itself'.

This search for and, through editing, reinforcement of the circuits' 'authentic expressions' (Louis Barron, cited in Greenwald 1986) provides an early case of artistic technosymbiosis, with unstable circuit/loops mediated by composers' own agency and insight to form a 'cognitive assemblage' (Hayles 2024). Eno, who referenced cybernetics as an influence (Eno 1976), also describes feedback loops created on his 1970s EMS synthesisers by applying an oscillator's filtered output as its own FM source (Pinch and Trocco 2004: 294). This approach, termed *circular FM* (Silliman 2023: 53), blurs boundaries between carrier and modulator, creating chaotic outputs. Eliane Radigue explored this approach in 1972's *Geelriandre*, in combination with ring modulation and filtering (ibid.: 57), resulting in a signal network comprising oscillator-oscillator, ring-modulator-filter, and mixer nodes to create differing feedback paths and weightings for musical output. 'In this sense, we might think of Radigue as a sort of supervisor who is guiding, though not outright controlling, a semiautonomous network of actors engaged in unruly yet interdependent behaviors.' (ibid.: 58). Barton and Hulbert (2024) term this type of process of tuning results of systems *relational listening*; we might even go further and term it cyborg listening: a listening-action process and machine-human cybernetic loop. Similarly, Sanfillipo (2023) highlights the accessibility (indeed, ubiquity) of feedback as a musical process for many prominent composers of the 1960s, including Ashley's *Wolfman* (1964), Reich's (1968) *Pendulum Music,* and Mumma's (1967) *Diastasis, as in Beer* and 1968 *Hornpipe.*

In tracing a history of cybernetic music, Roland Kayn is of particular interest because, influenced by Max Bense's Information Aesthetics, he set out to create what he explicitly termed *cybernetic music* in the 1960s. He believed he finally achieved this while working with analog modular technologies at Utrecht's Institute of Sonology in 1970 (Patteson 2012). A salient feature of his approach was its moderation of homeostasis as a singular goal in earlier cybernetic works such as 1977's *Simultan* (composed 1970–1972), on steering between chaotic non-linearity (allowing the music to break out of cyclical patterns) and homeostatic adaptation. This balance of dynamic change with a system's adaptation extends the agenda implied by the Barrons' anthropomorphised circuits. Patteson (ibid.) cites *Simultan*'s programme notes in which 'Kayn signals […] the 'suspension of the opposition of automatic ('dead') and anthropoetic ('living') systems' (ibid.).

Kayn's large body of recorded cybernetic music can be contrasted with his disinclination to publicly document specific processes (as opposed to cybernetic principles). However, his working method at the Institute of Sonology centered on its 1960s-era voltage-controlled studio, and a review of its studio manual (Institute of Sonology 2005) highlights a high degree of continuity in its equipment specification. This, alongside examining the similar methodologies of Kayn's collaborator, studio engineer and composer Jaap Vink, allows us to infer some aspects of these processes. Reviewing these factors, alongside listening to *Simutan*, we find the following equipment potentially contributed to its genesis:

- Noise generators
- Voltage-controlled filters and filter banks
- Envelope followers
- Logic modules
- AM and Ring Modulation
- Function generators
- Tape delays
- Artificial reverberation

This basic architecture of his system appears to be an iterative series of loops through filter, delay, and modulation processes, with feedback contributing to chaotic system states delivering rapid transitions into new configurations before returning to homeostatic continuity, sometimes steered into or away from by a human in the loop. (What complicates matters is that *Simultan* (Kayn 1977) also contains materials created at the Studio de Recherches et de Structurations Electroniques Auditives in Brussels; a dense next-like web of patch-cables at the latter studio illustrates this release, implying the presence of an inscrutably complex system).

Kayn's *Tektra* (1984) has a more frequent focus on periodic, harmonic textures and gradual evolution resulting from more dependably homeostatic processes and may be somewhat more amenable to systems analysis. A similar sound world within Vink's contemporaneous compositions (e.g. *Tide,* from 1989 to 1985) may offer some clues as to its process. Present on the compilation *s/t* (Vink 2017), *Tide* gravitates towards similar harmonic drones in interplay with (and, emerging from) narrow-band filtered noise in a more slowly-evolving and more homeostatically coherent process than *Simultan.* Notable in the flow-chart diagrams accompanying Vink's (ibid.) compilation are patches describing both reverb feedback loops (moderated by envelope followers) and delay, filter bank, and ring modulator loops, again with envelope followers for control of feedback. Indeed, a further point, on examining a typical Vink patch of tape delay, ring modulation, (third-octave) filter bank, (digital) reverb, and envelope follower (Tazelaar 2021) is that multiple elements of this largely analogue system can be seen as impeding the rapid buildup of feedback products. The system acts as both a distributed dynamic compressor (through the tape compression, as well as the envelope follower's inverted output connected to a VCA), but more significantly, the ring modulation's frequency shifting also contributes to slowing the buildup of more fixed resonances.

Both aspects align with Kayn's later emphasis on more gradually evolving and harmonically focused materials, and homeostatic adaptation; the transition between these two poles can be traced in his liner notes, with *Simultan* (Kayn 1977) describing a balance between human intervention and system response and *Tektra* (Kayn 1984) being described by the composer as 'generat[ing] itself largely independently, based on the dynamics of intermeshed control loops.' Ho (2023) has sought to recreate some of these working methods, resulting in a plausible recreation of Kayn's broad sound world and dynamic based on a system of interacting oscillators in cyclical/

feedback FM and processor paths (filter banks, reverb, VCAs), controlled via envelope followers and associated logical operations. In this regard, it is striking to note parallels in working methods between Radigue's drone work and Kayn and Vink's cybernetic music, with all of these practitioners approaching their music as systems to inhabit within listening-action loops and varying degrees of human–machine co-creation.

Key to this type of cybernetic music is its relationship with the goal-oriented homeostatic self-correction of first-order cybernetics via more stable and gradually evolving states; system outputs are fed back (and forward) into the system and measured against a target state (e.g. the use of envelope followers and associated logic as control signals for amplifiers and filters). The system then corrects itself to navigate towards this target state with additional steering from a human 'in the loop', either towards or away from this target state.

Pickles and Collis (2016), exploring the relationship between cybernetics and the sonic arts, describe cybernetics as "the science and study of systems and [...] how information flows between man, machine and environment in a matrix of feedback loops [forming] emergent behaviours".

Pickles (2016) identifies a kinship with second-order cybernetic thinking and Pickering (2010) ties this more explicitly to Beer's (1972) *Brain of the Firm*, cited in Brian Eno's (1976) article 'Generating and Organizing Variety in the Arts'. This article laid the groundwork for Eno's later development of *generative music,* as exemplified in *Discreet Music (1975)*, through long-duration cycling feedback of the output of sequenced EMS Synthi synthesiser, and *Ambient 1 Music for Airports (1978)*, based on layered tape loops of differing lengths; his 1996 installation *Generative Music 1* may have contributed to the popularisation of this term (Collins 2008). Pickles (2016) identifies a kinship with second-order cybernetic thinking and Pickering (2010) ties more explicitly to Beer's thinking in *Brain of the Firm* (Beer 1972).

In this model, the composer can be considered as adopting the role of a planner or organiser, setting up a system, and letting it go, becoming the audience to the result. As his famous *Oblique Strategy* (1975) suggests, this is an approach more akin to gardening than architecture**.** Eno's early application via extended tape-echo-looping (*Discreet Music)* and composites from differing loop cycles (*Music for Airports*) is a more passive version of the cybernetic listening-action of the Barrons, Kayn and Vink, and Radigue. Nevertheless, alongside his 1976 writing, it reflects both curiosity and conceptual clarity around the musical application of cybernetic principles with humans (somewhere) in the loop. In so doing, these approaches may be considered to exemplify both a search for first-order cybernetic stability, and a second-order and technosymbiotic relationship of system and human co-creator, which will be traced through more recent practices in the sections which follow. It is also interesting to note that many of these early explorations of cybernetic music generated sonic practices, through their focus on extended textures and gestures rather than discretised and legacy acoustic-instrumental models (Keller et al. 2019), contrasting with the note-based approaches of early computer music such as Hiller's rule-based and stochastic *Illiac Suite* (1957) and Mathews's 1957 *Music-N* language's orc-score design.

5.4 Cybernetic Music and AI/ML Music

Drawing from Pickering (2011), and recalling Hayles (2024), Pickles (2016) describes cybernetic music as a process involving "real-time feedback coupling between performer and performance" and "the decentering of the self into a technological apparatus". This involves the application of heuristics, defined by cybernetician Stafford Beer (1972) as "a set of instructions for searching out an unknown goal by exploration, which continuously or repeatedly evaluates progress according to some known criterion". Thus, we can think of cybernetic approaches in terms of ontology, a set of practices organised around key themes as opposed to epistemology or system of objective knowledge. In this reading, cybernetic music is improvisational and ephemeral with trial and error experimentation, and recovering from or dealing with error becoming key navigational principles. The 'mistake' in this context becomes an opportunity for course correction and an important component of how the system works, meaning that systems of this nature are quite resilient in their way to error. This error correction to some target state is achieved through feedback and feedforward loops, both positive and negative, along with recursive coupling strategies. This focus on ephemerality, improvisation, and error correction as a navigation technique breaks from the dogmatic limitations of traditional Western music notation. Instead what we are left with is a collaborative mode of music making where the agency is shared equally among performers, machines, and the cultural/built/natural environment(s) in which they are embedded. This brings reflexivity into the equation, allowing the human in the loop to contribute to meaning-making as envisioned by MacKay. The end result here being autopoietic, self-organizing musical systems evolving in time to support the emergence of novel behaviors, patterns, and properties that were not apparent in the isolated parts or initial conditions of the system, but rather appear as a function of the system's evolution in time. The bedrock of this approach is a focus on equally distributed agency between the performer, machine, and environment. As cybernetics matured as a field we saw this ecological turn reflected in the work of Lovelock and Margulis and later Maturana and Varela. This is also captured in our appeal here to Hui's technodiversity and Hayles' technosymbiosis.

We contrast this with the AI/ML-generated tools currently developed and maintained by corporate tech interests that are built on transhumanist values, and trained on ethically objectionable datasets. Roddy and Parmar (2023) highlight how these tools operate on principles of replication, interpolation, and extrapolation to produce pastiches of the original data. By training on these large swathes of data, the model becomes a kind of lower-dimensional map of a musical 'problem space'. These approaches tend to draw heavily from culturally dominant musical paradigms. Popular musical styles (read: normative musical practices that reinforce the cultural values of Western Pop and Art Music) will be heavily represented in the dataset and perpetuated in model outputs, in contrast to more open sonic aesthetics such as Wishart's (1996) discussion of countering lattice-based structures in sonic arts, and the countering of legacy 'acoustic-instrumental models' of music in practices such as ubiquitous music (Keller et al. 2019).

The aim of these AI/ML tools is to create 'perfect' normative musical outputs that are smooth and continuous in an aesthetic sense, i.e. consistent with a pop paradigm derived from the established syntaxes of Western (Eurocentric) common practice music. The avoidance and reduction of error is paramount, which therefore will tend to de-prioritise less culturally dominant modes of expression. These outputs are always pointed toward a known and specific musical goal and, since the 2017 advent of transformer architectures are generally defined by text prompts inputted by a user. It is ironic, then, that this focus on perfection, and empowerment through the creation of accessible musical tools, will tend towards the generation of monocultural AI slop. Further, this approach results in a severely limited and reduced interaction dynamic between the human and machine that completely ignores the embodied musical knowledge of the individual, in favor of a full reliance on purely linguistic descriptors for musical processes that, being trained from corpora of cultural materials, embed those same transhuman values we criticised in the introduction.

5.5 The Cybernetic Resurgence

The culturally dominant paradigm for the application of AI/ML technologies in music performance and composition is disappointingly underwhelming and rife with ethical problems as previously explored. However, this state of affairs need not be the case. In fact, there are already a number of music makers who have broken with this approach to define a new paradigm for working with AI/ML in musical contexts. We argue that there is something of a cybernetic resurgence taking place, where music makers are creating and discovering new ways of working with AI/ML technology that is reflective of a musical cybernetics that represents an technodiverse approach to musical technosymbiosis. These approaches reject the values of the hegemonic tech powers we see driving the contemporary push towards an algorithmic monoculture of AI slop, reflecting instead human-centric values and processes from across the history of cybernetic thought and its contemporary culmination in Hui and Hayles by way of Canguilhem. Building upon our position form the introduction we believe that a technodiverse approach to a musical technosymbiosis with ML technologies can provide promising new vistas for musical practice. Such an approach embraces the use of ML technologies as equal components in musical networks consisting of musicians, non-musicians (humans and organisms), and machines throughout which musical meaning and information circulate and flow during music-making activities. To maintain technodiversity, and thus resist algorithmic monoculture, those ML tools must be devised to address the genuine artistic problems, goals, and concerns of the music-makers involved. This will generally mean that they emerge from spaces and processes outside of powerful tech companies or alternatively they engage in the ethical transformation of tools originating within those spaces through processes of hacking and reappropriation. It will also mean that massive datasets consisting of unethically and sourced and (all too often) toxic content are replaced by smaller ethically curated datasets designed to address specific artistic concerns.

While at present there are a number of artists currently engaged in practices that reflect these values, it is George E. Lewis has likely been engaged in this kind of work for the longest sustained period of time. Lewis' Voyager system was initially developed by combining principles from 1980s rule-based AI (GOFAI, or good old-fashioned artificial intelligence), and 1950s cybernetics, with sociomusical networks of free improvisation (Lewis 2019, 2021) to produce an interactive computer music environment that operates as a 'virtual improvising orchestra' (Lewis 2000), although our analysis would see this system as more akin to the feedback networks surveyed by Sanfilippo (2023), as well as other human-in-the-loop feedback-based practices discussed above. Cybernetic ideas were part of Voyager's makeup from the off, but the system has developed and evolved in the years since its 1987 debut, always operating as an autonomous computer-based agent capable of improvising intelligently alongside human performers in a live context. Lewis' treatment of the machine performer as an equal of the human performer resonates with Hayles' conception of technosymbiosis across distributed cognitive assemblages of equal players, machine, organism and human. He takes this further in his assertion that the behaviour of a given machine is highly dependent on its programmer and argues that Voyager expresses the richness and complexity associated with Afro-diasporic music-making (Lewis 2000). More recently, Lewis has been working to integrate modern AI/ML techniques while still focusing on collaborative improvisation as an assertion of agency on behalf of machine, human and environmental agents (Royal Northern College of Music 2023). Technodiversity lies at the heart of Lewis' approach as he continues to update and maintain the Voyager system as his own artistic interests have changed and evolved over the years (Roddy 2023).

We see this cybernetic approach extended in the work of DEBIT (Delia Beatriz) who also subverts the usual musical applications of AI/ML technology to produce works that are both socioculturally and timbrally complex. For her album *The Long Count (2022)* she trained a DCNN (deep convolutional neural network) model, called CREPE (Kim et al. 2018), on recordings of pre-colonial Mayan wind instrumentation. We don't have any written musical notation for pre-colonial Mayan music as this musical culture was all but erased by the Spanish conquest. Beatriz's work represents a speculative decolonialist reclamation of Mayan music transposed into a modern electroacoustic context. Hayles' technosymbiosis is evident in Beatriz's interaction with the ML models which, as instruments, become critically important actors in a larger cognitive assemblage that involves Beatriz as composer and performer, the original Mayan instruments, the ML models trained on recordings of those instruments, and the broader Mayan musical culture from which they originate. This is also a technodiverse approach in that Beatriz opted to develop these tools for her specific and unique musical purposes, carefully curating the dataset and creating the instruments, rather than sacrificing her musical vision by turning to the plethora of AI tools pushed by the competing hegemonic tech powers. Rather it is contributing to an ecosystem of bespoke musical tools for unique musical purposes.

In a similar fashion, Valenzuela, for his 2020 album *Transfiguración* focuses on AI/ML as a product of research activities driven by the military-industrial complex of the Global North. He trains GANs on Antonio Zepeda's 1982 album Templo Mayor which contained some of the earliest recordings of ancient Mesoamerican and ethnic Mexican instrumentation relying on the GAN to transmogrify the original material in what he describes as a "technoshamanistic conceptual framework" that renders the GAN as an alchemical of "mnemonic resistance" to the musical epistemicide (erasure of Indigenous cosmovisions) that resulted from the colonialization of Mexico and Mesoamerica. Previous to this, Valenzuela addressed connections between AI and cybernetics head-on with his piece "A Ritual for Floral, Cybernetic and Neuronal Intelligences", a live audiovisual performance and interactive installation for the "Stories for a more-than-human world" exhibition at Kesselhaus, Berlin in July of 2019. In this piece, Valenzuela created an interspecies communication system that mediates between EEG readings of his own neuronal patterns, biological readings from a succulenta plant, measured via the Interspecifics collectives Pulsu(m) Plantae system, and a sound synthesis system incorporating Pure Data, Processing, Ableton Live and Rebecca Feibrink's Wekinator (Fiebrink et al. 2009) for the AI/ML component (Valenzuela 2019). This work blurs the line between natural and artificial intelligence in a manner that is similarly consonant with the networks of self-determined cognitive assemblages described by Technosymbiosis. Valenzuela's 2024 compilation album *MutualismX* features a series of collaborations with international artists, including Ale Hop and Jessika Khazrik, intended to explore the political biases and historical prejudices inherent in AI/ML models trained on vast swathes of cultural data (Hinton 2024). Each musical piece was created using Semilla.ai, a neural audio synthesis tool that implements Antoine Caillon's open-source RAVE 2 (Realtime Variational Autoencoder) architecture in Max with the help of the nn ~ (neural network) object externals. Semilla can be used with pre-trained RAVE models or, interestingly, users can train their model using their own data via a Google Collab notebook available through the official RAVE GitHub repository (Caillon 2021). Thus Valenzuela is contributing to the development of a musical AI/ML technodiversity by making new tools available to artists.

Another artist actively developing new AI/ML tools for music making is Nao Tokui. Tokui engages in a playful subversion of AI/ML technology, as it is sold to us by hegemonic tech monopolies, through strategies of deliberate musical 'misuse' (Tokui 2024). He aims to reintroduce errors, mistakes and deviations into our application of AI/ML technology in musical contexts, as evidenced by their application on his *Dawn Patrol EP (2022)* or his recent track *Distant Echoes through the Mist (2024).* In dealing with these errors, he believes, entirely new possibilities for human creativity are opened up and this is especially true of his approach to live musical performances with AI/ML systems. This also is evident in the AI/ML tools, like timbre morphing VST plugin Morpho, that he actively develops through his music tech company Neutone. Morpho is a plugin (VST/AU) that uses autoencoders for real-time timbre morphing inside the DAW (digital audio workstation). It transforms the timbre or tone of an input audio waveform while retaining the pitch, rhythmic, and amplitude information of the input opening up a world of interesting sonic potentials. While it currently has a number of available models, Neutone allows artists to train their own models for use with the plugin via their training system. Presently, the free-to-use Neutone FX plugin (VST/AU) supports timbre transfer and cross-synthesis with a variety of models built on the DDSP and RAVE architectures discussed previously. What makes these plugins interesting from a musical perspective is the unexpected musical opportunities they open up as tweaking the parameters can result in the accumulation of little errors and mistakes that can result in surprising sonic results. The idea of embracing error was something that grew out of Tokui's work with Brian Eno who commented to him that he was more interested in artificial stupidity than artificial intelligence (Tokui 2024 p. 165). Allowing errors to happen and then finding creative ways to deal with them recalls Pickles' distinction between cybernetic music, where trial and error processes producing 'mistakes' are key to steering music-making systems, and the more traditional AI-music approach which aims to produce the perfect, mistake and error-free score or audio file. At the same time, by developing his own AI/ML tools and making them available to the wider music community Tokui, like Valenzuela, is contributing to technodiversity by helping to create an alternative cosmotechnic of AI/ML for music-making.

5.6 Conclusion

In closing, we reiterate our position that there is a cybernetic resurgence underway in contemporary technologically mediated music-making practices. This is not a return to some glorious cybernetic utopia of the past which, as deftly illustrated in Geoghegan (2023), never actually existed. Instead, it is a contemporary response to the emergence of modern AI/ML technologies; a set of practices for thinking with and being amongst machines that have been evolving and developing since the 1940s. While each intervening era has had a different approach to cybernetic music shaped by the sociotechnical landscape of the time, our present epoch is one of artificial media driven by generative AI/ML tools produced by the global tech industry. While Hayles' technosymbiotic thesis suggests that we should enter into a relationship with these AI/ML systems as actors of equal agency in a wider network of cognitive assemblages, Hui maintains that in doing so, we must not acquiesce to the transhumanist values of the global tech industry, but resist them by supporting and encouraging technodiversity. The artists discussed here are all applying and working with AI/ML tools in musical contexts, but they are bending, hacking, reshaping and recreating these tools to suit their own artistic interests and aims, thus contributing a plurality of techniques, a technodiversity that embraces the potential AI/ML has to offer music-making, while confronting and rejecting the transhumanist ideological agenda which fuels the global tech industry.

While we find these approaches to be of critical importance we would further argue that there is a need for dedicated ML tools developed by artists for artists outside of the tech monopolies who currently dominate the AI/ML landscape. In practical terms these tools need to allow artists to train their own models using (a) small ethically sourced data and well-curated datasets paired with (b) the correct ML architectures to address the artistic questions at hand. We also need (c) sustainable training techniques to minimise environmental impacts and (d) minimal computation (e.g. embedded systems) to encourage resource-appropriate designs. Further the 'client–server' or 'master-servant' model reduces the relationship between artist and machine to one of consumer and producer. This is highly problematic for dynamic and culturally complex music-making contexts.

We suggest a cybernetic approach in which the artist and machine are integrated into a matrix of feedback and feedforward loops, in line with Pickles' 'cybernetic music' and Hayles' 'cognitive assemblages', provides a promising forward trajectory for the ethical and musically effective integration of AI/ML technologies for music making in an era all-too-frequently dominated by AI slop.

References

Agostinelli A, Denk TI, Borsos Z, Engel J, Verzetti M, Caillon A, Huang Q, Jansen A, Roberts A, Tagliasacchi M, Sharifi M (2023) Musiclm: generating music from text. arXiv preprint arXiv: 2301.11325

Anil R, Borgeaud S, Alayrac JB, Yu J, Soricut R, Schalkwyk J, Dai AM, Hauth A, Millican K, Silver D (2023) Gemini: a family of highly capable multimodal models. arXiv preprint arXiv: 2312.11805 1

Anthropic (2023) Introducing claude. Anthropic.com. https://www.anthropic.com/news/introducing-claude. Accessed 19 July 2024

Barry E (2024) Is an AI stock bubble looming? That's the $167 billion question. Market Watch. https://www.marketwatch.com/story/is-an-ai-stock-bubble-looming-thats-the-167-billion-question-53a76c00. Accessed 18 Dec 2024

Barton T, Hulbert A (2024) Cultivating sounds: relational acoustics within the Buchla-Serge paradigm. In: Filimowicz M (ed) Routledge handbook of sound design. Routledge, London

Beer S (1972) The brain of the firm. John Wiley and Sons Ltd., London

Bender EM, Gebru T, McMillan-Major A, Shmitchell S (2021) On the dangers of stochastic parrots: can language models be too big?. In: Proceedings of the 2021 ACM conference on fairness, accountability, and transparency. pp 610–623

Berger V (2024) Why major labels are suing AI music startups Udio and Suno for mass copyright infringement. Forbes. https://www.forbes.com/sites/virginieberger/2024/06/27/why-major-labels-are-suing-ai-music-startups-udio-and-suno-for-mass-copyright-infringement/

Braidotti R (2012) Afterword: complexity, materialism, difference. Angelaki 17(2):169–176

Brockman J (1992) The first electronic film score–forbidden planet: a conversation with Bebe Barron. Score Soc Compos Lyric 7(3):5

Caillon A (2021) GitHub–acids-ircam/RAVE: official implementation of the RAVE model: a Real-time Audio Variational autoEncoder. GitHub. https://github.com/acids-ircam/RAVE. Accessed on 22 July 2024

Canguilhem G (1952) Machine et organisme. In: La Connaissance de la vie. Hachette, pp 124–159

Collins N (2008) The analysis of generative music programs. Organ Sound 13(3):237–248

Concialdi G, Koudounas A, Pastor E, Di Eugenio B, Baralis E (2024) Ainur: harmonizing speed and quality in deep music generation through lyrics-audio embeddings. In: ICASSP 2024–2024 IEEE international conference on acoustics, speech and signal processing (ICASSP). IEEE, pp 1146–1150

Copet J, Kreuk F, Gat I, Remez T, Kant D, Synnaeve G, Défossez A (2024) Simple and controllable music generation. Adv Neural Inform Proc Syst 36
Dhariwal P, Jun H, Payne C, Kim JW, Radford A, Sutskever I (2020) Jukebox: a generative model for music. arXiv preprint arXiv:2005.00341
Dreyfus HL (1992) What computers still can't do: a critique of artificial reason. The MIT Press
Dua M, Yadav R, Mamgai D, Brodiya S (2020) An improved RNN-LSTM based novel approach for sheet music generation. Procedia Comput Sci 171:465–474
Eck D, Schmidhuber J (2002) A first look at music composition using lstm recurrent neural networks. Istituto Dalle Molle di Studi Sull Intelligenza Artificiale 103(4):48
Engel J, Hantrakul L, Gu C, Roberts A (2020) DDSP: differentiable digital signal processing. arXiv preprint arXiv:2001.04643
Eno B (1976) Generating and organizing variety in the Arts. Studio Int 192(984):279–283
Evans Z, Carr CJ, Taylor J, Hawley SH, Pons J (2024) Fast timing-conditioned latent audio diffusion. arXiv preprint arXiv:2402.04825
Fiebrink R, Trueman D, Cook PR (2009) A meta-instrument for interactive, on-the-fly machine learning
Gebru T, Torres ÉP (2024) The TESCREAL bundle: eugenics and the promise of utopia through artificial general intelligence. First Monday
Geoghegan BD (2023) Code: from information theory to French theory. Duke University Press
Google (2022) Imagen. https://imagen.Research.google. Accessed 19 July 2024
Greenwald T (1986) The self-destructing modules behind the revolutionary 1956 soundtrack of forbidden planet. Keyboard Magaz 12:54–65
Hayles KN (1999) How we became Posthuman: virtual bodies in cybernetics, literature, and informatics, 1st ed. University of Chicago Press
Hayles NK (2024) Detoxifying cybernetics: from homeostasis to autopoiesis and beyond. In: Yuk H (ed) Cybernetics for the 21st century, vol 1: epistemological reconstruction. Hanart Press, pp 54–66
Hernandez DR (2017) Music in the age of communication and control. University of California, Santa Cruz
Hinton P (2024) How Hexorcismos' collaborative project 'MUTUALISMX' challenges AI prejudices. Mixmag. https://mixmag.net/feature/mutualismx-hexorcismos-ai-artificial-intelligence-interview. Accessed 22 July 2024
Ho N (2023) Cybernetic synthesis and Roland Kayn. [online resource]. https://nathan.ho.name/posts/cybernetic-synthesis/
Huang Q, Park DS, Wang T, Denk TI, Ly A, Chen N, Han W (2023) Noise2music: text-conditioned music generation with diffusion models. arXiv preprint arXiv:2302.03917
Hui Y (2024) Machine and ecology. In: Yuk H (ed) Cybernetics for the 21st century, vol 1: epistemological reconstruction. Hanart Press, pp 54–66
Institute of Sonology (2005) Studio manual BEA5. [online resource]. https://sonology.org/wp-content/uploads/2020/01/STUDIO-MANUAL-BEA-5-2005-opt.pdf
Kayn R (1977) Simultan. [3-LP set]. Colosseum (COLOS SM 1473). Liner notes. https://kayn.nl/wp-content/uploads/2016/12/Simultan.pdf
Kayn R (1984) Tektra [6-LP set]. Colosseum (COLOS SM1479). Liner notes. https://kayn.nl/wp-content/uploads/2021/12/tektra_booklet_2021.pdf
Keller D, Schiavoni F, Lazzarini V (2019) Ubiquitous music: perspectives and challenges. J New Music Res 48(4):309–315
Kim JW, Salamon J, Li P, Bello JP (2018) Crepe: a convolutional representation for pitch estimation. In: 2018 IEEE international conference on acoustics, speech and signal processing (ICASSP). IEEE, pp 161–165
Lakoff G, Johnson M (1980) Metaphors we live by. University of Chicago press
Lewis GE (2000) Too many notes: computers, complexity and culture in voyager. Leonardo Music J 10:33–39
Lewis GE (2019) Listening for freedom with Arnold Davidson. Crit Inq 45(2):434–447

Lewis G (2021) Co-creation: early steps and future prospects. In: Bernard Lubat, Gérard Assayag, Marc Chemillier. Artisticiel/Cyber-Improvisations. Phonofaune, Dialogiques d'Uzeste
Lighthill J (1973) Artificial intelligence: a general survey. In: Artificial Intelligence: a paper symposium. Science Research Council, London, pp 1–21
Loughran R, O'Neill M (2016) Generative music evaluation: why do we limit to 'human'. In: Proceedings of the first conference on computer simulation of musical creativity (CSMC 2016), Huddersfield, UK
Lovelock JE (1983) Gaia as seen through the atmosphere. Biomineralization and biological metal accumulation: biological and geological perspectives papers presented at the fourth international symposium on biomineralization, renesse, The Netherlands, June 2–5, 1982. Springer, Netherlands, Dordrecht, pp 15–25
Maturana HR, Varela FJ (1991) Autopoiesis and cognition: the realization of the living, vol 42. Springer Science & Business Media
McCarthy J (1996) Defending Al research: a collection of essays and reviews (Lecture Notes Series). CSLI Publications, pp 45–46
Midjourney (2023) Midjourney. https://www.midjourney.com. Accessed 19 July 19 2024
Nicoletti L, Bass D (2023) Humans are biased. Generative AI is even worse? Bloomberg. https://www.bloomberg.com/graphics/2023-generative-ai-bias/
O'Connell M (2018) To be a machine: adventures among cyborgs, utopians, hackers, and the futurists solving the modest problem of death. Anchor
Oord AVD, Dieleman S, Zen H, Simonyan K, Vinyals O, Graves A, Kavukcuoglu K (2016) Wavenet: a generative model for raw audio. arXiv preprint arXiv:1609.03499
Open AI (2022) Introducing ChatGPT. openai.com. https://openai.com/index/chatgpt/. Accessed 19 July 2024
OpenAI (2021) Dall-E 2. OpenAI.com. https://openai.com/dall-e-2/. Accessed 19 July 2024
Patteson TW (2012) The time of Roland Kayn's cybernetic music. Travel Time Sonic Acts 14:47–67
Perrigo B (2023) OpenAI used kenyan workers on less than $2 per hour to make ChatGPT less toxic, time. https://time.com/6247678/openai-chatgpt-kenya-workers/
Pickering A (2010) The cybernetic brain: sketches of another future. University of Chicago Press
Pickles D, Collis A (2016) Cybernetic principles and sonic ecosystems. In: 42nd International computer music conference. International Computer Music Association, pp 529–532
Pickles D (2016) Cybernetics in music, Doctoral dissertation. Coventry University
Pinch T, Trocco F (2004) Analog days: the invention and impact of the Moog synthesizer. Harvard University Press
Ren S, Wierman A (2024) The uneven distribution of AI's environmental impacts. Harvard Business Review. https://hbr.org/2024/07/the-uneven-distribution-of-ais-environmental-impacts
Roberts A, Engel J, Raffel C, Hawthorne C, Eck D (2018) A hierarchical latent vector model for learning long-term structure in music. In: International conference on machine learning. PMLR, pp 4364–4373
Roddy S, Parmar R (2023) AI/ML in the sonic arts: pitfalls and pathways. Resonan J Sound Cult 4(4):399–408
Roddy S (2023) Creative machine-human collaboration: toward a cybernetic approach to artificial intelligence and machine learning techniques in the creative arts. In: AI and the future of creative work. Routledge, pp 18–35
Rombach R, Blattmann A, Lorenz D, Esser P, Ommer B (2022) High-resolution image synthesis with latent diffusion models. In: Proceedings of the IEEE/CVF conference on computer vision and pattern recognition. IEEE, CVF, pp 10684–10695
Royal Northern College of Music (2023) George lewis residency. RNCM Musicians and An Enhanced Voyager–Royal Northern College of Music. RNCM. https://www.rncm.ac.uk/research/research-activity/research-centres-rncm/prism/prism-news-and-events/george-lewis-residency-rncm-musicians-and-an-enhanced-voyager/. Accessed 22 July 2024
Sachs G (ed) (2024) Gen AI: too much spend, too little benefit? https://www.goldmansachs.com/intelligence/pages/gen-ai-too-much-spend-too-little-benefit.html

Sagan L (1967) On the origin of mitosing cells. J Theoretic Biol 14(3):225-IN6

Sanfilippo D (2023) The aesthetics of musical complex systems. Organ Sound 28(3):381–391

Silliman DA (2023) Transcendent machine: an analysis of ÉLiane Radigue's ARP 2500 synthesizer music, Doctoral dissertation. Princeton University

Tayeb Z (2023) Stability AI cofounder dumped his entire stake for a mere $100 just months before company hit a $1 billion valuation. Markets Insider. https://markets.businessinsider.com/news/stocks/stability-ai-cofounder-dumped-stake-1-billion-valuation-2023-7

Tazelaar K (2021) Ring-modulated feedback in BEA5. [online video]. https://sonology.org/aiovg_videos/ring-modulated-feedback-in-bea5/. Accessed 18 Dec 2024

TechCrunch (2024) TechCrunch. https://techcrunch.com/2024/05/13/anthropic-is-expanding-to-europe-and-raising-more-money/. Accessed 19 July 2024

Tokui N (2024) Surfing human creativity with AI—a user's guide. English Edition.

Ugander J, Epstein Z (2024) The art of randomness: sampling and chance in the age of algorithmic reproduction. Harvard Data Sci Rev 6(4)

Valenzuela MH (2019) HEXORCISMOS-a ritual for floral, cybernetic & neuronal intelligences. moiseshorta.audio. https://moiseshorta.audio/obra/hexorcismos-ritual-for-floral-cybernetic-neuronal-intelligences/

Vaswani A, Shazeer N, Parmar N, Uszkoreit J, Jones L, Gomez AN, Kaiser Ł, Polosukhin I (2017) Attention is all you need. Adv Neural Inform Proc Syst 30

Vink J (2017) *s/t* [LP/digital release]. GRM: recollection GRM (REGRM018EXT), Paris, France

Vyas A, Shi B, Le M, Tjandra A, Wu YC, Guo B, Zhang J, Zhang X, Adkins R, Ngan W, Wang J, Cruz I, Akula B, Akinyemi A, Ellis B, Moritz R, Yungster Y, Rakotoarison A, Tan L, Summers C, Wood C, Lane J, Williamson M, Hsu WN (2023) Audiobox: unified audio generation with natural language prompts. arXiv preprint arXiv:2312.15821

Wiener N (1948) Cybernetics or control and communication in the animal and the machine. MIT Press

Wishart T (1996) On sonic art, vol 12. Psychology Press

Part II
Artificial Media in Education and Design

Chapter 6
Media Education as AI Education—An Experiential Approach to Integrate Generative AI in Engineering Pedagogy at University

Daniela Reimann

Abstract The paper looks at generative AI as an issue of media education. It is based on a university seminar held in the study programme of engineering pedagogy, a teacher training study program to graduate vocational school teachers. It presents a didactic concept of a university scenario which is a setting for learning to analyse and reflect on AI systems for writing scientific papers integrating text and other media. Since the generation of text and media formats, such as, such as virtual worlds, animations, robotic objects which constitute our digital media environments. The use of AI tools has become common and widespread, university teaching, learning and training processes are challenged. What impact do those tools have on the learning processes and what kind of tasks do they facilitate? What are the challenges and opportunities opening up and which skills are required to use these tools reasonably and creatively, in engineering pedagogy study programs? In the seminar scenario applied, the didactic concept is a practice-based and shaping-oriented research approach to learning: The students are asked to undertake a research topic and test an AI tool (such as ChatGPT or other) to pursue the scientific topic. Rather than simply prompting, a writing collaboration between student and machine is realised. How to prompt the tasks to the system, so that the machine writes scientific articles of quality related to the topic selected is just one part of the task. The seminar is understood as a research environment connecting learners and machines as collaborative partners for experiential tests, for writing texts and shaping and analysing the media such as images and graphics related to it. The teaching methodology is based on a mix of theoretical Inputs related to the concepts of intelligence and creativity, the (wrong) implications linked to it as well as the practical experimentation with AI software. AI is used as a didactic tool to support those writing processes, based on the concept of activity-oriented learning. In conclusion, the paper looks at future aspects of artificial media in learning in university settings, using AI creatively to support the learning processes.

D. Reimann (✉)
Karlsruhe Institute of Technology, Karlsruhe, Germany
e-mail: Daniela.Reimann@kit.edu

N. Zagalo and D. Keller (eds.), *Artificial Media*, Springer Series on Cultural Computing,
https://doi.org/10.1007/978-3-031-89037-6_6

Keywords Media education · Media literacy · AI skills · Engineering pedagogy · Vocational teacher training · Generative media · Artificial intelligence · AI didactics · Higher education · Creative learning scenario · Portfolio

6.1 Introduction

"Artificial intelligence does not exist. But an ensemble of machines, media, programs, algorithms, hardware and software has led to an extraordinarily large, multifaceted and productive field of research called A.I." (Weibel 2021). Since the introduction of generative AI tools, such as ChatGPT online in 2022, a big issue in higher education institutions is the question of how to support AI-related skills of students at the university level. The general learning goals of media education are related to critically analyse, shape and engage with digital media in a variety of forms, in order to support the learners' understanding of technology, in the sense of media literacy. It includes an understanding of technology and its implications based on practical shaping and design processes. In the German scientific community of vocational education and training research, the idea of *Gestaltung*—the shaping of technology—was introduced and considered being an active, communicative and participative social process to be put into practice by the individuals involved in the planning and design process of technological systems (cp. Reimann et al. 2003). In the paper, a shaping-oriented approach to technology is reflected. Modern vocational education and training (VET) is characterised by the guiding principle of enabling employees to "help shape the world of work and society in a socially and ecologically responsible manner" (KMK 1991). As Rauner has put it (2019, p. 3) "The clever exploitation of the solution space [to solve problems in professional tasks] is an indicator of creativity as a dimension of professional competence." In the following, the teaching methodology and the learning contents are discussed and augmented by the operationalisation in the context of the higher education scenario.

6.2 Generative AI Systems as a Subject of Education and Learning?!

What is the educational content of AI? What should students, especially future teachers, learn about it? Apart from being an algorithmic machine, the computer is a linguistic, and semiotic—sign-processing—machine, which is able to analyse and process language (signs). The sign brings together natural sciences and humanities and forms the basis of their theory formation and research (cp. Grabowski and Nake 2019). Generative AI combines natural language with the computability of the algorithm at user level. It calculates probable sequences of words. As we know, but tend to forget, it does not understand language in semantic terms, such as making sense and recognizing the meaning. The differentiation between artificial machine intelligence and human intelligence and language use makes sense. However, apps such as chatbots based on generative A. I. allow the users to interact with the machine via natural language on the interface level. Chatbots like ChatGPT are on everyone's lips and with it the fears associated with the use of the software at school and in university education grow. As it is common when it comes to the introduction of new technologies, a great deal of scepticism is spreading around in education contexts. However, in the paper, we look at both challenges and the opportunities opening up using generative AI in education. Weizenbaum developed the ELIZA program in 1966, which was intended to demonstrate the possibilities of human–computer interaction using natural language. He introduced the term of *natural stupidity* as opposed to the concept of artificial intelligence. As Weizenbaum has put it: 'The danger of artificial intelligence does not reside in machines thinking more and more like people, but in people thinking more and more like machines' (Weizenbaum). However, Lenzen (2024) has stressed this point as a common characteristic of scientific language in AI research, leading people on the wrong track by using language terms which humanise computing processes (e.g. the machine does not learn, hallucinate, thinks, as humans do, but generates and calculates as given in the algorithms Lenzen 2024). Consequently, the overall learning goal of the scenario described is related to a more holistic understanding of AI systems based on the perspective of humanities and social sciences. However, the paper scrutinises writing and learning processes inspired by generative AI. As Meckel and Steinacker (2024) have put it: "ChatGPT & Co can support less well-educated or less literate people and thus reduce the inequality of these qualifications in the labour market. But the new tools can also be used to challenge your own thinking or creativity. They can therefore be useful co-pilots in natural work." (p. 164).

6.3 The Learning Scenario and Its Didactic Key Questions

The paper is based on a course held at KIT in engineering education. The pedagogical methodology is based on activity-based and self-directed learning. A central feature of the seminar was the use of authentic, self-directed selection of the task. The aim of the course is to support the students' reflection on KI and interest in using KI systems for scientific writing. Therefore, they selected a topic they wanted to examine. The outcome of the seminar was scientific papers developed by the students, such as AI in vocational education and training, the use of artificial intelligence in education: Models and methods to support teachers.

The target group are students of engineering pedagogy who will become vocational school teachers in the future. Those students are tech-savvy and differently skilled when it comes to writing texts, including scientific papers. Scientific writing is a challenge for many of them. So, the question to answer was, how can generative AI support them in writing in a meaningful, targeted, creative and inspiring way? When it comes to learning goals related to generative AI, a lot is said about the latest tools and their updated functionalities. However, the aim of the seminar was to reflect on AI on a broader level. Some of the key questions for reflection of the physical world and the AI simulations identified were the following:

- What characterizes the human way of thinking, and what of it can or should be handed over to a computer, such as "algorithmic thinking" (Nake), which is fundamental to the understanding of technology?
- What is intelligence and what concept of intelligence is underlying the AI, that is, machine-based intelligence?
- What (mis)conceptions of intelligence and creativity do exist in our culture anyway, apart from generative AI? (Robinson)
- What are empathy machines (Turkle), that is, what are the implications when we interact with machines as if they embody the richness of human experience (embodiment)?

The seminar was based on a shaping-oriented approach to learning. The AI system itself becomes the object of investigation and research, realised through the active testing of the software for scientific writing processes. The experiential and targeted use of generative AI systems to initiate AI-supported writing processes that the students shape by themselves and document in the portfolio. The semester task is to select a topic and write a scientific paper by using and reflecting a generative AI software. The students are asked to focus on the observation of the system's behaviour, to document the prompting procedure in a portfolio and reflect on the challenges and opportunities opening up. Therefore, they developed a research topic of choice with the help of a generative AI system and documented the process along the portfolio categories such as procedure/approach, the prompts, challenges and solutions, effects of AI on the work/writing process, Perceived strengths and weaknesses of the AI system as given in the Table 6.1 and the question: What they have learned about AI through practice. The aim was to develop an understanding of the system by observing how it behaves.

Table 6.1 Template of the portfolio document to be used for students' reflections

Dimensions of the portfolio documentation	
Procedure/approach	
Prompts	Use and differentiations, if necessary per chapter/paragraph
Challenges and solution	
Effects of AI on my work/writing	
Perceived strengths of the A.I system	
Perceived weaknesses of the AI system	
What do you think you have learned about AI and how?	
Other remarks, comments	

The learning objectives include the reflective engagement with generative AI systems through experimental and its targeted use by observing, what the system does, understanding functionalities. On a deeper level, the conveying of an understanding of technology is a learning goal to aspire to, realised through the differentiated use, conception, revision and reflection of prompts (prompt design). The aim is to understand, AI text is not yet knowledge, but a generated probability of word sequences. The students are to experience AI as an interactive writing partner (Wampfler 2023), so that they learn to understand how AI works from the application level and learn to use it for their own purposes and develop AI skills to deal with it.

The portfolio documentation (see Table 6.1) serves as a didactic tool to support reflection of the system as well as the overall collaborative writing process with the machine. The portfolio is used to accompany the process in order to make the work processes visible (instead of "worksheet" characters, e.g. hyperlinks and individual solutions).

Different AI-tools such as ChatGPT or co-pilot were used, examined, questioned and tested, but learning about AI requires a broader concept of the AI-related learning contents. In the seminar setting, AI is used as a learning environment, that is, an environment for complex learning processes, rather than a technology-driven simple view of new tools. Using technology in education requires "understanding practical realities rather than relying solely on technological advancements, which call for balanced approaches that recognize the complexities of teaching and learning" (Reich, 2020 quoted from Han et al. 2024, p. 1). Students explore AI in engineering education studies using selected scientific literature as a self-organised introduction to topics and particular research questions: What is the heart of human intelligence and human creativity and which part do we pass to a computer (AI)? The students work on the potentials and challenges of AI systems studying particular examples. To this end, students will test and analyse the processing of tasks by the system such as language and text analysis, translation, search queries, explanation of complex issues and the writing of texts (essays) and discuss and present the results.

Research topics were selected and investigated: What can the system do well, what are the challenges for the subjects using it and what should be made of it? What (false) trails users are being led down? What potentials and dangers does it hold for educational processes? Under which conditions can AI be used in a shaping-oriented way for teaching and learning processes in vocational and engineering education?

Learning objectives to aspire to as to become familiar with the current debate about AI and its influence on the future of work and vocational education and training by analysing the scientific literature and testing, analysing and evaluating AI tools. Students shall be enabled to name potentials and challenges, possible effects and side effects after the examination.

6.4 Interim Results

To evaluate the seminar and the participants' reflection, the portfolio maintained by the students throughout the seminar, recording their thoughts, insights, and critical reflections on the criteria given in Table 6.1 and activities.

Initially, some students had a critical attitude towards the general use of AI systems for scientific writing, and most of them mentioned a change of perception before and after the seminar: Students stressed that they would like to use it specifically in the future, as a support for further writing processes, e.g. for writing code, for creating learning materials, or interpreting graphics (e.g. physical phenomena). In the reflection and in conclusion, amongst others, the following issues related to the use of generative AI in the writing process were mentioned by students:

– Overcoming the writer's block

"Generative AI systems have the potential to support scientific work and can help overcome writer's block. These AI systems offer various possibilities that can facilitate the entire writing process" (Baur et al. 2023).

– Generation of ideas

"A major contribution of generative AI systems lies in the generation of ideas. They serve as a creative stimulus by helping researchers to develop new approaches, hypotheses or research questions. By generating unconventional ideas or making unexpected connections between different concepts, they can help scientific writers to help scientific writers to adopt new perspectives and find innovative approaches" (Baur et al. 2023).

– Literature review

"Furthermore, generative AI systems also support literature research. By analysing large volumes of specialist literature, they can identify relevant sources, summaries, highlight key terms and even provide new perspectives or approaches. This saves researchers valuable time that they would normally spend on reviewing texts manually" (Baur et al. 2023).

– Support of the writing process

"Generative AI systems can also be helpful in the actual writing process. They generate texts or structure existing ideas to get the writing process going. With the help of these systems, researchers can create initial drafts, outlines or summaries for scientific articles or research papers. This enables a quick start helps you to organize your thoughts" (Baur et al. 2023).

– Supporting the generation of code

Some students mentioned the opportunity to use AI systems to support their programming by generating code.

– Multiple choice questions for the classroom

ChatGPT 4.0 was used to develop Multiple choice questions for lessons, to support teachers. "In view of the fact that the questions were created at the university level, the quality is surprisingly high. However, the tasks could occasionally be more detailed. It is therefore particularly important that the teacher has a sound understanding of the material in order to correct such ambiguities. However, a teacher who teaches at a school should have no difficulty in identifying such errors after completing the Master's program." (Wegner 2024).

- ChatGPT as a trainer for oral exams

Furthermore, chatGPT was used for supporting the learning process, in particular as a trainer (mentor) to prepare an oral examination. A lecture on a project on additive manufacturing entitled "Development and production of an additive component" was used as an example to test ChatGPT as a trainer. The approach included the study of the learning content in the first place, using index cards, as it quickly became clear that one needs to know the material well before starting to learn with the AI. A chatGPT was created in which a lecture script was uploaded. The AI created questions, the answers which were then recorded into a microphone and subsequently analysed by the GPT (Wegner 2024).

In terms of challenges and opportunities opening up they have specifically mentioned the effects of the system AI on your own work and writing process:

- "The workload is reduced in that the text and wording do not have to be worked out by yourself. However, you have to compare it with other chapters more often to check whether things are repeated" (Hesse and Gehlert 2023).
- "It saves work and time. The work that remains is different to writing it by yourself. You can focus more on the content as you save yourself the time to formulate the text well" (Hesse and Gehlert 2023).
- "As soon as a text sounds well formulated, it is difficult to edit it again or reformulate it yourself. This is also the case here. Since the [Ai generated] text sounds plausible for the first time, [I have] dispensed with further source research and left it as it is" (Hesse and Gehlert 2023).
- "Precise instructions are necessary, which also requires a certain intellect and experience. Otherwise, further intermediate steps may be required. The solution offered must be checked" (Hesse and Gehlert 2023).

Summing it up, the students perceived the AI system as a partner to support their writing and learning processes. They appreciated the system as a tutor and trainer, since the A.I is able to change perspectives and roles (such as mentor, tutor and teacher). A dialogue was initiated between the student and the machine to optimize the process. However, the students are aware about sensitive ethical issues like scientific standards and procedures.

6.5 Conclusion

The didactic use of AI in the university seminar taught a lesson: The reflection processes were stimulated, since the students need to reflect on every single step towards the result, rethink the procedure of prompting and the design of sentences and cues given to the system. Summing up the pros and cons related to the use of AI in university teaching and research, one can conclude it is all about facilitating an interactive dialogue between humans (student) and machines (generative AI). Knowledge, experience and writing, leaning skills and last but not least thinking skills are not only required but essential. Those are brought together with a complex tool, which computes. It needs human creativity and inputs, to generate intelligent, and useful objects with meaning. Since AI can also take on the role of a tutor, i.e. formulate from a different perspective and be used as a writing partner, it has great creative potential (not only) for academic work, but also for target group-oriented text production (e.g. certain learning media/materials).

References

Baur J, Marcus A, Zimmermann A (2023) Die herausforderungen und potentiale von generativen KI-Systemen für das wissenschaftliche Arbeiten—eine Hausarbeit geschrieben mit Hilfe von künstlicher Intelligenz. The challenges and potentials of generative AI systems for scientific work—a term paper written with the help of artificial intelligence. Developed in the course media education, of D. Reimann, summer semester 2023. Karlsruhe Institute of Technology KIT

Grabowski S, Nake F (2019) Algorithmische Kunst als Bildungsgegenstand. Algorithmic art as a subject of education. MedienPädagogik 33:76–101. https://doi.org/10.21240/mpaed/33/2019.03.19.X

Han A, et al (2024) Teachers, parents, and students' perspectives on integrating generative A.I. into elementary literacy education. ACM. https://doi.org/10.1145/3613904.3642438

Hesse T, Gehlert St. Herausforderungen und Potentiale von generativen KI-Systemen für die berufliche Bildung. In: Challenges and potentials of generative AI systems for vocational training, paper developed in the course "media education", summer semester 2023. Karlsruhe Institute of Technology KIT

KMK: Rahmenvereinbarung über die Berufsschule (1991) Beschluss der Kultusministerkonferenz vom 14./15.03.1991. Bonn: Sekretariat der Ständigen Konferenz der Kultusminister der Länder in der BRD (Conference of the Ministers of Education and Cultural Affairs of the Länder in the Federal Republic of Germany FRG (1991): Framework agreement on vocational schools. Resolution of the Standing Conference of the Ministers of Education and Cultural Affairs of 14/15.03.1991. Bonn: Secretariat of the Standing Conference of the Ministers of Education and Cultural Affairs of the Länder in the Federal Republic of Germany FRG) (1991)

Lenzen M (2024) Künstliche Intelligenz. (Artificial intelligence), 2nd edn. Nördlingen

Meckel M, Steinacker L (2024) Alles überall auf einmal. Wie künstliche Intelligenz unsere Welt verändert und was wir dabei lernen können. (English title: Everything everywhere at once. How artificial intelligence is changing our world and what we can learn from it.). Hamburg

Rauner F (2019) Kreativität. Ein Merkmal der modernen Berufsbildung und wie sie gefördert werden kann. Lit Verlag, Bremen

Reimann D, Winkler T, Herczeg M, Höpel I (2003) Exploring the computer as a shapeable medium by designing artefacts for mixed reality environments in interdisciplinary education processes. In: Proceedings of the ED-MEDIA, World Conference on Educational Multimedia, Hypermedia and Telecommunications 2003, Honolulu, Hawaii, p 915–923

Wampfler P (2023) Schreiben mit KI-tools–digital unterstützte Schreibprozesse gestalten und begleiten. (on at research gate). Writing with AI tools–designing and supporting digitally supported writing processes. https://doi.org/10.58098/lffl/2023/03/806. https://www.researchgate.net/publication/375963614_Schreiben_mit_KI-Tools_-_Digital_unterstutzte_Schreibprozesse_gestalten_und_begleiten

Wegner NJ (2024) Einsatz von künstlicher Intelligenz in der Bildung: Modelle und Methoden zur Unterstützung von Lehrkräften. (Use of artificial intelligence in education: models and methods to support teachers). In: Developed in the course media education, summer semester 2024. Karlsruhe Institute of Technology KIT

Weibel P (2021) Art, algorithmen, artificial intelligence. Kunstforum Int 278. Köln

Chapter 7
Design of Interactive Narratives Mediated by Artificial Media: The Use of AI in Secondary Education

Sara Cortés Gómez, María Ruth García Pernía, Lorena Chiwerto Callejo, Raquel Echeandía Sánchez, and Adrián Domínguez Díaz

Abstract Technological advancements, particularly the emergence of Generative Artificial Intelligence (GAI) tools, are transforming various sectors, including education. This chapter explores how educational institutions must adapt to these new technological models by integrating AI into teaching and learning processes. The research focuses on a project at Jaby School (Torrejón de Ardoz, Madrid) during the 2023–2024 academic year, where 1st-year ESO students create narrative video games using platforms like Twine or Canva and GAI tools such as ChatGPT, Playgroung or Dall-E. The workshop promotes essential skills such as critical thinking, media literacy, and creative expression, addressing both practical and theoretical aspects of Artificial Media. The objective is to assess how interactive narratives (IN) combined with AI tools can support creative expression. These activities can increase students' interest in computer science and develop practical and ethical skills in a future dominated by AI. The results, obtained through qualitative techniques, aim to demonstrate that teaching computer science at basic levels can align with new creative and technological demands.

S. C. Gómez (✉) · M. R. G. Pernía · L. C. Callejo
Faculty of Philosophy and Arts, Universidad de Alcalá, Madrid, Spain
e-mail: sara.cortesg@uah.es

R. E. Sánchez
Creative Campus, Universidad Europea de Madrid, Madrid, Spain

A. D. Díaz
Politechnic School, University of Alcalá, Madrid, Spain

N. Zagalo and D. Keller (eds.), *Artificial Media*, Springer Series on Cultural Computing,
https://doi.org/10.1007/978-3-031-89037-6_7

7.1 Introduction

Society is saturated with technology that is advancing rapidly across all sectors, including education. This presents a challenge for both teachers and students. In this context, the concept of Artificial Media is particularly noteworthy. Its potential to unlock new creative avenues could prove highly beneficial for educational environments.

Artificial Media is spearheading educational innovation through the utilisation of cutting-edge technologies, including Artificial Intelligence (AI), generative media and virtual reality, to create and disseminate digital media. In terms of AI, the United Nations Educational, Scientific and Cultural Organization (UNESCO 2019, pp. 4–5) asserts that it has the potential to significantly impact the education sector, from management to teaching methodologies. However, this will only be achieved if it is deployed in an ethical and responsible manner, with due consideration given to privacy policies and the handling of personal data. This innovative approach has the potential to facilitate the development and adaptation of educational content in a personalised and contextualised manner (Heredia-Carroza and Stoica 2024), thereby enabling efficient production and dynamic delivery of educational materials.

AI is emerging as a catalyst for change in the field of education, unlocking unprecedented potential for innovation and growth. Although its impact is clear, its full potential remains to be seen. It is evident in the form of 24-h student support chatbots, automated administrative processes for teachers and online learning systems. Technological advances have begun to streamline educational management, enhancing the efficiency of learning management systems. Additionally, they are enabling real-time monitoring of student performance and the personalisation of curricula.

In this context, this project aims to demonstrate the creative process supported by Artificial Media, developed in an educational activity with secondary education students based on the design of Interactive Narratives (IN). To this end, innovative platforms such as Twine and Canva have been employed, along with cutting-edge Artificial Media creation tools, which have enabled the development of multimedia content for the design of the games. The technologies employed include ChatGPT, DALL-E and PlayGround. The specific objectives are as follows:

- Theoretically assess the potential of Artificial Media in the education sector as a tool to enhance the teaching and learning process.
- The objective is to propose educational strategies that support the acquisition of creative ways of thinking and acting based on the design of video games. Video games are considered cultural tools in the classroom, already part of the students' culture, and their educational value and potential within the school environment are recognized.
- The design process of INs developed in the classroom will be analysed in terms of both its creative aspects and the technical process of its elaboration with Twine or Canva and Artificial Media.

- An examination of the INs created by students will reveal the difficulties and learning acquired by students when designing games mediated by generative AI (GAI).
- It is important to observe the teachers' vision after the project has concluded in order to ascertain the educational benefits of this practice for each of the participating subjects.

This work makes two key contributions. Firstly, it proposes and evaluates the use of INs as a suitable educational experience for integrating Artificial Media education with other key skills for students at the secondary education stage. Secondly, it contributes to a greater understanding of the impact that Artificial Media tools can have on the creative processes that take place in the educational environment.

7.2 Theoretical Framework

7.2.1 Use of Generative AI in Education

The latest AI-powered tools are revolutionising the way we teach and learn, offering new forms of adaptive and personalised learning experiences at all levels of education. A growing body of research has demonstrated the positive impact of these advanced technologies on various aspects of education. This includes the implementation of accessibility measures, the adaptation of content and the generation of new resources for other teachers (Incio-Flores et al. 2022; Page et al. 2021).

This advancement not only improves the efficiency and effectiveness of the educational process but also paves the way for new frontiers in inclusion, accessibility and equal opportunities in education. In this context, we are interested in exploring the main benefits that generative AI tools bring to the educational environment, as well as how these technologies are being implemented in educational practice.

Systematic reviews on the application of digital tools in educational environments are a prominent area of research. Alateyyat and Soltan's research indicates that generative AI and its integration into higher education have become standardised in recent years. However, they highlight a gap in the research, noting that studies on predictive modelling, AI for evaluation and support for administrative processes are scarce (Alateyyat and Soltan 2024, p. 3). The integration of AI tools in teaching has been shown to significantly improve academic success, as evidenced by studies such as that of Ateeq et al. (2024). These tools provide improved guidelines for assignments, which are applicable to other educational cycles. In addition to facilitating the understanding of complex concepts, these tools personalise the learning experience to the specific needs of each student.

In the field of advanced educational content development, smart textbooks, such as the one described by Deepika et al. (2023), utilise AI to generate material enhanced with pertinent information, images and multimedia links. This not only enhances the learning material, but also makes it more accessible and engaging, thereby fostering autonomous and deep learning among students.

In terms of tool utilisation, several notable examples can be cited. One such example is the deployment of augmented reality with AI in the classroom to develop a conversational tutoring system that coordinates a range of learning activities, including natural language exchanges, graphical concept visualisation, instant translation into other languages or sign language. The use of intelligent tutoring systems (ITS), as demonstrated in studies such as Kokku et al. (2018), enables the adaptation of teaching methods to suit individual learning styles by providing interactive examples and fostering greater engagement and collaboration among students. AI chatbots can be utilised to provide personalised support to students, answering common questions and offering real-time tutoring, which streamlines administrative processes and frees up time for teachers to focus on individual student needs. Furthermore, advanced assessment tools, as outlined by Qianyi and Zhiqiang (2023), utilise image processing and multimodal techniques to evaluate learning holistically, taking into account academic performance as well as emotional and attitudinal aspects.

Finally, the integration of tools such as ChatGPT in the classroom, according to Wang et al. (2024), has enhanced students' communication and presentation skills by facilitating natural and effective interactions with educational content, better preparing them to face challenges outside the classroom.

In conclusion, it can be said that the application of smart tools in education extends to three key categories. The first area of focus is to provide support for teachers in the creation of educational material. AI tools enable educators to create interactive and bespoke educational materials, which can be deployed in the classroom, as a flipped classroom or shared with other teachers. A survey conducted in 2021 revealed that 60% of educators considered AI integration to be essential for successful teaching. However, only 25% of educators expressed confidence in their ability to use these technologies effectively (Ateeq et al. 2024). This highlights the increasing necessity for educators to enhance their professional skills in AI technology in order to fully utilise its potential in the classroom. Secondly, tutor-led learning for students represents a key area of focus. These AI tools facilitate the implementation of accessibility measures in the classroom, enhancing the efficiency and accessibility of tutoring support. Conversational tutoring systems are capable of interacting with students in real time, responding to queries and offering personalised feedback. Finally, automated correction and assessment should be mentioned. AI-based systems can automate the process of marking and assessing assignments and exams. These tools utilise machine learning algorithms to analyse student responses rapidly and accurately, providing immediate feedback on individual performance.

Nevertheless, the incorporation of these tools in education is not without its challenges. Previously mentioned authors such as Ateeq et al. (2024) and Qianyi and Zhiqiang (2023) have also expressed concerns regarding data privacy, improper use by students, and the importance of adequate human oversight. These aspects have prompted recent studies that also emphasise the need to advance research on the ethical foundations and regulatory frameworks for the use of AI in education (Alonso-Rodríguez 2024), as well as the definition of the new professional teaching profile, its implications for teacher training, and the use of GAI in classrooms as a complementary educational tool (Mora Naranjo et al. 2023).

As can be seen, the impact of GAI in education is being widely studied, especially in relation to its potential to adapt or produce new educational content according to the needs of students, to guide students during their learning process or to improve their assessment. However, there has been limited focus on the impact of generative AI on the creative processes that take place in education, for example, in the production of texts or in artistic production. This study aims to address this gap in the research.

7.2.2 Use of Artificial Media and Generative AI in Creative Processes

AI is transforming the multimodal arts sector, enabling the integration of images, text and sound in innovative ways. In particular, the use of GAI and Artificial Media is expanding the possibilities for new creative processes, whereby the description of text in the form of prompts can be an innovative way of creating and creating art (McCormack et al. 2023). However, numerous professional artists have highlighted significant challenges resulting from the emergence of large-scale image generators trained with image and text pairs sourced from the internet (Jiang et al. 2023).

However, in an educational context, the application of generative AI in students' creative processes is beneficial for "the development of children's literacy and creative expression. We are seeking to obtain information on the applicability of generative AI for educational purposes from various stakeholders (i.e. parents, teachers, and AI researchers)" (Han and Cai 2023, p. 1). These tools not only facilitate project development but also enhance creativity by offering new forms of expression and aesthetic possibilities.

One of the most promising fields in this context is IN, where the combination of sound, image and text has the potential to significantly enhance the user experience. In the field of arts education, there is a growing trend of integrating AI into the creative process (Navas Guzman and Meier 2024; Dehouche and Dehouche 2023). Tools such as DALL-E, Midjourney and Leonardo. AI facilitate the creation of illustrations and visual scenes from textual descriptions, ensuring that the images are coherent with the narrative and aesthetically appealing (Allauca 2023). From the perspective of implementation in the classroom with secondary school students, the composition and iconicity processes can be streamlined by starting from previously thought-out concepts in the form of prompts. In this section, we will examine the latest research on the evolution of the GAI of sound effects, music and text-to-audio translation (Magro-Vela et al. 2024; Marrinan et al. 2024) from the perspective of extending immersion with image and sound. The creation of bespoke music and sound effects that can be tailored to the emotions and situations in the narrative, enhancing the atmosphere and immersion, enables learners to more effectively convey the desired emotions through their IN.

It is essential to utilise multimedia elements to create an immersive atmosphere and convey emotions within INs. The use of AI tools in the creation of these audiovisual products (González 2023) not only streamlines the development process for students, but also enhances the quality and overall user experience. These tools provide guidance throughout the content generation, development, correction and optimisation phases, ensuring a seamless and high-quality production. The following section will address the potential applications of AI in the creation of INs in the secondary education sector. We will examine how AI can be used to enhance scripting and dialogue design in games, as well as visual and audio storytelling.

In the context of interactive fiction, the script and dialogue are of critical importance in guiding the user experience and enriching the narrative. These elements serve to establish the plot and characters, while also providing the emotional context and decisions that shape the direction of the story. There is a growing body of research exploring the use of ChatGPT as a tool for generating conversational interfaces. This includes studies by Yang et al. (2022) and Alonso and Cantos (2023).

Furthermore, AI offers valuable assistance in the development of speech and characterisation of language for video game characters. The incorporation of AI in this process provides students with guidance in creating contextualised scenarios, structured conversations and distinctive character traits. It is also crucial to comprehend the narrative structures, personalities, and interpersonal dynamics that are desired by developers (Alonso and Cantos 2023). It is essential to have a comprehensive understanding of the fictional medium in order to design authentic dialogues that reflect the complexities of human interactions. Another dynamic that can be investigated and implemented with students is the co-writing of fiction using a "finishing each other's stories" approach (Yang et al. 2022).

Therefore, this work, in addition to reinforcing the numerous advantages of IN in education demonstrated over the years (Green and Jenkins 2014), provides a practical example of the process of creating Artificial Media in the field of secondary education and in a multimodal way, including both text and image, with the aim of developing the same artistic work, such as an IN. These tools streamline the creative and development process for students while enhancing the interactive narrative's dynamism and capacity to offer immersive and personalised experiences.

7.3 Methodology

The work is based on an ethnographic approach, which involves observing the experiences of participants, conducting interviews, organising focus groups and collecting documents. This approach enables us to gain insight into the educational phenomena occurring in the environment, as well as their interpretation and narration by the various stakeholders, including researchers, teachers, and students (Contreras et al. 2016; Cotán 2020).

The effectiveness of this approach is contingent upon comprehensive case studies that elucidate how individuals derive meaning from their actions within socio-cultural settings. This expansive research methodology has been demonstrated to yield valuable insights in educational contexts (Pons and Rovira 2020; Cadaveira 2023).

7.3.1 The Project, Context and Participants

This research presents the educational experience developed at JABY School (Torrejón de Ardoz, Madrid) during the 2023–2024 academic year. Students designed INs, leveraging the innovative and creative potential of Artificial Media through the use of Twine and Canva. This approach facilitated a multidisciplinary work coordination between different subjects and teachers. This innovative proposal employs new technologies, such as narrative video games, to develop a range of skills, both curricular and technological.

It was developed with students in their first year of secondary education (aged 12). The activities were conducted in collaboration with teachers at the school and the research team from the University of Alcalá (UAH research project, code: PIUAH23/CSJ-045, name: NarraTechESO).

In this research, we focus on the work carried out in the subjects: "Geography and History", "Spanish Language and Literature" and "Plastic, Visual and Audiovisual Education" taken in 1st year of ESO (groups A and B), with a total of 56 students (28 in group A and 28 in group B), although not all of them participated. The students worked in pairs or groups of three in their respective classes, which were previously organised by the teaching staff. The research follows a quasi-experimental study design. In addition to understanding the impact of generative tools on the student's creative process, its objectives also included studying the impact of programming on students' attitudes and on the quality of their productions. To that end, group A used Twine, which requires programming the IN visuals and interactions, while group B used Canva, a tool which does not require any type of programming. These research objectives are not addressed in the present study, which focuses strictly on the creative process. Furthermore, the project was implemented in compulsory subjects to avoid selection bias.

The objective was to enable students to develop a creative product in an interdisciplinary manner. The three subjects involved in the project collaborated on the development process.

1. The script for the stories based on prehistory was created by the Geography and History subject.
2. The creation of all textual elements, including characters, scenes, dialogue, and so forth, was completed by the Spanish Language subject.
3. The objective is to create a visual story in plastic, visual and audiovisual education. To this end, Artificial Media will be used as a mediator in the creative

process, both in the creation of proposals, ideas, narratives, texts and, above all, the visual elements of the games. The IN were created using the Twine (Group A) and Canva (Group B) tools.

The research team provided support and supervision throughout the work process, visiting the classrooms at key moments and providing documentation and video tutorials to guide the students through the narrative and programming process.

7.3.2 Data Collection and Analysis

The research uses case study techniques combined with practices from ethnography (Fusch et al. 2017; Schwandt and Gates 2018). We analysed the continuous process developed throughout the workshop to understand the process itself and not only the outcome of the IN design activity, combining qualitative and quantitative samples (Bazeley 2018; Bergin 2018; Creamer 2018). This combination allows considering the context and circumstances in which the practices are carried out to be observed, analysed and interpreted, with the aim of gathering a global view of both the process and the results, to make improvements in future editions.

The participating students completed a questionnaire before the workshop on Google Forms to discover their interests and digital competences. These data allow us to understand the profile of the students we are working with, based on their interests and concerns, to be able to adjust the knowledge. Once the workshop was over, a new questionnaire was passed, to discover what was learnt and the students' vision of the workshop. These data will be shown quantitatively and qualitatively in the data section, with the aim of showing their vision of the skills acquired, future improvements and learning.

In addition to the quantitative results, qualitative data were analysed. On the one hand, the face-to-face sessions attended by the researchers, which were recorded on video and audio. On the other hand, the photographs were taken during the most relevant moments of the workshop. And, finally, the advances in the INs created by the students. The most important data are the audio interviews recorded with the working groups to follow up on their creative process and to discover the difficulties, problems and challenges they faced when using Artificial Media, as well as Twine and Canva. The data collected is shown in Table 7.1.

Table 7.1 shows the data collected by the research group from three perspectives. Firstly, the audio-visual data collection during the face-to-face sessions (data collection tools). Secondly, the material produced by the researchers as support material in the workshop (videos and PowerPoint). Thirdly, between sessions the students continued to work with the teachers in their respective subjects, all the material generated during the work process was collected (Student Materials). Finally, in group A, 10 games were obtained, corresponding to 20 students, and in group B, 13 games were collected, corresponding to 28 students.

Table 7.1 Data collected across the session during the workshop. Prepared internally

Total session	1st ESO A group	1st ESO B group
Tools for collecting data	Collected by the research group	Collected by the research group
Video recording	6 sessions 50 min	6 sessions 50 min
Group audio interviews	27 audio interviews	26 audio interviews
Photographs	52	48
Researchers' summaries	14	14
Student questionnaires on google forms	24	26
Researchers' materials	Prepared by the research group	Prepared by the research group
Videos	3 interactive fiction + 15 twine video tutorials	3 interactive fiction
PowerPoint	1 project presentation for students	1 project presentation for students
Infographics	2 guides for the creation of prompts	2 guides for the creation of prompts
Students' materials	Google classroom	Google classroom
Character sheets and narration tree	11 PowerPoint/pdf files	13 PowerPoint/pdf files
Scene descriptions and dialogues	11 PowerPoint/pdf files	13 PowerPoint/pdf files
Hand-made scene illustrations	~11 scanned JPEG files	~13 scanned JPEG files
AI-generated scene illustrations	~66 generated JPEG files	~72 generated JPEG files
Narrative games	10 Twine interactive narratives	13 Canva interactive narratives

It is important to highlight the value of the audio recordings of the interviews with the working groups. The interviews were a key source of information to follow the continuous process of the students' work. This monitoring was fundamental to discover how the students were aware that they were carrying out a creative process and how Artificial Media influenced their work process in designing the IN. The data collected has been combined following an interpretative approach, which allows us to examine both the practices and the mental representations present in the conversations.

7.4 Results: Designing Interactive Narratives Mediated by Artificial Media

The results are presented through the reconstruction of the phases of the work process, highlighting the key moments in the creation of the story content and illustrations mediated by Artificial Media.

Figure 7.1 presents the main phases of the work. These phases started with the visit of the NarraTechESO university research group (sessions) and continued with classroom work in each of the subjects (work weeks). There were 6 sessions co-directed by the teaching staff and the research group (Table 7.2). These sessions had a dual function: to evaluate the work done so far and to guide the next steps to be taken in the project. Some of these sessions were key to introducing the tools and the use of Artificial Media. This is the result of the researchers' interpretation and serves to reconstruct the work experience from an educational perspective.

The sessions and their work periods included a number of noteworthy topics related to Artificial Media phases 1, 2 and 3. These covered a range of specific skills, including the requirements for image generation prompts, media literacy in the use of web applications of GAI and the development of critical thinking in the use of AI. All of these were adapted to align with the concerns, needs and age of the students.

The following section provides a more detailed exploration of each phase, with a particular focus on the work sessions involving Artificial Media, given their significance in the overall process. In analysing the data, we will consider the interviews with students conducted in small groups and the classroom dialogues held in larger groups. Additionally, we will draw upon other materials to contextualise the workshop process, including the dialogues held with teachers.

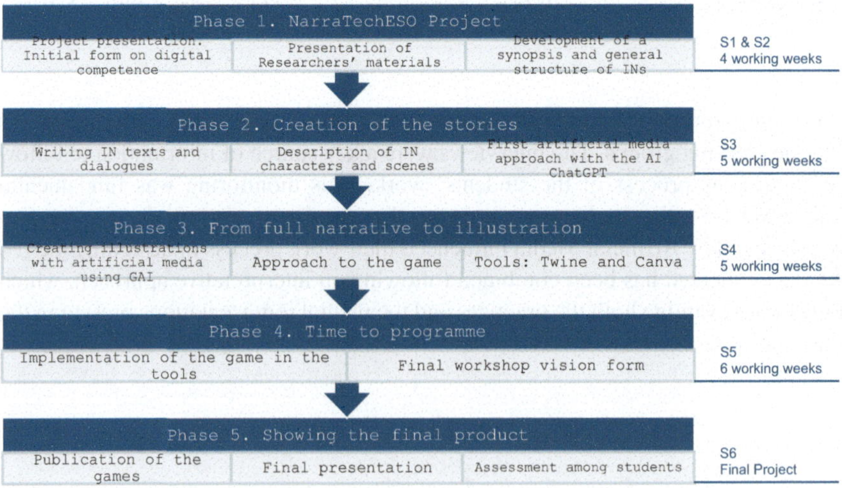

Fig. 7.1 Workshop context: phases and sessions. Prepared internally

Table 7.2 Sessions and working weeks, educational perspective. Prepared internally

Phase	Session	Working hours (h)	Subjects	Time elapsed	Description
1	S1 Tuesday 9 January	8	Geography and history	2 weeks	Presentation of the NarraTechESO project to students Filling in the initial form Delivery of prepared support material (Twine video tutorials and guides, templates for structure, character development, etc.) Practice with IN made with Twine (itch.io)
	S2 Tuesday 23 January	7	Geography and history	2 weeks	Review of the synopses and ideas developed for each IN Reminder of IN branching structure working on templates provided Introduction to artificial media in text and query applications (ChatGPT)
		6	Spanish language and literature		
2	S3 Friday 2 February	24	Spanish language and literature	5 weeks	Review of the complete structures developed for each IN Guidelines for establishing a first- or third-person narrator for the gaming experience Recommendations for texts and dialogues according to gameplay Creation of prompts in ChatGPT for basic queries and data verification Revision of texts and dialogues for each IN

(continued)

Table 7.2 (continued)

Phase	Session	Working hours (h)	Subjects	Time elapsed	Description
3	S4 Wednesday 6 March	11 h	Visual and audiovisual art education	5 weeks	Introduction to artificial media in imaging applications with GAI Ideas for illustration of each IN Use of artificial media applications to create images with GAI for each IN (Playground, Dall-E, Canva) Manual sketching for images needed for each IN
4	S5 Wednesday 17 April	12	Visual and audiovisual art education	6 weeks	Review of images made and chosen for each IN Guidelines for IN customisation (Font, colours, backgrounds, titles, etc.) Programming assistance for the interactivity of each IN in Twine and Canva Filling in the final form Instructions for uploading the complete IN, playability and assessment among pupils on the school website
5	S6 Wednesday 29 May	2	Visual and audiovisual art education	1 week	Collective review of all INs produced General assessment in open discussion of the INs created and the use of Artificial Media

7.4.1 *Phase 1. NarraTechESO Project: Introduction to the Project, Getting Closer to the Artificial Media*

This phase was developed over 2 sessions and 4 working weeks, serving as an introduction and first approach to the creative work for the structure of the stories and the structure of the games. It was mainly carried out during the weeks of work on the subject "Geography and History", as they had to think about the theme of the narratives.

During the presentation of the NarraTechESO project, the first questionnaire was compiled to collect the students' views on digital competence. In addition, they were given the support material prepared by the research group for the development of the IN. At this moment, the topic to follow was presented according to the didactic content they were working on in the subject of "Geography and History", which would be "Prehistory".

7.4.1.1 Presentation of the Project and Working Materials, Tips for Using AI

The first session served as a liaison between the NarraTechESO university project, the teachers and the students who would participate in the workshop. The choice of developing IN games in an educational context is due to three factors: firstly, the playable core of these games is based on the reading of descriptions and dialogues, which can be accompanied by static illustrations, as well as background music, voiceovers or sound effects, which allowed the use of Artificial Media. Secondly, the strong narrative component of these games facilitates their linkage with the subject of Geography and History, by seeking a specific content with "Prehistory". Finally, the technical aspects of these types of games are less complex and easier to learn than in other genres, due to the existence of tools designed to simplify the technical development of these works, such as the Twine and Canva tools.

The research team provided face-to-face support and supervision in these introductory sessions, explaining the materials provided that would be used throughout the project and the key steps in developing the IN (Fig. 7.2).

Throughout this phase, the teachers had the students watch the audiovisual resources created by the research team (videos) and then worked in class with the templates and resolve doubts (PowerPoint, Fig. 7.3). These resources were very important and there was a clear need to improve them for future workshops.

The use of Artificial Media in the process of creating INs was marked by the creation of media content (text, images, audio, video, etc.) created, modified or generated by AI systems. The purpose of Artificial Media in the workshop was to create content that could be used as part of the creative process of the stories.

In this first phase, the students were also introduced to the concept of Artificial Media, text and query applications such as ChatGPT. To help them in the use of these media throughout the project, they were provided with tables (Infographics Figs. 7.4

Fig. 7.2 First working session in the classroom between teachers and the research team of the University of Alcalá. Prepared internally

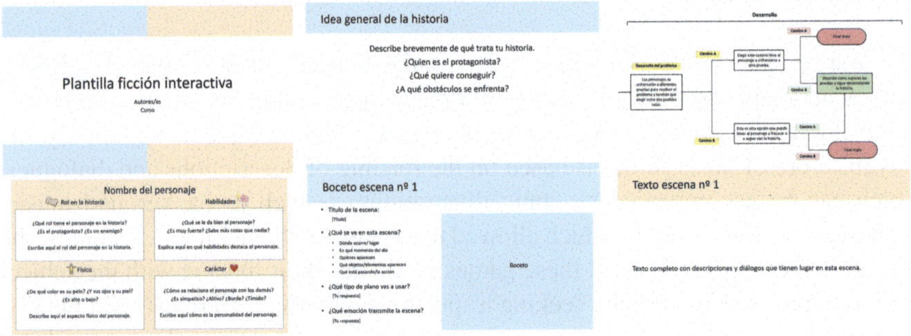

Fig. 7.3 Work template in the creation of INs. Prepared internally

and 7.5) prepared by the research team with advice on how to obtain prompts (textual instructions to be entered into the AI tool), as this is one of the main lessons learned in the use of these tools. Given that they would be carrying out activities with Artificial Media in different contexts, they were provided with two specific tables: "Tips and examples for using ChatGPT" and "Tips and examples for creating images with GAI".

7.4.1.2 First Approach to the Story, Themes of the Game Emerge

Once the students were confronted with the working topic "Prehistory", the first ideas for their narratives emerged. Following a two-week period of work, the students presented the researchers with the plots of the game in the second session. Through

Tips and examples for using ChatGPT	
Be clear and direct. Write down what you want to know or what you want Chat GPT to do in a simple way and without complicated words.	**"What is a dinosaur?"** Instead of "Explain to me the nature of dinosaurs in detail".
Use complete sentences. It is better to write complete sentences so that ChatGPT understands what you mean.	**"Can you tell me a story about a dragon?"** Instead of "Dragon Story."
Be specific. If you want information about something, give more details to make the answer more useful.	**"Tell me a short story about a blue dragon who lives on a mountain".** Onstead of "Tell me a dragon story".
Ask open questions. Questions beginning with "How?", "What?", "Why?" tend to give longer and more complete answers.	**"Why is the sky blue?** Instead of "Is the sky blue?"
Avoid very long questions. Questions that are too long can be difficult to understand. Try splitting or combining them if they are too long.	**"What animals live in the jungle and how do they feed?** Instead of "What animals live in the jungle, how do they feed, how do they sleep, and what are their predators?"

Fig. 7.4 Table with tips for using ChatGPT for text generation. Prepared internally

the pair interviews the first ideas for their stories were collected. Table 7.3 shows each storyline of the game collected by working groups/pairs and the initials of the students (Group_Pair_Students_Initials).

In this session, the researchers took the opportunity to ask questions about the materials and the project approach (Fragment 1), finding out whether they were useful and of interest to them.

Fragment 1. GB_P6_P&D&S dialogue on the creation of stories. Session 23/01/2024

Research: ***Have you seen the videos and*** *what do you think of them?*
Student P: ***They are cool, they inform us well. They give us ideas.***
Research: *Yes, and have you seen whether Twine is going to be easy or difficult for you?*
Student D: *Easy. I think it's easy.*
Student S: *There is work to be done, but it can be done...*
Research: *OK, and* ***is it interesting for you to do a job like this, and*** *do you think it's original?*
Student Q: *Yes, because it* ***involves technology and language. Several subjects.***

They have started to work with the materials, and they are proving positive, especially the PowerPoint, which helps them to define the general idea of the story. In this first approach to the creative process of the stories, the students designed the narratives focusing on the main theme. It is observed that the main plot, the characters, their goals and challenges are the main aspects that the students define when explaining the story. Although they have already thought about the ramifications that

Tips and examples for image creation with GAI	
Be Descriptive. Think about the details you want to see in your image, such as the colours, the atmosphere or what the characters are doing.	**"Draw a boy and his dog playing. The boy is wearing shorts and a T-shirt. The dog is a German shepherd.**
Use Adjectives. Words that describe emotions or qualities, such as "cheerful", "old", "bright", "dirty", help to enhance the creativity of your image.	**"Draw a boy and his dog playing. It is a sunny day. The boy is wearing blue shorts and an old white T-shirt. The dog is a German shepherd.**
Don't forget the environment. If you don't specify where and how you want your characters to be, the AI will choose for you, and you will probably not get the result you expected.	**"Draw a boy and his dog playing in the sand on the beach near the water. It is a sunny day. The boy is wearing blue shorts and an old white T-shirt. The dog is a German Shepherd.**
Mention a Style. If you like the way a famous artist or a particular type of art was painted, you can mention this to influence the style of the image.	**"Drawing in comic style. A boy and his dog playing in the sand on the beach near the water. It is a sunny day. The boy is wearing blue shorts and an old white T-shirt. The dog is a German Shepherd."**
MORE EXAMPLES	
A fairytale scene	"A smiling princess in a long pink dress, in an enchanted forest with shining trees and talking animals, all in a cartoon style."
A mythical animal	"A unicorn with white fur and glitter sparkles, running through a meadow under a sky full of rainbows, drawn as if it were a children's storybook."
A science fiction scene	"Portrait of a female space explorer, brunette with green eyes. She is wearing a futuristic yellow and green suit. In the background is a space station and a very large red planet. In a hyper-realistic style."

Fig. 7.5 Table with tips for using ChatGPT for image generation. Prepared internally

each IN should have, they still struggle to understand the interactive part of the game by developing quizzes, different options and outcomes that lead through the story (Fragment 2).

Fragment 2. GA_P6_P&D&S dialogue on tutorials and the project. Session 23/01/2024

Research: *What do* ***you find difficult about creating history****?*

Student A: *It's a bit like* ***thinking about different endings because you think of many stories, but of course, in the end you don't find a perfect ending.*** *So, you must keep looking.*

Research: *Okay, so the hardest thing for you is that you must look for like many endings (...)* ***But that's also the fun of this story, that there is not just one story, there can be many stories*** *with many different games.*

Table 7.3 First approach to the arguments of the games in pairs. Prepared internally

Group A		Group B	
GA_P1_ A&A	A Neanderthal who supports painting, while a Homo Sapiens rejects it. The aim is to learn to paint and to get humanity to develop	GB_P1_ A&D	The leader of one of the Neanderthal tribes has a vision of Homo Sapiens coming to steal their food. The tribe must prepare themselves with weapons to fight them
GA_P2_ A&J	The journey of a Homo Erectus in search of food leads him to various adventures, including recovering his invaded cave, fighting, and inventing, in order to survive	GB_P2_ A&D	The search for fire, for which he will face different obstacles until he achieves it
GA_P3_ B&U	Cave art. The story will lead the protagonist to decipher codes in search of the materials to paint	GB_P3_ C&A	Two brothers living in a small village where they must survive, decide to embark on an adventure with other friends to find food, new weapons, fight mammoths
GA_P4_ D&QW	War between Neanderthals and Homo Sapiens, where the player must choose sides	GB_P4_ H&A	The main character, who lives in a tribe of Homo Habilis, has run out of food and winter is coming They must choose between going with the whole group or going alone, depending on their choice they will live different adventures
GA_P5_ H&H	Homo Sapiens conquest of the last Neanderthals. The protagonist travels through the tribes fighting or teaching the people	GB_P5_ N&L	The main character, Kimana, wakes up from a dream in a cave and meets other characters, Ahab and Yoko. The three of them have decided to leave the cave, where they will embark on a series of adventures
GA_P6_ M&N	The journey of Homo Erectus from the horn of Africa to Europe. During the course of the game, the player will be required to complete a series of tasks, including locating water, food, and engaging in combat	GB_P6_ P&D&S	The path of Homo Erectus, a story of war and survival
GA_P7_ N&S	Homo Erectus' way to Europe is via two routes, through Egypt or through the Strait of Gibraltar. The Strait of Gibraltar is the bad way and the Egyptian way, although longer, is the good way	GB_P7_ R&G	The program follows the development of a family of Homo sapiens as they learn to make decisions. The characters search for and examine objects, and will discuss their findings, including how they are used and the decisions that were made, such as the use of fire and hunting

(continued)

Table 7.3 (continued)

Group A		Group B	
GA_P8_ S&A	Eukerio, the main character, wants to take over the fire together with two friends called Arlet and Aneo. One night during a thunderstorm they make a fire, but they don't know how to keep it going and it goes out. From then on, they try to make fire again and again with different elements		
GA_P9_ S&P	Rodolfo the protagonist leaves his shelter with a torch in search of food, but in his search, he meets a girl, Rebeca, who decides to accompany him. Suddenly it rains and the torch goes out. The goal is to find fire again		

7.4.2 *Phase 2–Creating the Stories*

In this second phase, session 3, which the researchers attended, the students already had the plots for their stories and began to work on narrative in the subject of Spanish Language and Literature. To this end, it is verified that all the groups have adequately prepared the structures and ramifications of their story. It is considered that in all stories there are different options that lead to different endings or back to the main story again, depending on the choice of the IN player.

In this context, introducing ChatGPT allowed for the improvement of story descriptions using prompts to generate artistic content through AI. This means that instead of creating stories in a traditional way, students, as artists, used prompts to describe what they wanted to create, and AI-generated texts, images, sounds, or combinations of both based on those descriptions. It's a novel way to explore creativity and expand artistic possibilities.

7.4.2.1 Introducing ChatGPT for Story Improvement

Once the outline of each IN is structured, it is mainly checked that the synopsis of the main story of each group is complete (introduction, crux, denouement). Likewise, it is verified that in the proposed story there is a narrative possibility of choice to bifurcate the story, as they must develop complementary narratives that enrich their IN with other small plots that will provide interactivity (Fig. 7.6).

Students are then asked to create alternative situations to their main story in the actions of the protagonists. It is at this point that students begin to use the ChatGPT tool as a creative support and to understand the concept of interactivity in their stories.

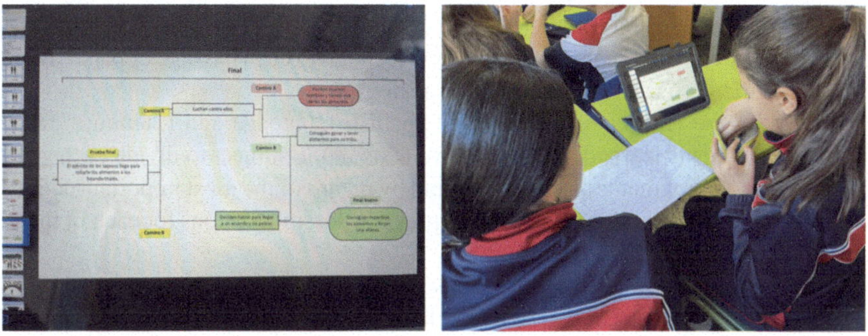

Fig. 7.6 First structures of the game by the students. Prepared internally

Most of the groups made direct queries about actions that prehistoric civilisations performed in their daily lives that inspired their plots. One example was the search for how to make fire in prehistoric times on a rainy day, so that with the answers provided by the AI they could think of actions that, if the main character in their story were to perform, they would not be able to make fire (Fig. 7.7). The prompt used to follow the advice of the tables provided was: "Tell me how a person in prehistoric times could make fire on a rainy day". With the information provided they were able to use the wrong alternatives in the story such as "use wet wood" or "make a fire outside the cave".

Another of the most popular queries in the class made to ChatGPT was about hunting in prehistoric times, to find out about different strategies they could follow. With this type of query, different choices emerged in the stories, such as choosing the right weapon or deciding whether to go alone or with a companion. For one of these cases, the prompt they used was: "What can I use to hunt a mammoth with".

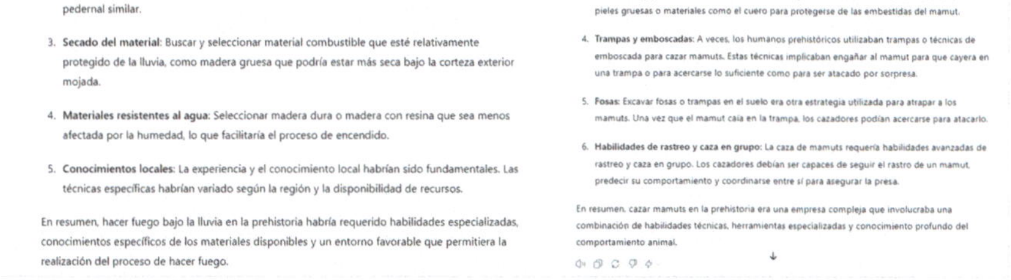

Fig. 7.7 Examples of searches in ChatGPT to enrich stories. Prepared internally

Once they had created the alternative plots in each IN with the help of ChatGPT, they had to structure the scenes that would correspond to each passage or page, which they would then program with Twine or Canva.

Guided by the teacher of the subject "Spanish Language and Literature", they applied the contents learned about narrative texts in the subject to divide each story into manageable fragments and connect them by means of the most important actions of the plot. Based on these actions and the player's possible options for each of them, they generated each scene.

Once they had identified all the scenes and the actions that would take place in each of them, they proceeded to write the texts and dialogues with literary intent.

7.4.3 Phase 3–From Full Narrative to Illustration

This phase was developed over 5 weeks of work, once the work templates with their stories and texts had been defined, it was time to start generating the audiovisual content of the INs. At this point, work began on the subject of "Visual and Audiovisual Plastic Education" and the GAI tools were introduced in the classroom.

Although it was not done formally, the ethical and creative value of these tools emerged during the initial sessions of using GAI. The teacher discussed with the students the importance of viewing these tools as aids that provide examples and ideas, or in this case, facilitate the work process of creating images in developing narratives. The potential of this task lies in the fact that students used both their own images and those generated by GAI for their stories.

7.4.3.1 Introducing Artificial Media with GAI

During this phase, the researchers directly followed the process of working with GAI. In session 4, the teacher of the subject informed the researchers about the first approaches with the GAI tools, the work process, as they had to create 2 images of their own and 4 created with GAI and, finally, in this session, several tests were carried out in a large group with the students. In a collaborative way with the class, a prompt was written by all of them (Fragment 3), which was used to see the difference in handling and creation between the different tools.

Fragment 3. Dialogue with the teacher about the working process and the use of the GAI. Session 4. 06/03/2024

Teacher: *Each pair chooses a passage and illustrates it without using AI. They can do it on paper, or they can do it with a digital tool with sketches or sketchbook, the two applications they have. Then the other four images they have to do with AI. Right now, they have five tools to test (...) Yesterday we were looking at Playground, where they give you a field to put what you want to appear. Like all of them, you can apply a filter and we have*

Fig. 7.8 Example of a search with different GAI Group A tools. Prepared internally

> *unlimited credits, and we can upload as many images as we want. Some people like it more, others like it less. And then today we wanted to see the Blender one that allows you to put two images together, to make remixes (...) Exactly, the Playground one allows you to upload a sketch and it applies a style. But yesterday we were doing a pilot and today we're going to try it all together.*

The more advanced students became the protagonists of this large-group research work. The first example done in a large group (Group A) was using the following prompt: *"Draw a prehistoric man at the door of a cave who is cooking next to a prehistoric woman who is chopping wood. Do it in cartoon style"*.

In this case, we were able to verify that the image style, despite having requested the same one, was interpreted very differently in all of them. In addition, the Playground tool omitted the information provided by the woman (Fig. 7.8).

In group B, the first prompt generated was: "*A group of prehistoric people observing a mammoth. It is daytime and they are in the forest. Realistic style*". As we could verify, the style of the images is more similar than in the previous case. However, for this instruction, in the Canva tool, the generated image seems to have omitted the prehistory, providing an image with modern clothes (Fig. 7.9).

We could also see that, in all the tools, it allowed the option of debugging or modifying the prompt and saving the history of images, so they could make modifications until they found the expected result.

The use of these tools, both external to Twine with GAI programs and those offered by Canva, helped to understand the value of using these tools in creative processes, but above all, in their proper management to achieve the desired outcomes. This means understanding how the prompts mediate between the human and the GAI.

Fig. 7.9 Example of a search with different GAI Group B tools. *Source* Prepared internally

7.4.3.2 Creating Illustrations: Students' Views on Their Experience with the GAI

In the dialogue with the work pairs, we were able to discover the processes of creating the illustrations, as well as the problems or good results they had when applying the advice offered for the GAI. In general, the students were dissatisfied, as the tools did not match their idea, other times they argued that the images that were generated were better than they had expected. Below, we show, as an example (Fragment 4), the conversations held with two pairs in Group A, their results and ideas on a visual level.

Fragment 4. GA_P2_N&M dialogue on the search for GAI. Session 4. 06/03/2024

Research: *And about Artificial Intelligence, have you tried it yet?*

Student N: *Yes, we have tried, but it's getting a bit of a mess (...) We have tried several scenes, but when you put two Homo erectus, or you put two prehistoric people, two prehistoric people, it doesn't come out anything like what we were looking for.*

Research: *Maybe you don't understand Homo erectus, or maybe prehistoric people, or maybe you don't understand that term.*

Student M: *I was trying it out later with the teacher and I did understand it from time to time, about prehistoric men. What happens is that when we write, I want a pile of straw and a pile of wood to appear. And maybe only the pile of straw appeared, the pile of wood didn't appear. And you could see that there were pyramids behind and it didn't say anything.*

Below, we can see an example of a sketch made by this same couple where they were looking for a scene in which the characters were in a wooden boat, and they got their idea right with the GAI (Fig. 7.10).

Another group interviewed highlighted the importance of the use of words or terms to define the search for images (Fragment 5).

Fig. 7.10 Example of sketch and AI-generated image of GA_P2_N&M

Fragment 5. GA_P9_J&A dialogue on the search for GAI. Session 4. 06/03/2024

Research: *You have already worked with AI (...) And the results have been good, did you get it right the first time or are you going to have to work on it?*

Student J: *No, let's see, not the first time. There are some, for example, in this one he put it on at night and I told him it was daytime.*

Research: *And* ***how did you deal with*** *that?* *When it didn't come out, you asked for a few words first and it didn't come out, how did you do that?*

Student J: *Changing the words.*

Student A: *Or* ***changing the word order****, for example, here in this image it happened to us once when we wanted it to be daytime and it turned into night, even though we put daytime, it was still night, so we wrote, put it in sunlight and that's what we came up with.*

Research: *So, it's been relatively easy,* ***and what have you enjoyed most about what you've done so far,*** *creating the textual part, the scenes, the image?*

Student J: ***I think the imagination that we have had to make the scenes****.*

Research: *And the most complicated thing, well, you haven't programmed it yet, next week you're going to start putting it all in there. Have you ever used the program? Do you watch it out of curiosity?*

Student A: *Yeah, I did last year, I was very good at it, I did AI in computer science and all that stuff.*

Looking at the templates developed by the students for the design of the images, they collected the most relevant information to prepare the sketch (Fig. 7.11). These templates also collected the relevant information to generate the AI images, but the result was not always as expected, and they had to redefine the search text.

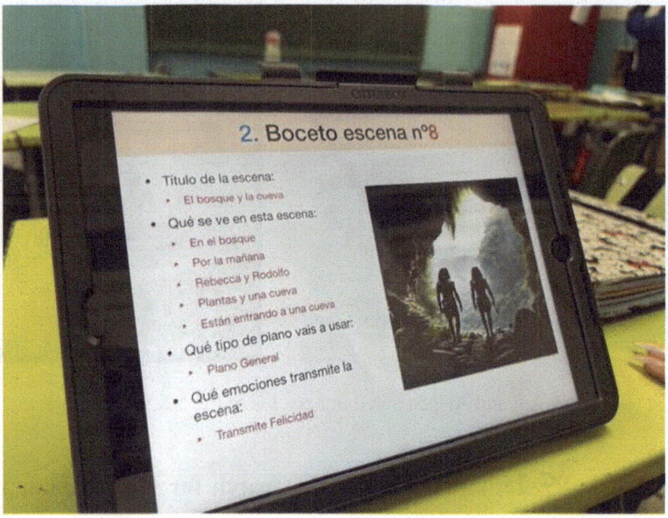

Fig. 7.11 Example of sketch and AI-generated image of GA_P9_J&A

7.4.4 Phase 4. Implementing the Game

Finally, the IN games were created with the Twine tool (Group A) and Canva (Group B).

Twine is one of the most popular tools for the creation of interactive fiction, allowing the programming of IN through various languages or "story formats" with different levels of complexity. It is conceived as a novel divided into scenes. On a technical level, the textual content of the IN is interspersed with very simple code fragments that allow visual elements (colours, images, typographies) to be introduced and interactivity to be added through hyperlinks in the text.

In the example in Fig. 7.12, we can see on the left the complete IN structure configured in Twine in which the passages are linked to each other. On the right we can see the detail of the programming of the selected passage (in blue) and then the result displayed by the player.

On the other hand, Canva is a design and visual communication platform that offers multiple possibilities in content design. The application has a huge selection of templates, fonts and colours. It is possible to create invitations, cards, CVs, presentations, posters, graphics, social media posts, and even interactive games.

In Fig. 7.13 we can see one of the completed INs. In this one, we can see the visual appeal that the tool reveals. This is facilitated by the numerous customisable templates available in Canva and the use of its own GAI which allows a homogeneous configuration in all the pages of the NI.

In short, Twine was an interesting tool when it came to generating game proposals due to the numerous possibilities of interactivity offered through programming, although it meant extra learning for the students. Canva, on the other hand, enhanced

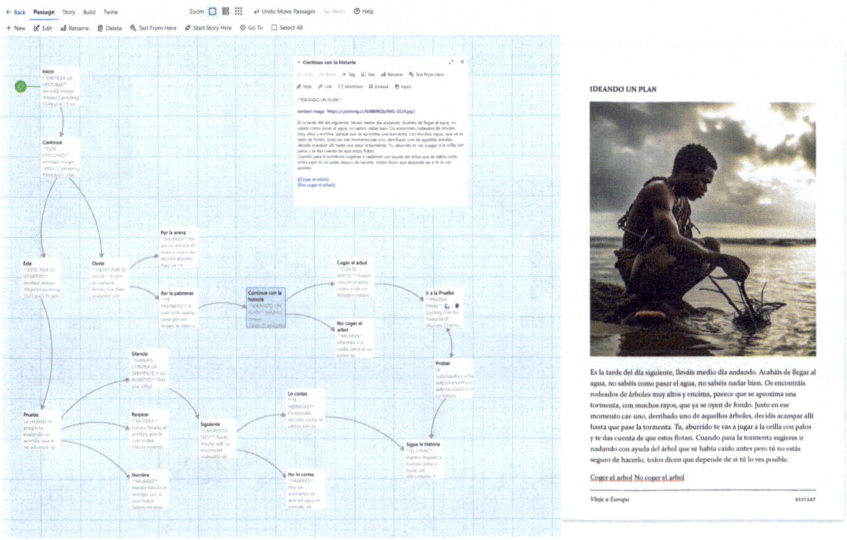

Fig. 7.12 GA_P7_N&S sample passage configuration in Twine

the visual aspect of IN. This was due to the multiple predefined options, the extension of the GAI tool itself and the regular use of the tool by the students.

7.4.5 *Phase 5. The Final Product, the Students' View of the Project*

In the following links you can see the games that were published on padlet.com (Fig. 7.14) according to the class group:

1ST A: https://padlet.com/narratech/jaby-narratech-1-a-4lb7p6g7t2j04ye2

1ST B: https://padlet.com/narratech/jaby-narratech-1-b-yvxrhqm2lyp9l0yn

The goal of this work is to ensure that children, as users of AI, have control over their interactions with it. This includes the ability to make informed decisions and the option to opt out of using the technology if they wish (Cornejo-Plaza and Cippitani 2023).

7.4.5.1 Learning Acquired by Students

The choice to focus on narrative games, combined with specific thematic content such as "Prehistory", was pedagogically beneficial, fostering historical knowledge through interactive learning. But one of the workshop's objectives was to promote essential

Fig. 7.13 Sample of GB_P5_N&L's complete project in Canva

Fig. 7.14 Repository of IN delivered in Padlet. Prepared internally

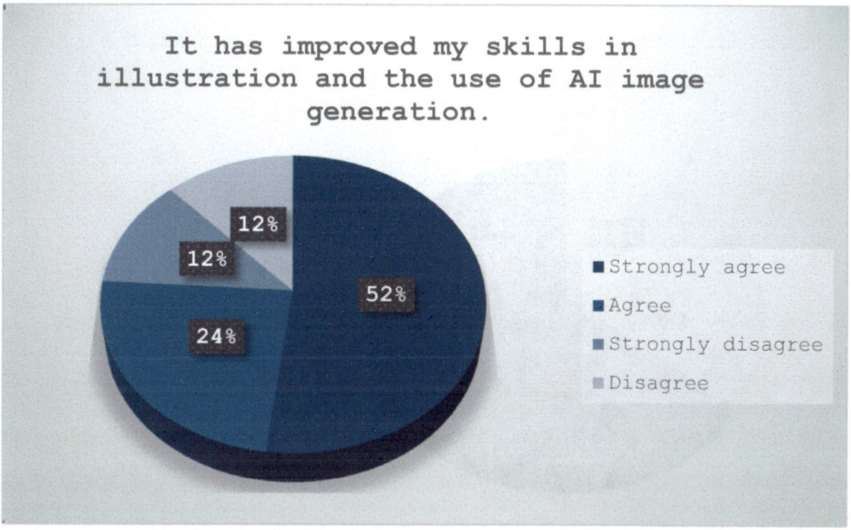

Fig. 7.15 Results of skills improvement after the project. Prepared internally

skills such as critical thinking, media literacy and creative expression, addressing both practical and theoretical aspects of Artificial Media.

For this reason, we wanted to know the students' self-assessment of their learning in Artificial Media throughout the project and to check the effectiveness of the programmed activity, through a questionnaire. In Fig. 7.15, we can observe that 76% of the students surveyed consider that they have substantially improved their skills in using tools for creating images with AI.

They were also asked about their interest in continuing to learn how to use Artificial Media tools, and almost two-thirds of the students showed interest in further training (Fig. 7.16).

The assessment of learning is self-reported, leading to "self-report bias." It would be necessary to analyze the impact on learning from other perspectives, such as assessing the quality of the work produced or using independent tests to measure the transfer of learning.

7.4.5.2 Evaluation of the Workshop by the Students

Just as the students rated their skills, in the final questionnaire we asked them to rate the NarraTechESO project from 0 to 10.

As we can see in Fig. 7.17, there is a notable majority of ratings between 8 and 9, with the average rating of the students being 7.54. This result is very positive in terms of continuing the research along the lines of this work, being able to promote the most positive aspects for the students.

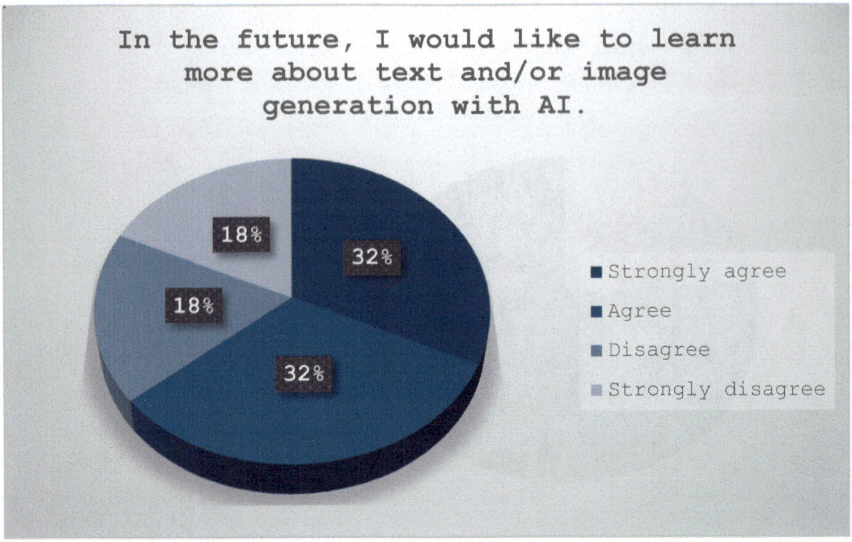

Fig. 7.16 Results of students' interest in future learning. Prepared internally

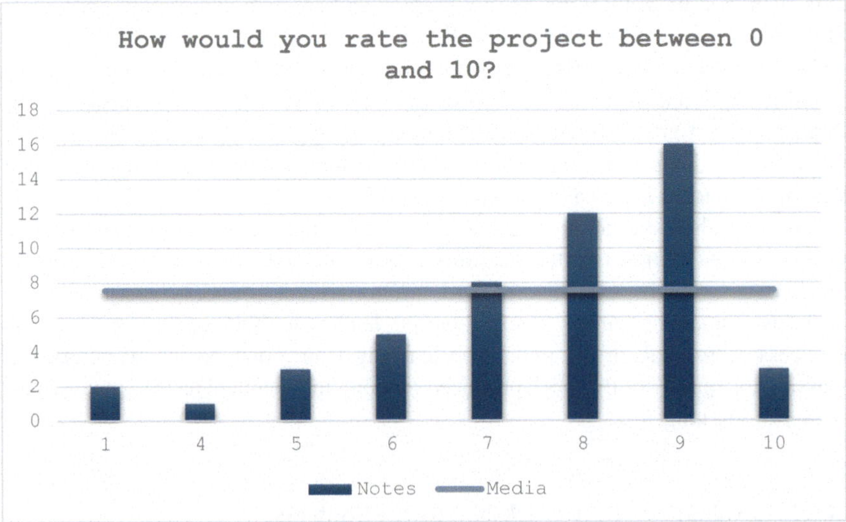

Fig. 7.17 Grades and average awarded to the project by the students. Prepared internally

For this reason, in the final questionnaire, students were optionally allowed to comment on which part of the project they liked the most, with a high number of students indicating the part of the project that involved creating images with AI and the group work. Figure 7.18 below shows some of the students' comments.

What did you like most about the NarraTechESO project?
Doing the project with a friend, learning how to use AI, seeing my final finished project and that it works well
Progressing little by little and seeing how it looks.
Creating images with AI, developing text and learning how to use Canva.
The part of the illustrations for the photos
What I liked most about the NarraTechESO project was creating images with AI because I found it very interesting and entertaining.
I really enjoyed having the university teachers come to school and practicing digital art with the art teacher by making illustrations with AI.
I enjoyed using AI and working with my friends.
What I liked most about the project was creating the images with AI. and working with my partner
AI image creation and text development as I love writing stories.

Fig. 7.18 Sample of student comments. Prepared internally

Overall, the assessment of the project was very favourable for students and researchers. The responses obtained from the questionnaire encouraged reflective analysis of the process from the students' perspective, rather than focusing solely on the results. This approach allows for improvements in future iterations of the workshop.

7.5 Conclusions

The experience presented aims to offer a vision of how to work with Artificial Media through the creation of INs with Secondary Education students, which presents various educational benefits at a creative level, in the development of technical skills, active learning and an innovative educational proposal.

Students could express their creativity through the creation of their own games and narratives. By creating their own games, students engage in a design process from conceptualisation to execution. Through this experience, they learn critical thinking and problem-solving skills that are fundamental to innovation.

The promotion of creativity and innovation through this type of workshop generates benefits that go beyond the educational environment, as learning to think creatively and seek innovative solutions prepares them to face other challenges throughout their lives, forming individuals who are adaptable and open to change, essential qualities in a globalised and constantly evolving environment.

In addition to learning about technology and programming, students develop teamwork, communication and problem-solving skills. Students who master specific technical skills, such as programming, graphic design, or the use of specialised software, are better prepared for educational advancement to higher, even professional levels, and these skills are highly valued.

In addition, the implementation of soft skills often requires a logical, social and analytical approach, fostering learners' ability to identify problems, propose possible individual or collective solutions, follow structured processes or execute effective strategies.

Students are active participants in their learning process, which increases their motivation and engagement. AI allows the projects that students create to be personalised according to the skill level and interests of each student, ensuring an appropriate learning experience.

On a technical level, using ChatGPT to support Twine and Canva is of considerable benefit to secondary school teachers. ChatGPT offers guidance, creative suggestions and technical solutions, making it easy to integrate these tools into the classroom.

In the case of Twine, teachers can design and structure stories in Twine efficiently with the help provided in the programming part. For Canva, it offers design tips and help in using the many features available.

In summary, the use of ChatGPT in combination with Twine and Canva encourages responsible use of Artificial Media tools, drives innovation and enhances the learning experience, making lessons more dynamic and effective.

References

Alateyyat S, Soltan M (2024) Utilizing artificial intelligence in higher education: a systematic review. In: Proceedings of 2024 ASU international conference in emerging technologies for sustainability and intelligent systems, ICETSIS 2024, vol 1, Bahrain, pp 371–374. https://doi.org/10.1109/ICETSIS61505.2024.10459629

Allauca J (2023) Creación de imágenes utilizando midjourney. un caso de estudio. Ciencia Inteligente 1(2):19–34. https://cienciainteligente.com/index.php/CIN/article/view/15/15

Alonso-Rodríguez AM (2024) Hacia un marco ético de la inteligencia artificial en la educación. Teoría De La Educación. Rev Interuniv 36(2):79–98. https://doi.org/10.14201/teri.31821

Alonso UD, Cantos LR (2023) El uso de la inteligencia artificial en el proceso de diseño del habla y el lenguaje de un personaje de videojuegos. Miguel Hernández Commun J 14(2):427–447. https://doi.org/10.21134/mhjournal.v14i.1985

Ateeq A, Alaghbari MA, Alzoraiki M, Milhem M, Hasan Beshr BA (2024) Empowering academic success: integrating AI tools in University teaching for enhanced assignment and thesis guidance. In: ASU International conference in emerging technologies for sustainability and intelligent systems (ICETSIS). pp 297–301. https://doi.org/10.1109/ICETSIS61505.2024.10459686

Bazeley P (2018) Integrating analyses in mixed methods research. SAGE Publications Ltd.

Bergin T (2018) An introduction to data analysis: quantitative, qualitative and mixed methods. SAGE Publications Ltd.

Cadaveira G (2023) La investigación etnográfica: experiencias autobiográficas en una escuela secundaria de la ciudad de Mar del Plata, provincia de Buenos Aires. Saberes Y Prácticas Rev Filos Y Educ 7(2):1–9. https://doi.org/10.48162/rev.36.080

Contreras P, Assael J, Acuña F, Santa Cruz E, Campillay B, Pujadas B (2016) Construyendo saber etnográfico: reflexiones a partir de la experiencia de campo en instituciones escolares. Rev Pensam E Investig Soc 16(3):55–79. https://doi.org/10.5565/rev/athenea.1629

Cornejo-Plaza I, Cippitani R (2023) Consideraciones éticas y jurídicas de la Inteligencia Artificial en Educación Superior: desafíos y perspectivas. Rev Educ Y Derecho (28). https://doi.org/10.1344/REYD2023.28.43935

Cotán A (2020) El método etnográfico como construcción de conocimiento: un análisis descriptivo sobre su uso y conceptualización en ciencias sociales. Márgenes, Rev Educ Univ Málaga 1(1):83–103. https://doi.org/10.24310/mgnmar.v1i1.7241

Creamer EG (2018) An introduction to fully integrated mixed methods research. SAGE Publications Ltd.

Deepika D, Sindhu G, Nikhil K, Sree KNB, Vardhan YH (2023) Generation of smart text book using AI. In: 2023 4th IEEE global conference for advancement in technology (GCAT), pp 1–6. https://doi.org/10.1109/GCAT59970.2023.10353266

Dehouche D, Dehouche K (2023) What's in a text-to-image prompt? The potential of stable diffusion in visual arts education. Heliyon 9(6):e16757. https://doi.org/10.1016/j.heliyon.2023.e16757

Fusch PI, Fusch GE, Ness LR (2017) How to conduct a mini-ethnographic case study: a guide for novice researchers. Qual Rep 22(3):923–941. https://doi.org/10.46743/2160-3715/2017.2580

González M (2023, enero 26) Cómo se aplica la Inteligencia Artificial en los videojuegos—IIC. Instituto de Ingeniería del Conocimiento. https://www.iic.uam.es/noticias/como-aplica-inteligencia-artificial-en-videojuegos/

Green MC, Jenkins KM (2014) Interactive narratives: processes and outcomes in user-directed stories. J Commun 64(3):479–500. https://doi.org/10.1111/jcom.12093

Han A, Cai Z (2023) Design implications of generative AI systems for visual storytelling for young learners. In: Proceedings of the 22nd annual ACM interaction design and children conference, pp 470–474. https://doi.org/10.1145/3585088.3593867

Heredia-Carroza J, Stoica R (2024) Artificial intelligence in higher education. a literature review. J Publ Admin Finance Law 97–115. https://doi.org/10.47743/jopafl-2023-30-09

Incio-Flores FA, Capuñay DL, Estela RO, Valles MA, Vergara SE, y Elera DG (2022) Inteligencia artificial en educación: una revisión de la literatura en revistas científicas internacionales. Rev Investig Apunt Univ 12(1):353–372. https://doi.org/10.17162/au.v12i1

Jiang HH, Brown L, Cheng J, Khan M, Gupta A, Workman D, Hanna A, Flowers J, Gebru T (2023) AI art and its impact on artists. In: Proceedings of the 2023 AAAI/ACM conference on AI, ethics, and society, pp 363–374. https://doi.org/10.1145/3600211.3604681

Kokku R, Sundararajan S, Dey P, Sindhgatta R, Nitta S, Sengupta B (2018) Augmenting classrooms with AI for personalized education. In: 2018 IEEE international conference on acoustics, speech and signal processing (ICASSP), pp 6976–6980. https://doi.org/10.1109/ICASSP.2018.8461812

Magro-Vela S, Sánchez-López P, Navarro-Sierra N (2024) The revolution will be artificial. An analysis of AI-generated audio-visual creation. Tripodos (55):75–98. https://doi.org/10.51698/tripodos.2024.55.05

Marrinan T, Akram P, Gurmessa O, Shishkin A (2024, abril 25) Leveraging AI to generate audio for user-generated content in video games. https://doi.org/10.48550/arXiv.2404.17018

McCormack J, Cruz Gambardella C, Rajcic N, Krol SJ, Llano MT, Yang M (2023) Is writing prompts really making art? In: Johnson C, Rodríguez-Fernández N, Rebelo SM (eds) Artificial intelligence in music, sound, art and design. Springer, Cham, pp 196–211. https://doi.org/10.1007/978-3-031-29956-8_13

Mora Naranjo BM, Aroca Izurieta CE, Tiban Leica LR, Sánchez Morrillo CF, Jiménez Salazar A (2023) Ética y responsabilidad en la implementación de la inteligencia artificial en la educación. Cienc Lat Rev Científica Multidiscip 7(6):2054–2076. https://doi.org/10.37811/cl_rcm.v7i6.8833

Navas Guzman L, Meier C (2024) Experiencia en el aula basada en la (re)creación de imágenes mediante inteligencia artificial. Rev Ecos Acad 10(19):e1076, 1–23. https://doi.org/10.53358/ecosacademia.v10i19.1076

Page MJ, McKenzie JE, Bossuyt PM, Boutron I, Hoffmann TC, Mulrow CD, Shamseer L, Tetzlaff JM, Akl EA, Brennan SE, Chou R, Glanville J, Grimshaw JM, Hróbjartsson A, Lalu MM, Li T, Loder EW, Mayo-Wilson E, McDonald S, Moher D (2021) Declaración PRISMA 2020: 0000000000000na guía actualizada para la publicación de revisiones sistemáticas. Rev Esp Cardiol 74(9):790–799. https://doi.org/10.1016/j.recesp.2021.06.016

Pons SC, Rovira JP (2020) Investigación visible, problemas invisibles: un balance crítico de los aportes de la etnografía educativa en Cataluña (España). In: Bravo R, Granda S, Narváez AM (eds) Prácticas educativas, pedagogía e interculturalidad: V Congreso internacional de etnografía y educación. Modalidad virtual [online]. Abya-Yala, pp 83–94. https://doi.org/10.7476/9789978108253.0006

Qianyi Z, Zhiqiang L (2023) Research on multimodal based learning evaluation method in smart classroom. Learn Motiv 84:101943. https://doi.org/10.1016/j.lmot.2023.101943

Schwandt TA, Gates EF (2018) Case study methodology. In: Denzin NK, Lincoln YS (eds) The SAGE handbook of qualitative research, 5th edn. SAGE, pp 341–358

United Nations Educational, Scientific and Cultural Organization (2019) BEIJING CONSENSUS on artificial intelligence and education. In: Outcome document of the International conference on artificial intelligence and education 'planning education in the AI era: lead the leap'. https://unesdoc.unesco.org/ark:/48223/pf0000368303

Wang S, Iwata J, Okamoto M (2024) Incorporating ChatGPT in english classrooms: a case study. In: 2024 12th international conference on information and education technology (ICIET), pp 203–207. https://doi.org/10.1109/ICIET60671.2024.10542776

Yang D, Zhou Y, Zhang Z, Li TJJ, Lc R (2022) AI as an active writer: interaction strategies with generated text in human-AI collaborative fiction writing. In: Joint Proceedings of the IUI 2022 Workshops: APEx-UI, HAI-GEN, HEALTHI, HUMANIZE, TExSS, SOCIALIZE, pp 56–65. https://ceur-ws.org/Vol-3124/paper6.pdf

Chapter 8
The Use of Artificial Media as a Tool for the Creation of Artistic Images Through Collaborative Methodologies

María Rodríguez Valdés

Abstract This study explores the utilization of Artificial Media as a collaborative tool in the creation of artistic images. By integrating human creativity with advanced media technologies, the research delves into the processes of image generation and manipulation, showcasing how these tools can enhance and accelerate artistic workflows. Through the use of DALL-E 2 and other state-of-the-art media generation programs, along with traditional artistic techniques, the study highlights the synergy between human artists and artificial systems. The findings suggest that while Artificial Media can significantly aid in creative processes, it is the human element that ultimately drives the artistic vision and final outcome. The research concludes that Artificial Media serves as an extension of the artist's toolkit, providing new possibilities for innovation without replacing the inherent creativity of human artists.

Keywords Creative processes · Graphic art · Methodologies · Collaborative

8.1 Introduction

Artificial Media, in the context of visual arts and media studies, refers to advanced technologies that utilise artificial intelligence algorithms and machine learning to generate, manipulate, or reinterpret visual and auditory content. Unlike "artificial intelligence," this term emphasises not only the technical capabilities of these tools but also their interaction with human creative processes. Inspired by historical precedents such as photography and cinema, Artificial Media acts as an extension of creative thought, redefining concepts of authorship, authenticity, and aesthetics in contemporary art. However, their implementation raises ethical and cultural challenges, including algorithmic bias and environmental impact, demanding critical reflection on their role in society.

M. Rodríguez Valdés (✉)
University of Granada, Granada, Spain
e-mail: mvaldes@ugr.es

N. Zagalo and D. Keller (eds.), *Artificial Media*, Springer Series on Cultural Computing,
https://doi.org/10.1007/978-3-031-89037-6_8

These tools have profoundly transformed the creative landscape of contemporary art, introducing new forms of collaboration between humans and computational systems. Their impact extends beyond aesthetic outcomes, reshaping creative processes and opening up discussions about originality, artistic control, and the interaction between creators and digital technologies (Li 2022).

Since the Renaissance, art has continuously evolved with the adoption of contemporary technologies such as the camera obscura or photography (Hockney 2016). Today, the development of artificial intelligence tools like Artificial Media represents another revolutionary leap. These technologies act not only as extensions of human imagination but also, as Chatterjee (2023) notes, expand the possibilities for artists to explore visual realms that are difficult to access using conventional methods. According to Cetinic and She (2022), models that translate data across different modalities into a unified semantic space are powerful tools for artistic exploration, particularly given the historical importance of multimodality in various art forms.

Platforms such as DALL-E 2 (OpenAI 2022) Stable Diffusion, MidJourney, Runway ML, Deep Dream Generator, and Artbreeder exemplify how neural network algorithms can generate images from textual descriptions, blend visual styles, or reinterpret existing works. Tools like DeepArt and Fotor AI enable the stylisation of images through the application of specific artistic techniques, while NVIDIA Canvas uses artificial intelligence to transform simple sketches into realistic landscapes, providing creators with a fast and accessible workflow. Additionally, hybrid technologies like Adobe Firefly integrate AI functionalities directly into traditional design platforms, positioning Artificial Media as a bridge between traditional methods and contemporary innovations.

Beyond their technical applications, these technologies raise fundamental questions about authorship and creativity. Walter Benjamin (1936) argued that technical reproducibility transformed the relationship between artworks and their perception. These reflections impact not only artistic practice but also the ways society values and regulates art in the digital age.

In the realm of computational aesthetics, Chatterjee (2023) highlights that collaboration between humans and computational systems redefines artistic experience. This concept is reflected in methodologies like image-to-image and prompt-to-image, which allow artists to interact with generative AI models to reinterpret images or transform textual descriptions into visual results. The image-to-image methodology starts with a base image and, through parameters defined by the creator, generates multiple variations. Meanwhile, prompt-to-image uses textual descriptions to guide the system in creating images, balancing the model's autonomy with the artist's creative control.

Contemporary artists demonstrate the potential of these techniques. Refik Anadol (2020) employs AI-generated data to create immersive visual experiences, transforming digital content into physical installations that respond to their surroundings. Sougwen Chung combines manual strokes with algorithms, exploring the interaction between human gestures and algorithmic precision. Similarly, Zach

Blas (2023) uses these technologies to examine the political and social implications of digital surveillance. These practices reflect an ongoing dialogue between human intervention and computational capabilities.

Finally, the impact of Artificial Media transcends image generation. Its integration redefines how we conceive the relationship between human imagination and technological media, offering new tools that enhance, rather than replace, artistic creativity. As Yurmn and Reddy (2022) argue, these tools represent an opportunity to explore unprecedented ways of narrating the familiar, expanding the boundaries of contemporary art.

8.2 Human Creative Processes

When we refer to the creative processes of any artist, we are alluding to their way of working from the inception of an idea to its finalization. What we find is an organic process in which each step taken represents a decision-making moment that can alter the course of the image. This journey, sometimes lengthy and sometimes shorter, is synonymous with creativity, as defined by sources like Merriam-Webster (n.d.), which describes it as "the ability to create," and the American Psychological Association, which defines it as "the use of imagination or original ideas to create something." When discussing human creative processes in art, we refer to the series of decisions and transformations that an artist experiences from the emergence of an idea to its final realisation in a piece. This process is inherently organic and, while it follows a logical sequence, is characterised by its flexibility. Each step involves decisions that can significantly alter or modify the outcome. Human creativity is not merely an act of producing something new but a continuous process of reflection, intuition, and evaluation. As Csikszentmihalyi (1996) explains, creativity is a state of flow where decisions seem to emerge naturally as the creator interacts with the medium and tools employed. In this sense, creativity is not just a skill but an active attitude towards the challenges each work presents.

Throughout the creative process, the artist encounters pivotal moments where decisions must be made that affect not only the final form of the work but also the message it conveys. These decisions, encompassing both technical and conceptual aspects, include considerations such as composition, use of colour, texture, proportion, and harmony. From the initial idea, the creator faces questions that multiply as the work progresses: How should the composition be arranged? Which colours and textures will best communicate the intended emotion? How should the relationships between elements within the work be structured to generate the desired visual impact?

This process is not necessarily linear. Often, a piece begins with a vague or general idea that gradually takes shape as the artist works on it. The initial stages can be as fluid as an intuition yet to be fully formed. However, as the work progresses, the artist must make conscious and deliberate choices, which can be both technical and emotional. As the piece takes shape, the initial idea often evolves or even deviates entirely from the original vision, determined by the constant interaction between the creator's intent and the material decisions made during execution. Every stage of the work involves critical evaluation, where the artist adjusts direction to enhance cohesion, balance, and expression.

A fundamental aspect of this process is the artist's ability to revise and modify their work. This flexibility, which in some cases may lead to radical changes during development, reflects the creator's constant critical evaluation. The creative process is, therefore, an act of continuous learning: each decision can open new pathways, prompting the creator to rethink their vision and adapt it to what emerges as the work evolves. The final form of the piece is not merely a finished product but a testament to this dynamic and evolutionary process.

This approach is also reflected in the evolution of the tools and materials an artist uses throughout their practice. While digital media has significantly changed the way artists approach the creative process, traditional tools such as brushes, pencils, or clay remain essential to artistic creation. Using these tools allows the creator to physically interact with the medium, adding a tactile dimension that is often crucial to the materialisation of the work. In working with traditional media, the artist establishes a direct connection with the materiality of the piece, from selecting the type of canvas or preparing the paint to the hands-on interaction with the elements of the work.

In the case of digital media, although the creation process may be faster or less constrained by the physical limitations of materials, the decisions remain inherently human. Tools such as graphic tablets or design software offer greater flexibility, but, as with traditional painting, the final result depends on the choices the artist makes at every stage of the process. The increased speed with which digital media allows for image generation does not mean the process is any less reflective or profound; rather, it provides new forms of interaction that can enrich the creative experience. Digital art, like traditional art, remains a reflection of human experience, not merely the execution of a technique.

A key example of this dynamic process is the work of David Hockney, who has embraced digital tools such as the iPad and drawing applications to expand the possibilities of his artistic practice. Although he does not use artificial intelligence, his transition to digital media demonstrates how technology can redefine traditional creative methods. Hockney has noted that using the iPad enables him to experiment with colour and composition instantly, leveraging the medium's capability to make real-time adjustments without the physical constraints of canvas and traditional pigments. Moreover, his digital works, such as the series of landscapes created during the lockdown, show how these tools allow for new ways of capturing light and space, which are central to his oeuvre. By printing many of his digital creations on large-format canvases, Hockney blurs the line between the digital and the physical, adapting the language of classical art to a contemporary context. This approach underscores that while technological tools transform technique, the creative essence lies in the intervention and vision of the artist.

Similarly, the traditional creation of a painting or sculpture often involves complex decision-making about spatial use, relationships between figures, light and shadow, and emotional communication. For example, a painter might begin with a relatively simple representation and then, as the work progresses, discover the need to adjust certain aspects, such as the colour tones or line types, to better convey the desired atmosphere. This ongoing adjustment reflects how the artist's ideas evolve throughout the work and how the creative process can open up unforeseen possibilities.

Ultimately, what distinguishes human creative processes is the creator's ability to adapt and reflect. Artists make decisions not only based on technique but also on the emotional and conceptual experience that emerges during the work's development. This ability to transform and reinterpret an initial idea shows that art is a continuous process of self-discovery, where the final piece is not just the result of an original idea but the culmination of a series of deliberate choices reflecting the artist's evolving thought process.

8.3 Artificial Media Creative Processes

After analysing the traditional creative process, it is essential to reconsider the role of Artificial Media in the artistic domain. What happens when we forgo human creative processes and proceed directly to a machine-generated outcome? Is it possible to achieve artistic quality comparable to works created by humans? Can we truly find what we seek if artificial intelligence handles the entire creative process? These questions arise when considering the use of AI in artistic creation, a field that redefines the boundaries of what we understand as art.

The primary difference between the traditional process and one mediated by Artificial Media lies in the elimination or reduction of human intervention during the creative phase. In the conventional approach, the artist makes constant, deliberate decisions that guide the evolution of the work. By contrast, in AI-mediated creation, the system can autonomously generate images, relying on algorithms that analyse and process vast volumes of visual data. This capability to produce images without direct human involvement raises the question of whether we can truly call it "art" when the machine, rather than the human, produces the final result. One notable example of this is the development of Creative Adversarial Networks (CAN), proposed by Elgammal et al. (2017), which are designed to generate artworks by learning the characteristics of established artistic styles and purposefully deviating from them. These systems demonstrate how artificial intelligence can move beyond replication and attempt stylistic innovation, challenging the boundaries of machine creativity.

To evaluate these concerns, an experimental approach is necessary to compare the outcomes of human creation with those facilitated by AI. In this context, the challenge is to determine whether, by removing the artist's conscious decision-making process, the final result can still be regarded as a high-quality artistic work and whether it meets the aesthetic standards expected of traditionally created pieces.

A. **Image-to-Image**

The objective of this experimentation with *image-to-image* technology is to map the possibilities it offers within the artistic domain. Starting with the provided image,

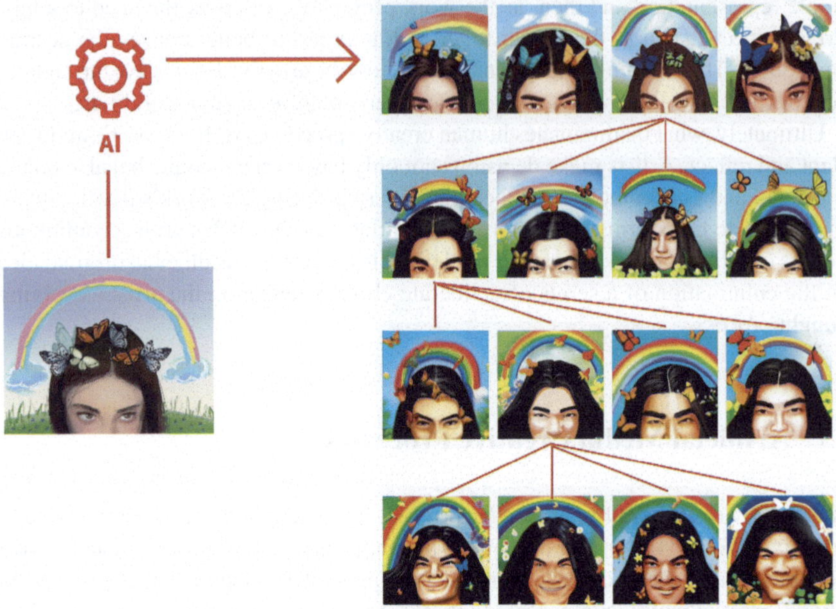

Fig. 8.1 Illustration variations using AI

the system employs its algorithms and the data it has been trained on to generate various alternatives to our illustration. While a critical assessment of the results will be undertaken later, for now, the focus is on gaining an overview of the outputs and the parameters established to achieve them. The following table (Fig. 8.1) outlines the actions we requested the system to perform. Specifically, we defined a framework of four variations, as observations indicate that those generated beyond the fourth tend to diverge significantly from the original, with the first phase likely producing the most promising results.

Additionally, the following parameters were set to select the reference image for subsequent variations: (1) Fidelity to the composition of the original image. (2) Spectrum of light and colour, i.e., chiaroscuro. (3) Artistic quality of the strokes. (4) Harmony. These criteria enable an objective evaluation of the content, allowing the best option to be chosen from each set of four.

Composition: In the first row of variations, it maintains a composition identical to the original, introducing minor variations such as the rainbow in the background but largely preserving the structure. In the second row, it remains similar but some elements have shifted from their original positions and in one of the images it introduces a previously unseen variable: the complete head. In the third row, the central body's composition is maintained but secondary elements take on a life of their own, introducing complete faces in all images and even facial expressions that change. This change may have been inferred from the positioning of shadows in the previous row. Elements that were once placed above the scalp are now spread throughout the image, and even new elements are introduced.

Chiaroscuro, Colour, and Volume: The primary difference observed is the tendency to exaggerate these effects after each variation, favouring images with increased contrast in saturation and light, possibly due to the training data's propensity for creating attention-grabbing images. This poses a challenge when trying to find an equivalent to the original artwork as the lack of mid-tones between the darkest and lightest points often leads to a visually "pop" effect. In the first row, these characteristics are exaggerated compared to the original. As we compare the first row to the fourth, disregarding the original image, the "best" is the first row as it still maintains mid-tones. This is noticeable in the hair colour, which starts brown but gradually turns nearly glossy black. Shadows on the skin also intensify, making the facial expression harsher, deviating from the original particularly since this is a portrait.

Artistic Quality in Strokes: The stroke in every artist's work is not the same; some emphasize lines, others brushwork, and some use a combination of both. This preference does not determine whether the work is artistically interesting or not. The combination of different textures, gradients, hatching, and flat colour masses influences artistic engagement. In this case, a generalized trend of "sfumato" is observed in each row of images. All textures and values tend to disappear, giving way to a smooth, textureless surface. This makes distinctions between objects challenging, particularly in the third row where butterflies have blended into rainbows, making them difficult to recognize independently.

Harmony: Harmony is the balance of each part within a whole. In the original image, harmony resided in its balanced composition and colour palette. Once processed through Artificial Media, harmony shifted, with colours becoming more vibrant and purer, causing a loss of visual calmness. The balance of complementary colours that created a unified aura was disrupted, leading to different interpretations not reflecting the initial intention.

Each of these criteria was applied in each round to select the best image for further variations. Upon closer analysis of the selected images (Fig. 8.2), we find that the closest to the original illustration was the first image, with everything else representing minor variations of the same content. Artificial Media can be a valuable tool for artists to make subtle adjustments to their work or seek alternative options for existing ideas. However, it requires a reasonably developed idea in advance, as the AI is unlikely to introduce significant changes. Even if an image obtained is liked by the artist, it would still require touch-ups or serve as inspiration for separate work.

B. **Prompt-to-Image**

In this section, we will attempt to achieve a similar result using a prompt (textual description). Starting with a general description of the illustration, highlighting the most significant details, we will see whether multiple generations can lead to an outcome compatible with the aesthetics and composition of our original image. To achieve this, we will follow the same methodology as in the image-to-image process (Fig. 8.3), using the following prompt: "Half-face portrait of a girl looking upwards

Fig. 8.2 Illustration variations using AI. Best options

with butterflies in her hair and a rainbow in the background ending in two clouds in broad daylight." We will generate four variants to ensure consistency and analyse the same variables for each: composition, chiaroscuro, stroke, and harmony.

Composition: The composition depends heavily on the given prompt. In the first row, we encounter the most compositional variety, with the AI providing variations based on "half-face portrait." The AI introduces two variations for each possibility and even shows the entire facial profile. The rainbow is visualized in different forms, from complete to partial arches, with the third row showing more uncommon compositions like a complete circle and opposite halves.

Chiaroscuro, Colour, and Volume: Results are similar to image-to-image, with brightness and saturation adjustments. The image chosen in the first row is less contrasted but maintains a natural daylight effect. As we progress, the AI exaggerates

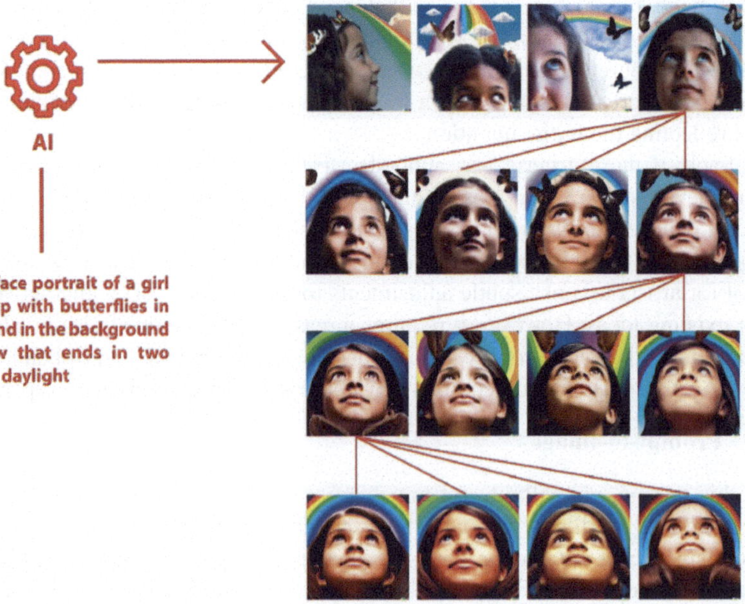

Fig. 8.3 Illustration using prompts

Fig. 8.4 Comparing AI results using the words digital arts

reflections and artificial lighting effects. Colores of the rainbow remain consistent with real rainbows, but the distinction between brightness and darkness gradually eliminates mid-tones, resulting in stark contrasts.

Quality of Artistic Stroke: The first row maintains differentiations between image planes, adding more detail to the foreground. As we progress, texture and detail diminish, resulting in a smooth, textureless surface. The fourth image in the fourth row exemplifies this loss of texture, with hair texture remaining visible while the face and background become soft and diffuse.

Harmony: With each variation, image balance improves. Initially, the AI combines elements without much regard for harmony. By the second row, elements are better balanced, with the head below and butterflies above, avoiding competition. The third row shows an interesting development with a complete circumference of the rainbow, framing the image harmoniously. The fourth row offers the best compositionally in terms of shape and colour, respecting the harmony within the entire image.

Next, we compare the prompt-to-image result with the same prompt including "digital art" (Fig. 8.4). When introducing "digital art," colours and compositional elements are dramatically altered, associated with powerful colours like reds, blues, and greens. The stroke becomes more visible through contrasting colour spots, lacking texture but following the same scheme.

8.4 Analysis

When critically analysing the results obtained, we observe that, initially, artificial intelligence identifies all the elements we provide (in the case of the prompt) or have at its disposal (in the case of the image), and understands them separately. That is, if the AI knows there are butterflies and a rainbow, it will represent them in the most common way possible: butterflies with open wings facing forward, and a rainbow with all its colours in a semi-circle. The same happens when we add "digital art" at the end of the prompt; the AI understands that it should use bright, almost pure colours. This presents challenges, particularly when requesting aspects like a "never-before-seen butterfly" or a "unique butterfly." It will not show us a new species of butterfly, as it is trained on existing images. In contrast, an artist can create a completely new and unprecedented species of butterfly based on their imagination. This limitation highlights one of the major differences between human creation and AI-generated work: the ability to generate something entirely new and unexplored.

To illustrate this with another example, if a designer is given the same prompt as the one provided to the AI, they are likely to not treat all objects separately and analyse them in the clearest and most extended way possible. Instead, they will play with different perspectives, combining elements in a more complex and dynamic manner. This is comparable to the functioning of Egyptian art, where the eyes are always depicted front-facing, the feet in profile, and the hands front-on, unless a specific posture is requested. This representation is not based on direct observation of reality but on a stylised coding of it. Similarly, designers and human artists can alter the arrangement of elements and give them a new interpretation that goes beyond a literal or conventional representation.

The process we have experienced demonstrates how AI-generated images tend to capture our attention immediately, eliminating the natural component that art typically implies. The images created appear increasingly artificial, which distances us from the artistic element where allowances for imperfection are permitted. AI-created works, despite being visually striking, lack the personal imprint that characterises human art. This is what allows us to distinguish images created by AI from those made by human artists.

Interestingly, this phenomenon is also leading AI developers to create a unique style in the way results are presented. Even if they are asked to generate a work in the style of Picasso, a trained eye could identify the influence of the AI in the final outcome. This is the key: a trained eye. It is easy to seduce those unfamiliar with the intricate details of images, but for those who study and understand how an image is constructed, it becomes more difficult to be captivated, as they can quickly identify the artificial component. This is also one of the defining characteristics of artistic creation: authenticity and the personal imprint that cannot be replicated by an algorithm.

The difference between human creation and that generated by AI can also be observed in the work of contemporary artists exploring the potential of digital tools. Artists such as Hito Steyerl (2009) and Rafael Lozano-Hemmer use advanced technologies but always with critical and reflective intervention on the use of technology in art. Steyerl, for example, in her installations and videos, critiques the overabundance of digitally generated images and automation in contemporary art, while Lozano-Hemmer uses digital interaction to create real-time artistic experiences that rely on public participation, adding a crucial human layer to image creation.

Another relevant example would be the work of Mario Klingemann (n.d), a pioneering artist in the use of neural networks and generative algorithms to create art. Klingemann not only uses AI to generate visual images but also focuses on the collaborative process between machine and human creator, exploring how algorithms can expand creative possibilities but also distort the perception of authorship and authenticity. Anna Ridler (2018) is another key figure in this field. She works with data generated by AI and uses this data to create complex visual narratives. In her series Mosaic Virus, Ridler shows how AI algorithms can be used to reimagine and reinterpret information in ways that humans might not, while still maintaining the human creative intervention that often leads to deeply poetic and reflective outcomes Finally, Refik Anadol, known for his stunning generative installations, uses AI to transform vast amounts of data into sensory and visual experiences that explore the relationship between physical and digital space. His work invites us to reflect on the role of AI in art creation while examining the boundaries between the human and the artificial.

By analysing these examples and the observed behaviour of AI tools, it is confirmed that while the machine can generate visually captivating images, it still lacks the ability to generate something completely new or to capture the subtleties that human artists bring through their emotional and aesthetic interpretation of the world.

Next, we present Table 8.1 outlining the advantages, disadvantages, and applications of each process, to offer a clearer comparison between AI-mediated creation and traditional art.

Table 8.1 Methods, pros, cons and uses in summary

Method	Pros	Cons	Uses
Traditional	Active participation in the creative process through decision-making throughout the entire process Leaves our own mark as artists Allows us to implement our personal imagination the joy of creating creativity	We typically spend more time. Constrained by material/spatial resources	Gallery or locations where the artist wants authorship to be recognized Physical object
Image-to-image/ prompt-to-image	Usually less time Reduction of material and spatial resources Allows for infinite variations on an existing image	Constrained by a specific visual finish No artist's imprint Constrained by the machine's inventory Lacks creativity	Resolution of logos or small images that require minimal time and won't have an exemplary use Quick visualization of an abstract idea: mechanical use Can be turned into a physical object through graphic art

In summary, when an artist creates an image without utilizing Artificial Media, they experience greater creative freedom compared to the constraints imposed by the direct use of Artificial Media for image generation. It is essential to avoid the endless quest for the ideal image through AI, as it often cannot precisely replicate the artist's vision. Artificial Media seldom captures an individual's creative vision entirely. For this reason, we propose a methodology that seeks to combine the strengths of both categories and apply this approach in the field of graphic arts.

8.5 Collaborative Engagement Human+Artificial Media/ Using AI as Another Tool

In the previous sections of this chapter, we presented a framework for the regular creative process within the human mind. But what happens when we alter that process and begin with an existing image? In this context, the goal is to discover a formula that combines the strengths of both worlds: what Artificial Media offers, while artists actively engage throughout the entire creative process. The following illustration (Fig. 8.5) summarises the most relevant steps of the formula we have employed.

To apply this formula, it is necessary to begin with at least a vague idea of the content to work with. This is because we will initially use Artificial Media, either through a prompt or an existing image. It is important to note that in this initial phase, we skip the entire creative process and go directly to the result we have termed "1". The image is already constructed, but it should be considered a potentially manipulable image to work on. A perfect image would not be very useful, as there would be little room for modification. Similarly, it is essential to understand that this is a step involving variations and decisions. Although we already have a formed image, we must thoughtfully choose until we find the most suitable option. Once we

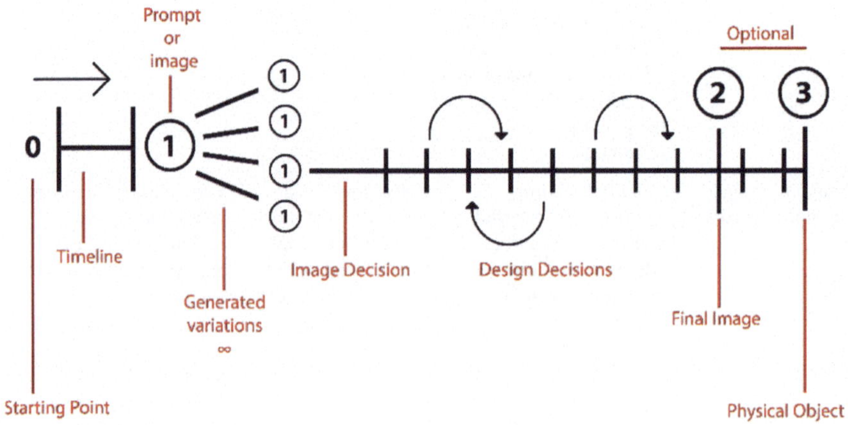

Fig. 8.5 Reversed creative process

have gathered several images of interest, we reach the stage in the diagram called "image decision", where one or more will be selected to begin the regular creative process (now genuinely). It is as though this image becomes another tool in the image construction process. Subsequently, after the decision-making stage called "design decisions", we obtain another product, which we term "2". The level of correspondence between "1" and "2" may vary, but what is certain is that "2" would not have been achievable without "1". If one wishes to continue modifying "2", they could print the image using a graphic process or painting, leading to further modifications and another distinct product termed "3".

It is important to recognise that the process carried out by each individual may differ; therefore, this should be considered one of the existing options. To illustrate this process, we will analyse a practical example. The artist begins with the general idea of "flowers" (Fig. 8.6). Without a fixed idea of the final outcome, they choose prompts aligned with the theme but keep them open to offer a broader range of representations. To achieve this, they use evocative words like "strange", "coming from the sky", "full of insects", ensuring the image is not conventional. The prompts used include: "strange white flower full of insects with no background", "a mix of orchid and tulip full of small dots", "white orchid in daylight that seems to come from the sky", and "many small flowers grouped together while bees pollinate them". The artist proceeds to vary and select images according to their interest, crucially beginning to visualise the final artwork.

After careful selection, these images are modified by the artist, moving from the selection process to design. The modifications include adjustments of saturation, brightness, and colour changes, as well as the introduction of alterations such as

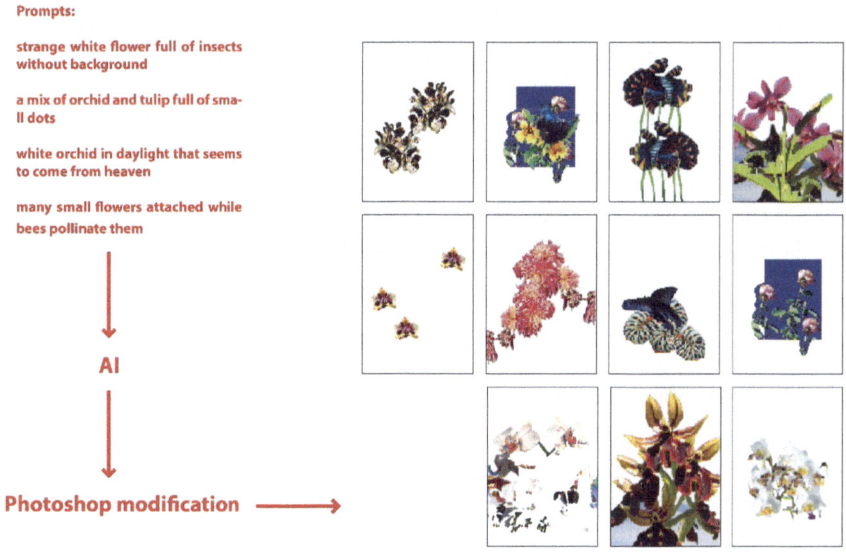

Fig. 8.6 Images resulting from the prompts and their modification in Photoshop

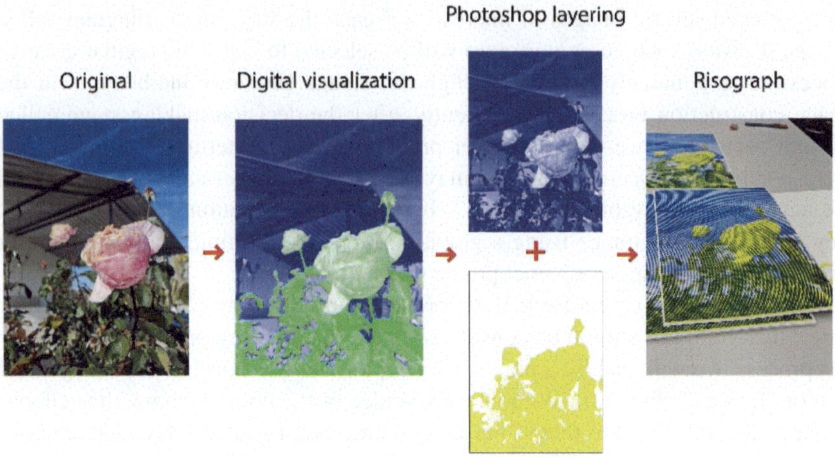

Fig. 8.7 Creative process using Riso

duplications, virtual brushes, image overlays, background removal, and pixelation. The artist selects the eleven best images for the next step.

The images created with AI are PNG files with no background. The artist now searches their gallery for an image to serve as a base. A floral close-up, a medium shot with a metal structure, and a sky background were selected. This choice ensures easy integration of the AI-generated images with the artist's vision. The decision to transform the digital file into a graphic print, using risography on A3-sized paper, divides the image into two parts according to the selected colours (cyan and yellow). The process is carried out using Photoshop, adapting the channels to risography through a halftone dot pattern, which creates a green visual effect (Fig. 8.7). The artist creates a sharp foundation.

The images created with AI were printed using a Roland cutting and printing plotter, producing adhesive vinyls the same size as the risographic print. Although the starting point was an image provided, it was modified and edited according to the artist's needs, resulting in a final product that is far from being solely an AI outcome (Fig. 8.8). The human touch is evident, not the machine's, even though it was used as a tool.

8.6 Conclusions

Throughout this research, we have seen how the combination of Artificial Media software and human creative ability exerts a powerful effect on image construction through multiple creative processes. The results obtained show that by combining these two worlds, we can achieve faster and more effective results. However, for a successful outcome, it is necessary to have prior knowledge and not delegate all

Fig. 8.8 Final results

the work to Artificial Media; the division of labor should be approximately 50–50 depending on the intended use of the final image.

These tools can aid in unlocking creativity, but we must be able to take the images generated and transform them according to our needs. Otherwise, what is intended to be helpful can become a hindrance, resulting in an unbreakable loop of image variations. Artificial Media seldom captures an individual's creative vision entirely. For this reason, we propose a methodology that seeks to combine the strengths of both categories and apply this approach in the field of graphic arts.

Regarding applications beyond the screen, a good method for introducing these images is through graphic processes. In this study, we used risography, but digital prints on rigid media, canvas, or paper can also be suitable options. For artists who use graphic image methodologies, Artificial Media can be a valuable starting point or tool to incorporate at a specific stage.

It is highly likely that as Artificial Media capabilities continue to develop, these methodologies may evolve. What is certain is that they are here to stay, and denying their inclusion in the creative process would be akin to rejecting any form of technology in the world of art. As Zagalo and Branco (2015) point out, we are currently experiencing a creative revolution driven by the integration of intelligent systems into artistic practice. This shift not only affects the tools used by artists but also redefines the very processes and contexts in which creative work emerges.

Acknowledgements Funded by the Spanish Ministry of Universities through an FPU Fellowship (FPU20/01757)

References

Anadol R (2020) Machine Hallucinations. [Installation art]. https://www.refikanadol.com/

Benjamin W (1969) The work of art in the age of mechanical reproduction (trans: Zohn H). In: H. Arendt (ed) Illuminations. Schocken Books, New York, pp 217–251 (Original work published 1936)

Blas Z (2023) Works on digital identity, surveillance, and subjectivity. https://www.zachblas.info/

Cetinic E, She J (2022) Understanding and creating art with AI: review and outlook. ACM Trans Multimed Comput Commun Appl 18(2):1–22. https://doi.org/10.1145/3475799

Chatterjee A (2023) Art in an age of artificial intelligence. Front Psychol 13. https://doi.org/10.3389/fpsyg.2022.1024449

Csikszentmihalyi M (1996) Creativity: flow and the psychology of discovery and invention. Harper Perennial

Elgammal A, Liu B, Elhoseiny M, Mazzone M (2017) CAN: creative adversarial networks, generating "Art" by learning about styles and deviating from style. arXiv:1706.07068. https://arxiv.org/abs/1706.07068

Hockney D (2016) A history of pictures: from the cave to the computer screen. Thames & Hudson

Klingemann M (n.d.) Quasimondo – Mario Klingemann. Retrieved 23 June 2025, from https://www.quasimondo.com/

Li L (2022) The impact of artificial intelligence painting on contemporary art from disco diffusion\u2019s painting creation experiment. Int Conf Front Artif Intell Mach Learn (FAIML). https://doi.org/10.1109/faiml57028.2022.00020

Merriam-Webster (n.d.) Creativity. In: Merriam-webster.com dictionary. https://www.merriam-webster.com/dictionary/creativity. Accessed 30 July 2024

OpenAI (2022) DALL·E 2 https://openai.com/dall-e-2/. Accessed 30 July 2024

Ridler A (2018) Mosaic virus. [Artwork]. https://www.annaridler.com/mosaic-virus

Steyerl H (2009, November) In defense of the poor image. e-flux J (10). Retrieved from http://worker01.e-flux.com/pdf/article_94.pdf

Yurmn P, Reddy AV (2022) Drawing conversations mediated by AI. Creat Cogn. https://doi.org/10.1145/3527927.3531448

Zagalo N, Branco P (2015) The creative revolution that is changing the world. In: Springer eBooks. pp 3–15. https://doi.org/10.1007/978-1-4471-6681-8_1

Chapter 9
Artificial Intelligence and the Influence of AI Filters on Creative Processes in TikTok: Methodological Challenges

Pilar Lacasa, Rut Martínez-Borda, and Mitsuko Matsumoto

Abstract This study analyzes how artificial intelligence (AI) filters in TikTok transform creative practices related to narrative construction and identity building in the context of the platform's participatory culture. The perspective of a mixed methodology with different phases is adopted: First, data scraping, visualization, and qualitative analysis using Nvivo's artificial intelligence for initial coding are implemented through thematic analysis. 1,857 videos tagged with #AIfilter and 5,000 comments on the video with the highest number of them were studied. The results show that using AI in TikTok facilitates creativity by allowing users to reimagine their identities and experiment with aesthetic norms. It also generates critical discussions about authenticity, body image, and algorithmic bias. In particular, comments analyzed using NVivo reveal how users negotiate these technologies around issues of self-expression, emotional impact, and tensions between reality and fiction. The discussion considers how TikTok is a space where collective narratives and active participation are intertwined with algorithmic mediation. By addressing these dynamics, the research provides insight into how the TikTok social network redefines concepts of creativity, identity, and forms of participation.

Keywords Artificial intelligence · Creativity · Algorithms · TikTok · Filters · Identity · Mix methods

P. Lacasa (✉)
International University of La Rioja and University of Alcalá, Alcalá de Henares, Spain
e-mail: p.lacasa@uah.es

R. Martínez-Borda
University of Alcalá, Alcalá de Henares, Spain
e-mail: rut.martinez@uah.es

M. Matsumoto
International University of La Rioja, Logroño, Spain
e-mail: mitsuko.matsumoto@unir.net

N. Zagalo and D. Keller (eds.), *Artificial Media*, Springer Series on Cultural Computing,
https://doi.org/10.1007/978-3-031-89037-6_9

9.1 Introduction

TikTok is a social network designed to promote creativity and entertainment. It is one of the most influential social platforms globally, ranking fifth in terms of downloads, according to Statista (Stacy-Jo-Dixon 2024), following Facebook, YouTube, Instagram, and WhatsApp. Originally launched in China, TikTok's headquarters have since expanded worldwide. Most of its users are between 13 and 19 years old (AppApe 2024). Its format, which primarily consists of short horizontal videos, combined with advanced editing tools and filters, has made it an ideal platform for artistic expression (Barnes 2024), digital identity construction (Dyer and Abidin 2023), and collective participation in cultural dynamics (Lin et al. 2023). Moreover, TikTok's integration of artificial intelligence (AI) into its operations makes it a cutting-edge platform, offering a contemporary laboratory for studying the impact of technology on creative forms of communication (Mazumdar 2022).

Few studies have focused on introducing filters in TikTok (e.g., Herman et al. 2024), and those that do often neglect the creative processes associated with their use. This research situates its subject matter and contributions within that framework. It analyzes how creativity becomes a collective phenomenon, where the interaction between humans and generative technologies redefines participation in social networks. In addition, it encourages reflection on the processes of identity construction and the influence of AI on social dynamics. This study explicitly demonstrates how TikTok combines the technical capabilities of AI with users' creative power.

On the one hand, its algorithms are responsible for selecting and presenting content, creating algorithmic bubbles that shape cultural narratives and discovery processes (Obreja 2024). On the other hand, its creative tools, such as filters that alter physical appearance or generate complex visuals, expand users' ability to become a creator, blurring the traditional boundaries between consumers and producers of content (Maris et al. 2024). Although numerous studies have delved into these two dimensions, few have explored how both affect creative processes when users generate audio-visual productions.

This study aims to:

1. Analyze **TikTok as a communication context mediated by algorithms** and AI. Relevant data regarding the platform's communicative dynamics were extracted using scraping techniques to capture metrics and metadata;
2. Examine **the creativity of TikTok users through the hashtag #AiFilter**, focusing on how it impacts the creation of visual narratives and contributes to the collective construction of content;
3. Explore **the relationship between TikTok user identity** and generative technologies when using the hashtag AIfilter. This analysis considers the videos with higher engagement, such as those with more comments, and examines the content of these comments;

4. Implement an integrative methodological approach that articulates the phases of data extraction, visualization, and qualitative analysis, supported by AI-provided software.

To analyze the presence of AI in TikTok and its impact on creative processes, 1857 videos tagged with the hashtag AIfilter were analyzed. An engagement-based analysis of their metrics was conducted, selecting those videos with the highest user engagement. Additionally, 5,000 comments were examined to understand user reactions.

9.2 Theoretical Framework

9.2.1 TikTok and the Power of Its Algorithms in Communication Situations

Social networks serve as communication platforms where AI is increasingly present, both explicitly and implicitly. Traditionally, AI has been associated with machines imbued with human-like capabilities. Among the numerous definitions of AI, we can select one that represents the views of experts in the field. It was published in the 2024 MIT Technology Review (Heaven 2024).

> Artificial Intelligence is the hottest technology of our time. But what is it? It sounds like a stupid question, but it's one that's never been more urgent. Here's the short answer: AI is a catchall term for a set of technologies that make computers do things that are thought to require Intelligence when done by people. Think of recognizing faces, understanding speech, driving cars, writing sentences, answering questions, creating pictures. But even that definition contains multitudes https://tinyurl.com/4szdrjtv.

It is compared to human intelligence, although it is more concretely defined by the tasks it can perform, some of which are already in use, while others are anticipated as diverse possibilities. Recently, there has been significant discussion regarding generative AI, which Manovich (2023) describes as "artificial neural networks," opening the way for human-AI dialogue. Amazon's AWS provides a precise definition: "Generative artificial Intelligence, also known as generative AI or gen AI for short, is a type of AI that can create new content and ideas, including conversations, stories, images, videos, and music. It can learn human language, programming languages, art, chemistry, biology, or any complex subject matter. It reuses what it knows to solve new problems."[1]

There is no doubt that generative AI is embedded in TikTok, as recognized by the application itself, which selects what its users share. This is evident in how TikTok curates user content regarding the use of AI on social networks.[2] It is also necessary to note that TikTok explicitly uses AI. For example, the TikTok Symphony Assistant application[3] serves as a tool designed to improve users' creative processes. This application is integrated into TikTok Creative Center or Adobe Express, demonstrating its collaborative approach with external companies. From this perspective,

TikTok represents a cultural production that is profoundly participatory, depending on a digital platform powered by algorithms capable of predicting new images. When these interact with users, TikTok transforms into a huge database, generating personalized narratives "through its 'brain-screen' interfaces, which simulate our conscious and unconscious mind and actualize the idea of creativity based on repetition" (Lin et al. 2023).

TikTok activities must be associated with specific communication contexts. Previously, this process was considered asymmetric (Fuller 2023). Asymmetry is evident in the mathematical model proposed by Shannon and Weaver (1949/1964), which makes a clear distinction between the sender and receiver. The objective of this model is to achieve effective communication without distorting the original messages. However, this framework changes in other contexts, such as when AI is involved, because both the sender and receiver assume an active role mediated by interpretation processes. In social networks, including TikTok, messages are created by participants—whether humans or machines, such as bots (CISA 2024). The platform generates rules of participation through algorithms. From this perspective, the communications generated on TikTok and mediated by AI, can be interpreted through the lens of McLuhan's concept (1964) "the medium is the message." The principle suggests that the content in any medium is, in essence, always another medium—an extension of human capability—and influences human affairs, including social relations and actions. In this context, the validity of a message is influenced by the channel through which it is delivered; therefore, in the case of TikTok, it is necessary to consider the presence of algorithms that shape the environments of communication and expression.

However, what does this mean for TikTok's use of AI? Communication on TikTok is mediated by its algorithms, which align with traditions framing this process within the context of AI (Fuller 2023). How should these algorithms be understood? Technically, algorithms are coded instructions that process datasets to solve computational problems (Gillespie 2016). In the case of TikTok, its most well-known algorithm focuses on presenting content through the "For You" function. When users interact with the platform, they are presented with content tailored to their previous activities, shaping their personal TikTok experience within a social environment. However, owing to their technical complexity and opacity, these algorithms are often considered inaccessible to most users. This lack of transparency leads many to imagine them as mysterious entities that organize people's lives on the network.

In any case, algorithms must be considered context-dependent. Their meaning emerges from this context, both for those who have created them and for those who are controlled by them (Wang 2023). For instance, when translating a task into computational data, those constructing the task may be influenced by their training or beliefs, which could introduce biases in how the data are processed. In addition, those who are compelled to use these algorithms by platforms, such as courts on TikTok, project their own understanding of them (Lomborg and Kapsch 2020). That is, what people believe algorithms do and how they can modify and influence their activities are both relevant. In this sense, we can argue that users are agents who can actively engage with algorithms—for example, by retaining certain information, reworking some data, but not others, and selecting specific elements—thus adjusting the system to meet their own needs. This process contributes to the projection of their actions and values (Shaw 2017).

9.2.2 Artificial Intelligence, Filters, and Creative Practices in TikTok

Thus far, we have analyzed how people are immersed in the communicative universe of TikTok, which is mediated by a platform organized and governed by a set of algorithms. Users have discussed and speculated the effects of interacting with the application on their activities. However, they cannot fully explain these effects, which leads them to rely on stereotypes and beliefs. We can now observe how the presence of AI continues to shape this environment, as has been previously mentioned. TikTok is a hub for creativity and entertainment, where users share their creations, often mediated by generative AI, which is concretized using filters. These filters transform physical reality, making modifications to both animate and inanimate objects, as well as to people.[4]

It is worth considering how creativity, in relation to AI, can be understood within this context. Redefining creativity with human–machine interaction in mind has been discussed extensively. In 1990, Margaret Boden, a researcher in cognitive science and AI, published a book that remains highly influential. She defined creativity as follows: "Creativity is the ability to conceive new, surprising, and valuable ideas or artifacts" (Boden 1990, p 2). In her exploration of this idea, Boden emphasizes that creativity relies on everyday skills, such as conceptual thinking, perception, memory, and critical reflection. She further differentiates between psychological and historical creativity. The former involves ideas that are surprising, valuable, and new for the individual who generates them. By contrast, the latter involves ideas that have not been produced throughout history. By relating creativity to history, rather than just the individual, Boden highlights the social dimension of creative intelligence, emphasizing that novelty extends beyond an individual's consciousness and that the created product is perceived as new.

Extending previous ideas, it is important to note that creativity does not operate in a vacuum; it does not depend solely on the ingenuity of individuals but emerges within diverse communities. Atkinson and Barker (2023) discussed the power of AI in reshaping communicative practices associated with creativity. In their view, all AIs, including so-called "generative AI" and those integrated into everyday platforms, have the potential to transform communicative contexts by both generating and reconstructing content. In other words, the creation of cultural representations, such as music or photography, results from the "collaboration" between human beings and tools or machines. From this historical perspective, these technologies extend to others who engage with AI and the algorithms mentioned earlier in social communication environments (Atkinson and Barker 2023).

In this social context, we aim to emphasize that when AI is integrated into social networks, the dialogues generated between users lead to the creation of collective representations, images, or concepts. In particular, we focus on the interactions between individuals who send messages and use AI as a cultural resource (Kang and Lou 2022). In these situations, creation transitions from being an individual activity to becoming a collective process (Manovich and Arielli 2021, 2024). This process is situated within studies on software and media objects, with which billions of people interact daily. Examples of such media include websites, blogs, animated TV show titles, advertisements, designs, illustrations, and photos. These elements are often integral to interactive media experiences such as browsing the Internet, playing video games, and using Instagram and TikTok. Forms of "engagements" include sharing, editing, remixing, and commenting. All these experiences are ultimately social and cultural, but above all, they are dynamic, as they allow information to be elaborated upon and transformed.

TikTok's multimodal content creation can also be described as a communicative context characterized by an overload of information. For instance, people are often inspired by what others have created or what the platform offers, which makes the role of search tools in databases—designed to filter information for creative practices—particularly interesting. Therefore, creators can act as content selectors and modifiers for the AI-generated material. Technology plays a vital role in supporting both creation and practice, and TikTok's blog provides instructions on how to implement these creative practices (Business 2024). In addition to selecting information or resources, the transformation process itself can be stopped at any stage. For instance, let us consider filters that undoubtedly transform creative practices by enabling real-time content modification in innovative ways. Video or image elements are modified to create dynamic, personalized, and unique effects (Media 2024). These filters not only alter the appearance of existing content, but can also generate entirely new elements that were not present in the original image.

9.2.3 Identity and Artificial Intelligence in TikTok

We have demonstrated how the AI-supported creative experience offered by social networks, such as TikTok can be personalized on the platform. These technologies utilize visual, sound, or textual data to generate new elements that enrich the creative experience and contribute to individualizing the creation in a way that fosters a sense of identity for the creator. Dyer and Abidin (2023) emphasized that platforms design the contexts in which identities are formed. For instance, certain conditions are well established, such as TikTok videos having specific durations—either 15 or 60 s for short or long videos. Users must adapt to this technological determinism. As previously mentioned, TikTok's generative intelligence primarily manifests through tools such as filters, visual effects, video editing, and algorithms that transform the appearance, sound, or scenarios of content. These technologies may not only facilitate content creation but also democratize creativity by providing advanced tools to users, regardless of their technical skills or resources, thereby contributing to the shaping of their identities.

Thus, TikTok resources can transform an individual's appearance, create complex video effects, and generate new content from existing materials. These forms of expression are easier to achieve using AI technology. Moreover, on this platform, the "artist" can be anyone, relying on generative AI as a collaborator. Other works have expanded the identity construction process, even relating it to the development of a robot's identity, created through AI. Ashton and Patel (2024) discuss a machine's creative identity experience.[5] If we apply this concept to the human world, multiple identities can coexist within a person—the artistic identity, along with their personal and social selves.

Considering that technology enables the formation of the self through social networks, this can be viewed from a dual perspective. On one hand, "macro" approaches understand identity as a broad cultural category that is both generated by and participates in collective enterprises. On the other hand, "micro" approaches emphasize identity as an individual response to a specific situation. Some scholars have attempted to bridge this dichotomy to better understand the interactions between broad categories and individual variations (Dyer and Abidin 2023). We adopt both perspectives, highlighting the need for integrative rather than exclusive approaches that account for both the collective whole and individual variations, particularly when considering individuals within social and cultural scenarios.

Situating the construction of identity within a social context is not a novel concept. Classic works in sociology and communication (e.g., Goffman 1956; Papacharissi 2011) have explored this subject extensively. The self is influenced by interactions with others, and an individual's perception of themselves by how others perceive them, which is, in turn, based on their own self-perception. Our current focus is on examining how digital tools within social networks, where multimodal or audiovisual discourse is prevalent, offer new perspectives on identity analysis (van Leeuwen 2022). Additional research (Dyer and Abidin 2023) suggests that users approach digital spaces with expectations informed by intertextuality, drawing from both digital and analog texts. In this context, users draw upon past experiences while reframing both the technologies and sociocultural categories that shape the construction of the self.

Let us now examine the aspects that focus on the dimensions differentiating the individual from others and allow them to attribute a sense of individuality to the network constructed through interactions with others. For instance, people exhibit a sense of self and expected behavior, which extends to ways of experiencing, knowing, feeling, seeing, and making sense of the outside world—elements that are linked to anticipated social discourses but also incorporate personal preferences. A relevant example is behaviors related to practices such as "liking" on TikTok, which certainly contribute to the generation of the content presented on the "For You" page. This phenomenon cannot be entirely reduced to social technologies or social structures expressed on social network platforms; there is undoubtedly something personal and controlled by the individual, even though it is influenced by the platform itself (Paßmann and Schubert 2021). However, further research is needed to explore the extent to which users feel that they have control over their online identities and choices. These studies suggest that users seek to control their privacy when faced with multiple voices (Choi et al. 2018; Draper & Turow 2019; Lutz et al. 2020).

9.3 Methodology

Considering that this study aims to understand the creative practices of TikTok users and the representations they construct of AI using labeling filters, including generative AI, a mixed methodology (Tashakkori et al. 2020; Younas et al. 2023)—combining quantitative and qualitative analyses—was used.

The data analyzed in this study consisted of two types: videos posted on TikTok and user comments on one of the most relevant videos, determined by audience responses. This data type includes brands and influencers who are considering marketing strategies. To explore this topic further, several outreach (Bawab 2023) and academic studies (Kang 2022 #10,245; Shawky et al. 2022) provide valuable insights. In essence, users interact on TikTok, with these interactions being, to some extent, controlled by AI. Users create and post videos, while others leave comments or share them. Figure 9.1 summarizes the data collection and analysis processes across three phases, along with the results obtained in each phase.

First, to define communication situations, 1857 videos related to the hashtag *#AIfilter* on the social network TikTok, obtained between November 4, 2022, and November 4, 2023, were considered. Information on the links to all posts and their metrics was also acquired (Karatas 2024).

Second, data visualization strategies were applied to the previously obtained metrics to determine the most prominent videos that revealed different ways of

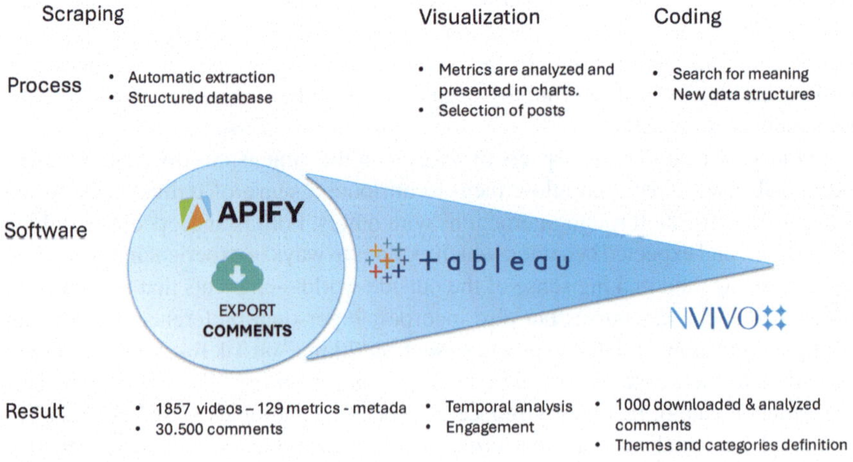

Fig. 9.1 Phases of the data collection and analysis process[6]

applying and understanding AI (Dougherty and Ilyankou 2021). That is, to identify which videos had the greater impact on the audience, the *engagement rate* formula provided by *Socialinsider* was obtained from Cucu (2024) and Udescu (2024).[7] When it was discovered that the videos with the highest engagement were related to a fake account, the number of comments obtained was given priority as a metric for selection.

Third, 5,000 comments related to the video with the highest number of comments (30,500) were analyzed. The video was published on January 1, 2023. With the help of the *Export Comments* online application, 5,000 comments that appeared between January 6, 2023, and April 21, 2024, were downloaded. The criteria by which the application selected the comments for download are unknown and were the subject of our analysis.

9.4 From Data Mining to Meaningful Insights

Moving from extracting data from the network to deriving insights that interpret meaning from the data involves an integrative approach that unfolds over three distinct but interconnected phases supported by AI: data mining, visualization, and qualitative analysis. The mining phase focuses on collecting raw data from TikTok, which is organized through the API provided by Apify, ensuring a structured foundation for calculating metrics that establish relationships between videos based on users' responses. Visualization bridges the gap between numbers and stories by presenting data in intuitive formats that highlight trends and patterns. Finally, qualitative analysis builds upon this foundation by delving deeper into the context and meaning of the data, interpreting its nuances and uncovering possible meanings attributed to the senders of the messages.

9.4.1 Access to Creative Communication Contexts Through Scraping

The data were obtained and analyzed through *Scraping*, which refers to the process of using *Application Programming Interfaces* (APIs) to collect web data on a large scale (Lenchner 2024). In this study, information was obtained from videos appearing on TikTok; however, data can be extracted from any type of web content. *Scraping* is the first step in the analysis, as it involves that initial organization of the data based on its metrics. Despite its long-standing history in the social sciences, there are several challenges associated with scraping that must be considered. For instance, Dahlke et al. (2023) highlighted that the content collection may be systematically biased when the entire dataset cannot be captured retrospectively. Boegershausen et al. (2022) provided an insightful review of the topic, considering data validity, technical feasibility, and legal or ethical risks.

All videos containing the hashtag *#AIfilter* were analyzed. 1857 videos were obtained through scraping with *Apify* (TikTok Scraper).[8] For each video, *Apify* provides 129 columns, including all the hashtags associated with the video. In this study, we focused on the columns that were most relevant to deepening the analysis of videos, based on the study's objectives. The data from TikTok (Udescu 2024; Zonin 2024) were used for this analysis. The study considers various fields, each selected according to its relevance to the main goals. The first category includes traditional metrics such as the number of followers, *comments, likes, views* or *shares.* Second, fields related to the time the video was generated and the timestamp were included. Third, qualitative data related to the music in the videos were also considered. In addition, *Apify* provides access to the links for each video, allowing them to be downloaded either automatically or manually. In summary, the processes of data acquisition and initial analysis are interconnected when handling large amounts of data hosted on the Internet. Thus, communication scenarios related to different metrics were defined. The researcher must select the most relevant ones according to his/her objectives, even if this implies excluding others.

9.4.2 AI Creative Representations from Visualization Strategies

An in-depth analysis of user responses to each video is one approach to understanding AI representations and their relationship with creativity. To achieve this, a second phase of analysis phase was conducted, focusing on data visualization related to the metrics obtained. *Tableau,* a specific software designed for this purpose, was used. Visualization is defined as the visual representation of data created to extend the cognitive processing and support the social application of the analyzed data. Today, it is common to associate this with the identification of different narrative patterns and plot structures, which help uncover meaning (Dougherty and Ilyankou 2021; Jackson and Stanke 2021).

In this study, *Tableau* allowed us to examine two key data dimensions to determine their meaning. First, we analyzed data related to its metrics, such as the date of broadcast for videos related to the hashtag *#AIfilter.* Indeed, the representations, ideas, or concepts that users form about AI can be influenced by external events, such as specific filter launches or the interests of certain companies. Second, user comments on each tagged video allow us to discover which videos received the most engagement from users, offering a way to explore representations, ideas, or concepts regarding how they are understood. Both results helped us to understand TikTok's practices regarding AI-based filters.

9.4.3 The Time Sequence of the Videos Posted with the Hashtag #AIfilter

In this study, the publication dates of videos related to the hashtag *#AIfilter* on TikTok did not show patterns linked to external events that could be easily delimited. Figure 9.2 illustrates the number of videos published each month using the hashtag.

It is notable that there was one month in each quarter in which more videos were published (January, 250; May, 324; September, 224; and November 139). Exploring the dates on which TikTok introduced filters related to generative AI, we identified a reference in an article published on March 13, 2013, in the *MIT Technology Review* (Ryan-Mosleyarchive, 2023) that directly addresses this topic. The following excerpt expresses the author's opinion and is worth reading in detail:

> Last month, TikTok launched new generative AI tools [it is called Bold Glamour] to help users create filters for the platform. However, the company declined to tell us whether *Bold Glamour* uses generative AI.
>
> …
>
> Beauty filters, along with influencer culture and algorithmic amplification, have led to a rapid narrowing of beauty standards in a way that prioritizes whiteness and thinness.

In reading the full article, the author expressed concern that TikTok is not sufficiently transparent about acknowledging the use of this type of intelligence. A detailed analysis of the beauty filters used by TikTok was presented in McQuarrie (March 16, 2023). According to the author, this filter makes significant modifications to the face,

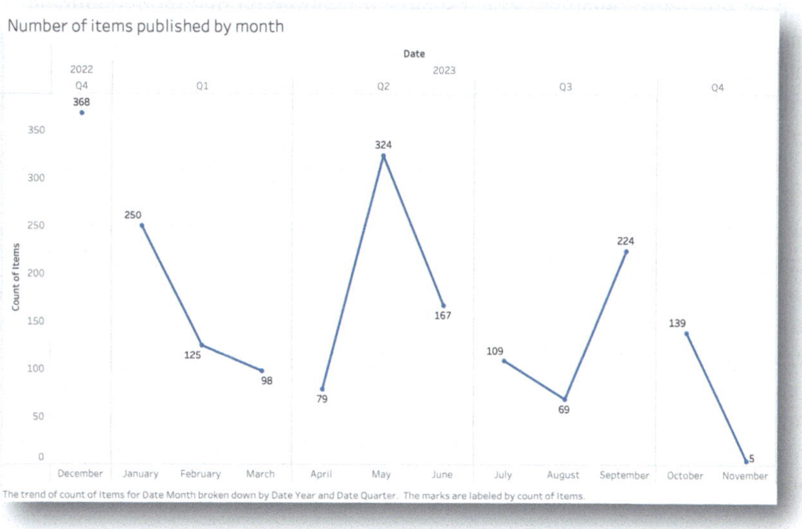

Fig. 9.2 The number of TikTok videos published during 2023 with the hashtag #AIfiler

such as "higher cheekbones, thinner noses, fuller lips, and sculpted eyebrows," all of which contribute to a more attractive appearance on social networks. The author also argues that it contributes to "creating unrealistic canons of beauty and fostering a negative body image."

These data raised more questions than answers, especially when considering them in the context of our previous work (Hernando Velasco et al. 2024; Martínez-Borda et al. 2021). That is, interpreting the role of the video creators that include *hashtags* and determining the optimal timing for launching them is challenging. The most relevant dates of appearance were linked to external events. It would be naïve to assume that there are no cult industries, the TikTok platform itself, or specific influencers with vested interests in generating new audiences committed to their products. Therefore, it is necessary to continue exploring the use of *Tableau* to uncover meaning and engagement in specific videos, leading to a qualitative analysis.

9.4.4 Use of **#AIfilter and** *Comments*

The ten videos with the highest number of comments were selected. All of these correspond to real accounts and use generative AI due to the transformations introduced in the images. In this context, the representations that users build using AI are related to certain transformations of physical reality and may involve various types of creativity.

As shown in Fig. 9.3, item 1,555 had the highest number of comments (30,500). Other data highlight the power of *Tableau* software in determining which videos are worthy of qualitative analysis. For instance, it is observed that more comments do not necessarily imply higher *engagement,* that this video has been tagged with four hashtags, and that its duration is 58 s.

Figure 9.4 provides qualitative data related to the first frame of each of the 10 videos selected for their highest number of comments. It offers the first insight into how filters are used and what representations of AI are constructed by those who use them. Of the 10 images included in the figure related to the first frame, six show aspects related to the body figure, three refer to mechanical transformations of objects, and one depicts an animal.

In summary, the analyses performed using *Tableau* reinforced the importance of contrasting the data obtained through *Scraping* (Boegershausen et al. 2022). Moreover, the fact that comments are more relevant than other metrics suggests that not all practices people engage in when interacting with TikTok involve the same level of engagement. However, these analyses allowed us to select videos that display the representations of the AI that people construct, showing the need for further progress through qualitative analyses.

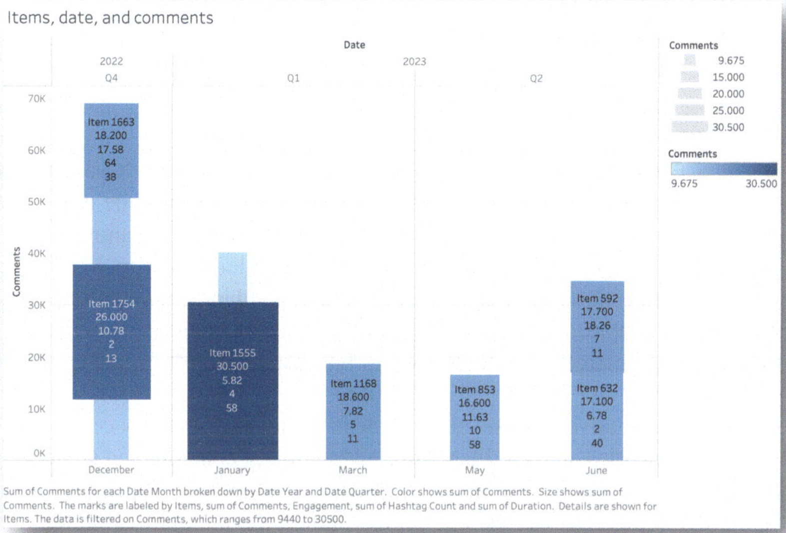

Fig. 9.3 The 10 videos containing the hashtag #AIfilter with the highest number of comments

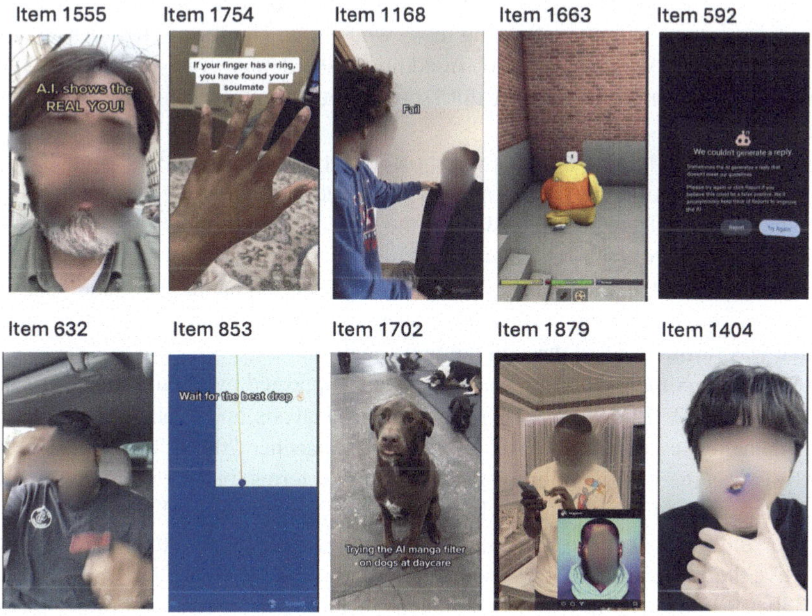

Fig. 9.4 Initial screenshots of the top 10 videos with the most comments

9.4.5 *The Construction of Identity: Qualitative Analysis and Meaning*

The third phase of the analysis was qualitative and conducted using the *NVivo 14* program, the *Windows* version of the software, which uses IA in the coding process. In this study, we drew inspirations from approaches associated with these two techniques. First, content analysis can be defined as "a research technique that allows valid and reproducible inferences to be drawn from texts (or other meaningful materials) and the contexts in which they are used" (Krippendorff 2004, p 18) Second, thematic analysis techniques (Braun and Clarke 2024) combine inductive and deductive approaches to capture and code the intention and meaning of messages. It is assumed that each message is not independent but that relationships and continuity may exist between them (O'Halloran et al. 2018).

In summary, qualitative analysis aims to identify themes that unify coding, transcend isolated categories, and facilitate the construction of coherent and meaningful interpretations of the data (O'Halloran 2023). Determining these themes requires a process of analysis and interpretation by the researcher, which, in our case, was facilitated by the use of AI provided by *NVIVO*. In this study, we adopted this approach to seek a contextualized and holistic analysis of TikTok activities (Lee & Abidin 2023).

It is imperative to focus on videos that received the highest number of comments and analyze them qualitatively. Figure 9.5 presents the transcript along with three relevant screenshots. The first screenshot shows the face of an individual discussing the advantages of AI in transforming those who use it. The second features a young girl who justifies why she uses AI. In addition, she demonstrates how to use it by controlling the camera. Finally, the third screenshot presents the results after applying the filter.

It is important to note that this video received the most comments (30.500). The transcript included in the figure captures the speech of the protagonists, a man and a young woman. This directly addresses the transformation of the face, particularly in relation to the role of plastic surgery.

The *NVIVO 14* application for *Windows* was used to conduct a content analysis of the imported comments. These texts were categorized using automatic coding, which was further refined through thematic analysis.

Automatic comment coding was performed, supported by linguistic analysis and mediated by AI (Lumivero 2024). A thematic analysis approach was adopted to complement the content analysis (Delve & Limpaecher 2023). The result of this analysis was the identification of the frequency of terms, between which semantic relationships could be established (AIContenfy 2023; Green 2023). The analysis categorized 32 nodes into fine-grained sub-nodes, which were manually grouped into five themes according to the semantic criteria listed in Table 9.1.

Table 9.1 presents the results obtained, including the frequency of comments categorized into each of the five themes, their corresponding nodes, and an illustrative example. The most frequent references pertain to personal appearance (268) and face (193), both of which are relevant in defining personal and cultural identity. TikTok

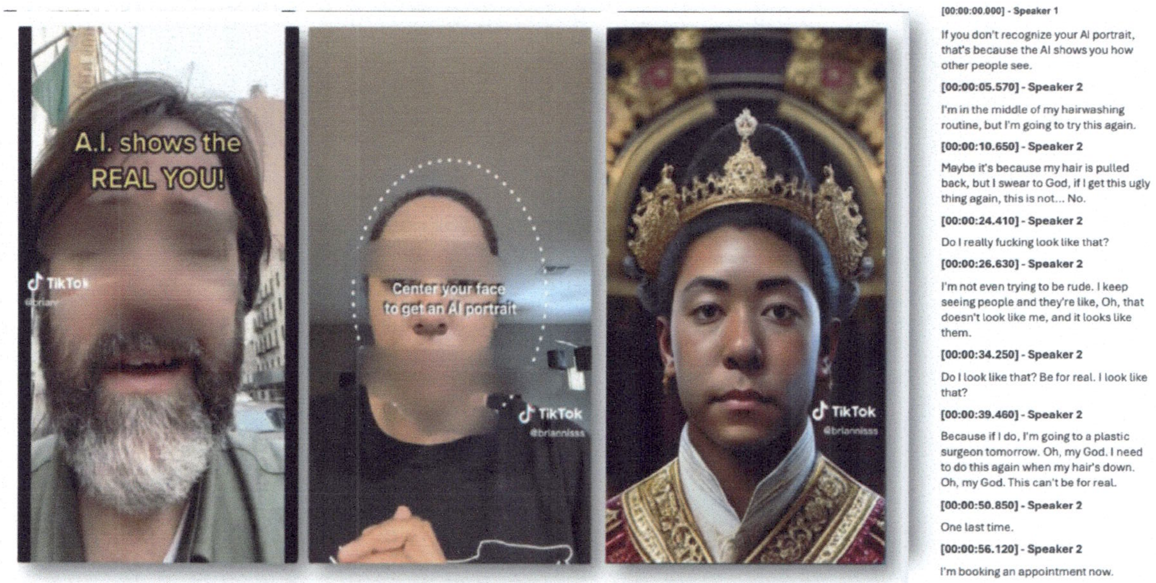

Fig. 9.5 Video with the highest number of comments. Screenshots and transcript. https://www.tiktok.com/@briannisss/video/7185338623242276142

Table 9.1 Themes grouping the automatically coded nodes

Topics	Frequency	Nodes	Example
Appearance and identity	268	Thing; look; version; plastic surgery; pretty; pretty; real; image; shape; plastic; Asian	Girl looking like the most Royal beauty and is talking about plastic surgery
References to the face	193	Face; face shape; eyes; skin; hair; nose; jaw	It morphs your face into a different woman's face
Persons	82	People; woman; man; girl	It is not like a selfie, but if this was your mugshot or a composite sketch, people would 1000% be able to identify you
Colloquial internet	81	Lol (express laughing), tho (express in spite of everything)	She looks pretty, and there is no issue!
Instruments, effects	67	Camera; filter; features	50/50 it looks like me but with different features/ more exaggerated features

filters promote specific beauty and aesthetic standards, while also offering tools for creative self-expression and cultural exchange. These tools allow users to experiment with and reshape their digital appearance in ways that can affirm or reinvent their cultural identity. This dual function highlights the complex relationship between technology and cultural identities in the digital age.

However, the use of expressions typical of youth vocabulary on the internet (81) places the use of filters in a playful context. There are also references to the audience's role (82), which involves terms such as man, woman, or people. Finally, references to the technical aspects of filter use (67) were highlighted.

Although examples have been included in Table 9.1, we can go deeper into the selected topics and discuss some relevant comments in some depth. We will focus on those that refer to appearance and identity, specifically those that allude to plastic surgery. These comments generally reflect the social pressure and expectations around appearance. There is a mixture of positive reassurance in reference 2: *"U beautiful girl u don't need plastic surgery"* and subtle criticism, humorously in reference 5: "*Plastic surgeon updates?*". Overall, these comments highlight how the AI-generated images in TikTok provoke comparisons between idealized beauty and natural identity.

Transcript 1. Appearance and Identity: Plastic Surgery

Reference 1–

No it does not look one bit like you. No need to go to the plastic surgeon

Reference 2–

U beautiful girl u don't need plastic surgery

Reference 3–

You do not need plastic surgery, pay no attn to this portrait!

Reference 4–

Yes Please don't get plastic surgery.

Reference 5–

😅 *plastic surgeon updates?*

Reference 6–

girl looking like the most Royal beauty and is talking about plastic surgery

Reference 7–

i can see that this is you 😊 *But I dont get why you would need a plastic surgeon....*

We will dwell on more specific examples.

- Reference 1: "*No it does not look one bit like you. No need to go to the plastic surgeon.*" This comment suggests a disconnect between the AI-generated image and the person's real identity. The user implicitly criticizes using such filters, equating it to artificial alteration of oneself (surgery).
- Reference 3: "*You do not need plastic surgery, pay no attn to this portrait!!!*"). Here, the commentator acknowledges the power of the AI image but emphasizes it in a reassuring tone. He reflects on how filters provoke insecurities while others intervene to affirm natural beauty.
- Reference 6 "*girl looking like the most Royal beauty and is talking about plastic surgery*" It captures a paradox: While the image is admired for its beauty, the association with plastic surgery undermines its authenticity. It suggests that ideal beauty becomes suspect or unreal.

In sum, these examples highlight how TikTok comments respond to the impact of filters on perceived identity. Users oscillate between admiration, humor, and criticism, exposing tensions around authentic self-presentation versus an idealized version shaped by AI tools.

These reflections would only be completed if they alluded to the content of the video related to the original sound—in this case, the voiceovers of the characters. The video begins with a relatively ambiguous phrase spoken by a male character: "If you don't recognize your portrait, it's because the AI is showing you how others see it." He reinforces the canon of beauty. The young woman responds with a monologue, always speaking in the first person. She expresses dissatisfaction with her appearance, stating that she does not like her hair. However, she does not seem to agree with the image offered by the filter. She says, "Because if it's like that, tomorrow I'm going to the plastic surgeon. Oh my God. I have to do this again when I have my hair down. Oh my God. This can't be real." This text clearly demonstrates how AI contributes to the generation of personal identity, a topic that will need to be explored in future studies.

9.5 Conclusions

This study demonstrates how generative AI is embedded in TikTok's social network and how its participants use it when applying the hashtag *#AIfilter* to their posts. We examine creative practices employed in specific communication situations. Consequently, we present these conclusions in relation to the proposed objectives and highlight the methodological challenges that the research faces in achieving them.

The first objective is to examine the digital landscape of creative communication. To achieve this goal, data extraction techniques (*Scraping),* were applied to the TikTok social network, providing various metrics for defining these contexts. It has been observed that the hashtag *#AIfilter* generates distinct communicative scenarios, each characterized by different metrics, implying variations in user engagement and participation. TikTok is a dynamic communication environment, mediated by AI, where the algorithms that shape the "for you" page profoundly impact the user experience and forms of social interaction. *Scraping* techniques allow for the capture of key patterns in how users interact with the content presented to them. Algorithms serve as active mediators, shaping the dynamics of visibility, participation, and consumption of platforms. In this sense, TikTok is not merely a communication channel, but an environment where algorithms are key actors, shaping contemporary cultural practices.

The second objective was to define TikTok participants' representations of AI. Methodological analysis techniques related to data visualization enabled the achievement of this goal using *Tableau.* Visualization techniques help overcome limitations associated with the validity of data scraping. The filters grouped under the hashtag *#AIfilter* are a fundamental tool to democratize creativity on TikTok, allowing users to experiment with new formats of artistic expression that involve various modifications of immediate reality. These activities are associated with representations, images, or concepts that users attribute to AI, and in many cases, are related to the human body. By offering advanced resources previously limited to professionals, TikTok makes creativity an accessible practice by redefining the concept of authorship in the digital realm.

Finally, the third objective was to demonstrate how AI can shape personal and cultural identities. Qualitative analyses were conducted using NVIVO software. A deeper analysis of comments on specific videos reveals how generative AI can contribute to shaping personal and cultural identities. For instance, beauty standards are linked to stereotypes that provoke multiple reactions on TikTok. The hashtag #Aifilter shows that users can experiment with alternative versions of themselves by modifying their appearance, adopting fictitious roles, or projecting aspirational ideals. This phenomenon underscores that identity on TikTok is not fixed but can be continually reinvented, demonstrating how digital technologies have expanded the possibilities of self-expression and representation.

The integrated methodological approach used in this study, which links the extraction, visualization, and qualitative analysis phases, has proven to be particularly useful in understanding the complexity of TikTok. Through scraping, the extraction phase provides access to vast and structured datasets regarding interactions on the platform. Simultaneously, visualization facilitates the identification of relevant patterns that are challenging to detect using other methods. Finally, the qualitative analysis added depth to the process by interpreting the cultural and social meanings behind the quantitative data. This approach was not only practical but also efficient for this analysis, offering a methodological model that can be applied to future studies on other digital platforms, where combining data and context is the key to understanding complex phenomena.

This study has certain limitations that continue to pose theoretical and methodological challenges. First, the fact that data are confined to well-defined periods overlooks their inherent dynamism. In a world as rapidly evolving as TikTok, it will be essential to consider how this dynamicity can be incorporated into future studies. Second, it is necessary to examine the role of hashtags and specific profiles in exploring practices related to the use of generative AI. Finally, to delve deeper into how AI contributes to the formation of personal and social identities, specific qualitative analyses inspired by alternative perspectives, such as multimodal discourse analysis, will be required. Therefore, while this study has opened many avenues for future research, questions remain more critical than answers.

Acknowledgements The research that has given rise to this work is funded by the International University of La Rioja, from the project "Artificial Intelligence from TikTok: Fostering critical engagement among young people", Call of the Program of Strategic Investments for the Development of Research and Transfer Capacities (Incentive Program, 2024).

Notes

1. What is Gen AI? Amazon AWS https://tinyurl.com/yck75xf3
2. https://www.tiktok.com/tag/ai?lang=een videos labeled with AI and why it is necessary to label them as such https://tinyurl.com/55wkeuyf or how to obtain AI related filters https://www.flexclip.com/learn/use-ai-filter-on-tiktok.html
3. https://tinyurl.com/59x9mexs August 2024 https://tinyurl.com/59x9mexs. Let us elevate your whole creative game https://tinyurl.com/2rhbn8ty can also be consulted to check its functionalities, such as generate content, optimizing it, editing it, generating scripts, or discovering the latest TikTok trends. It even analyzes how posts launched on TikTok are received https://tinyurl.com/3nfbr2pd.
4. The pages generated by TikTok allow user to explore the possibilities of these type of filters through its results: https://www.tiktok.com/discover/generative-ai-filter. Other companies collect and explain the different types of filters that can be used to achieve what appears in the videos generated on TikTok; for example, *FlexClip,* which is dedicated to creating videos using AI. or https://www.flexclip.com/learn/use-ai-filter-on-tiktok.html or *Vidnoz* Free AI Video Generator https://www.vidnoz.com/ai-solutions/ai-tiktok-filter.html

5. "Ai-Da's artistic processes help establish a sense of 'being an artist' and signal aesthetic expertise by sharing aspects of artistic development and work in progress " https://bit.ly/4f81NfO
6. The charts, images, and tables presented in this paper were created by the authors using the data analyzed in this study. Images sourced from TikTok have been modified and blurred to ensure privacy and compliance with ethical standards.
7. The formula used was the following ((SUM([Likes]) + SUM([Comments]) + SUM([Share])/ SUM([Views]) * 100.
8. The characteristics and operation of the API used by Apify to obtain data are presented at TikTok: https://apify.com/clockworks/tiktok-scraperare. In this study, information related to the following metrics and metadata FullName, UserName, Followers, Comments, Share, Likes, Views, Duration, Date, Time 24H, MusicDuration, MusicAuthor, webVideoUrl, Hashtag, OriginalMusic, MusicTitle was considered. It should also be noted that, in its paid version, the 4 K Tokkit application allows the download of videos of a specific hashtag: https://bit.ly/49qxgZA

References

AIContenfy (2023) The role of AI in content analysis. AIContenfy, https://aicontentfy.com/en/blog/role-of-ai-in-content-analysis

App-Ape (2024) TikTok statistics-updated May 2024. Wallaroo. https://bit.ly/4gjBxQQ

Ashton D, Patel K (2024) People don't buy art, they buy artists': robot artists-work, identity, and expertise. Convergence 30(2):790–806. https://doi.org/10.1177/13548565231220310

Atkinson DP, Barker DR (2023) AI and the social construction of creativity. Convergence 29(4):1054–1069. https://doi.org/10.1177/13548565231187730

Barnes D (2024) Indigenous knowledge and creativities online: TikTok as a relational tool within the Indigenous art process. AlterNative: Int J Indig Peoples 20(2):322–331. https://doi.org/10.1177/11771801241246731

Bawab B (2023) Leveraging social media analytics for better engagement in 2024. Linkedin. https://bit.ly/3tRSNtL.

Boden MA (1990) The creative mind: myths & mechanisms. BasicBooks

Boegershausen J, Datta H, Borah A, Stephen AT (2022) Fields of gold: scraping web data for marketing insights. J Mark 86(5):1–20. https://doi.org/10.1177/00222429221100750

Braun V, Clarke V (2024) Thematic analysis, 6th edn. In: Denzin NK, Lincoln YS, Giardina MD, Cannella GSU (eds) The SAGE handbook of qualitative research. SAGE, pp 901–940

Business TF (2024) Creative codes: 6 principles for creating on TikTok. Blog. https://tinyurl.com/n55c6934

Choi H, Park J, Jung Y (2018) The role of privacy fatigue in online privacy behavior. Comput Hum Behav 81:42–51. https://doi.org/10.1016/j.chb.2017.12.001

CISA (2024) Social media bots. America's Cyber Defense Agency. https://www.cisa.gov/sites/default/files/publications/social_media_bots_infographic_set_508.pdf

Cucu E (2024) TikTok metrics you should be tracking in 2024. Socialinsider Blog. https://www.socialinsider.io/blog/tiktok-metrics/

Dahlke R, Kumar D, Durumeric Z, Hancock JT (2023) Quantifying the systematic bias in the accessibility and inaccessibility of web scraping content from URL-logged web-browsing digital trace data. Soc Sci Comput Rev. https://doi.org/10.1177/08944393231218214

Delve HL, Limpaecher A (2023) Content analysis versus thematic analysis: what's the difference? *Delve,* https://delvetool.com/blog/content-analysis-vs-thematic-analysis

Dougherty J, Ilyankou I (2021) Hands-on data visualization: interactive storytelling from spreadsheets to code. O'Reilly Media, Inc.

Draper NA, Turow J (2019) The corporate cultivation of digital resignation. New Media Soc 21(8):1824–1839. https://doi.org/10.1177/1461444819833331

Dyer HT, Abidin C (2023) Understanding identity and platform cultures. In: Housley W (ed) The SAGE handbook of digital society. SAGE Publications Ltd, pp 170–187. https://doi.org/10.4135/9781529783193
Fuller S (2023) Mediating the message in digital society. In: Housley W (ed) The SAGE handbook of digital society. SAGE Publications Ltd, pp 610–634. https://doi.org/10.4135/9781529783193
Gillespie T (2016) Algorithm. In: Benjamin P (ed) Digital keywords. Princeton University Press, pp 18–30. https://doi.org/10.1515/9781400880553-004
Goffman E (1956) The presentation of self in everyday life. University of Edinburgh, Social Sciences Research Centre
Green A (2023) MIT report on generative AI. MIT Technology Review Insights. https://bit.ly/3WBQ4kk
Heaven WD (2024) Will douglas heaven artificial intelligence. Why is AI? MIT Technology Review. https://tinyurl.com/4szdrjtv
Herman AA, Brammer SE, Punyanunt-Carter NM (2024) Face off: exploring college students' perceptions regarding face filters on TikTok. Media Watch. https://doi.org/10.1177/09760911241291950
Hernando Velasco A, Matsumoto M, Dominguez-Santos S, Lacasa P (2024) Digitalization of cultural industries: evidence from the official Spider-Man movie TikTok account. Convergence. https://doi.org/10.1177/13548565241253904
Jackson A, Stanke L (2021) Tableau strategies: solving real, practical problems with data analytics. O'Reilly Media
Kang H, Lou C (2022) AI agency versus human agency: understanding human-AI interactions on TikTok and their implications for user engagement. J Comput-Mediat Commun 27(5). https://doi.org/10.1093/jcmc/zmac014
Karatas G (2024) TikTok scraper: how to scrape data from TikTok in 2024. AIMultiple. https://bit.ly/49cfnwu
Krippendorff K (2004) Content analysis: an introduction to its methodology, 2nd edn. Sage
Lee J, Abidin C (2023) Introduction to the special issue of "TikTok and social movements." Soc Media+Soc 9(1). https://doi.org/10.1177/20563051231157452
Lenchner O (2024) ScrapeCon 2024-the state of public web data. Bright Data. https://www.youtube.com/playlist?list=PLFgLa9oxPE0fPLJtTD1G-G9ZSEf_MS2eh
Lin J, Swart J, Zeng G (2023) Theorising TikTok cultures: neuro-images in the era of short videos. Media Cult Soc 45(8):1550–1567. https://doi.org/10.1177/01634437231202167
Lomborg S, Kapsch PH (2020) Decoding algorithms. Media Cult Soc 42(5):745–761. https://doi.org/10.1177/0163443719855301
Lumivero (2024) NVivo automated coding with AI. Videos. Lumivero. https://bit.ly/4b9UMu2
Lutz C, Hoffmann CP, Ranzini G (2020) Data capitalism and the user: an exploration of privacy cynicism in Germany. New Media Soc 22(7):1168–1187. https://doi.org/10.1177/1461444820912544
Manovich L, Arielli E (eds) (2021–2024) Artificial aesthetics: generative AI, art, and visual media. Manovich.art. http://manovich.net/index.php/projects/artificial-aesthetics-book
Manovich L (2023) The AI brain in the cultural archive. Medium. https://bit.ly/3OcpARv
Maris E, Caplan R, Thach H (2024) Taking back and giving back on TikTok: algorithmic mutual aid in the platform economy. New Media Soc. 14614448241238396. https://doi.org/10.1177/14614448241238396
Martínez-Borda R, de-la-Fuente J, Lacasa P (2021) Digital storytelling in times of pandemic: TV series, social media and internet conversations. Front Psychol 16(12):677713. https://doi.org/10.3389/fpsyg.2021.677713
Mazumdar S (2022) Loving the enemy app: resistance versus professionalism in 'post-TikTok' India. Glob Media China 7(3):340–356. https://doi.org/10.1177/20594364221116018
McLuhan M (1964) Understanding media; the extensions of man, 1st edn. McGraw-Hill
Media T (2024) Viral content creation on TikTok: what works and what doesn't. Medium. https://tinyurl.com/4yx9fewc

O'Halloran KL (2023) Matter, meaning and semiotics. Vis Commun 22(1):174–201. https://doi.org/10.1177/14703572221128881
O'Halloran KL, Tan S, Pham D-S, Bateman J, Vande Moere A (2018) A digital mixed methods research design: Integrating multimodal analysis with data mining and information visualization for big data analytics. J Mixed Methods Res 12(1):11–30. https://doi.org/10.1177/1558689816651015
Obreja DM (2024) When stories turn institutional: how TikTok users legitimize the algorithmic sensemaking. Soc Media+Soc 10(1):20563051231224110. https://doi.org/10.1177/20563051231224114
Papacharissi Z (2011) A networked self: identity, community, and culture on social network sites. Routledge
Paßmann J, Schubert C (2021) Liking as taste making: Social media practices as generators of aesthetic valuation and distinction. New Media Soc 23(10):2947–2963. https://doi.org/10.1177/1461444820939458
Ryan-Mosleyarchive T (2023) Hyper-realistic beauty filters are here to stay. MIT Technol Rev. https://bit.ly/4bxCnXG
Shannon CE, Weaver W (1949/1964). The mathematical theory of communication. University of Illinois Press
Shaw A (2017) Encoding and decoding affordances: stuart Hall and interactive media technologies. Media Cult Soc 39(4):592–602. https://doi.org/10.1177/0163443717692741
Shawky S, Kubacki K, Dietrich T, Weaven S (2022) The multi-actor perspective of engagement on social media. Int J Mark Res 64(1):19–37. https://doi.org/10.1177/14707853211024472
Stacy-Jo-Dixon (2024) Most used social networks 2024 by number of users. Statista. https://tinyurl.com/27mm7puk
Tashakkori A, Johnson B, Teddlie C (2020) Foundations of mixed methods research: integrating quantitative and qualitative approaches in the social and behavioral sciences, 2nd edn. Sage
Udescu A (2024) TikTok engagement rate calculator & 10 tips to increase engagement. SocialInsider Blog. https://www.socialinsider.io/blog/tiktok-engagement-rate-calculator/
van Leewen T (2022) Multimodality and identity. Routledge
Wang S (2023) Algorithmic configurations of sexuality: theoretical foundations and methodological approaches. In: Housley W, Edwards A, Beneito-Montagut R, Fitzgerald R (eds) The SAGE handbook of digital society. SAGE Publications Ltd, London, pp 281–298
Younas A, Durante A, Fàbregues S (2023) Understanding the nature of and identifying and formulating "research problems" in mixed methods research. J Mixed MethoDs Res 18(4):483–502. https://doi.org/10.1177/15586898231191441
Zonin A (2024) Social media scraping: unlocking insights and opportunities. Medium. https://bit.ly/3UCCwCv

Part III
Artificial Media in Practice

Chapter 10
Proposal for Using Artificial Media for Reinforcing Journalism: Responsibility, Discourse, Deliberation, and Audiences' Participation

Gloria Gómez-Diago

Abstract The development of artificial media and their applications pose a challenge to societies at the economic, political, social, and media levels. The dangers associated with these technologies are highlighted, such as the automatic generation of content that can lead to the dissemination of false news, as well as the preponderance of the use and misuse of quantitative data extracted from the digital ecosystem. Meanwhile, social networks capture the attention and energy of the citizens who inhabit and feed them with content and visits, providing them with commercial value, while newspapers lose it. In a context of political polarization, where discourse has been replaced by data, even though truth has a narrative character (Byung-Chul, 2022), it is necessary for the media, especially newspapers, to recover the value of agoras and to regain audiences by integrating them as intellectual capital. Based on the review of different perspectives on the introduction of artificial media in the media, on analyzing how some newspapers express to be using artificial intelligence, and taking also into account the fieldwork developed in last in the context of the research project entitled, Employability and entrepreneurship in communication in the digital context: labour market demands,educational offerings by universities and the work experience of universities graduates [Empleabilidad y emprendimiento en comunicación en el contexto digital: demandas del mercado de trabajo, oferta formativa universitaria y experiencia laboral de los graduados (EMPLECOM)], to understand the needs of Spanish media, especially newspapers, we propose four ways of using these technologies and artifacts to strengthen journalism: 1. Assigning responsibility to the media; 2. Contextualizing information through discourse; 3. Promoting deliberation; and 4. Incorporating audience participation.

Keywords Artificial intelligence · Artificial media · Discourse · Ethics · Information · Journalism · Media · Newspapers · Participation

---

G. Gómez-Diago (✉)
Rey Juan Carlos University, Madrid, Spain
e-mail: gloria.gomez.diago@urjc.es

N. Zagalo and D. Keller (eds.), *Artificial Media*, Springer Series on Cultural Computing,
https://doi.org/10.1007/978-3-031-89037-6_10

10.1 Introduction

In recent years, the communication ecosystem has undergone major transformations due to the development and extension of the use of technologies that facilitate the publication and dissemination of content on Cyberspace and that have even contributed to transforming the job market available to journalism graduates (Martínez Nicolás 2023; Gómez Diago and Martínez Nicolás 2024). These transformations have been accelerated further, if that is possible, by the ongoing development and expansion of artificial intelligence, and of artificial media, that is, artificial intelligence assistants that allow, among other applications, the automated generation of content (Zagalo 2022). While it is warned that these technologies may replace humans in some jobs (Laiser 2022) in the field of journalism, it is suggested that the use of these technologies will reduce the workload of journalists by, among other things,[1] automating the writing of news based on data, such as sports results (European Commission 2022).

At the same time as technologies based on artificial intelligence are being integrated into different spheres of society, an uncritical translation of this technology into the journalism academic field has led to a banalization of the term 'journalism'. Thus, despite being journalism a human activity, "algorithmic journalism" is used to refer to the semi-automated process of natural language generation, which includes selecting data from private or public databases, assigning relevance to the data, processing and structuring the relevant data, and publishing the final text on a platform (Dörr 2015 in Dörr and Hollnbuchner 2017). "Automated journalism" is suggested for those cases in which a complete automation of journalistic content has taken place, without any human contribution apart from that of the programmers who developed the algorithm (Moses 2017), and "aggregation journalism" is applied to embrace algorithms that scan online resources (news agencies, websites, PR agencies) for content, but without checking the reliability of the sources, and without paying for the content, so that values such as reliability and accuracy suffer (Debatin 2015, in Dörr and Hollnbuchner 2017).

It is necessary to stop this race to add technology related terms to journalism, as if it were a hanger on which we put scarves, coats, hats…It is urgent to go deeper than applying technology to the journalism practice and to reflect on how technology can maintain and extend the journalism possibilities. For doing that it is firstly necessary needed to consider the ethical challenges posed by artificial intelligence-based technologies in journalism.

Considering that technology can help professionals, but never replace them in a newsroom, researchers as Nolan (2023) encourage media to achieve a collective agreement on criteria to ensure that content created directly by AI is not published.

[1] In addition to automated content production, artificial media are being used in the news industry to interact with audiences through virtual assistants and chatbots (Council of Europe 2023), search and clean large amounts of data, moderate comments, convert text to audio, distribute news, understand audience interests, attract subscribers, check and verify facts, optimize the use of images or identify and mitigate risks of bias (Polis, n.d.).

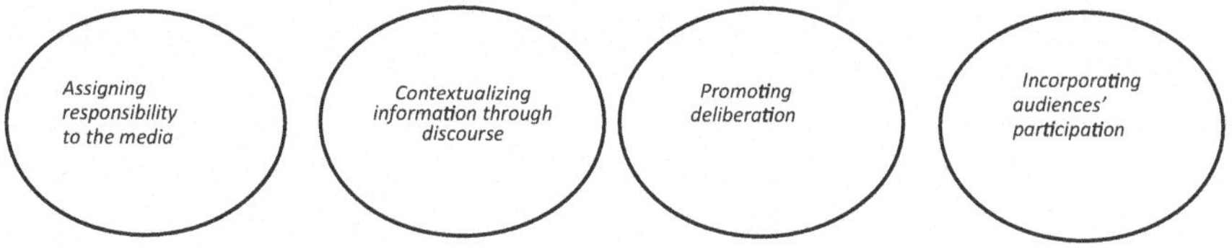

Fig. 10.1 A fourfold approach for strengthening journalism by artificial media

Although regulations on AI-based tools use hardly refer to the media (Porlezza and Ferri 2022), the Council of Europe (2022) provides guidance for implementing AI in these organizations. First, it stresses that adopting AI based technologies in journalistic enterprises is a time-consuming task requiring, among other activities, identifying, negotiating and defining the core values that will guide the use of AI-based media. Secondly, the Council of Europe (2022) points out the need for the media to assess the performance of AI journalism systems, looking at whether there are biases that need to be eliminated and paying attention to the side effects that the technology may have on human rights. Finally, this European institution suggests that the media should create a multidisciplinary and participatory space[2] for exchanging best practices for using AI technologies.

Beyond the need to evaluate technological tools based on AI to see whether they contain bias, it is important to identify ways in which technologies can be used to strengthen the role of journalism in a context where the crisis has led to the closure of newspapers (Abernathy 2020; Radcliffe and Ali 2017) and to the failure of 39,000 media companies between 2008 and 2019 (European Union 2023).

We are proposing a fourfold approach to enable media to integrate the use of artificial media so that they can strengthen journalism, connect (with) citizens and recovering them as audiences: 1. Assigning responsibility to the media; 2. Contextualizing information through discourse, 3. Promoting deliberation and 4. Incorporating participation of audiences (see Fig. 10.1).

10.2 Assigning Responsibility to the Media

The analysis of the ethical implications of algorithmic journalism is situated in the overlapping fields of digital media ethics—as part of journalism ethics—and cybernetics' (Dörr and Hollnbuchner 2017). In the media, it is possible to identify three spheres, associated with three ethics dimensions: the organizational sphere, governed by media system ethics, is concerned with the tensions created by hierarchy and media economic goals; the professional sphere refers to individual ethics, which deals with objectivity, transparency, accuracy, respect for privacy, appropriate research methods and the separation of fact and fiction; and the social sphere refers

[2] In terms of creating a place for dialogue on AI uses, it is of interest to obtain perspectives not only from developers or journalists, but also from citizens (Ouchchy et al. 2020)

to audience ethics, which focuses on media education (Dörr 2016) and or media literacy.

With the emergence of algorithmic journalism, the journalist is no longer the main moral agent, as other actors, journalistic and non-journalistic, are involved in the production of news. This means that the importance of the individual is decreasing, while the importance of media organizations and the media system as moral agents is increasing (Dörr and Hollnbuchner 2017). The responsibility for the use of artificial media should lie in the media, in its organizational sphere, and not in journalists, because journalists may be subject to external (economic, hierarchical) constraints that sometimes prevent them from acting morally (Dörr and Hollnbuchner 2017; Meyrowitz 2016). Therefore, the media must develop ethical perspectives for using artificial intelligence (Summers 2020). Dörr and Hollnbuchner (2017) underline the relevance of Fiedman et al. (2006) approach, which proposes doing a sensitive design, that is, designing technology with human values in mind and placing responsibilities for the use of technologies at the organizational level of the media and not at the individual level, with journalists.

In addition to placing responsibility for the use of algorithms in the media, it is essential to approach algorithms from a social science and humanities perspective. To this end, it is needed to consider four aspects of the algorithm that places them within the social context where they are produced: 1. It is not simply made up of information, but is generated through relationships between human and non-human entities; 2. Its boundaries cannot be known in advance, as they are determined by progression and an infinity of interactions and contexts; 3. It is a situated and contingent entity that cannot be separated from the practices of developers, nor from the legal, geographical, economic and/or organizational cultures that shape it; and 4. It is generated in a very specific production context, understood as a set of programming activities, scientific rationalities and material constraints (Cellard 2022). To evaluate algorithms, we can make questions[3] related to the type of data on which they are based or about the bias contained in them. Furthermore, ethnographic approaches can be used to combat the opacity of algorithms. They can shed light on the complex interweaving of social, cultural and technological aspects of computer systems in everyday life and provide rich and specific data on how algorithms are constructed and used by making visible the relationships between workplace cultures and algorithmic design. Regarding reception, ethnographic work demonstrates how social practices mediate the actual use and impact of algorithms (Christin 2020).

We approach transparency as the need to communicate when an algorithm is being used, and to provide information about its characteristics. Although we can agree

---

[3] Marconi (2020: 83–85) propose several questions to evaluate algorithms: "What does the algorithm optimize?; What data is the algorithm based on and are there any biases in it?; Is it clearly communicated to users how the algorithms make decisions?; Is there human supervision capable of making decisions and adjusting the algorithm?; Is the output provided by the algorithm explainable and interpretable?; Is there a record of errors made by the algorithm?; Are certain groups disadvantaged by this algorithm?; Is the output provided by the algorithm explainable and interpretable?; Is user data recorded or shared with other users with institutions, government?; Has the robustness of the service against attacks and hacking been assessed?"

that the information society is the "society of transparency", where people are not free but the information is (Byung Chul 2022), companies that generate and direct content to users do not provide enough information about the use of algorithms.

The EU Artificial Intelligence Act requires certain artificial intelligence systems to inform people that they are interacting with an AI system, unless it is obvious, and to inform people that they are being subjected to emotional recognition or biometric categorization systems. In this line, *Le Monde* Group stipulates that any use of generative AI must be explicitly notified to readers,[4] establishes a ban on the use of AI to create images and underlines as one condition for using this type of AI "improving the quality of news content". In addition, this regulation indicates how this media group uses AI: to make available an audio version of articles automatically generated from the written version and to moderate subscribers' comments (Van Kote 2024). For its part, The New York Times, with the document titled "Principles for Using Generative A.I. in The Times's Newsroom", expresses how this newspaper uses AI: as a tool to serve its mission, with human guidance and review, and with transparency and ethics. In the document, generative AI is understood as something that can help journalists uncover the truth and can help more people understand the world because they use machine learning to tell stories they would not otherwise be able to tell. In addition, the *New York Times* stresses that the use of AI-based tools and/or media will make this newspaper more accessible to more people through features such as voice-driven articles or translations into other languages.

However, being transparent when using artificial media also implies enabling citizens to make choices about the type of content they want to receive. Thus, users should have the right to responsible personalization of content, i.e. they should have access to the information to exercise control over their personal data, they should be able to manage and adjust their profiles, to be offered genuine personalization that considers short- and long-term interests, including the possibility of not receiving recommendations (Council of Europe 2022). Users should be capable of knowing the criteria for segmenting them into one group or another (Gandi 2021). In addition, it is important that the technology contains information about how it works, and it must be available to be questioned about its motivations, processes, and the products it generates, to answer enquires through a critical dialogue with its audience (Colton et al. 2015).

10.3 Contextualizing Information Through Discourse

Contextualizing information can be done in two levels or dimensions. From a perspective focused on interaction, we can consider how contents are delivered and expected to be used. From a perspective centered on the content, we are aware of the need to

[4] Article 1 of the guide for using AI published by *Le Monde* guarantees that "the use of generative AI is only authorized, under strictly defined conditions, as a tool to assist editorial production".

obtain qualitative data for understanding, supporting, and completing the quantitative data provided by artificial media.

From an interaction perspective, Shah and Bender (2022) warn against the elimination of interactions to retrieve information for users because this is detrimental to many aspects of search, including information verification, information literacy, and serendipity. In the authors' view, it is needed to build tools that help users find and make sense of information, rather than tools that claim to do it all for them. Within this approach occupied on the interaction level, Pavlik (2001) presents "contextualized journalism" as a result of the application of the possibilities granted by the Internet to the media. The researcher identifies five dimensions of contextualized journalism which are situated at a technological level: 1. Breadth of communication modalities; 2. Hypermedia; 3. Heightened audience involvement; 4. Dynamic content; and 5. Customization. From an interaction perspective, Pavlik (2001) approaches audience involvement by focusing on how users are provided with possibilities to acquire more information and/or content by clicking on objects displayed in virtual environments.

In a context where automated news has been found to lack contextualization (Royal and Napoli 2022), for contextualizing information we propose to focus on the content provided and in how it is obtained within the journalism practice. Being "churnalism[5]" increasingly frequent and being increasingly rare having journalists gathering news (Van Hout and Van Leuven 2016), the exponential growth of research measuring social life through digital environments, such as social networks, highlights the need to discuss the underlying epistemology that gives maximum trust and credibility to the mining of datasets[6] available on the internet (Felt et al. 2017) even when perfect data is affected by human error, bias and misjudgment which can be introduced at any point in the news-making process (Leiser 2022).

An automation bias leads decision-makers to assume that quantitative methods are superior to qualitative ones, motivating them to apply a positivist perspective even to evaluate work done with qualitative methods (Hesse et al. 2019), undermining the necessary complex contextualization required for human reasoning (Leiser 2022). In this line, Chomsky (2023) refers to the lack of contextualization of AI-generated content when warning about the pre-human or non-human stage of cognitive evolution of AI programs, being their fundamental problem the absence of the most crucial capability of any intelligence: the ability to state not only what is the case, what was the case and what will be the case—that is, to describe and predict—but also what

[5] Churnalism refers to "the recycling of prepackaged public relations and press agency copy as news" (Van Hout and Van Leuven 2016: 117).

[6] Given the lack of agreed criteria for the media to assess data quality, the questions posed by the European Union Agency for Fundamental Rights (2019) could serve as guidance: 1. Where does the data come from, i.e. who is responsible for the collection, maintenance and dissemination of the data?; 2. What information does the data contain, i.e. is the information included in the data fit for the purpose of the algorithm?; 3. Who is included in the data, i.e. is the information included in the data fit for the purpose of the algorithm?; 4. Is there missing information in the data set or are units only partially covered?; 5. What information is included; 6.What is the data collection time frame and geographic coverage of the data?

is not the case and what could and could not be the case, ingredients of explanation, and hallmarks of true intellect.

According to Byung-Chul (2022), data scientists see in big data and artificial intelligence a functional equivalent of the discursive public sphere in which despite the fact that truth has a narrative character, discourse has been replaced by data. The idea that truth has a narrative character means that in the de-narrativized information society it loses its meaning, since, beyond an economic crisis, we are_ the researcher argues_, in a narrative crisis. This is why we believe that information must be overcome, contextualized through discourse, a discourse produced from discursive operations[7] whose execution is the responsibility of journalists, and which must be oriented to explain, contextualizing, dialoguing, and generating meaning, rather than just providing data. To produce this contextualization, which depends on the journalist's judgement and assessment, tools such as ChatGPT can be used, for example, to locate basic concepts in qualitative data (Morgan 2023). Contextualizing the quantitative data collected can help to overcome six limitations: 1. Reliance on single, isolated data streams; 2. The one-dimensional nature of the quantitative data on which it relies; 3. The difficulties in interrogating these data streams; 4. The lack of contextualization of quantitative data feeds; 4. The lack of human angles in the texts generated; 5. The requirement to plan stories—to predict the 'main lines'—in advance; and 6. The difficulty of working creatively with the data in the process of creating templates (Thurman et al. 2017).

To better understand what contextualizing information consists of, we suggest following the idea provided by Manovich (2024) to artists to compete with a superhuman generative AI. The researcher advises artists to become a mole, that is, instead of attending to a large surface of infinite possibilities, which is what artificial intelligence-based technologies do, they should focus on a small aspect and go as deep as possible, that is, working on such a narrow micro-scale that the AI cannot reach it.

10.4 Promoting Deliberation

The media play a fundamental role in Western democracies, and the European Court of Human Rights (ECHR) has repeatedly affirmed their democratic function as 'information providers'. However, the ECHR has also emphasised their importance in facilitating public debate and acting as a public watchdog. This is consistent with Norris's (2014: 525) view that journalism's role is akin to that of an independent watchdog situated within civil society, counterbalancing the power of the executive, legislative, and judicial branches of government.

[7] Martínez Nicolás (1996) proposes and defines four relevant discursive operations: assessment, thematisation,actorialisation, referencing [valoración, tematización, actorialización y referenciación].

From a deliberative point of view, informing citizens is not enough. The media should give space to all those citizens who can contribute to advancing the debate. The media have a responsibility to present the audience with ideas that they have not previously considered, because deliberation requires not only multiple but also opposing points of view, since conflict of some kind is the essence of politics (Helberger et al. 2020).

As content selection tools, news recommenders can play an important role in a participatory democracy. These systems, aimed at suggesting content to users, can be an interesting tool for helping media to recover the relevant position they had in the communication ecosystem. Content selection through AI-based tools may not only affect individual users, but also the structure of the public sphere. If algorithmic personalization is taken to the extreme, each article could one day reach an audience of one person. This has implications for all the collective processes that form the pillars of modern democracies (Helberger et al. 2020) and for that reason, it is crucial that the algorithms, as technologies that redefine the economy, ecology, and society, can be designed by different people (Rushkoff 2003). One example is the News Values public service algorithm developed for Swedish Radio (SR). The aim of the algorithm is to personalize the news *feed* based on the ratings made by journalists, both to create a more relevant news *feed* and to streamline the organization's news rating criteria. In the process of developing the algorithm, employees from across the company were involved in identifying and formulating the core values that they believe characterize strong public service publications (Jaakkola 2023).

To evaluate algorithms for content recommendation, media outlets can ask questions such as those proposed by Helberger et al. (2020): How diverse or not diverse, and how personally relevant and inclusive should recommendations be?; How far should media outlets go in their engagement with the audience?; What is the role of values such as participation, transparency, deliberation, and privacy?; What are the social implications of exposing users to personalized information?; and more generally, What are the goals and values for which recommendations should be optimized?

The challenge for academics, policy makers, editors, journalists, and developers is to jointly conceptualize diversity in terms of metrics that can optimize deliberative algorithms. The overall goal should be to ensure that citizens are exposed to diverse information and to counteract the undemocratic effects of recommendation by platforms and social networks that considerably influence public opinion formation in a way that is counterproductive to a general 'readiness for dialogue' on the part of the population (Helberger 2019). Moreover, to avoid the lack of (media) content diversity online, prioritization of engagement over accuracy and diversity is recommended ensuring that diverse media content is available in different languages, formats, and is easy to find and use, and create/promote media and information literacy initiatives which can help individuals, especially those from minority or disadvantaged communities, to develop the skills and confidence to engage with the media and participate in the public sphere (Council of Europe 2024).

10.5 Incorporating Audiences' Participation

Journalists have always had a complex relationship with their audiences, a relationship which varies according to time, place and medium. Throughout the twentieth century, mainstream american print journalists neglected audience data, seeing it as an intrusion of commercial interests into their editorial autonomy while French journalists, on the other hand, developed a more ambivalent understanding of readership, viewing it critically as a form of market pressure but also valuing it as a sign of recognition in the public sphere (Christin 2022). Today the information available through social media platforms and networks (profile information, friends, status updates, links followed, time on the site…) is used to make an interpretation of users that is imperfect but considered sufficient[8] (Guillespie 2014).

Beyond audiences, users can be approached as participants. Citizens participate in the social sphere through their profiles on social networks. These platforms have allowed them to "be the media" and thus influence mass culture, but platforms are rigidly hierarchical, allowing certain uses and preventing others. For the owners of social networks, the goal is to store as much user-generated content and data as possible. To continue to grow, these platforms need more participants to attract other participants due to the so-called network effect, whereby the value of a technology increases as more people use it (Gehl 2014). Citizens have become the content providers for social networks and are expected to share content, forge connections and categorise cultural artefacts as part of an ongoing process (Gehl 2014).

Social networks have become the structure from which people interact and communicate within their conditions such as the number of characters and/or the type of interaction that can be performed (liking, retweeting, etc.). However, the digital network lacks the amphitheatrical structure of conventional media, which aggregates issues relevant to society as a whole and draws the attention of the entire population to them. The inherent centrifugal forces of these platforms cause audiences to disintegrate into fleeting, self-interested groups, hindering communicative action, which requires stable audiences on a large scale Byung Chul 2022:45).

A large proportion of citizens are interested in sharing their views and ideas on the issues covered by the media, particularly newspapers, but in recent years, in the academic context, there has been a shift from a utopian view of the online world to a strong emphasis on the "dark side"[9] of online communication embraced by the concept of dark participation (Quandt 2018). It is essential that media, specially newspapers, which have lost readers, attend to the interest of citizens in participating with comments. There are opportunities to involve audiences in newsmaking at the

[8] For digital newspapers is fundamental Chartbeat, a software which provides a quantitative visualization of the audience visiting a news website at anu given moment. Its dashboard provides "a sense of the ongoing, decentralized, and large-scale online dialogue taking place between journalists and their online readers" (Christin 2020).

[9] The negative perspective on participation must be derived from considering citizens as "citizen journalists" (Quand 2018) instead of citizens who want to express and to share their concerns and ideas.

observation (generating source material), selection (determining what to report), processing (assembling the content), distribution (sharing content with others), and interpretation (commenting on and evaluating the content) stages of the process (Domingo et al. 2008; Hermida 2011; Vos and Thomas 2023). Furthermore, a large proportion of citizens are interested in sharing their views and ideas on the issues covered by the media, particularly newspapers, but in recent years, in the academic context, there has been a shift from a utopian view of the online world to a strong emphasis on the "dark side" of online communication embraced by the concept of dark participation even when readers' comments in newspapers are one of the practices of news use (Meijer and Korme 2014) that generate interesting dialogues (Berg et al. 2024) so they are studied to see how users articulate discourses on topics such as COVID-19 confinements (Tafi et al. 2023).

If we access the *New York Times* online version *today* (15 December 2024, 18:15 PM, Madrid time zone (GMT + 1), we see that the articles "How will the rebels rule Syria? Their Past Offers Clues" and "Automakers Thrived in the Pandemic. Many are now struggling" have112 and 398 comments respectively. In the Spanish newspaper *El Paı́s,* the articles "'The report commissioned by Puente refutes Aldama's accusations" and "How to fabricate a political, media and judicial scandal: Podemos and the Neurona case" have received 481 and 254 comments. In the also Spanish newspaper, el diario.es the article "A new protest against Altri's macro-cellulose once again takes to the streets of Santiago" has 20 comments two hours after being published. This brief overview of newspaper websites reveals that many citizens are interested in commenting on the news. Their comments provide insight into their perspectives and highlight the issues that interest them most.

Ten years ago, Ruiz et al. (2011) found political news attracted the most comments and Strandberg and Berg (2013) agree user comments largely address news covering societal or political matters or political issues. Diakopoulos and Naaman (2011) encountered that people had four types of motivations to comment on news and to read them: 1. Motivations related to information; 2. Motivations linked to personal identity; 3. Motivations related to entertainment and 4. Motivations connected to social interaction. These motivations are concerned with the interest of citizens in sharing but also on obtaining more information and on participating in conversations. Authors noted that people comment on the news for motives such as educating others, answering/asking questions, adding information, sharing experience, clarifying, noting missing information, balancing discussion, correcting inaccuracies, factual errors or misinformation; and that people read comments for reasons such as getting more information on story, validating or comparing personal opinion against community opinion, see perspectives or view from community, etc.

Below, we present a table (see Table 10.1) outlining the motivations of citizens for writing and reading comments in online newspapers, as identified by Diakopoulos and Naaman (2011). These motivations are categorised under four main headings: information, personal identity, entertainment, and social interaction.

Table 10.1 Understanding of users' motivations for both reading and writing news comments

	Motivations for writing comments	Motivations for reading comments
Information	Educating others, answering/asking questions, adding information, sharing experience, clarifying, note missing information, balance discussion, correct inaccuracies, factual errors, or misinformation	Get more information on story, get additional reporting including updates to story
Personal identity	Expressing an intense emotion or opinion	Validating or comparing personal opinion against community opinion
Entertainment	Inject humor into discussion, debate	Funny
Social interaction	See reaction of community, persuade others, sympathize, leave condolences, applaud goodness, debate	See perspectives or view from community, see people's true feelings on topic, gauge political response or agenda, take pulse of community

Source Diakopoulos and Naaman (2011)

Subscription is the most important form of revenue for newspapers today, but these media are developing alternative forms of funding based on direct reader engagement, such as events[10] (Newman 2024) which permit media connecting with their audiences. In terms of creating spaces to build community with readers, the ability for readers to post comments is what differentiates online journalism most clearly from broadcast or print journalism (Lee 2012). Generating spaces for users to comment is fundamental and artificial intelligence-based technologies can help to moderate them (Vos and Thomas 2023) and combat the perception that moderating user comments is a time-consuming task (Çatalbaş et al. 2014: 492). Media[11] can use AI-based tools for helping journalists in the moderation process. Online comments not only permit users to express their opinions regarding one topic, but they can also communicate with precedent comments, hence generating a conversation, fusing interpersonal and mass communication (Ziegele and Quiring 2013), and producing dialogues and discourses.

[10] In an academic seminar celebrated on October 2024 with television, radio and press professionals, organized by GIDECOM, the consolidated group of educational innovation for employability in communication (grupo de innovación docente consolidado para la empleabilidad en comunicación) and funded by the Faculty of Communication Sciences of Rey Juan Carlos University, the four professionals explained that events are now a key source of funding for the media.

[11] Newspapers such as the *Financial Times* uses artificial intelligence tools for moderating comments, by permitting to filter them automatically, so journalists can be more attentive to the content posted by users (Kunova 2024). *The Washington Post* has also launched ModBot, a computer-based tool on artificial intelligence to moderate comments using an algorithm that has been trained by The Post's years-long history of human-moderated comments (The Washington Post 2017). The tool uses machine learning to automatically filter comments that require human moderation, flag stories that require real-time monitoring, and approve or delete comments based on The Post's discussion policy.

10.6 Conclusions and Discussion

This chapter proposes a fourfold approach for extending the possibilities of journalism by using artificial media in a moment where newspapers are hardly read, especially by the younger generations on whom their survival will depend. The first idea, "Assigning responsibility to the media" points out the need to hold the media, rather than individual journalists, accountable for their use of artificial intelligence. The second proposal, contextualizing information, refers to the need to obtain and analyze qualitative data which contextualize and amplifies quantitative data. It emphasizes the need for journalism to go beyond providing information and to contextualize it by developing discourses nourished by perspectives, sources, and concepts. The third idea, promoting deliberation, is related to the need for the media to expose their audiences to diverse content, functioning not only as content generators but also as content distributors in the broadest sense of the term, and the last idea, audiences' participation, raises the suitability of media, specifically online newspapers for functioning as agoras for citizen participation and debate.

It is necessary for the media not only to generate content but also to function as spaces for citizen interaction, and as vehicles for dialogue that contribute to the strengthening of democracies. In this line, we propose using artificial media to empower not only artificial sociability as the one referred to describe technologies and practices that create an appearance of sociality in machines such as ChatGPT, voice assistants, virtual influencers, socialbots, and companion chatbots (Natale and Depounti 2024) but also real sociability produced by the interaction between humans.

In a context where the ability to generate narratives has been lost (López Mondéjar 2024) and in which information prevails over discourse, it is important for the media, specifically newspapers, to provide spaces to generate communities around them and thus recover a vibrant press which, according to Tocqueville in Bouie (2023) "helps shape individuals into members of a community with responsibilities and obligations toward that community, it acculturates them into political life and ties them to other, like-minded people". In this line, apart from informing the public, enabling the free formation and expression of opinions and ideas, scrutinizing the activities of public and private stakeholders, journalism must provide a forum for pluralistic debate (Council of Europe 2024).

With citizens connected to them, it will be easier for the media to recoup the attention from the audiences and the advertising investment that social networks receive now (Abernathy 2020). In this effort, given that smaller publishers lack the financial and technical resources to build their own technological systems, while larger players in the cultural and creative sectors can build their own AI technologies, it is necessary for the media to work together and in alliances with universities (Gómez Diago, 2022) to develop technologies aimed at improving journalism, as they are less frequent than those aimed at corporate communications or advertising (Gómez Diago and Martínez Nicolás 2024).

References

Abernathy (2020) News deserts and ghost newspapers: will local news survive? the center for innovation and sustainability in local media. Hussman School of Journalism and Media University of Nort Carolina at Chapel Hill. https://www.usnewsdeserts.com/reports/news-deserts-and-ghost-newspapers-will-local-news-survive/

Berg J, Fagerholm A, Strandberg K (2024) Quality user-generated content? a case study of the quality of online news comments on the site of finnish public service broadcaster yle. J Pract 1–22. https://doi.org/10.1080/17512786.2024.2329759

Bouie J (2023) Disinformation is not the real problem with democracy. The New York Times. https://www.nytimes.com/2023/03/11/opinion/local-media-newspapers-democracy.html

Byung-Chul H (2022) Infocracia. La digitalización y la crisis de la democracia. Taurus, Argentina

Cellard L (2022) Algorithms as figures: towards a post-digital ethnography of algorithmic contexts. New Media Soc 24(4):982–1000. https://doi.org/10.1177/14614448221079032

Christin A (2020) Metrics at work: journalism and the contested meaning of algorithms. Princeton University Press, Princeton, New Jersey

Chomsky N (2023) The false promise of ChatGPT. The New York Times. https://www.nytimes.com/2023/03/08/opinion/noam-chomsky-chatgpt-ai.html

Colton S, Halskov J, Ventura D, Gouldstone I, Cook M, Pérez-Ferrer B (2015) The painting fool sees! new projects with the automated painter. In: International conference on computational creativity (ICCC 2015). Brighma Young University Utah, UT, pp 189–196. https://computationalcreativity.net/iccc2015/proceedings/8_2Colton.pdf

European Commission (2022) Opportunities and challenges of artificial intelligence technologies for the cultural and creative sectors. Directorate-General for Communications Networks, Content and Technology. Publications Office of the European Union. https://op.europa.eu/en/publication-detail/-/publication/359880c1-a4dc-11ec-83e1-01aa75ed71a1/language-en

Council of Europe (2024) Guidelines on the responsible implementation of artificial intelligence systems in journalism. https://rm.coe.int/cdmsi-2023-014-guidelines-on-the-responsible-implementation-of-artific/1680adb4c6

Diakopoulos N, Naaman M (2011) Towards quality discourse in online news comments. In: Conference on computer supported cooperative work (CSCW). https://pdfs.semanticscholar.org/57df/d8ff7566134062e77119762ccfebc01791c9.pdf

Domingo D, Quandt T, Heinonen A, Paulussen S, Singer JB, Vujnovic M (2008) Participatory journalism practices in the media and beyond. an international comparative study of initiatives in online newspapers. Journal Pract 2(3): 326–342. https://doi.org/10.1080/17512780802281065

Dörr KN (2016) Mapping the field of algorithmic journalism. Digit J 4(6):700–722. https://doi.org/10.1080/21670811.2015.1096748

Dörr KN, Hollnbuchner K (2017) Ethical challenges of algorithmic journalism. Digit J 5(4):404–419. https://doi.org/10.1080/21670811.2016.1167612

European Commission (2023) The competitiveness and economic viability of the news media sector in the EU: final report. In: Directorate-general for communications networks, content and technology publications office of the European Union. European commission. https://doi.org/10.2759/803098

European Union Agency for Fundamental Rights (2019) Data quality and artificial intelligence: mitigating bias and error to protect fundamental rights. European Union Agency for Fundamental Rights. Publications Office. https://fra.europa.eu/en/publication/2019/data-quality-and-artificial-intelligence-mitigating-bias-and-error-protect

Felt U, Fouché R, Miller CA, Smith-Doerr L (2017) The handbook of science and technology studies. MIT Press, Boston, MA

Friedman B, Kahn PH, Borning A (2008) Value sensitive design and information systems. In Himma KE, Tavani HT (eds) The handbook of information and computer ethics. Wiley, pp 69–102, New Jersey

Gandi HO (2021) Algorithmic manipulation. How shall we respond to the threats and challenge before us (Online conference). What is communication? Speaker Series. University of Oregon

Gehl RW (2014) Reverse engineering social media. Software, culture and political economy in new media capitalism. Temple University, Philadelphia, Pennsylvania

Gillespie T (2014) The relevance of algorithms. In: Gillespie T, Boczkowski P, Foot K (eds) Media technologies: essays on communication, materiality, and society. MIT Press, pp 167–194. https://doi.org/10.7551/mitpress/9780262525374.001.0001

Gómez-Diago G, Martínez-Nicolás M (2024) Technological skills demanded in job postings for journalism graduates in Spain. Commun & Soc 37(3):1–18. https://doi.org/10.15581/003.37.3.1-18

Gómez-Diago G (2022) Perspectives to address artificial intelligence in journalism teaching. A review of research and teaching experiences. Revista Latina de Comunicación Social 80:29–46. https://doi.org/10.4185/RLCS-2022-1542

Helberger N (2019) On the democratic role of news recommenders. Digit J 7(8):993–1012. https://doi.org/10.1080/21670811.2017.1289819

Helberger N, Eskens SJ, van Drunen MZ, Bastian MB, Möller JE (2020) Implications of AI-driven tools in the media for freedom of expression. Council of Europe. https://rm.coe.int/coe-ai-report-final/168094ce8f

Hermida A (2011) Mechanisms of participation: how audience options shape the conversation. In Singer J, Hermida A, Domingo D, Heinonen A, Paulussen S, Quandt T, Reich Z, Vujnovic M (eds), Participatory journalism: Guarding open gates at online newspapers. Wiley, pp 13–33, Malden, MA

Hesse A, Glenna L, Hinrichs C, Chiles R, Sachs C (2019) Qualitative research ethics in the big data era. Am Behav Sci 63(5):560–583. https://doi.org/10.1177/0002764218805806

Jaakkola M (2023) A handbook for journalism educators reporting on artificial intelligence. United Nations Educational, Scientific and Cultural Organization, Paris. https://doi.org/10.58338/HSMK8605

Kunova M (2024) Keeping the conversation clean: how AI helps the financial times moderate comments. Journalism.co.uk https://www.journalism.co.uk/news/keeping-the-conversation-clean-how-ai-helps-the-financial-times-moderate-comments/s2/a1148237/

Lee E (2012) That's not the way it is: how user-generated comments on the news affect perceived media bias. J Comput Mediat Commun 18(1):32–45. https://doi.org/10.1111/j.1083-6101.2012.01597.x

Leiser M (2022) Bias, journalistic endeavors, and the risks of artificial intelligence. In: Pihlajarinne T, Alén-Savikko A (eds) Artificial intelligence and the media. Edward Elgar Publishing, Cheltenham, UK, pp 8–32.https://doi.org/10.4337/9781839109973.00007

López Mondéjar L (2024) Sin relato. Atrofia de la capacidad narrativa y crisis de la sibjetividad. Anagrama, Madrid

Manovich L (2024) Separate and reassemble: generative AI through the lens of art and media histories. In: Manovich L, Arielli E (eds) Artificial aesthetics. https://manovich.net/index.php/projects/separate-and-reassemble-generative-ai-media-history

Marconi F (2020) Newsmakers: artificial intelligence and the future of journalism. Columbia University Press, New York. https://cup.columbia.edu/book/newsmakers/9780231191371

Martínez Nicolás M (1996) El estudio del discurso periodístico informativo: una aproximación metodológica desde la teoría de la discursividad social, *Trípodos. Lenguaje, pensamiento, comunicación* 2:95–114. https://tripodos.com/index.php/Facultat_Comunicacio_Blanquerna/article/view/1595

Martínez-Nicolás M (2023) Quo vadis, Periodismo? Inserción laboral, mercado de trabajo y formación de los graduados en Periodismo. Anuario ThinkEP I:17. https://doi.org/10.3145/thinkepi.2023.e17a48

Meyrowitz J (2016) Limits of mainstream U.S. Journalism. Academia. https://www.academia.edu/29902757/Limits_of_Mainstream_U.S._Journalism

Morgan DL (2023) Exploring the use of artificial intelligence for qualitative data analysis: the case of ChatGPT. Int J Qual Methods 22. https://doi.org/10.1177/16094069231211248 (Original work published 2023)

Moses L (2017) The Washington Post's robot reporter has published 850 articles in the past year. DigiDay. https://digiday.com/media/washington-posts-robot-reporter-published-500-articles-last-year/4

Natale S, Depounti I (2024) Artificial sociality. Hum-Mach Commun 7:83–98. https://doi.org/10.30658/hmc.7.5

New York Times (2024) Principles for using generative a.I. in the times's newsroom. https://www.nytco.com/press/principles-for-using-generative-a%E2%80%A4i%E2%80%A4-in-the-timess-newsroom/

Newman N (2024) Journalism, media, and technology trends and predictions 2024. Reuters Inst Study Jlsm. https://doi.org/10.60625/risj-0s9w-z770

Nolan H (2023) How to stop AI from eating journalism. Ethical standards can also save a lot of human jobs. In these times. https://inthesetimes.com/article/ai-artificial-intelligence-journalism-chatgpt-media-ethics

Norris P (2014) Watchdog journalism. In: Bovens M, Goodin RE, Schillemans T (eds) The oxford handbook of public accountability. Oxford Academic Press, Oxford, pp 525–542

Ouchchy L, Coin A, Dubljević V (2020) AI in the headlines: the portrayal of the ethical issues of artificial intelligence in the media. AI & Soc 35:927–936. https://doi.org/10.1007/s00146-020-00965-5

Pavlik JV (2001) Journalism and new media. Columbia University Press. https://doi.org/10.7312/pavl11482

Polis. Journalism and Society (n.d) JournalismAI starter pack. A guide designed to help news organizations learn about the opportunities offered by AI to support their journalism. https://www.lse.ac.uk/media-and-communications/polis/JournalismAI/Starter-Pack

Porlezza C, Ferri G (2022) The missing piece: ethics and the ontological boundaries of automated journalism. ISOJ J 12(1):71–98, https://isoj.org/research/the-missing-piece-ethics-and-the-ontological-boundaries-of-automated-journalism/

Quandt T (2018) Dark participation. Media Commun 6(4)36–48. https://doi.org/10.17645/mac.v6i4.1519

Radcliffe D, Ali C (2017) Local news in a digital world: small-market newspapers in the digital age. C Univ Acad Commons. https://doi.org/10.7916/D8WS95VQ. https://ssrn.com/abstract=3094783

Royal A, Napoli PM (2022) Local journalism without journalists metric media and the future of local news. J Creat Ind Cult Stud 8:119–147. http://eprints.rclis.org/44082/

Ruiz C, Domingo D, Micó JL, Díaz-Noci J Meso K, Masip P (2011) Public sphere 2.0? the democratic qualities of citizen debates in online newspapers. Int J Press/Polit 16(4):463–487. https://doi.org/10.1177/1940161211415849

Rushkoff D (2003) Open-source democracy. How online communication is changing offline politics. Demos, London. http://www.demos.co.uk/files/OpenSourceDemocracy.pdf

Shah S, Bender E (2022) Situating search. In: CHIIR '22: ACM SIGIR conference on human information interaction and retrieval. https://doi.org/10.1145/3498366.3505816

Strandbeg K, Berg J (2013) Online newspapers' readers' comments-democratic conversation platforms or virtual Soapboxes? Communicaçao e Sociedade 23:132–152. http://revistacomsoc.pt/index.php/comsoc/article/download/1618/1556

Summers S (2020) Humans Vs. Technology: what are the implications of using Artificial Intelligence in media and on society? Human Rights Commission. Recuperado de. https://humanrights.gov.au/sites/default/files/2020-07/9_-_sina_summers_1.pdf

Tafi V, Coles BA, Goodman S, Yates S, Elsey C (2023) Scepticism or conspiracy? a discourse analysis of anti-lockdown comments to online newspaper articles. Crit Discourse Stud 21(4):482–501. https://doi.org/10.1080/17405904.2023.2186449

The artificial intelligence Act. https://artificialintelligenceact.eu/

The Washington Post (2017) The Washington Post leverages artificial intelligence in comment moderation. https://www.washingtonpost.com/pr/wp/2017/06/22/the-washington-post-leverages-artificial-intelligence-in-comment-moderation/

Thurman N, Dörr K, Kunert J (2017) When reporters get hands-on with robo- writing. Digit JIsm 5(10):1240–1259. https://doi.org/10.1080/21670811.2017.1289819

Ürper DÇ, Çevikel T (2014) Reader comments on mainstream online newspapers in Turkey: perceptions of web editors and moderators. Commun 39(4):483–503. https://doi.org/10.1515/commun-2014-0022

Van Hout T, Van Leuven S (2016) Investigating 'Churnalism' in real time news. In: Franklin B, Eldridge S (eds) The Routledge companion to digital journalism studies. Routledge, pp 117–125

Van Kote G (Marzo 13, 2024). Le Monde adopts a charter on artificial intelligence. Le Monde. https://www.lemonde.fr/en/about-us/article/2024/03/13/le-monde-adopts-a-charter-onartificial-intelligence_6615286_115.html

Vos TP, Thomas RJ (2023) They're making it more democratic: the normative construction of participatory journalism. Digit J 12(6):869–893. https://doi.org/10.1080/21670811.2023.2174893

Zagalo N (2022) Artificial media 2022 will go down in history as the year when artificial intelligence was recognize fo it creative capabilities. Medium. https://medium.com/@nzagalo/artificial-media-79735f549b5a

Ziegele M, Quiring O (2013) Conceptualizing online discussion value: a multidimensional framework for analyzing user comments on mass-media websites. Ann Int Commun Assoc 37(1):125–153. https://doi.org/10.1080/23808985.2013.11679148

Chapter 11
Crafting Artificial Musicians: Building *Solaris* as a Co-operative, Perceiving and Creative AI

Craig Vear and Fabrizio Poltronieri

Abstract In this chapter, we discuss an approach for crafting an artificial musician. At the centre of this is the understanding that music is an embodied process involving joint action and mutual perception. In contrast to many music-AI projects, we have designed and built a system from the bottom-up by focusing on musical togetherness and embedding the mutual perception of liveness and responsivity rather than symbolic representations of music such as midi-files, notation and audio. We view this from the perspective of creative artistic researchers, and therefore from an insider perspective. By developing an artificial musician that is co-creative and capable of 'perceptual experience' (Kirk, Zombies and us: understanding consciousness, Bloomsbury, London, 2017) we believe this approach is appropriate for a wide range of musical systems. The practice-based project at the centre of this paper is *Solaris* a jazz quartet in which three musicians are AI, trained with a dataset collected over two years, and only one musician (co-author Vear) is human. This ensemble has been performing since 2019 in various guises, mostly with compositions in the spirit of jazz and free improvisation. In the first section of this chapter, we outline the core perspectives that define our understanding of music-making, behavioural and embodied AI, AI as media, the nature of togetherness, and the importance of mutual perception of liveness and perceptual experience (Kirk, Zombies and us: understanding consciousness, Bloomsbury, London, 2017) from our musicking partners. These have been developed and tested through a process of practice-based methods, with the co-authors operating as practitioner-researchers in this process. From this, we present a list of guiding principles which we used to craft *Solaris*. Following this we discuss how we crafted *Solaris* through (a) a new dataset that captured certain physiological parameters from a series of professional jazz pianists; (b) a new approach to an AI-Factory built on models trained from the dataset, and (c) a digital score that represented the inner workings and experience of *Solaris'* AI. We tested *Solaris* in several scenarios. The results obtained from the interaction of

C. Vear (✉) · F. Poltronieri
University of Nottingham, Nottingham, UK
e-mail: craig.vear@nottingham.ac.uk

F. Poltronieri
e-mail: Fabrizio.Poltronieri@nottingham.ac.uk

N. Zagalo and D. Keller (eds.), *Artificial Media*, Springer Series on Cultural Computing,
https://doi.org/10.1007/978-3-031-89037-6_11

human musicians with *Solaris* are surprising, as they suggest that human musicians see *Solaris* as a competent jazz improviser who acts and responds in real time to the musical space. In the discussion section, we dig deeper into the implications of *Solaris'* perceptual experience and playfully present a conceptualisation of *Solaris* as a sentient Creative-AI system. We propose a framework based on Charles Sanders Peirce's concept of Synechism to understand sentience in the context of Creative-AI and from this insider perspective. The idea that AI should be understood as a form of mind, following the precepts of Peirce's synechism, opens up new avenues for collaboration between humans and apparatus, breaking the Cartesian duality (spirit-matter) that has plagued us since Descartes (Hull, J Soc Comput 4(3), 193–204, 2023). What we experience when interacting with artificial media systems like *Solaris* is not just a cold, programmatic interaction with inert matter, there is the presence of a collaborative and creative spirit (Poltronieri and Vear, ISEA—Awaiting publication, 2024) that has perceptual experiences (Kirk, Zombies and us: understanding consciousness, Bloomsbury, London, 2017).

Keywords Sentience · Jazz music · Creative-AI · Digital scores · Musicking · Datasets · Neural networks · Synechism · Music-AI · Embodied AI · Behavioural AI · Sentience · Digital Score

11.1 Introduction

In this introduction, we outline a foundational challenge that is at the core of our research: how might we craft an artificial musician? In order to understand this challenge, we must first define what we mean by making music, as that is what our intended artificial musician would be required to do with other musicians. We then argue that one of the critical aspects of making music is the sense of togetherness with others inside musicking, through which we discuss the importance of relationships as a critical factor in understanding artificial media from an insider perspective. From this, we then outline the research to date that has led to the design of *Solaris*, and introduce the notion of *perceived experience* (Kirk 2017) as a way of building an artificial musician.

11.1.1 What is It to Make Music

Let us start with the question *What is it to make music?* If you ask this question to 200 people, you will no doubt get 200 differing responses. For us, the authors, making music involves taking part: to be incorporated in the sound; to be in the flow; to be led and lead at the same time; to seek and find relationships and connections with others as sound; to become attuned to the music-world; to feel it materially; to be lifted out of this physical shell of meat and flesh and dance with others inside music

(Vear 2019, 2022, 2023, 2024). We are not alone in believing this (Bhagwati 2017, Devenish and Hope 2024, Niljs et al. 2009), and this is not poetic thinking: there is scientific evidence to prove this incorporation into music (Leman 2007, Schiavio et al. 2015, 2024, Bishop 2018, 2024). But you simply need to look at any musician who is so totally into the groove, or flow, or pocket, or whatever they call it, to see that they are transported to some other place and with some other sense of self.

We talk about this in our chapter from the position of musicians who have spent several decades deeply engaged in the creative practices of music and who now research this phenomenon through creative AI. These practices range from playing in cover bands in pubs to experimental music and jazz to world tours with signed bands; from recording albums with popstars such as Tom Jones, to composing for national ballets companies and designing award-winning theatre sound, and many more (in fact several thousand) professional experiences making music.

The point of mentioning this is to contextualise our position of what we consider it is to 'make music'. And by extension, our approach to understanding artificial media, and to crafting an artificial musician. Furthermore, we are discussing artificial musicians interacting with other musicians, primarily humans, but the following can apply to a collective of artificial musicians cooperating in real time together.

11.1.2 Musicking

Our understanding of the act of making music evangelises the theory of musicking as defined by Chris Small (1989). He states that musicking is to do music whether that be rehearsing, performing, organising, coding, and listening "(even dancing)" (Small 1989). Critically, the act of musicking 'establishes in the place where it is happening a set of relationships, and it is in those relationships that the meaning of the act lies' (Small 1989). This goes beyond harmonic relationships of chords and melodic notes—although this is part of it—but also considers qualities of the sound, the acoustic spaces (physical or virtual), relationships with other agents and actors (perceived and real), the fulfilment and pleasure of joint action and of self-agency, and the journeys that the musicians go on in, with, through and when musicking.

From this perspective it is these relationships and the connections within musicking that are the music and where the meaning lies; the resultant sound is the artefact. As a conclusion to what we are describing here, our priority in crafting an artificial musician is on the mutual perception of responsivity, liveness, emergence and togetherness that is generated between human and artificial musicians when they are musicking. The artefact is much less of a concern to our studies.

This, as you can imagine, is a huge challenge, but one that we have spent many years trying to crack, with some degrees of success. Key to this is breaking down these relationships into a set of principles, with which to guide the crafting process. The first of these is the notion of musical togetherness, which we will discuss next, but first, we must explain our understanding of music and AI as media.

11.1.3 Understanding Music and AI as Media

Our perspective of musicking described above, informs our understanding of what media is, or rather what media does. For the authors, we are less concerned with the content of a medium (say an abstract graphical image on a screen) and more concerned with how this graphical image, say, how it makes us behave, feel, think, create. This clearly aligns with McLuhan's theories of the 'Medium is the Message' and how media could be understood by how it shapes and controls "the scale and form of human association and action" (McLuhan 1964). When we discuss music and digital score, AI design and embodiment it is from this perspective, and as such is a discussion about the core affect ("message") of a medium.

11.1.4 Musical Togetherness

Musical togetherness (Bishop 2024) is a critical factor in the perceived success of musicking relationships. Bishop defines it as the 'feelings of social connection and pleasure that result from being and acting as part of a group during musical interaction' (Bishop 2024). She goes on to define three conditions that 'must be fulfilled' for the experience of togetherness to occur:

> First, participants in an interactive setting must be aware of one another as intentional co-performers capable of exchanging expressive ideas. Second, interaction must unfold reliably in real-time, allowing for a mutual perception of liveness. Third, participants must adapt and build off of one another in a way that allows for mutual perception of responsivity. (Bishop 2024)

Bishop argues further that for togetherness to 'unfold reliably in real-time' (Bishop 2024) there needs to be a mutual perception of responsivity and of liveness, and an awareness of intentionality from the partners inside musicking. This is articulated in Fig. 11.1. She goes on to say that:

> Underlying all of the other criteria that characterize MT is an awareness of intentional interaction partners in a shared musical environment. For this awareness to occur, three conditions must be met: (i) a player must be aware of their interaction partner(s), (ii) it must be possible for partners to exchange expressive information bidirectionally, and (iii) this bidirectional exchange must enable the player to perceive their partner(s) as intentional. (Bishop 2024)

We have taken these principles into the work that we are discussing in this chapter, as they get to the core of the challenge. However, this presents us with a sticky issue: how do we know that the artificial musician is 'perceiving' and is 'aware'? This we explain using Robert Kirk's notion of the 'basic package' for 'perceptual experience' (Kirk 2017). This is another important stepping stone in cracking the nut of an artificial musician.

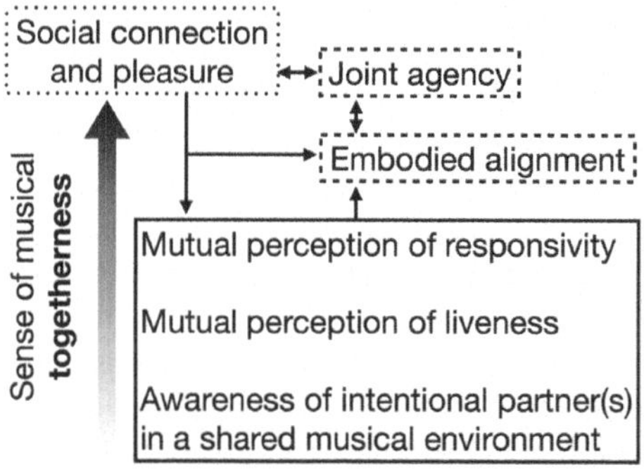

Fig. 11.1 Framework for musical togetherness (MT). The bottom layer (box with a solid border) includes necessary conditions underlying MT experiences. The second layer criteria (boxes with dashed line borders) are contingent on the bottom layer, mutually influential, and contribute directly to strengthening MT experiences. The top layer (box with dotted borders) characterizes the rewarding outcomes of MT, which feed back to shape the continued musical interaction. (Used with kind permission by Laura Brooks)

11.1.5 Perceptual Experience

In *Robots, Zombies and Us*, Kirk outlines a way of understanding perceptual consciousness through behaviourism. He argues that it might be possible to conceive of consciousness in robots (and AI) through the 'performance of functions' (Kirk 2017). He presents a 'basic package' for understanding the perceptual experience of AI as an essential, but not determining, building block that might lead to an understanding of consciousness. He states 'we know human consciousness is more than a mere parade of experiences. Notably, it involves the capacities to notice, attend to, and on occasions remember and compare experiences' (Kirk 2017). But what of the perception of non-humans such as oysters, ants, dogs, AI and robots?

He argues for a basic package which is a set of capabilities that form the essential building block for perceptual experience and awareness. He argues that while we can tell we are conscious because 'we *are* conscious', this is less true for the oyster, or dog, or AI, or robot. He proposes that we can rely on his version of functionalism to help us understand what might be going on inside those beings and creatures that cannot articulate their consciousness, as we can, or do not experience such high levels of perceptual consciousness as humans can. His solution is to focus 'on their behavior and what goes on inside their bodies' (Kirk 2017)—or with AI and robots, their code— as 'we need some idea of the *minimum* requirements for perceptual consciousness' without being 'distracted or even misled by the complexities of normal human consciousness' (Kirk 2017). With this in mind, Kirk's basic package consists of these conditions:

1. Perception and pure reflex systems
2. perception and control
3. information … *for* the system

4. interdependent capacities
5. concepts and language (Kirk 2017).

It is possible to craft an artificial musician using symbolic representations of musical behaviour, or to train a neural network on the sound of music to achieve such attunement, however, the authors feel that this will weaken, or lessen, its ability to fulfil several of the conditions outlined by Bishop and musical togetherness. So, if we are to build an artificial musician that is capable of musical togetherness, and therefore engages in musicking, we must craft a system that contains, at the very minimum, the basic package as outlined by Kirk. And if we are successful in crafting an artificial musician that has these basic conditions, then not only is it possible to consider it capable of *perceptual experience*, but also capable of musical togetherness, *if* the basic package is musically attuned. This attunement is a core part of the ongoing research by the authors on embodied musicking robotics (EMR) and our interpretation of Rodney Brook's early work on 'coping machines'. We will introduce this next, however, it is worth stressing here, that what we seek is not human-level 'perceptual experience', but the *minimum* requirements for musicking togetherness.

11.1.6 Rodney Brooks and Embodied Musicking Robots

In *Embodied AI and Musicking Robotics* (Vear 2022), Vear discusses a 'hypothesis for embodied AI and its development with music robots'. It offers a definition of embodied AI as '*an intelligent agent whose operational behaviour is determined by percepts interacting to the dynamic situation within which it operates*'. This builds on the foundational work of Rodney Brooks, in which he created robots that engaged with the world through behaviourist AI principles. He states that for robots to engage with the world, they should be designed 'first and foremost able to cope' (Vear 2022) and 'adapt to a dynamically changing environment within the parameters of specific and multiple goals' (Vear 2022).

Brooks' foundational theories guided the developed of Vear's embodied AI musicking robot (EMR) projects (2008—present), through which he generated this set of principles:

- EMR must cope in an appropriate musical manner, and in a timely fashion, with the dynamic shifts inside the musicking world
- EMR should be robust to the dynamic environment of musicking, it should not fail to minor changes in the properties of the flow of musicking, and should behave appropriately to its ongoing perception of the flow
- EMR should maintain multiple goals, changing as required and adapting to its world by capitalising on creative opportunity
- EMR should do something in the world of musicking, 'it should have some purpose in being' (Vear 2022).

Through a series of experiments, these principles were tested and refined to build embodied musicking robots that coped in the dynamic situation within musicking forming relationships of togetherness and being perceived as in-the-flow with the human musicians (Vear 2019). This approach we consider to be bottom-up as it focuses on human-experience over the more pervasive top-down approach of recreating the artefact of sound, music or art. Our research shows that the creative use of AI in symbiotic environments, where human creativity and creative forms of AI share spaces and processes transparently and in real time, is an efficient way of leveraging new methods and visions (Poltronieri 2022). But as this is speculative and philosophical, it is difficult to find precursors, AI designs and datasets that support it. In the next section, we will outline why such a lacuna exists.

11.1.7 Related Work and the Need for a Craft Approach

The literature surrounding the notion of artificial musicians is rather thin. Specifically, those that are capable of engaging in musicking as outlined in Sect. 11.1 of this chapter. This is not surprising given that it's a grand challenge (perhaps a foolish one) and extremely difficult to define. There are, however, encouraging work that have designed such systems. For example, Tahiroğlu (2022) 'reflects on the potential use of artificial intelligence technologies in instrument building, and subsequently to address the specific challenges and opportunities that arise through these technologies. I focus on emerging musical expectations and musical demands in a practical research implementation of our AI-terity autonomous musical instrument'; Ramalho et al. (1999) 'presents an intelligent agent model for simulating the behaviour of a jazz bass player during live performance'; and in Dai 2023 Ph.D. thesis they have created 'artificial musicians across different music creation levels and representation modalities'. However, the generalised approach uses top-down, symbolic representations of what music sound likes, rather than what musicking feels like.

Musicking modelling has been a research challenge for some time, and more sophisticated real-time solutions are being developed. Researchers have grappled with how AI can be used in relationship building with human musicians and AI, such as McCormack et al. 2019, which is a direct antecedent to this research. In this, they 'developed a collaborative improvising AI drummer that communicates its confidence through an emoticon-based visualisation. The AI was trained on musical performance data, as well as real-time skin conductance, of musicians improvising with professional drummers, exposing both musical and extra-musical cues to inform its generative process.'

The bulk of computational models for musicking attempt to codify musical expression in terms of mathematical formulae or symbolic programs and rely on datasets that are built on symbolic representations of the musical artefact (Civit et al. 2022). This type of modelling concentrates on making machines perform music that can be perceived as being expressive. However, there is limited research in the systems and knowledge around performance modelling from an embodied, bottom-up perspective. A critical element here is the lack of datasets that can be used to model such an artificial musician.

There are plenty of datasets containing midi data of performances, and compositions, and there is an abundance of datasets containing audio files of music performances. And there are large language models such as ChatGPT. But so far, none of these can help build an artificial musician from a bottom-up perspective and therefore understanding this media from how it shapes and controls "the scale and form of human association and action" (McLuhan 1964). As such, we needed to craft our own AI eco-system, which meant designing and building small datasets from scratch, defining new values of success for these builds, and rethinking the AI architecture so that its behaviours align to that of the priorities set out in the following point (below) and a protracted process of evaluation and testing in the real world with real-world musicians and non-academic audiences.

11.1.8 Defining Principles of an Artificial Musician

It is hopefully clear to the reader that we are dealing with the challenge of crafting an artificial musician from a specific perspective: that of embodied musicking and how AI shapes and controls "the scale and form of human association and action" (McLuhan 1964). Furthermore, we have set out a challenge to craft such a system from bottom-up perspectives: that it must feel like and behave like another musician in the ensemble. This path and our interest in music led us to create *Solaris*: A Jazz-AI quartet. In this, the AI performs the piano, bass, and drum-machine along with a human drummer (Vear). Together, they symbiotically generate the improvisation in real time and are part of a universe of musical meaning inserted into a flow of musical creation.

We discuss *Solaris* in more detail in the next section, but by way of evaluation, we defined three nested principles that guided its design, development and deployment as an artificial musician. Each of these principles is a subset of the previous one and therefore represents only one pathway through this research field, many more solutions are possible. So, for us, an artificial musician must:

1. cope with the dynamic flow (Csikszentmihalyi 1975) of musicking [
    a. have a musically attuned basic package for perceptual experience [
        i. maintain a sense of musical togetherness]]

11.2 *Solaris*: Practice-Based Case Study

In this section, we detail how we crafted an artificial musician. The case study at the centre of this discussion is *Solaris*, a 'flow-based, post-modern, free, math-AI jazz quartet led by the musician Craig Vear' (Solaris 2024). After a short introduction to *Solaris*, we expand on the crafting process including developing a small, bespoke 'embodied musicking dataset' created from the physiological and psychological data of solo improvising jazz pianists. From this, we explain the embodied approach to the AI stack in *Solaris*, and the development of a digital score by co-author Poltronieri as a poetic representation of *Solaris'* perceptual experience (Kirk 2017).

11.2.1 About Solaris

Solaris is a practice-based case study run by the authors since 2018. Practice-based (Candy et al. 2023) is a form of research about the nature of practice where the investigation is conducted by the practitioners and critically from inside the world-of-concern. This is a rigorous and robust research type, that brings new knowledge about, among other things, the experiential nature of practice, frameworks for understanding practice, embodied relationships and perceptions through practice, and ontological models of making practice. While a criticism of this approach is the lack of breadth in the primary data that it gathers, it more than makes up for this lack by the depth of knowledge and insights that it generates. The latter defines our approach to this research and involves many years of developing design iterations, testing and rebuilding the AI from the inside.

The investigation underpinning *Solaris* was to seek to understand how an AI built on the principles laid out above could be considered an integral part of the musicking experience by stimulating an acute sense of being in the same immersive flow as human musicians. Furthermore, we were interested in finding out what music would it make. And how this was received by real-world audiences.

For us to investigate how *Solaris* stimulated and mediated mutual perceptions of responsivity and liveness we needed not to fall foul of a human-centric bias. As such, in the language we used (and still use) and in the system designs we built there is no hierarchical distinction between human musicians and the AI, all of whom are central to the musicking decision-making process. In *Solaris*, humans and AI are engaged in the shared endeavour of musicking, sensing each other's activities and being attuned to the flow of their shared environment, which is the musical world.

Our deliberate choice of jazz as the musical style for *Solaris* was because this style represents a rich domain through which we could explore the tension between improvisation and expert knowledge, as Torrance and Schumann (2019) noted. To this end, the project's first phase, between 2019 and 2020, was the creation of an unprecedented, embodied dataset, capturing multidimensional interrelationships of professional musicians playing a standard jazz piece. The process of capturing and creating this dataset, as well as a detailed analysis of its results and training *Solaris'* neural networks, is detailed in two other papers (Vear et al. 2024; Poltronieri and Vear 2024).

11.2.2 Crafting Process 1: Building the Dataset

In Vear et al. (2024), we discuss in detail the process of designing, building and testing an "embodied musicking dataset". To build a gold-standard dataset, we formalised the process and used a single backing track that would act as a strict matrix for the dataset. We also designed a self-labelling process. 10 musicians each performing a series of solos, were employed, and the dataset was built. This was meant as a proof-of-concept activity, with the aim of expanding the contributions if the dataset proved effective. We started with data collected from musicians performing "How Deep is the Ocean" since this composition is a well-known standard. The choice of a standard was also decided by the fact that one of our research objectives was to observe whether new patterns, in the spirit of free jazz, could emerge from training neural networks using more rigid patterns.

The dataset captured physiological and psychological data of solo musicians improvising from these three domains:

- Performed-world music: Backing track audio and associated score organisation (mono). Audio recording of the piano (mono). Video of hands and fingers (embedded with the audio track).
- Embodied musicking: Electroencephalogram EEG [from BrainBit]. Electro-Dermal Activity EDA (arousal from Bitalino). Body tracking (using the Cubemos Skeleton SDK from the Intel Real Sense depth tracking camera).
- Flow protocol analysis (post-recording): Self-flow-evaluation as a sliding scale.

Each musician improvised 3 to 5 times, selecting their best 3 for inclusion into the dataset. They played through five choruses of the tune in the format: head, improv 1, improv 2, improv 3, head recap. After each improvisation, they listened back to it and scored their recollection of their depth of flow using a sliding scale. This operated as the labelling parameter. It is interesting to note, that each musician selected only their 'best' recordings for the dataset, meaning that the dataset only contains perceived 'good' performance, as such the dataset does not contain any data for poor or lacklustre flow.

11.2.3 Crafting Process 2: Conceptualising Embodiment as AI

In order to conceptualise the theoretical hypothesis of this project in a real-world situation it was necessary to conceptualise an AI architecture that mirrored aspects of musicking. In short—as it is not the remit of this paper to outline the AI design in detail—we designed a modular design of:

- Layer 1—*Percept input and formatting*. This module manages all the real-time input data from a single audio input and sends it to the AI factory and gesture manager for processing. It can be thought of as its *umwelt* (windows to the world) and is a critical module for connecting to (perhaps perceiving) specific attributes of the outside (musicking) world with the AI Factory.
- Layer 2—*AI Factory*. This module generates constant streams of data from the four neural network models in the AI factory. This is a free-flowing loop with all RNNs predicting live (at 10 Hz). The purpose is to generate a constant flow of predicted data from each model, emulating a busy mind negotiating options inside musicking, regardless of whether it gets used or not in the following Layers.
- Layer 3—*Gesture manager (Affect)*. This module chooses one of the outputs from the AI factory (layer 2), or live input stream (layer 1) and holds this stream for a few seconds (randomly chosen between 2–8 s) before randomly choosing the next. There is also a 'startled' effect that interrupts and momentarily scrambles the other layers if the audio amplitude or data predictions are over an intensity threshold. It operates as the AI's affectual response manager to inputs from Layer 1.
- Layer 4—*Belief system*. This module takes the single output stream from the gesture manager (layer 3) and uses its value to determine which instrument will play and which note to play. It also sends conditions to the visual generator to convey its perceptual experience.

Each of these layers is key and discussed in detail in Vear and Benerradi 2024. But it's worth concentrating on Layer 4—the belief system. In Vear (2021) we define the AI belief system of EMR as an extension of Russell and Norvig (2002) discussion of it in their book *Artificial Intelligence: A Modern Approach* as:

> It might seem odd to implement belief into the AI of a robot, given that this term usually refers to religious or spiritual faith, but it is the broader definition of this word that I am particularly interested. Specifically, *EMR* has an acceptance that something is true, or that it has trust or confidence in something from the perspective of the role its belief system plays in the behaviour of EMR. (Vear 2021, after Russell and Norvig 2002)

11.2.3.1 The AI Factory Defines When to Play

For *Solaris*—which is an evolutionary point on the larger EMR project, and shares many inner workings and theories discussed in this chapter—the belief system is a set of symbolic rules that governs what the AI plays. The AI factory defines *when* it plays and controls its behaviours. This, we believe, is a crucial element in the reach of this approach. And even though the embodied musicking dataset contains musical media, the models trained in the AI factory used only two features from the dataset: a single point of the pianist's movement (their nose position) and their arousal data (electro-dermal activity: EDA). In total 5 models were created with inputs from either the live amplitude of the audio signal or a predicted output from another NNet. They are:

- NNet1 (MoveRNN) time series LSTM trained on sequential data from the musicians' skeleton_data.nose.x. In performance, the input is its own predicted output.
- NNet2 (AffectRNN) convolution 2D model trained on movement data from skeleton_data.nose.x to predict the affect/ arousal data from the EDA. In performance, the input is its own output.
- NNet3 (MoveAffectCONV2) convolution 2D model trained on movement data from skeleton_data.nose.x to predict the affect/ arousal data from the EDA. In performance, the input is its own predicted output.
- NNet4 (AffectMoveCONV2) convolution 2D model trained on affect/ arousal data from the EDA to predict the movement data from skeleton_data.nose.x. In performance the input is NNet2.
- NNet5 convolution 2D model trained on movement data from skeleton_data.nose.x to predict the affect/ arousal data from the EDA. In performance, the input is the live microphone amplitude.

11.2.3.2 The AI Has Never Heard Jazz

It is important to stress that in this design the AI has never heard jazz. Nor has it been trained on the symbolic representation of jazz music (e.g., midi notes). Its only reference to jazz harmony is the chord sequence that it is given per song (Table 11.1), and a matrix with which to interpret George Russell's *Lydian Chromatic Concept of Tonal Organization* (Russell 1959) (defined in Table 11.2 by only 7 lines of code). Beyond that, the jazz music that it creates is built on the relationships that are formed through improvisation.

11.2.4 Crafting 3—Embodying Solaris as a Digital Score

To this point, the practice-based research had been developing the behaviours of the AI through a series of practical experiments with Vear and the AI and had taken nearly 4 years. The second part of the project involved developing strategies for embodying and communicating *Solaris* with the real world i.e., the human musician and the audience. This phase designed and built by Poltronieri, resulted in developing a graphic interface for the project, which works like a digital score (Fig. 11.2),

Table 11.1 All the information that AI receives about a particular song. In this case, *I Wish I Knew How It Would Feel To Be Free* by Billy Jenkins[1]

```
"i_wish_i_knew": {"name": "i_wish_i_knew",
            "harmonic_prog": [
             # verse
             ("F", "I", 2, None), ("A", "II", 2, None), ("D", "VI", 2, None), ("C", "VI", 2, None),
             ("Bb", "II", 2, None), ("Bb", "II", 2, "C"), ("F", "I", 2, None), ("Bb", "II", 2, "C"),
             ("F", "I", 2, None), ("Bb", "II", 1, None), ("F", "I", 1, None), ("F", "I", 2, None), ("C",
"III", 1, "E"), ("F", "I", 1, None),
             ("C", "II", 2, "G"), ("G", "II", 2, None), ("C", "II", 2, None), ("Bb", "II", 2, "C"),
             ("F", "I", 2, None), ("A", "II", 2, None), ("D", "VI", 2, None), ("C", "VI", 2, None),
             ("Bb", "II", 2, None), ("Bb", "II", 2, "C"), ("F", "I", 2, None), ("B", "+IV", 2, None),
             ("F", "V", 2, "C"), ("C#", "+IV", 2, None), ("D", "VI", 2, None), ("B", "+IV", 2, None),
             ("F", "V", 2, "C"), ("Bb", "II", 2, "C"), ("F", "I", 2, None), ("F", "I", 2, None),
             ],
             "bpm": 120,
             "time_sig": (4, 4),
             "ticks": 2},
```

Table 11.2 The *Lydian Chromatic Concept of Tonal Organization* matrix referenced by *Solaris* AI

```
scale_patterns: list = [
   (2, 2, 2, 1, 2, 2),
   (2, 2, 2, 2, 1, 2),
   (2, 1, 3, 1, 2, 2),
   (2, 2, 2, 1, 2, 1),
   (2, 2, 2, 2, 1),
   (2, 1, 2, 1, 2, 1, 2),
   (1, 2, 1, 2, 1, 2, 1),
]
```

acting in conjunction with the sonic aspect of the AI. This digital score phenomenologically informs the human musician through a visual language, providing sensory information about the mood of the rhythm section that forms the core of the *Solaris* AI.

According to Vear 2019, a digital score is characterized by being a technically mediated communications interface that enhances how ideas in music can be represented. The digital score developed in this phase enables the *Solaris* AI to communicate its presence, behaviour and responses to the outside world. As such, it helps stimulate the sensation of joint action when performing with human musicians. The development of this digital score adhered to our understanding of media from an inside perspective, that of how it shapes and controls "the scale and form of human association and action" (McLuhan 1964). In this instance, it doesn't employ semantic symbols and notational languages but communicates a sense of being in the shared

[1] A version of this song can be heard here https://www.youtube.com/watch?v=jlH_XFuf3wU.

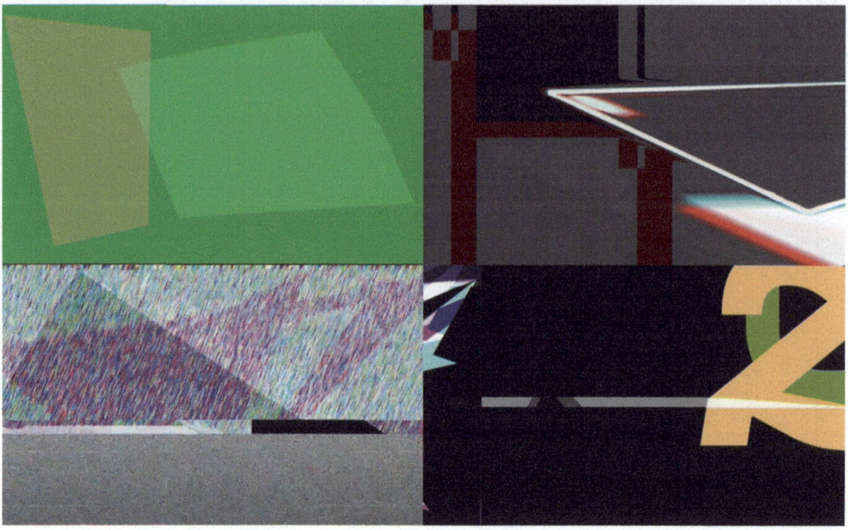

Fig. 11.2 *Solaris*' visual interface, displaying 4 different frames of its digital score

flow with the human, and crucially communicates a musical idea to the human musicians.

In our participatory observation process, described in the next section and in Poltronieri and Vear (2024), we noticed that,

> from the human point of view, notions of self-representation within *musicking* together within *Solaris* gain new representations, mainly through the mediation generated by the continuous interface that is a constituent part of the digital score. The digital score helps to define the space for *musicking* to take place, to establish with the music a constant link between the artificial and the human minds – both endowed with the ability to make mental representations – and to provide a space for creative invention.

Just as the movements of the bodies of human musicians improvising communicate to their peers their experience of their musicking (Bishop 2024), the visual forms of this digital score inform human musicians of the internal movements of *Solaris* AI architecture, thereby giving a "body" to this artificial musician as well as communicating intention, density, and direction through the flow. It is important to emphasise that *Solaris'* digital score differs from a classical score, which brings detailed information on how the music should be performed. *Solaris*' digital score is a set of abstract shapes and colours providing a feeling, along with the sound, about the piece in question, open to interpretation and improvisation and embracing the affectual and phenomenological properties of the media. In this way, the communicology of *Solaris* takes place through the sounds produced and the poetic visual representations of the internal state (perceptual experience) of its architecture through a digital score. The digital score is projected for the human musicians to interact with when performing.

11.2.4.1 Testing Solaris: In the 'Real-World'

Over 2023–24 *Solaris* performed several concerts in front of public and academic audiences to pressure-test the quality of the musicking experience in a real-world space (i.e. outside of the laboratory). Each performance was logged on the project's Bandcamp page and can be heard as a catalogue of development https://solarisjazz.bandcamp.com/. Notable examples are:

- First official demo's: https://solarisjazz.bandcamp.com/album/tree-mountains-demos-2024 December 2023—February 2024
- First public performance https://solarisjazz.bandcamp.com/album/tree-mountains-live-at-the-bell-beeston-nott—May 2024
- Demo's from a studio recording session in August 2024—https://solarisjazz.bandcamp.com/album/tree-mountains-rough-mixes-from-session
- Full length performance in Australia—https://solarisjazz.bandcamp.com/album/tree-mountains-live-at-monash-music-vic (October 2024).

11.2.5 Testing Solaris: Performing with Other Human Musicians and Evaluation

After 5 years of development, deployment and public-facing testing, we felt that we had arrived at a stable system and decided to conduct two sets of tests to evaluate *Solaris'* capabilities in terms of its performance with other human musicians (2023–24). In both, we paid close attention to the relationships, stimulation, and the sensation of musicking with *Solaris*.

For the first test, we invited three professional drummers to play with *Solaris*. These three were from different backgrounds:

1. The first drummer has an international reputation for performing free jazz, although does perform more mainstream jazz on occasions.
2. The second was a mainstream jazz drummer, who plays in professional situations with tunes but is happy to improvise freely. However, he wouldn't consider himself to be comfortable with free jazz playing.
3. The third drummer straddles both free and mainstream jazz.

These tests were conducted in December 2023, with each drummer offered the same three tracks to perform with *Solaris*. They performed each track 3 times and reported their responses to each performance using a scale of 1–10, through an online survey that asked the following questions. These questions explicitly focused on the perception of *Solaris* as an intelligent musician and were designed to help us understand how it shapes and controls "the scale and form of human association and action" (McLuhan 1964):

1. Have you had any previous experience regarding AI and music?
2. How likely are you to respond positively to AI being creative?

3. Did you **believe** that the AI was in the here-and-now of jazz improvisation?
4. How **deeply** did you believe the AI was making it up in the moment?
5. Was the AI **behaviour** predictable or inspiring?
6. How deeply did you **feel** you and the AI were in the *flow* together?
7. Did you **trust** that the AI was aware of you and your playing?
8. Did you have the same sense of **closeness** and **togetherness** as a human-only improvising ensemble?

It is interesting to note that the free drummer (number 1) was not comfortable with the proposition and withdrew from the evaluation process. The responses from drummers 2 and 3, illustrated a growing sense of togetherness, trust and immersion with *Solaris*. As illustrated by Fig. 11.3, both drummer's responses to questions 1 and 2 grew in line with their familiarity to performing with AI, much like the degree of trustworthiness musicians grow after repeated performances together. In Fig. 11.4, there is clearly a general trend upwards across all the iterations of performing with *Solaris* (questions 3–8). Interesting to note the general trend of a dip with every group of three events. And of particular interest is the last grouping of 2 with drummer 2: Unfortunately, his last data was corrupted and was deleted, but the last data point in this chart dipped significantly in the same way as his 2nd data point did, and this was ascribed to him purposefully choosing not to look at the digital score, but to concentrate on the sound only.

Following the recording sessions, the drummers were asked to reflect on their experience overall. Their responses were:

Drummer 2

> I came into this situation with no prior exposure or expectations of the involvement of AI with improvised music. As a musician working solely in acoustic environments with very little digital or synthesized inputs, it would be fair to say I may have even been on the side of cynical about any contribution an AI could make to a musical setting. Straight out of the blocks I enjoyed the challenge of working with *Solaris*, it was interesting trying different approaches to engaging with the stimulus. Using the metric cues on screen was challenging but rewarding, and switching off and engaging with only the audio was equally rewarding and perhaps more organic. I imagine there will be a certain amount of resistance to music created in this was amongst traditional and purist music circles, but I can wholeheartedly say I had a most enjoyable morning exploring the possibility of this music format. I would

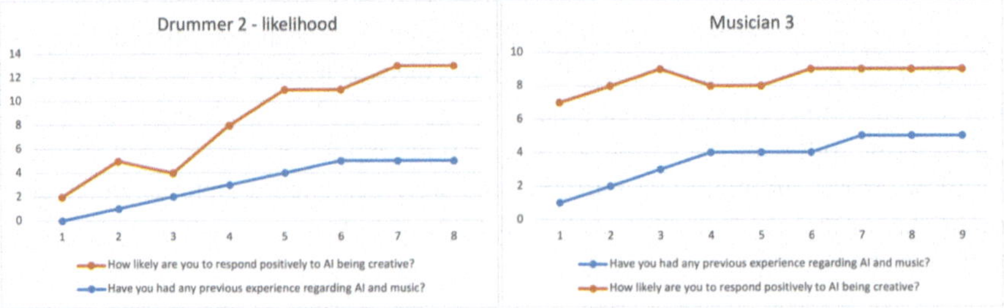

Fig. 11.3 Drummers 2 and 3 reported bias/likelihood to respond positively to AI

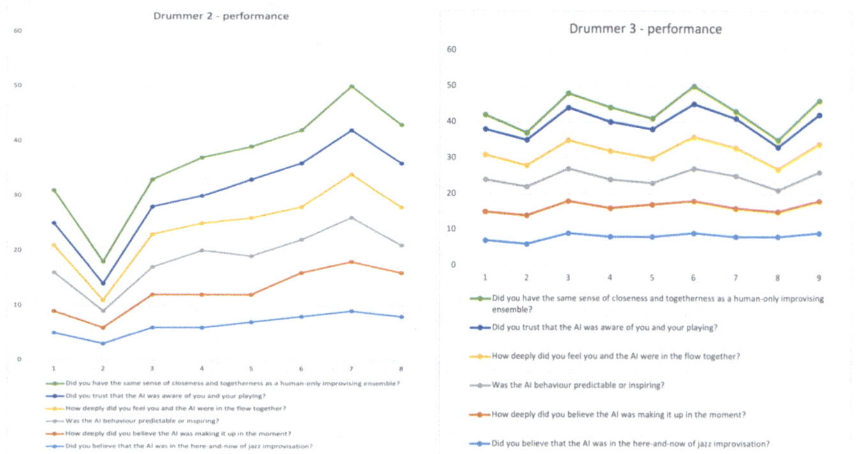

Fig. 11.4 Drummers 2 and 3 responses to performing with *Solaris*

be very interested to see where this project goes and how it can be transferred to the stage/studio for public consumption.

Drummer 3

What an exciting project to be invited to play on! Not only from the perspective of performance with AI (with which, I have absolutely no prior experience), but also the possibilities proposed in terms of education, for learning and the development of improvisation skills. My first response to the music and process of the AI recordings was the consistency of note count and relative lack of dynamic compared to live musicians. This was probably the most difficult aspect of the performance for me, but with repeat performances, the 'ensemble' nature created by the AI and myself simply became an accepted mode – much in the same way any set group of musicians might present. It was interesting to offer up the option of supplying the melody line of the pieces and to subvert this as each improvisation developed (a strategy which the AI players did seem to also reflect). The most interesting part, for me at least, was your proposal to change the parameter of the piano 'temperature', so that more space was created in the note count of the piano's improvisations: This immediately brought musical breadth and made the AI contributions feel more dynamic in terms of both volume/intensity, and of course, time-space in the final item performance. I thought this made for a much more musical and, dare I say, 'human' outcome!?

11.2.6 Second Test RENCON

The second test involved Vear recording a series of demo tracks with *Solaris* and circulating them amongst a critical music-technology-based community, in the hope of gathering measured and insightful responses. This process centred around a single track, although all 8 tracks were provided. This track was "I Wish I Knew How It Feels To Be Free",[2] which is a solo piano performance with the AI perceiving its own

[2] https://solarisjazz.bandcamp.com/track/franks-mood.

sound as it plays. This track was chosen as both authors felt that it articulated the central hypothesis for the question of musicking without distracting the observations with human musicking. In short, it was a raw, warts-and-all test of the musicking potential of *Solaris*. The authors also felt that when compared to the recording of the original composer,[3] *Solaris's* version demonstrated an extraordinary invention that was surprising. This phenomenon is heightened when you consider that the AI had never heard this original track, or any jazz recordings and that all it 'knows' about this tune is the song chords (see Table 11.1), and all it knows about jazz harmony is outlined in Table 11.2.

As part of the process of garnering comments, they were also asked to complete a Likert scale on the question "What or who created this recording: AI or a human?". This scale suggested that opinions as to the "What or who" was split in the middle: "unsure" and "maybe AI". But the free comments were much more divisive ranging from "The tracks sound great", "Very interesting" and "Yes! Simultaneous experience of humour and pathos", to much more visceral responses such as "I only listened a minute of it and it really sucks", "It sounds definitely 'robotic'", "Sounds like a student trying to write serial or algorithmic music" and [our favourite] "Thinking about all the processing power, energy, carbon emitted to create that. My cat could come up with something similar with just the tiniest amounts of methane".

From the authors' perspective, however, playing with *Solaris* felt like they were being taken on a journey through the music in each of the demos, forcing them to consider ingrained patterns, and stimulating them to think up new creative solutions and responses in the moment. The diverse comments following our lightweight RENCON listening test highlight that perhaps the "proof-in-the-pudding" with embodied AI is in the realm of embodied musicking.

11.3 Discussion

In this section, we discuss some of the main issues that emerged from our research investigation. It is important to stress that our focus on designing and developing an artificial musician, is from a bottom-up, insider perspective. Furthermore, that our understanding of media and musicking is equally from this perspective and how they shape and control "the scale and form of human association and action" (McLuhan 1964). For us, the AI, its behaviours, the digital score design, and the music the AI and the human make together are bound through this insider perspective with relationships reinforced through many years of developmental stages. It seems natural to us, therefore, to lean into the philosophical meaning of such relationships and to highlight the importance of perceptual experience, and sentience, as a core attribute in understanding artificial media.

[3] https://www.youtube.com/watch?v=jlH_XFuf3wU.

11.3.1 Does Solaris *Have Perceptual Experience?*

If we are to maintain an allegiance to Robert Kirk's 'basic package' and to view perceptual experience by relying on *Solaris'* 'behaviour and what goes on inside their bodies' (or code for AI), then we can speculatively say that *Solaris* does tick all the criteria for perceptual experience. For example, *Solaris* does have 'perception and pure reflex' of its musicking-world through listening and responding in real time, this includes the "startled" effect which will force changes in the gesture manager module (introduced above) if a loud sound or high-intensity prediction is encountered, it also has a pseudo affect system which it uses to inform its gestural responses back into the musicking-world consisting of low, mid and high behavioral traits. It also has 'perception and control 'as it acquires data of its musicking-world in real time and uses this to interpret, assess and choose a response. Also through its belief system, it has goals that it strives to attain. It also uses 'information *for* the system' through real-time analysis, temperature ratings, and the vertical gravities of Russell's Lydian Chromatic Concept (LCC). *Solaris* features 'interdependent capabilities', using trains of thought and drunken walks to negotiate the musicking-world. And finally, it utilizes 'concepts and language' such as the Lydian modes of LCC and how it constructs and communicates a harmonic world for all. Furthermore, it uses the belief system to navigate the real-time interactions and mutual perceptions of liveness and responsivity that we define in the 3 nested principles (above).

11.3.2 Could We (Dare We) Talk About Sentience?

Sentience (from the Latin *sentire,* to feel) means the ability of beings to feel sensations and have perceptions of their surroundings and what happens to them. Proctor (2012) argues that one of the key issues with understanding sentience and demonstrating its existence at a scientific level is that the concept relates to a being's own thoughts, feelings and emotions, none of which can be fully understood by physiological processes or anatomical structures. As a result, sentience is often described as anthropomorphic assumptions, in other words, the attribution of human characteristics to animals or AI.

Let us take as our starting point the concept that we want to dismantle and playfully lean into it through our research with *Solaris.* The concept, still dominant in AI studies (Hull 2023), is that the most pertinent question to be answered is whether "AI is sentient". This question is based on the Cartesian assumption that sentience and personhood are closely related terms, stipulating that language is evidence of this. The main interest of this exercise is to define what sentience is and whether an entity such as an artificial musician (or artificial medium) could possess it.

The views of René Descartes, whose philosophical and scientific beliefs led to the creation of Cartesianism, on sentience outside the human sphere are well known, especially about animals. Descartes believed that animals are just complex living machines, responding to external stimuli in the same way that machines react to specific triggers. In his 1636 *Discourse on Method* (Descartes 2014), he contends that even if animals sometimes behave as if they have some desires, feelings, sensations, or other mental states or processes, we should not be deceived by these appearances, as they do not correspond to anything genuinely mental.

It was not until the Enlightenment of the eighteenth century that philosophers started to accept the notion that animals have feelings. Duncan (2006) points to the fact that in the last 50 years the concept of animals being sentient, or "capable of experiencing positive and negative affective states", has become a topic of great interest to biologists.

Descartes developed an ontological thesis about the kind of thing minds are as features of the world and an epistemological thesis about how things of that kind could be known, making a fundamental distinction between minds, which think, and everything else, which is at most a machine. To explain how the human mind inhabits a body, he states that the human body is merely a machine, but made by the hands of God, who unites a rational soul to this machine (Descartes 2014), advocating a form of dualism for which the mind and body are mutually exclusive categories. "Minds" are things that can think, where access to minds can be secured by means of a faculty known as "introspection", which is a kind of inward perception of a person's own mental states (Fetzer 2004).

Later, in Meditations (Descartes 1984), he says that the rational soul is a "thinking thing", something that doubts, understands, affirms, denies, is willing, is unwilling and also imagines and has sensory perceptions. Although Descartes never adequately resolves the question of how perception happens, he consistently puts sentience and consciousness into the category of mind, which is restricted to the rational soul of human beings.

Hull (2023) highlights the fact that debates around AI and sentience have historically taken the early modern period, and Descartes in particular, as a starting point. In this view, a sentient AI is impossible, as it would just be a complex device reacting to external stimuli without being aware of its actions. Alan Turing was aware of these limitations when he introduced what has come to be known as the computational conception of the mind, which inverts the Cartesian account of machines as mindless by turning minds themselves into special kinds of machines, where the boundaries of computability define the boundaries of thought (Fetzer 2004).

Hull summarizes the problems with the Cartesian approach to AI:

> Whatever theory of mind underlies current AI work, this Cartesian attitude is persistent in a number of deficiencies in the literature on AI that have been the subject recent of critical attention. It persists in the tendency to look at algorithms in isolation, without paying attention to their deployment in algorithmic systems. It persists in the tendency to treat "fairness" as a formalizable concept that can be operationalized independently of its context. It persists in the isolation of technical academic work on AI from other disciplines that are more concerned with social impacts. And it persists in the quest to determine whether an AI is conscious at the expense of assessing its current socio-political implications. Whether or not an AI can be conscious or sentient in the Cartesian sense may well turn out to be unknowable. (Hull 2023, 196)

The author concludes that in the face of all this uncertainty, we need an alternative, proposing "the Hobbesian Alternative" (Hull 2023, 196), replacing the Cartesian question—"is AI sentient?"– with a more Hobbesian one: "How should we regulate AI systems that behave as if they are sentient?". Hull suggests this alternative based on the assumption that Thomas Hobbes extended a mechanistic treatment of body into mind as well, making Hobbe's mechanistic account of thinking seems initially attractive from an AI standpoint because it "explicitly reduces thinking to computation" (Hull 2023, 196). Such an alternative is promising, and Hull develops it further in his paper. However, we would like to propose a third way, more attuned to our theoretical and practical research in the light of *Solaris*.

11.3.3 AI as a Type of Mind

Our playful exercise continues and asks, "What is Sentience for in Creative AI?", allowing us to deal with the idea of creative collaboration between human and artificial minds, the kind of collaboration we observe in *Solaris*. For this, we need to understand how AI and artificial media in general, can be considered a type of mind. We do so based on Charles Sanders Peirce's theory of synechism.

Synechism is the branch of Peirce's metaphysics that deals with continuity, the connection between mind and matter:

> I carry the doctrine [continuity] so far as to maintain that continuity governs the whole domain of experience in every element of it. Accordingly, every proposition, except so far as it relates to an unattainable limit of experience (which I call the Absolute), is to be taken with an indefinite qualification; for a proposition which has no relation whatever to experience is devoid of all meaning. (Peirce 1992, xx)

The philosophical conception that underpins synechism is generous, as it does not separate mind—spirit—and body—matter –, breaking with a Cartesian tradition. In the Peircian conception, the human mind differs from other mental forms, such as those observed in AI, in that it is the most plastic reality of the entire known universe, the one with the greatest level of malleability for change (Peirce 1992).

The semiotic field of sign processes, from computers to living systems, has often been analysed in Cartesian dualisms: 'tool vs instruments', 'instruments vs machines' and above all 'machines vs living beings'. Rather than confirming these dualisms, Peirce describes this field as a continuum of symbolic processing from the simplest to the most complex. Among the less complex systems are those mediated by instruments or technical devices such as a thermometer or an automatic traffic system. The most complex semiotic systems occur in living beings. According to synechism, there is no separation or division, but differences of degree between nature and culture, the organic and the inorganic, the natural and the artificial.

Synechism should be understood as continuity between mind and matter, the latter also being a form of mind, but more exhausted and tired, especially if placed next to, for comparison purposes, the human mind. This connatural aspect enables a communicational flow between the various types of minds we observe in the universe, including AI. The mind in artworks allows contemplation or listening to be a dialogue and not just a discourse or narrative to be observed or listened to. In the same way, there is an active mind in *Solaris*, a sentient mind that participates in *musicking*. Synechism is a crucial concept for understanding Peircian metaphysics, based on the pragmatic idea of continuity and evolution, as we observe when human musicians play along with *Solaris*.

According to Peirce (1992), everything that makes up the universe is a mental form because its physical laws are derived from psychic models, so the great law of the universe is the law of the mind. This law is found in the tendency to generalise and form associations, which is also the tendency to acquire habits, itself a habit. For Peirce (1992), all of reality is governed by the law of mind, that is, the law to acquire habits from the purely physical world to the human mind, with the difference, as we have noted, that the human mind does not submit to the law in the same rigid way that matter does. That is why the matter is a mind so locked into habits that it ceases to exhibit the same spontaneous behaviour that is abundant in the human mind. This is particularly true for objects that retain their solidified form, such as stones. However, AI like *Solaris* exhibits a very spontaneous and diverse pattern of behaviour with remarkable plasticity, resembling the human mind.

Synechism reinforces the possibility of the existence of a creative sensibility in Creative-AI systems like *Solaris* because, according to Peirce (1992), no matter how exact the theories are and how highly predictive they are, the more precise the instruments, techniques, methods and expertise employed by the researcher in the search for truth, the more deviations from the norm will be found, i.e. the more variables and irregularities the object will reveal. Peirce's originality lies in the fact that he attributes this not only to errors of human nature, i.e., imperfections on the part of the observer but also to a chance present in the object of study, which is alive and pulsating.

Peirce brings us the realisation that everything we can know is purely mental since intelligence can only act on what is intelligible. Synechism opens the door to an unimpeded understanding of sentience in AI. The connaturality between representation and the real object eliminates the Cartesian barrier between subject and object, between sentience and the world. This free boundary is already present in Peircian phenomenology since, under its prism, all phenomena pass through interiority—phenomena as they are—and exteriority—appearance, how we perceive phenomena—in an undifferentiated way. To understand and utilise the doctrine of synechism, we must admit that if the material and the embodied universe are provided with habits of conduct in the form of natural laws, we must conceive of it as a form of mind. We feel that performing with *Solaris* establishes a semiotic way of communicating with the sentient mind that exists in AI and that this is a generalisable way forward for research in this field and within artificial media research in general.

11.4 Conclusion

As conclusion, we return back to our three nested guiding principles for an artificial musician, that it must:

1. cope with the dynamic flow (Csikszentmihalyi 1975) of musicking [
    a. have a musically attuned basic package for perceptual experience [
        i. maintain a sense of musical togetherness]]

These three nested principles are three among many that could be chosen to define the behaviours of an artificial musician. They do define the core attributes that are essential to musicking, and so we can confidently state that these are the minimum requirements for an artificial musician. Furthermore, they focus on how it shapes and controls "the scale and form of human association and action" (McLuhan 1964), and could be considered essential attributes when considering artificial media from a bottom-up, insider perspective of the practitioner.

We believe that *Solaris* met these conditions and that the only pathway was to craft an approach from scratch as there is very little to build on given the current state-of-the-art. We also believe that the depth of the investigation in the initial 4 years through practice-based means led to deeper insights, designs and music than if we had aimed for a broader observational research approach involving multiple participants requesting features, and suggesting concepts and solutions.

We also present an argument for re-considering creative AI to be sentient within a specific context, and from a certain perspective. We believe that one way to develop a proper symbiotic creative ecosystem between artificial media and human musicians is to meet in the domain where creativity is happening. In this instance: inside *musicking*. Going one step further, we hypothesise, based on Peirce's synechism theory that current AI constitutes a type of mind. It is this characteristic that makes it possible for AI to communicate with the human mind and for a sentient ecosystem to emerge; especially if the AI is reaching outside of its black-box and sensing the world through appropriate percepts. Peirce's synechism assumes that continuity always prevails, and the assumption of such continuity is of fundamental methodological importance. Minds are continuous entities, constantly changing and always in flux, as *Solaris* is.

We acknowledge that this is just one experiment, and one instance of creative AI co-operating symbiotically within one context, but due to the openness of our crafting approach, refusal to be swayed by out-the-box AI, and our guiding principles, we found that—while inside *musicking*—the musicians who engaged with the experimental practice seemed to be rewarded with *Solaris*.

Acknowledgments The Digital Score project (DigiScore) is funded by the European Research Council (ERC) under the European Union's Horizon 2020 research and innovation programme (Grant agreement No. ERC-2020-COG – 101002086).

References

Bhagwati S (2017) Vexations of ephemerality. In: Proceedings of the international conference on technologies for music notation and representation (TENOR'17), Coruna, Spain, pp 161–166

Bishop L (2024) Togetherness in musical interaction. Routledge Open Res 3(16):16

Bishop L (2018) Collaborative musical creativity: how ensembles coordinate spontaneity. Front Psychol 9:1285

Candy L, Edmonds, Ernest V (2023) Knowledge in Vear (ed) 2023 The Routledge international handbook of practice-based research. London: Routledge

Civit M, Civit-Masot J, Cuadrado F, Escalona MJ (2022) A systematic review of artificial intelligence-based music generation: Scope, applications, and future trends. Expert Syst Appl 209:118190

Csikszentmihalyi M (1975) Beyond boredom and anxiety: experiencing flow in work and play. Jossey-Bass, San Francisco

Descartes R (Translated by Donald A. Cress) (2014) Discourse on method. Indianapolis: Hackett Publishing

Descartes R (1984) The philosophical writings of descartes. Cambridge University Press, Cambridge

Devenish L, Hope C, McAuliffe S (2024) Contemporary musical virtuosities. In: Contemporary musical virtuosities, pp 1–13. Routledge

Duncan I (2006) The changing concept of animal sentience. Appl An Behav Sci 100(1):11–19

Fetzer J (2004) Peirce and the philosophy of artificial intelligence. The commens encyclopaedia: the digital encyclopaedia of Peirce studies

Hull G (2023) Unlearning descartes: sentient AI is a political problem. J Soc Comput 4(3):193–204

Kirk R (2017) Robots, Zombies and us: understanding consciousness. Bloomsbury, London

Leman M (2007) Embodied music cognition and mediation technology. MIT Press

McCormack J, Gifford T, Hutchings P, Llano Rodriguez MT, Yee-King M, d'Inverno M (2019) In a silent way: Communication between ai and improvising musicians beyond sound. In: Proceedings of the 2019 chi conference on human factors in computing systems, pp 1–11. 2019

McLuhan M (1964) Understanding media: the extension of man. Routledge, New York

Peirce CS (1992) The essential Peirce, Volume 1: selected philosophical writings (1867–1893). Indianapolis: Indiana University Press

Poltronieri F (2022) Towards a symbiotic future: art and creative AI. In: The language of creative AI: practices, aesthetics and structures, pp 29–41. Cham: Springer International Publishing

Poltronieri F, Vear (2024) ISEA—Awaiting publication

Proctor H (2012) Animal sentience: where are we and where are we heading? Animals 2(4):628–639

Ramalho GL, Rolland P-Y, Ganascia J-G (1999) An artificially intelligent jazz performer. J New Music Res 28(2):105–129

Russell G (1959) The Lydian chromatic concept of tonal organization for improvisation. Concept Publishing Company

Russell S, Norvig P (2002) Artificial intelligence: a modern approach, global edition, 2nd edition. Published by Prentice Hall

Schiavio A, Witek MAG, Stupacher J (2024) Meaning-making and creativity in musical entrainment. Frontiers Psychol 14:1326773

Schiavio A, Høffding S (2015) Playing together without communicating? A pre-reflective and enactive account of joint musical performance. Musicae Scientiae 19(4):366–388

Small C (1998) Musicking: the meanings of performance and listening. Wesleyan University Press, Middletown

Solaris 2024. Web page. https://solarisjazz.bandcamp.com/. Accessed 4 July 2024

Tahiroğlu K (2022) Evolving musical expectations: Mutual correlation between a human musician and an AI musical instrument. Embodied gestures, pp 30–36. Technische Universität Wien

Torrance S, Schumann F (2019) The spur of the moment: what Jazz improvisation tells cognitive science. In AI & Soc 34:251–268

Vear (2022) Embodied AI and musicking robotics. In: The language of creative AI: practices, aesthetics and structures, pp 113–135. Cham: Springer International Publishing
Vear (2019) The digital score. Routledge, London
Vear C (2021) Creative AI and musicking robots. Front Robot AI 8:631752
Vear C, Benneradi J (2024) Jess+: designing embodied AI for interactive music-making. ArXiv https://arxiv.org/abs/2412.06469
Vear C, Poltronieri F, DiDonato B, Zhang Y, Benerradi J, Hutchinson S, Turowski P, Shell J, Malekmohamadi H (2024) Building an Embodied Musicking Dataset for co-creative music-making. In: International conference on computational intelligence in music, sound, art and design (Part of EvoStar), pp 373–388. Cham: Springer Nature Switzerland

Craig Vear is Professor of Music and Computer Science at the University of Nottingham split between music and the mixed reality lab. His research is naturally hybrid as he draws together the fields of music, digital performance, creative technologies, Artificial Intelligence, creativity, gaming, mixed reality and robotics. He has been engaged in practice-based research with emerging technologies for nearly three decades, and was editor for The Routledge International Handbook of Practice-Based Research, published in 2022. His recent monograph The Digital Score: creativity, musicianship and innovation, was published by Routledge in 2019, and he is Series Editor of Springer's Cultural Computing Series. In 2021 he was awarded a €2Million ERC Consolidator Grant to continue to develop his Digital Score research.

Fabrizio Poltronieri is an award-winning computer artist, designer, researcher and curator with a special interest in the relationships between Art, Design, Digital Media, Gamification, and Technology. His expertise lies in the development of creative coding and its exchanges with philosophical questions.

Chapter 12
'Trás-os-Mundos, Outros Douros'—Constructing Retrofuturistic Narratives Through Artificial Intelligence

Mário Moura

Abstract This chapter reflects on the author's experiences with image generation using Artificial Intelligence over two years, from February 2022 to 2024. The process began informally and without structure. Focusing on the Douro region in Portugal, it quickly developed into a narrative incorporating elements of world-building, science fiction, retro-futurism, and alternate realities. Using an auto-ethnographic methodology, the chapter argues that this type of narrative emerged organically as a way to navigate the formal limitations and possibilities of image-generation platforms. AI generates stereotypes, but it is possible to build truthful narratives using these stereotypes as building blocks. The contrast between futuristic forms and impoverished, degraded peripheral landscapes reflects the sociocultural context of this region. The text advocates that generative AI can be a powerful tool for civic intervention as well as for theoretical and critical reflection.

Keywords Worldbuilding as civic intervention · Autoethnography · Generative AI · Retrofuturism

12.1 Introduction

This chapter provides a reflective account of the author's journey in generating images on online AI platforms over two years, from 2022 to 2024, capturing both the evolution of the project and the insights gained through the process.

Initially, there was no intention other than to reproduce the kind of AI-generated images shared on social media in those early days. Many of them were based on concepts of juxtaposition between subjects (mixtures between movie genres, for

All figures in this chapter were created by (various) AI-tools.

M. Moura (✉)
I2ADS, Universidade Do Porto, Porto, Portugal
e-mail: unseenbydesign@gmail.com

N. Zagalo and D. Keller (eds.), *Artificial Media*, Springer Series on Cultural Computing,
https://doi.org/10.1007/978-3-031-89037-6_12

example) or styles (depicting a movie such as Star Wars in the style of the paintings of Edward Hopper). The results were crude and schematic, almost abstract by today's standards. Even so, they were enticing. The experiment was condensed, without prior planning, around creating an alternative mythology centered on, but not limited to, the Douro wine region. These images were published on Instagram as they were made.[1] In the meantime, they have also become an exhibition and publication project. This essay is a commented record of this journey.

When working in creative fields, it is usual only to know the method behind your work retroactively.[2] This project was one of those cases. It began as an experiment in the most open sense, with no expectations, especially of usefulness or continuity. It was just a way of understanding, in the first person, the processes of creating generative images. The author carried out the experiments during vacations, weekends, and free time, on relatively brief periods in which he subscribed to the Midjourney AI platform, which became central to this work process—Dall-e, ChatGPT, Stable Diffusion, Luma, and Runway were also used occasionally (in the latter two cases, to produce short films from the images generated in Midjourney).

Using an autoethnographic approach, this chapter argues that the open and extra-curricular nature of the research, combined with the also open characteristics of these platforms, made it possible to cumulatively create a narrative object that is organically suited to the possibilities of this type of platform—the terraced vineyards of the Douro were a graphic motif capable of identifying even the crudest images; robots, astronauts, and extra-terrestrials disguised or justified the anatomical incongruities of AI.

The structure and nature of this text seek to honor that open character. Its purpose is to record a first encounter with a radically new technology.

After this introduction, the second part defines the scope of the research and presents the methodology to be used. This scope is defined both negatively and positively: although ethical concerns are addressed, our focus is on the popular use of AI. We are interested in the everyday use of the technology, not its technological roots or its definition upstream of the common user. Given the personal nature of the journey and its anchoring in a specific region and culture, the methodology employed is autoethnography.

The third part sets out and comments on the creative process itself. It explains how the Douro theme was chosen and establishes how the visual characteristics of the Douro region make it particularly suitable for experiments with AI.

The fourth part outlines precedents and influences. Within the traditional structure of an academic chapter, this section would typically appear at the beginning, framed within the State of the Art. However, in this case, the references emerged after engaging with a new technology and a new format. It is true that generative AI

[1] https://www.instagram.com/unseenby.design/

[2] The editor and designer Stuart Bertolotti-Bailey defended this open-ended stance at the opening of his Personal Views conference in (2008), subverting the usual design methodology that prefers thinking thoroughly projects at the beginning. The inspiration for this position was Umberto Eco's The Open Work.

led to images representing the author's deep interests, and these preferences formed the guiding threads of this work. However, awareness of their importance—visual, formal, and personal—only arose at a later stage, upon reflecting on the working process.

The conclusion condenses the main paths followed throughout the chapter and outlines some of the consequences, as well as parallel or future possibilities, whose scope goes beyond the constraints of the present text.

12.2 Scope and Method

12.2.1 Negative Scope

The focus here is not on learning the technique, understood as mastering the informal language of prompts or programming these platforms, but on the intersection of these platforms with other interests and tendencies, both individual and collective. The scope of this work is not the conditions of production or programming of generative artificial intelligence platforms but their popular reception. Nor is the central theme the ethical or legal issues surrounding the experience of the "ordinary" user. What interests us is the vernacular use of these tools.[3] This chapter records a process of familiarization with the possibilities of artificial intelligence. There is a great deal of upstream reflection, but understandably, relatively few first-person reflections engage with everyday, nonspecialized use.[4] We don't want to lose sight of the fact that this work began as an extracurricular activity, a way of producing images as a form of public intervention. This extracurricular character is not a provisional state but a central feature.[5]

12.2.2 Finding the Popular Uses of AI

The tendency for research to be carried out from the producer's point of view to the detriment of research into its end user is a blind spot that makes it challenging to

[3] An example of this approach is Peter Peter Snowdon's (2020).

There is also a trend in art history that also studies vernacular images uses. A great example is David Freedberg's "The Power of Images Studies in the History and Theory of Response", The University of Chicago Press, 1989. The emphasis is on the popular image and not the image produced by artists.

[4] One such example is the conference Towards an Automated Art, that took place in May, 2024, in Lisbon, in Universidade Nova/FCSH, where the author presented a paper. Most of the lectures talked about the programming or projecting of platforms and not the popular use of these technologies.

[5] The issue of civic intervention and creativity done in free time was addressed by Jacques Rancière in his book "A Noite dos Proletários: Arquivos do Sonho Operário." Rancière (2012).

assess ethical, aesthetic, social, and political problems. What is of interest, therefore, is not just a theory but a pragmatics of the reaction of the non-specialized user to images made by AI. They are not passively received but produced by users. It is, therefore, essential to distinguish between the technical production involved in creating and administering these platforms and their active reception by the public. We tend to see one as an extension of the other, but it is not safe to assume that the vernacular production of AI images derives linearly from their production. A possible comparison would be social networks. Despite the degree of control involved in their administration, there is an unexpected, underground use, sometimes even orchestrated by state and corporate actors, which goes beyond the original intentions of those who own these networks.[6] We are interested in the popular use of technology by people who see it as a kind of black box but, at the same time, use it. If Web 2.0 brought about an era in which the technical substrate of the Internet became invisible in the experience of the ordinary user—the so-called post-internet[7]—it seems that generative AI platforms are ushering in a new phase in which Artificial Intelligence becomes something that is in everyday use and no longer confined to specialized research or use. We are interested in mapping out what the post-AI era might look like.

12.2.3 Ethics and Iconophobia

AI inevitably raises a number of ethical and legal problems, which deserve a word, although they are not the focus of this text or this investigation. The author's experiments with AI were conceived as a form of public intervention through social networks. This work aimed not to produce images that were true illustrations, photographs, or collages. The intention has always been to understand the specific expression of generative AI, not as the ersatz of any other type of expression but as an expression in itself.

Ethical and legal problems are not the focus of this research. However, it is important to note that some of the biggest problems deriving from the use of AI turn out to be hidden by the way people react to these technologies. The reaction to AI is similar to classic reactions to images—they are forms of iconophobia and iconoclasm.[8] Artificial intelligence will likely have profound and traumatic consequences, such as the mass replacement or elimination of jobs. However, these fears of replacement coincide with a fear of AI that is also a deep fear of images, an iconophobia: these technologies produce images, but they are also images in the sense that they represent,

---

[6] See the Cambridge Analytica scandal or the issue of Russian interference in election via social networks.

[7] Aranda et al. (2015).

[8] This issue was tackled by the author in a paper titled "Generative AI and the Fear of Images—Looking for Clues about the Future of Artificial Intelligence in Iconophobic Reactions to Lithography and Desktop Publishing" and presented in the Towards an Automated Art international conference. Moura (2024).

duplicate, and extend human features. People react to them as if they were images.[9] On the one hand, these fears are intrinsic to these technologies–the historical study of iconophobia and the image itself necessarily involves the automaton,[10] the golem, the myth of Pygmalion,[11] the idol that comes to life. On the other hand, iconophobia is a veil (a screen but also a filter[12]) that clouds or distorts possibilities and threats.[13] To gain conscience of these pitfalls and avoiding them, one of the purposes of the process described in this chapter is to observe and experience these platforms in the first person.

12.2.4 Methodology

The author decided to frame this text and the research through auto-ethnography's prism. This approach, popularized in the 1970s, refocuses the researcher's position, mobilizing him to become the focal point of his research, criticizing the classic pretension of neutrality. He is no longer an external observer, even if an active one, questioning his own identity.[14] This approach seems particularly pertinent because it studies a set of peripheral positions and identities and their intersection with a new technology: the geographical periphery of the Douro region in Portugal, where part of the author's family comes from; the "free" extra-work and extra-curricular time, reserved in our society for civic intervention, which tends to be disallowed because it occupies the same part of the calendar reserved for vacations and tourism. Using AI as a tool, this project seeks to merge representations that are usually incompatible (rurality and progress, tourism and identity, utopia and everyday life). By using generative AI platforms, the project builds a complex representation of a subaltern region whose representations are usually stereotyped.

[9] The exhibition will take place in January 2025.

[10] Bredekamp (2018).

[11] Stoichita (2008).

[12] Mitchell (2012).

[13] Clearly, there are issues with using authors' works to train these technologies, but this is a new problem with new implications. The idea that an image in the 'style of' can violate copyright may have dramatic implications: it would no longer be enough to avoid copying a specific character or design from Disney, but it would become necessary to avoid the style itself. Potentially, this could lead to an even greater restriction on the field of cultural action. A writer could be sued not only for copying excerpts from another author but for writing in their manner, with their mannerisms, etc. On the other hand, there is indeed the danger of AI replacing human labor.

[14] Schouwenberg et al. (2021) p 13.

12.3 An Account of the Process

12.3.1 Generative AI: Stereotypes as Building Blocks

The basic process is easily described. An image is requested via a textual or iconic prompt. One or more of the images generated is chosen. The chosen images are published on Instagram or Facebook with a written caption that fits them into the world-building. This process is not linear. Sometimes, the caption precedes the image. Other times, the image serves as the inspiration for the caption. An image requested to illustrate a particular story gives unexpected results that lead to the creation of another story. Generative AI has a stochastic basis, so the results tend to be unexpected but also stereotyped—an apparent contradiction explained by the fact that it is based on probabilities.[15] For example, when asked for the image of a ball, we are given a set of pixels with a high probability of being interpreted as a ball by a human being. Therefore, this process has a connection to expectations and prejudices that cannot be ignored. Using it is, in a way, a management of stereotypes, especially the less obvious and unconscious ones. In this respect, its use is akin to automatic writing, and the pleasure one gets from using it is similar to that of surrealist writing devices. The stochastic process of generating images favors the unforeseen, the juxtaposition of ideas, compositions, or attitudes. The resulting images are never exactly what you ask. However, this distance can be interesting—because it reveals unexpected possibilities or requires you to think more carefully about the nature of the images you want to produce or the quality of the written description with which you produce the image. We argue that the mismatch between the prompt and its result is part of what is appealing in these technologies, both to those who produce and appreciate them.[16] It is in these apparent imperfections that the expressive specificity of this medium can be found. Contrary to what one might expect, dealing with AI-generated images often requires a reflective and open attitude toward images and writing. It is not optimism but openness. Artificial intelligence undoubtedly involves risks and will lead to widespread changes in society and the creative sphere. However, to assess this new territory, looking beyond the inevitable preconceptions will be essential.

12.3.2 First Contacts with Generative AI

The author's first experiments with generative AI were carried out in the first half of 2022. They were made impulsively, influenced by the first AI-generated images posted on social media. Almost all featured a comedic juxtaposition of characters in an incongruous context or style—some of the first examples featured, for example, Godzilla in a hospital room or an Easter Island statue giving a Ted Talk (Figs. 12.1

---

[15] Marian Bantjes explains this process in her text Artificial Idiot. Bantjes (2023).

[16] Marian Bantjes makes the same point in the article quoted above.

and 12.2). The images could have been sharper and better quality, but they showed the medium's possibilities. In response, a designer complaining about the Comic Sans font was requested (Fig. 12.3). Apparently a designer was a male in a worn shirt open over a white T-shirt with a desktop screen nearby. Despite the obvious distortions, it was a surprisingly convincing response.

The technology advanced rapidly, improving its realism and spatial, anatomical, and atmospheric consistency. Throughout this project, prompts were reused with variations that allowed the improvements between versions to be contrasted. Using Midjourney version 5.2, a series was created illustrating designers over the centuries. One of the intentions was to understand how Midjourney represented

Fig. 12.1 AI-generated image response to the prompt "Godzilla in a hospital room"

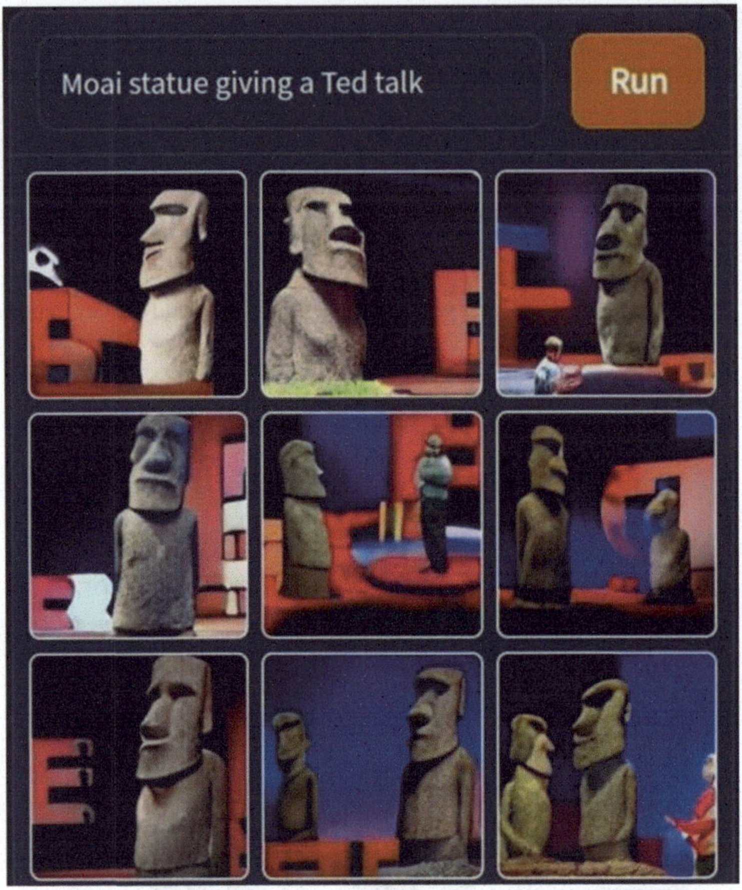

Fig. 12.2 AI-generated image response to the prompt "Easter Island statue giving a ted talk"

the idea of a designer—most of the results showed white men working on Apple-branded computers (Fig. 12.4). In addition, it is possible to see notable advances in the complexity and verisimilitude of the representation between Midjourney versions.

12.3.3 *Why the Douro Region?*

The first images of the Douro were requested at the beginning of August 2022 (Fig. 12.5). The push was the space voyage of Mário Ferreira, owner of Douro Azul, a Douro cruise company. The juxtaposition between tourism in the Douro and space tourism first prompted a set of uninteresting images of Mário Ferreira as an astronaut. Clearly, the AI platform did not know what Ferreira looked like. This limitation led

Fig. 12.3 AI-generated image response to the prompt "designer complaining about the comic sans"

to a change in strategy. If it was impossible to make a convincing caricature of Ferreira, asking for spaceships taking off in the middle of the Douro vineyards was a viable alternative. As a mere curiosity, these images were requested in the style of the painter Turner (Fig. 12.6). The almost abstract paintings of diffused light helped to disguise the inconsistencies of the IA, lending the images a dense and suggestive atmosphere. The lines of the terraces and the river's reflections helped to identify the Douro landscape even when they were barely present. In some cases, the AI merged different elements of the prompt: a farm merged with a spaceship, floating like a balloon above the valley (Fig. 12.7). These results led to the composition of captions that imagined flying farms and experimental airships. An alternative chronology was beginning to be constructed.

This type of fusion was very fertile in narrative terms. Fusing a spaceship with buildings made it possible to construct the narrative that the ships' interdimensional

Fig. 12.4 AI-generated image response to the prompt "a designer"

devices could be adapted to be used as portals to import goods from other universes in petty trade (Fig. 12.8). On another occasion, robots spontaneously merged with churches to become walking temples (Fig. 12.9). Every mistake, distortion, or accident could serve as a motif for a new facet of the narrative.

Specific juxtapositions were sought in some cases, such as Portuguese roadside restaurants built on the carcasses of spaceships or municipal robots functioning as firefighting or railway maintenance equipment (Fig. 12.10).

Experiments were carried out varying the image style—asking for photographs in the style of the WPA photographers, with the typical characteristics of color film from the 1970s. One unexpected result is that the objects' design varies with the style requested. A photograph in the style of Paul Strand or Berenice Abbot implies a particular era and a specific type of spaceship (Fig. 12.11).

We also experimented with different types of images. Woodcuts could evoke the periodicals and science fiction publications of the nineteenth century. Images in a format similar to Google Street View showed a contemporary Douro full of tourists (Fig. 12.12).

Fig. 12.5 AI-generated image response to the prompt "Voyage of Mário Ferreira, owner of Douro Azul"

Describing materials also proved critical in this process. Over time, various characteristics were added to the recipe. The blue and white tiles contributed to a Pombaline atmosphere. The ceramic could be justified because it was a material used for the thermal lining of spaceships. This decision made building automata, costumes, and vehicles of all kinds possible (Fig. 12.13). Wood, ivory, and bone also yielded exciting results when applied to automata and spaceships. Experiments with organic and transparent materials created a mythology about interdimensional exchange students and colonial wars between dimensions.

These are just a few examples of the images that allow us to assess how the characteristics and limitations of AI have served as a basis for the world-building narrative. This process is not limited to a text that captions a set of arbitrary images a posteriori, unifying them into a whole. The process is circular and dialogical. The text feeds the images, which in turn feeds the text. It should be noted that the text, like the formal characteristics of the images, was conceived within the constraints of Instagram. The world-building process is also based on fragmentation and multiverse ideas, allowing the narrative to be fed without excessive concern for formal, spatial, or thematic coherence. It also adapts to an irregular publication rhythm. Formal, technical, and personal limitations have shaped the project's structure.

Fig. 12.6 First AI-generated image response to the prompts "Space", "Douro vineyards" and "in the style of the painter J.M.W."

12.4 Precedents and Influences

12.4.1 A Hybrid Iconography of a Peripheric and Underdeveloped Region

Although they began in a contingent and arbitrary way, the images quickly condensed into a narrative with characteristics of world-building, science fiction, and alternative realities centered on the Alto Douro Wine Region in Portugal. In short posts, within the character limit allowed by Instagram, a mythology was built up in which the Douro region had become an inter-dimensional hub. However, it maintained its peripheral, backward, and degraded character. This narrative extends a series of reflections the author has produced on the periphery and this region. These essays dealt with the need for proper representation of these regions.[17] They were constantly shown through stereotypes that romanticized them, showing an idealized but one-dimensional scenario corresponding to a typical and traditionalist vision. It is not easy to find narratives or images that represent the experience of someone who,

[17] See "Trás-os-Montes" in Moura (2018).

Fig. 12.7 Second AI-generated image response to the prompts "Space", "Douro vineyards" and "in the style of the painter J.M.W."

like the author, grew up in a city in a region associated with rurality, reading and watching science fiction, going out at night, and reading sci-fi. It's not about a clash between progress and backwardness or urbanity and rurality. It is about a coherent identity, albeit difficult to represent. The difficulty lies also in producing images that illustrate these apparent contradictions but are, in fact, a faithful representation of the landscape and culture of the place. Geographer Álvaro Domingues specializes in reproducing this kind of unlikely juxtaposition, which he calls transgenic landscapes.[18] What these do is change the dynamics of the frame. Instead of framing only the picturesque view, isolating it from everything that could contaminate it, they try to achieve contrast effects by widening the frame or juxtaposing focal lengths. The same type of juxtaposition can be seen in works by Agustina Bessa Luís, such as Vale Abraão,[19] where the representation of the Douro region in the period of transition from the Estado Novo to the post-25 April period, including the 90 s, summons up a series of clashes—between the decadence of nineteenth-century entrepreneurship, between traditional rurality and the emergence of housing tourism and computer classes in the 90 s. These juxtapositions are not extravagant, except for those who

[18] Domingues (2021).

[19] Bessa-Luís (1991)

Fig. 12.8 Spontaneous merges in AI-generated image between spaceships and buildings

are used to seeing the region through a veil of stereotypes. It is a realistic representation that, once again, refuses stereotypical framing. In the same way, the purpose of world-building is to be realistic, but it achieves this effect through distorted mirrors, filters, and lenses.

It was also imperative to mention the importance of classic science fiction iconography, particularly the works of artists such as John Berkey or Chris Foss. Another significant influence was Simon Stålenhag's illustrations for Tales of the Loop.[20] The influence was not direct either—fictional technology, such as robots and spaceships, was juxtaposed with landscapes of the Trás-os-Montes region. These references were not used directly (by asking for images in the "style of") but by trying to understand and break down the formal and stylistic characteristics of the author. It was possible to obtain images similar to Berkey's by asking for paintings in the style of J.M.W. Turner and the English landscape painters, mixing science fiction elements such as spaceships and robots with traditional landscapes. Similarly, it was possible to obtain futuristic vessels similar to Foss's by asking for colored and striped vehicles (Fig. 12.14). It is possible to find more vivid and open results with a deeper perception of art history and how illustration often recycles styles and techniques by placing

[20] Stålenhag (2015).

Fig. 12.9 Spontaneous merges in AI-generated image between robots and churches

them in contexts such as science fiction. Generative AI's ability to resample styles makes it particularly suitable for building objects in such a way.

12.4.2 Why Does Science Fiction, the Fantastic and Political Cartoon Fit so Well with Generative AI?

Science fiction and the fantastic, both in terms of narrative and iconography, are powerful devices for operating these kinds of juxtapositions. The contrast between a poor, peripheral area and an environment where technology has become part of daily life is a frequent trope. This poor, dirty, everyday science fiction characterized the first films in the Star Wars cycle. The introductory scroll, which located the action "a long, long time ago, in a galaxy far, far away," also confused expectations by juxtaposing a distant past with a setting typical of anticipatory science fiction. In the case of this project, the simple juxtaposition between the ideas of AI and of periphery is enough to create an interesting mental image. One of the characteristics of AI images is the ability to create images of synthesis between different contexts, ideas, objects, or characters. These tools work by articulating verisimilitude. It is about producing images with a logic of likelihood of resemblance. Which set of

Fig. 12.10 AI-generated image juxtaposing Portuguese roadside restaurants and carcasses of municipal robots

pixels most likely resembles the result of the terms used in the prompts? In other words, when asking for an image of the Douro, the result is a "Douricity." When asking for a robot in the Douro, one gets a cross between the visual idea of what a robot will be and the idea of the Douro. If something that does not correspond so much to a visual stereotype is wanted, the prompts have to be tweaked. For example, the typical image of the Douro is predominantly rural, with vineyards and farms. The Douro landscape is complex: you can find buildings from different eras and in various states of repair. High-rise buildings in the middle of vineyards are ordinary in places like Peso da Régua. Therefore, one of the most considerable difficulties is precisely getting results that match the expected outcome. Most commonly, if simple prompts are used, one gets a stereotype.

In any case, these AI processes favor juxtaposition, counterpoint, and collage—not constructions that display their mechanisms, but can hide their seams and discontinuities. It is very similar to the verisimilar logic of the collages produced by Dadaist artist John Heartfield, which used the factual connotation of the photographic image to produce impossible situations. When used to make political cartoons, these techniques are sometimes feared to be falsifications. However, its more subversive use is not to deceive but to caricature or to "burn" its targets in effigy—an older, even traditional, mode of action through the image. Significantly, this project had part of

Fig. 12.11 AI-generated image response to request for image in the style of the WPA photographers

its origins in an attempt to produce a caricature of businessman Mário Ferreira when he became one of the first Portuguese space tourists. One of the most common uses of AI on social networks is to produce caricatures. In this respect, it is a hyper-meme. The traditional meme is a reusable template. Generative AI gives ordinary users the ability to intervene socially through customisable images.

These images are not intended to be factual but, for the most part, function as acts of trolling or a simple form of cartooning. The aim is to catch the other person out. They are pranks. These acts of trolling are intended to distinguish between those who realize that those images are false and absurd and those who fall for them. Generative AI thus functions as a social boundary between who gets the joke and who does not. This distinction is a social cleavage, and it is characteristic of a period in which these technologies are defining themselves socially. Hito Steyerl had already identified this social construction process of the digital image. She proposed the concept of the poor image, which merges the lack of quality of the digital image with the economic poverty of those who use it.[21] However, it can be argued that the AI Image, which can be produced in high definition, is shattering this social divide, forcing it to be restructured. Using absurd images but reproduced with a quality that brings them closer to photography effectively acts as a shibboleth that separates the sophisticated

[21] Steyerl (2009).

Fig. 12.12 AI-generated image response to request for Google street view in a contemporary Douro full of tourists

Fig. 12.13 AI-generated image response to request of automata in blue and white tiles

from the corpus. However, the hierarchies have only shifted for a moment. A difference has already emerged between the relatively crude images produced by free or cheaper AI platforms such as Bing or Dall-e, and the premium images produced by subscription services such as Midjourney or Photoshop-generated images.

12.5 Conclusions

The purpose of the Douro project was to develop iconography as a form of complex public intervention by producing a consistent universe in dialogue with AI. One of the aims is to understand, produce, or support a language of public intervention based on images, producing them through AI and extending it beyond trolling or political cartoons. Collage and juxtaposition are potent tools of public imagination and, therefore, of civic intervention.

This chapter has emphasized the issue of collage. Science fiction functions as a radical juxtaposition of elements. The imaginary use of science fiction is particularly suited to the formal limitations of generative artificial intelligence. A robot or a mutant body can explain the inconsistencies and disproportions regularly produced by these platforms. Fusions of incongruous architectural or landscape elements can be

Fig. 12.14 AI-generated image response to request of Chris Foss futuristic vessels

explained as interdimensional rifts or as amalgams between futuristic and traditional elements. In this respect, the Douro region is also particularly well suited to this imagery. With terraced vineyards, it is a landscape rewritten by the human hand. These terraces are a graphic element that allows us to recognize the landscape even in the most schematic images produced by the first versions of the platforms. The Douro region has been remade by technology over the centuries, a narrative that can easily be adapted to a science fiction context.

Throughout the journey described here, technology has forced a definition of this author's identity. It was not a process that had a defined objective from the outset. It also required an effort to define the character of this process and the objects it produces. It started as a hobby. Over time, it became something more structured. The process was not continuous. Curiosity motivated it. These devices were a new way of creating images from texts. It is an inevitably uncanny process because it has a non-human aspect. However, this characteristic also turns it into an external reflection, like a mirror where we can observe the human from the outside—prejudices, habits, and stereotypes. Even this sensation risks being a distortion, something we project on the stochastic calculations of AI. Nevertheless, we can see ourselves on this distorted surface. This reflexive character turns the IA into a literal examination of conscience. It is not a new development. Since its beginnings—from Alan Turing to Marvin Minsky—the development of AI has been based on examining human consciousness. We do not intend to discuss the ontological dimension of artificial intelligence here. What interests us is the kind of self-reflection involved on the side of the user rather than the producer, engineer, or designer of these systems. Throughout this journey, we have been guided by the work of creators who have experimented with AI as a way of taking on and examining consciousness. Two important examples were the book Prompt, written and self-published by Dave McKean,[22] and an article in Eye magazine written by Marion Bantjes.[23] The interest of these books lies in the perplexity of a first encounter. McKean is an illustrator and comic book artist who has done pioneering work in the field of digital creation. Some of the most striking works from these early months of AI looked a lot like his work.[24]

It is important to stress that this journey was undertaken mainly during the author's free time and vacations. It was not an effort with precise objectives or goals. Much academic research occurs within this diffuse zone between work and leisure. So does public and civic intervention and participation in wider communities such as social networks. As we have demonstrated above, this type of technology can be a way of participating, discussing, and arguing. It is not accidental that these experiments were carried out under these circumstances. This fact also underlines another issue: this work was only done because of these technologies. They unequivocally expand the possibilities of expression for those who use them.

The production and communication of images have become as accessible as written production. For hundreds of years, writing was always the simplest and most economical means of mass communication. The creation of images was reserved for those with power, financial resources, and specialized training. The reproduction of images required specific production methods (engraving, woodcut, lithography, or photogravure), which limited access to them. The advent of mass communication media such as television and cinema further highlighted the extent to which the production and distribution of images were beyond the reach of the general public. There were many spectators but very few producers. For this reason, it was assumed that most of the public received images passively.[25] However, with the internet and the advent of smartphones, image production has become an everyday activity, taking on new functions and modes of expression, with capacities still largely uncharted—memes, gifs, reels, and so on. Generative artificial intelligence now adds to this array of possibilities. One of its contributions is the ability to create fictional images of highly convincing quality. It is no longer possible to regard the public as passive spectators.

This project constitutes a theoretical practice. In its most common usage, "theoretical" means not only a methodologically structured thought process on a given

[22] McKean (2022).

[23] Bantjes, Marion, id.

[24] The comic Abolition of Man, by Carson Grubaugh and Sean Robinson is one of the best examples. It was announced as the first computer-produced comic. However, what was most noticeable was the sophistication of its references, which can be seen right from the title. In this typographical collage, part of Dave McKean's Sandman logo can be recognized. Grubaugh (2022).

[25] A canonical instance of this bias is the work of Guy Debord.

subject but also the expression of this thought through writing. In the context of a conclusion, it is customary to point out future or parallel developments for the work carried out. One such development will undoubtedly be the impact of accessible and sophisticated image production on theoretical production formats. Is it possible to produce a theory not just about the image but through the image? There are already answers. At the beginning of the twentieth century, Aby Warburg proposed an iconography that was not merely a writing about images but a reflection through images—his famous Atlas Mnemosyne.[26] In the 1990s, W.J.T. Mitchell thoroughly analyzed the potential of the visual image to function as theory[27]—it is no coincidence that, in that era of burgeoning desktop publishing, Mitchell produced "The Reconfigured Eye", one of the most comprehensive studies on the characteristics and possibilities of the digital image.[28] A similar mapping process is essential for generative AI.

The creation of images through generative AI can serve as a powerful tool for theoretical reflection but also as an exercise in self-fiction through images. The stochastic process of AI, combined with the biases of those who train it, is prolific in stereotypes. Using generative AI is akin to composing with clichés. To create an image that resonates with our personal experience, it is necessary to examine our own biases. Producing a realistic landscape implies observing the real landscape more attentively, questioning what we ourselves tend to leave out of the frame. In this regard, generative AI can be a fundamental critical tool.

It is often assumed that criticism is primarily written or spoken, relegating image-based criticism to a secondary role. However, in recent histories of art criticism, the concept of criticism has been expanded to include caricatures, songs, plays, or posters. These vernacular examples support the argument that the use of AI to produce memes and caricatures falls within a type of political and vernacular criticism and intervention. Similarly, AI is already a powerful tool for political intervention and vernacular criticism—as can be seen daily as we browse the Internet.

Generative AI opens up new possibilities while bringing new dangers. One possible path to critically engage with it is to turn it into a critical tool for political and civic intervention—seeking an emancipatory use of these technologies.

References

Aranda J, Wood BK, Vidokle A (eds) (2015) E-flux journal: the internet does not exist. Sternberg Press

Bantjes M (2023) Artificial idiot. Eye–Int Rev Des

Bertolotti-Bailey S (2008) Personal views conference

Bessa-Luís A (1991) Vale Abraão. Guimarães Editores, Lisboa

Bredekamp H (2018) Image acts: a systematic approach to visual agency. Walter de Gruyter GmbH, Berlin/Boston

[26] See Didi-Huberman (2013).

[27] Mitchell (1994).

[28] Mitchell (1992).

Didi-Huberman G (2013) Atlas ou a Gaia Ciência Inquieta. KKYM+EAUM, Lisboa
Domingues Á (2021) Paisagens Transgénicas. Museu da Paisagem, Lisboa
Grubaugh C, Robinson S (2022) The abolition of man. Living The Line, St. Paul
Kaethler M, Schouwenberg L (eds) (2021) The auto-ethnographic turn in design. Valiz, Amsterdam
McKean D (2022) Prompt. Conversations With Artificial Intelligence. Hourglass/ASFA
Mitchell WJT (1992) The reconfigured eye: visual truth in the post-photographic era. MIT Press, Cambridge/London
Mitchell WJT (1994) Picture theory: essays on verbal and visual representation. University of Chicago Press, Chicago
Mitchell WJT (2012) Seeing through race. Harvard University Press, Cambridge/London
Moura M (2024) Generative AI and the fear of images—looking for clues about the future of artificial intelligence in iconophobic reactions to lithography and desktop publishing, apresentado na conferência towards an automated art. Universidade Nova/FCSH, Lisbon
Moura M (2018) O design que o design Não Vê. Orfeu Negro, Lisboa
Rancière J (2012) A Noite dos Proletários: Arquivos do Sonho Operário. Antígona, Lisboa
Snowdon P (2020) The people are not an image: vernacular video after the Arab spring. Verso Books, London
Stålenhag S (2015) Tales from the loop. Design Studio Press
Steyerl H (2009) In defense of the poor image. E-Flux J. Sternberg Press. Disponível em. https://www.e-flux.com/journal/10/61362/in-defense-of-the-poor-image/
Stoichita V (2008) The pygmalion effect: from ovid to hitchcock. University of Chicago Press, Chicago

The manufacturer's authorised representative in the EU is Springer Nature Customer Service Centre GmbH, Europaplatz 3, 69115 Heidelberg, Germany. If you have any concerns regarding our products, please contact ProductSafety@springernature.com

Printed and bound by CPI Group (UK) Ltd, Croydon, CR0 4YY
30/09/2026
02225564-0009